ALGER HISS: THE TRUE STORY

JOHN CHABOT SMITH

ALGER HISS

THE TRUE STORY

HOLT, RINEHART AND WINSTON
New York

Published simultaneously in Canada by Holt,
Rinehart and Winston of Canada, Limited

Library of Congress Cataloging in Publication Data
Smith, John Chabot.
    Alger Hiss: The True Story
    Bibliography: p.
    Includes index.
    1. Hiss, Alger. I. Title.
E743.5.H55S58   364.1'31'0924   75-21462
ISBN 0-03-013776-4

Acknowledgment for permission to reprint material
is made to the following publishers:

    Random House for quotations from
    Witness by Whittaker Chambers, copyright
    1952 by Whittaker Chambers.

    Doubleday & Company, Inc. for quotations from
    Six Crises by Richard M. Nixon, copyright
    © 1962 by Richard M. Nixon.

Designer: Betty Binns

PRINTED IN THE UNITED STATES OF AMERICA
10 9 8 7 6 5 4 3 2

To my beloved wife,
Betty McCarthy Smith,
who has shared this work with me
in all the twenty-eight years
since it began

CONTENTS

Twenty-four pages of illustrations follow page 246.

ACKNOWLEDGMENTS

So many people have contributed in so many ways to this book that it would be hopeless to try to thank them all, and I hope those whose names are omitted here and those who are not fully credited for all they have done will forgive me. I most gratefully acknowledge my obligation to them, and in particular to some who have helped me in special ways:

To all those listed in the "Sources, Bibliography, and Notes" who gave so generously of their time and effort to answer my questions, and in many cases shared with me the fruits of their own research;

To Helen L. Buttenwieser, attorney for Mr. Hiss, who has in her custody the files accumulated by the defense lawyers during the long years of legal proceedings, and gave me unrestricted access to them as well as supplying office facilities for studying them; and to her partners and members of their staff who looked after my needs;

To Attorney Robert von Mehren, who opened the late Edward McLean's files on the case to me, and assisted me in many other ways from the beginning of the project; and to his wife, Marikay von Mehren, for her kindness and hospitality;

To William E. and Helene Arnstein, Visscher and Doris Boyd, Julian and Frances Falk, Daniel and Betsy Falk, Charles and Nellie Goodsell, Mac and Helen Morgan, Michael Chabot Smith, Anna Lord Strauss, and Harriet Van Horne, who gave generously of their hospitality and moral and material support;

To Representatives Bella Abzug, Robert F. Drinan, and Peter Rodino, who supported my efforts to gain access to government records;

To Dr. Philip A. D. Schneider and his staff in the Bureau of Manpower Information Systems, U.S. Civil Service Commission, who made it possible for me to examine Mr. Hiss's official personnel folder;

To the always helpful staffs of the Congressional Library, New York Public Library, Bridgeport Public Library, and Cyrenius H. Booth Library of Newtown, Conn.;

To Judie Johnston, who typed the manuscript with incredible

speed and accuracy, and to her husband William Johnston for his kindness and hospitality;

And to all the other helpful people who gave me information and assistance.

JOHN CHABOT SMITH
Newtown, Connecticut

1

THE BEGINNING

IT was on a Saturday that President Franklin D. Roosevelt was inaugurated for the first time, March 4, 1933. He was sworn in at noon, as the law provided; the last President to take his oath of office in March, and the first to repeat its solemn words as they were read to him by Chief Justice Charles Evans Hughes, instead of replying with a simple "I do." A symbolic gesture, drawing upon ancient ritual to reassure a frightened nation.

Noon was quitting time on Saturday for people with good jobs in 1933. The forty-hour week had not yet come; you worked five and a half or six days a week, if you weren't laid off, out of work, or on short hours, as more than one-fourth of the labor force were at that point in the Great Depression. Nobody really knew how many were unemployed, because there were no reliable statistics, and the guessing and arguing about it only made the situation more frightening. But everyone knew about the breadlines and soup kitchens, the wandering jobless in the hobo jungles, the rioting farmers and food wasted or rotting for lack of people to buy it, and the millions who were hungry or starving for lack of money to buy it. Most people had either been involved in such experiences themselves or knew someone who had, and the rest could see it happening before their eyes, or read about it in newspapers and hear it on the radio. On the Saturday morning of Inauguration Day even the banks had run out of money; every bank in the nation had closed its doors.

A few minutes before noon on that gray, chilly day, in New York, a young corporation lawyer emerged from the Wall Street offices of Cotton, Franklin, Wright & Gordon to meet his wife, who had come downtown to do some shopping, and ride with her in a taxi up Fifth Avenue to the Metropolitan Museum. They were a handsome couple, married only a little more than three years, with gilded youths' confidence in the future and concern for shaping a better world. He was a Phi Beta Kappa from Johns Hopkins, and a graduate of Harvard Law School in the top of his class, who was now engaged in buttoning up the details of an antitrust settlement involving such corporate giants as the Radio Corporation of America, General Electric, and American Telephone and Telegraph. She was a Bryn Mawr graduate, who had been awarded a scholarship to study English literature at Yale University Graduate School, in the days when comparatively few women did graduate work, and Yale was essentially a men's university. She was collaborating with her closest friend—a Bryn Mawr roommate now married to her brother—on a monograph, "Research in Fine Arts in American Colleges and Universities," with a grant from the Carnegie Corporation. Her friend was a curator at the Metropolitan, where the taxi was headed; but the young couple weren't thinking about friends or fine arts at this moment. The taxicab had a radio in it, an unusual phenomenon in those days, and they were listening to Roosevelt's First Inaugural Address, coming to them in thin, scratchy tones through a lot of static.

"This is a day of national consecration," the new President began, and the couple in the taxicab, like millions of others listening to other radio sets at the same moment, found nothing exaggerated in the phrase; it was exactly what they yearned for. "Let me assert my firm belief," the President said a moment later, "that the only thing we have to fear is fear itself—nameless, unreasoning, unjustified terror which paralyzes needed efforts to convert retreat into advance."

The young lawyer leaned forward in his seat, cupping his hand behind his ear to make sure no word was missed above the grumbling of the taxi's engine and the noise of outside traffic.

This was the voice he had been waiting for in the four-month long interregnum since the November election, the "lame duck" period, in which the Depression had steadily deepened. For the outgoing President and his successor had not agreed on what should be done, and until the new President took office nothing very helpful was done.

The reference to "fear" struck home; fear was all around. Young men like the one in the taxi were not greatly afraid, for with youth, knowledge, and health on their side why should they be? But they knew others who were, older men with more experience and more burdens; men less fortunate, with no jobs and no future; women dependent on men who were unable to provide for them; children, more dependent even than their mothers, suffering and uncomprehending. Young idealists who were spared these fears felt instead an urge to help the helpless, to put their knowledge and youth to work where it would do some good, to be part of this "national consecration."

Franklin Roosevelt was a country gentleman come to the rescue of the common man, or so he seemed to be saying in his Inaugural Address. There were some who resented it that day, and many more came to do so in the years that followed. But at this moment, as he had done before and would do forever after, the young man in the taxi identified with Roosevelt. He shared the traditions, if not the wealth of the country gentleman, and like him was moved by the sufferings he saw. As did most Americans that day, he responded to the new leader with hope, enthusiasm, and a vast sense of relief. For him, as for many others, it was a feeling almost akin to adoration.

More than forty years later Alger Hiss could still remember this experience and the impression it had made upon him. "It was almost like a holy moment," he said. "It was really like being in church. I thought the beauty of his delivery and the importance of what he said—this was just exactly like the finger of God pointing, even in the taxi. I was hearing his voice, speaking for the first time as President on Inauguration Day, and it was just the culmination of everything I'd been hoping for. His famous statement that we had nothing to fear but fear itself—he had a

3

gift for that kind of phrase, which struck you and then stuck to you."

And there was more in the speech to uplift frightened spirits: "This Nation asks for action now. . . . We must act and act quickly. . . . I shall ask the Congress for the one remaining instrument to meet the crisis—broad Executive power to wage a war against the emergency, as great as the power that would be given to me if we were in fact invaded by a foreign foe."

A crisis comparable to war—that was what Hiss remembered when the speech was over. They had arrived at the Metropolitan by that time, and the three of them sat in the taxi, Alger, his wife Priscilla, and the taxi driver, until the end. The driver was as enthusiastic as his passengers; there was a sense of fellowship among them, like fans at a football game rooting for the same team. All over America that day people were experiencing a kind of unity in crisis—whether it was the image of warfare that Roosevelt had used, the idea of banding together to vanquish a foreign foe, or whether it was the reality of the sudden bank closings, when rich and poor alike could get no money, and life could go on only if people trusted each other, extended credit, shared what cash they had, helped each other make do as best they could in a situation that nobody before had ever dreamed could possibly happen. Not least was the uplift of hope engendered by the new leader, who had used bold words and told America to abandon fear—it would be all right now, there was no need to be afraid— and there it was, a sudden outpouring of good fellowship, a return of courage, a sense of sunrise after a long, long night.

Thus began for Alger Hiss a course of events which brought him in a few weeks to Washington to join the sudden army of "New Deal lawyers." He went in the mood of a young man called to the colors, signing up for the duration of the emergency. But he was to stay there fourteen years and be involved in the shaping of government policy, both foreign and domestic. He was to go to Yalta with President Roosevelt and to San Francisco and London for the founding of the United Nations, and to become president

4

of the Carnegie Endowment for International Peace. Then, in a dramatic reversal that shocked the nation, he was to be denounced as a Communist spy, to deny it, stand trial for perjury, and be convicted and sent to jail.

It was the first of the great sensational political trials of recent years in America, and the arguments about it still go on. Although the Appeals Court upheld the conviction, the motion for a new trial was denied, and the U.S. Supreme Court twice refused to review the case, there are many who still believe in Hiss's innocence; and Hiss himself, now past seventy, continues to search for the evidence to prove it. In the more than twenty-five years that have passed, a great deal of such evidence has been found; but much is still hidden, and there are mysteries that remain.

Hiss's accuser Whittaker Chambers was a very different kind of man, and his reactions on that dramatic weekend of Roosevelt's inauguration were different too. They have been described by Matthew Josephson, author and biographer, who happened to meet Chambers that Sunday in a friend's apartment in Greenwich Village. Josephson had never seen Chambers before and never met him again, but the incident made such an impression on him that he remembered it when Chambers became a public figure fifteen years later, and he wrote it down in his notebook for later use in his memoirs.

Josephson had come to New York that day from his farm because of his own sense of excitement over the closing of the banks—and his hope of getting some cash from his publisher, since he couldn't cash a check anywhere else. He headed for his friend Robert Cantwell's apartment, where he rented a room for his weekly visits to the city. He was surprised upon arrival that the door was not immediately opened to his knock, for Cantwell was an affectionate friend, and always home at that time of a Sunday with his wife and baby. He heard voices inside, then silence; so he knocked again and called out his name. Then he heard Cantwell say to someone: "It's perfectly all right. It's Matty Josephson. You can come out." Cantwell opened the door, and

Josephson entered to find a man he didn't know coming out of the bedroom with an embarrassed, sheepish air, as if he'd been hiding there. Cantwell introduced the stranger as Chambers.

Josephson recognized the name as one Cantwell had mentioned before: a young left-wing writer (as was Cantwell in those days), who had contributed some pieces to a pro-Communist magazine called *New Masses*. Josephson had read them without much interest, but he remembered Cantwell's statement that Chambers "either fancied himself or actually was" a secret agent of the Russians in the Communist underground.

When they sat down to talk over a bottle of bootleg whiskey, Chambers became highly excited over the implications of the banking crisis. "Isn't this the great debacle of the American financial system—with all the banks closing their doors?" he asked.

Josephson didn't think so; he argued that the new President would get the banking machinery running again, that there might be a recovery in trade, and the business system might be saved.

"Why, man, you're crazy!" Chambers exploded. "With no money, no work, no food, everything stopped, there's going to be a revolution here right now! This is it—the big smashup. There'll be barricades the end of this week in Union Square, I tell you!"

The argument grew hot and heavy, as such arguments generally did. Josephson quoted Karl Marx, the apostle of Communism, against this Communist revolutionary, and Chambers protested "all the sacrifices" he had made over the years for the revolution. Josephson heard himself denounced as a "bourgeois stooge," a "tool of the capitalists," even a "spy," and the quarrel almost came to blows. Then Cantwell and his wife intervened, and Chambers left the apartment without another word.

Josephson didn't take Chambers seriously as a secret agent; he thought of him as "one of those Bohemian neurotic rebels one sometimes meets in Greenwich Village or Montparnasse, all emotion and noise and nonsense." But Chambers took himself very seriously. When he wrote his own memoirs, *Witness*, in 1952, he didn't mention the incident or Josephson at all, but he did say that he was a member of the Communist underground in 1933, attached to what he called the Fourth Section of the Soviet Military Intelligence.

Chambers had joined the Communists in 1925, while a student at Columbia University; he had become disillusioned with the state of the world after World War I, and found inspiration in the writings of Marx and Lenin. Leaving Columbia without waiting to graduate, he got a job on the *Daily Worker*, then the official organ of the Communist Party in the United States, but gave it up a few years later in a dispute over political tactics. He wrote some short stories expressing his own ideas about Communism and sold them to *New Masses*, which was not an official Communist publication but one that enjoyed wide Communist readership, many Communist contributors, and some ill-defined support from the Communist Party. The stories were an instant success, not only inside but outside Communist circles; the first of them, "Can You Hear Their Voices?", dealt with the farm crisis, and was made into a play by Hallie Flanagan, then head of Vassar's Experimental Theater, and performed at the Yiddish Theater in New York as *The Drought*. It was also reprinted in pamphlet form and sold by a Communist publishing house; Chambers boasted that it was translated even into Chinese and Japanese, and "played in workers' theaters all over the world."

This success earned him a job; first, as contributing editor and then editor of *New Masses*, the job he held until 1932, when, according to Chambers, he was recruited into the underground by Max Bedacht, then a member of the Secretariat of the Communist National Committee. Bedacht, Chambers wrote twenty years later, "had been for years a permanent link between the Central Committee of the American Communist Party and the Soviet Military Intelligence in the United States." Bedacht denied the whole story; he told journalist Elinor Ferry it was a flat lie, and that he had never had any connections with an underground of any sort, Russian or American. If Chambers was in the underground, Bedacht didn't know about it, and hadn't recruited him for it.

Chambers described his activities in this period as consisting mainly of carrying messages back and forth between the Communist Party (which at that time enjoyed the same legal status as any other political party in the United States) and his superior in the underground, whom he identified as "Ulrich." He learned how to photograph documents on microfilm and to develop them; how to make enlarged prints from microfilms, and to develop and fix them; and how to develop messages written in invisible ink. He discovered he was part of a communications network that employed sailors and stewards on the Hamburg–American and North German Lloyd steamships to smuggle messages in from the German Communists; the messages were on single frames of microfilm slipped behind the glass of pocket mirrors, or were written in invisible ink between the lines of typewritten letters. The couriers were identified by lapel pins in the form of scorpions and lizards, which Ulrich's wife bought, along with the pocket mirrors, at the local dime store. What the messages contained, and why they had to be smuggled in with such secrecy, Chambers didn't explain.

Also in this period, Chambers learned what he called "underground organizational techniques." Most important was discipline; whatever he was told was a military order, to be obeyed absolutely without question. All meetings were to be prearranged, but he was never to make a note of an appointment without disguising the time and place. He must be punctual at all meetings, but must spend from thirty minutes to two hours beforehand wandering about the city, using a variety of conveyances to give the slip to anyone who might be following. He must never notice the address of any place he was taken but must memorize the route so he could reach it again, but be careful not to know where it was. Nor should he give any sign of recognition if he met another underground worker in public; and he should have no further contact with anyone he knew on the *Daily Worker* or *New Masses*, or anyone else who knew him as a Communist. As an underground Communist spy he was to use only the code names "Bob," "Carl," or "Eugene"; to the outside world he was to be a "respectable bourgeois." For that purpose he was to receive an allowance to cover rent, telephone, transportation, medical expenses and other such items, enabling him to live at a more comfortable standard than the openly Communist proletarian could afford. To start with he was given fifty dollars to buy new clothes. And he was forbidden to drink, at least in public or on duty, and was warned by his superiors that if he did anything wrong, "we will soon find out."

Chambers found it dull work after the novelty wore off. The mystery of it all became a bore, the secrecy a burden, and the involved way of doing things a nuisance. Yet he responded, too, to the "melodrama working itself out so close at hand, among half a dozen people intimately known, in familiar rooms and streets, in a shared darkness and secrecy." And he also responded to the "sense of participating directly in the revolutionary transformation of our time, for which a Communist exists."

Whittaker Chambers and Alger Hiss: two men who sensed in 1933 that great changes were about to be made and wanted to be part of the making of them—Chambers in secret, Hiss in public. Two men so different from each other it would have been hard to imagine in 1933 that they would ever meet.

But they did meet, not once but many times, and at first Alger Hiss, like Matthew Josephson, didn't take Chambers very seriously. When he discovered his mistake he was in deep trouble; how he got into that trouble, and why he was never able to get out of it, is the subject of this book.

2

YOUNG NEW DEALER

WHEN Hiss got back to his office the Monday after Inauguration Day, he didn't get much work done on the Radio Corporation of America (RCA) case. He and his friends at Cotton, Franklin—men like Gerard Swope, Jr., son of the then president of General Electric, and Blackwell Smith, later assistant general counsel of the National Recovery Administration—"caucused and chortled" over the President's speech and argued about what it all might mean for the future. Hiss was in a state of mild euphoria; the new Gospel according to FDR was fine, exactly what he believed in.

He didn't expect to go to Washington and become a part of it, at first. He had turned down a Department of Justice appointment during the Hoover Administration, because he wanted to make his career in the private practice of law. He had a promising position with a good firm, and had been with them less than a year. They had been good to him, and Hiss didn't want to be accused of running out. True, his work on the RCA case was nearly done, but there were other cases coming up, just as important and as interesting.

The first thing that happened to change Hiss's mind was a phone call from Jerome Frank, then a highly successful corporation lawyer with a zeal for public service, who had established himself in the Department of Agriculture and was busy recruiting a legal staff to handle a new farm program. Hiss thought he knew something about farming, because he had spent most of his child-hood summers on a farm on the Eastern Shore of Maryland. Frank didn't care about that; he was simply looking for good lawyers, and he had been given Hiss's name by Felix Frankfurter, one of the new President's closest friends and advisers.

This was heady stuff for a young man of twenty-eight. Frank-furter was one of Hiss's heroes, a professor at Harvard Law School under whom he had studied and whom he greatly admired, a leader among liberals who had championed Sacco and Vanzetti in the great "Red Scare" of the 1920s, and an architect of the Norris–LaGuardia Act, which had opened the doors to modern labor legislation, while Hiss was at Harvard. And Frankfurter was a friend of Supreme Court Justice Oliver Wendell Holmes, whom Hiss had served as a secretary in 1929–1930 and whom he revered as a father. It was not an appeal to be ignored.

Nevertheless, Hiss told Frank that as much as he would like to be a part of the New Deal, he felt he had an obligation to his present employers, and couldn't leave them so suddenly. He was sorry, but he was not in a position to ask his employers about it, and he didn't think they would approve.

This was toward the end of March, three or four weeks after the Inauguration, when the bill creating the new Agricultural Adjustment Administration (AAA) was running into heavy weather in the Senate Agriculture Committee. Frank needed staff in a hurry to help draft compromise amendments if the bill was to get through before the planting season was too far advanced. At the beginning of April, as the Committee was sending the bill to the full Senate for what became nearly six weeks of debate, Hiss received a telegram from Frankfurter himself. On the basis of the "national emergency," the wire read, he must accept Frank's offer and join his staff.

Frankfurter knew his old pupils—this was an order Hiss couldn't refuse. And to Hiss's pleased surprise, his superiors at Cotton, Franklin raised no objection. Indeed, they gave him their blessing almost as though they had expected his departure for Washington; they weren't exactly "gung-ho for Roosevelt," as Hiss puts it now, but they didn't think he was doing the devil's work either. After all, there was already talk about relaxing some of the antitrust restrictions to help business on the recovery road, and this could help a firm that handled so much antitrust business. If one of their juniors went to Washington for the emergency, he would gain experience and make contacts that would increase his usefulness when he returned. All the bright young men were doing it, so why not Alger Hiss?

The decision was made suddenly, in a mood of excitement, and Hiss lost no time acting on it. He had family arrangements to make, but they didn't delay him long. His young wife Priscilla had been married before and had a son Timothy, now six and a half and in school; and she was engrossed in research for her book. So Priscilla and Tim stayed in the apartment on Central Park West at 98th Street until the end of the school year, while Alger packed his bag and headed for the Racquet Club in Washington and three months of bachelor living.

It wasn't the first time Hiss and his wife had been separated like this; she had come to New York ahead of him in the fall of 1931, while he spent the winter in Boston finishing his work there before starting the new job with Cotton, Franklin in the spring. He had commuted to New York on weekends then, and it hadn't been too bad; now in Washington he was to be working at the frenetic pace of Roosevelt's Hundred Days, and there would be no time for weekending.

On a bright sunny afternoon in early April, Hiss stepped off the train at Washington's Union Station, and walked through the huge vaulted lobby and triumphal arches that formed in those days a gateway to the nation's capital. It was the beginning of Washington's spring, when the blossoms were opening on the magnolias around the Capitol and the Japanese cherry trees beside the Tidal Basin.

Hiss checked in at the Racquet Club, up 16th Street from Lafayette Park opposite the White House, and then went straight to the old Agriculture Department building on the South Mall to report to Jerome Frank, his new boss. Rex Tugwell was there, one of Roosevelt's original brain trust and now Assistant Secretary of Agriculture; and Paul Appleby, a newspaper editor turned staff assistant to Agriculture Secretary Henry Wallace. It was a shirt-sleeves working party, eager young men crowded together in one ill-furnished office in the old marble building, because quarters had not yet been found for the new operation in the modern annex across the street.

There was no formal appointment yet for Hiss, because the bill that would create his new job hadn't passed Congress; it was to be part of his job to help get that done. There was no pay for the first six weeks, and even when the bill was passed on May 12, it took time for a payroll department to issue checks. But there was the exhilaration of being part of the new order of things, working with other talented young men to reform and rebuild the agricultural system, rescue the nation from disaster, and right some ancient wrongs in the process.

The young men Hiss met were all fired with the same kind of zeal, and he thought of them as sharing his views on everything. He describes them as fresh from law practice like himself, men who all thought they knew a lot, who were arrogant, brash, full of energy, working like the devil and taking pride in their work. Some were men he already knew—Gerry Swope and Blackie Smith soon came to Washington, and Tommy Corcoran, another veteran of Cotton, Franklin, was already there; he had joined the Reconstruction Finance Corporation (RFC) under Hoover and was more than delighted to find Hoover replaced by Roosevelt, whose close friend he quickly became.

There were others Hiss had known at Harvard Law School, including Lee Pressman, whose association with Communists was to add to Hiss's troubles in later years, and Harold Rosenwald, who was to come to Hiss's defense. And there were those who were later to be accused, like Hiss, of Communism, who managed to stay out of trouble by issuing general denials of the charge and refusing to answer specific questions on Fifth Amendment grounds. They were Nathan Witt, whom Hiss had met the previous year in New York but never knew very well; Henry Collins, a Harvard Business School graduate he had known since boyhood days at Camp Wildwood in Maine; lawyer John Abt and economist Charles Kramer, Agriculture Department employees whom he met on the job.

In later years, when Whittaker Chambers proclaimed that this group of men had been a "Communist apparatus" seeking to influence government policy in treacherous ways, much was made of the fact that they did indeed know each other and had dealings with each other in the course of their work. Ralph de Toledano and Victor Lasky wrote in *Seeds of Treason* (1950) that Pressman was the one who brought Hiss and the others to Washington; Arthur M. Schlesinger, Jr., in *The Coming of the New Deal* (1959), wrote that on the contrary, Pressman was brought to Washington "at the insistence of Mr. Hiss."

Either version suggests a picture of "planned Communist infiltration" of the government, one Communist recruiting another in a secret plot to take over the government by subversion, if not violence. Schlesinger, however, repudiates that idea and asserts that the men were hired by the government simply "because of the accident that Jerome Frank had jobs to fill." Since Pressman and Hiss had been classmates at Harvard Law School, it would hardly be surprising if Frank had consulted one about the other, and since they were friends they would each have given the other a good recommendation; but if Frank had consulted them, neither of them remembered it afterward. Frank already knew Pressman when he hired him; he had never met Hiss before, but hired him on Felix Frankfurter's recommendation. And it is hardly likely that Frank would have bowed to the "insistence" of a twenty-eight-year-old subordinate when he could consult Frankfurter, the President's adviser, to check his own impressions of Pressman. Hiss remembers Frank mentioning Pressman's name to him in their first phone conversation, as an inducement to come to Washington and join his friend; but it appears from the records that Hiss actually got to Washington before Pressman did.

The two were not exactly close friends at any time, though they probably saw more of each other in the two years they were in the Agriculture Department than at any other time before or after. Hiss liked Pressman, but then Hiss is the kind of man who likes everybody if he can; he hardly ever introduces a name into an anecdote without saying "lovely man," or "lovely woman," as the case may be. People he doesn't like he doesn't talk about if he can help it. But he remembers Lee Pressman as an extremely attractive young man, tall, handsome, well built, and well spoken. He wasn't one of Hiss's social crowd; he didn't ride horseback or play tennis, and he didn't enjoy music and the theater as Hiss did. There was a season's subscription to the Boston Symphony that some generous music-lover had donated to the Harvard Law School, enabling six or seven seniors each year to hear the concerts every week, and as each class graduated the tickets were passed on to another group in the next class. Hiss was one of those who used the tickets, and was extremely pleased with the privilege; Pressman wasn't interested.

What they had in common at Harvard was intellectual brilliance and an interest in some of the newer and more exciting things that were happening in the law, especially the new developments in labor law. Pressman was to make his career in this field; he became general counsel of the Congress of Industrial Organizations (CIO) and built a reputation for ruthlessness, which Hiss considers undeserved. "He was a good fighter, and he was hard," Hiss says, "but I've never known him to be dishonorable."

Communists were active fighters in the labor movement in those days, and Pressman made no bones about accepting their support whenever it was useful to him; in 1934 he joined a Communist group himself, but even after leaving it the following year he didn't break off contact with his Communist friends or repudiate them, as long as they were fighting for things he was fighting for. As a Jewish intellectual, Pressman's most passionate campaign was against Adolf Hitler, whose persecution of the Jews became a world issue after he seized power as German Chancellor in early 1933. Hitler hated Jews and Communists with equal fury, and persuaded his supporters that there was no real difference between them. As Hitler's most outspoken and, for a time, his best-organized enemies, the Communists were natural allies for Pressman, and he accepted them as such. And in explain-

ing his reasons for joining the Communists, he put "the destruction of Hitlerism" ahead of "an improvement of economic conditions here at home."

Alger Hiss had no such emotional involvement in 1933; his
family were of German origin, though American citizens for five
generations, and the "old Baltimore families" among whom he'd
grown up were mildly anti-Semitic without giving the matter
much thought. He had no particular prejudice of his own that he
was aware of, and had been trained to consciously exclude prejudice from his life; he did not inquire if Pressman was a Jew, and
in the same spirit didn't ask if he or anyone else was a Communist. He found Pressman's interest in labor law exciting, and
while at Harvard he wrote a note in the *Law Review* about
"yellow-dog contracts," an antiunion device which his favorite
Professor Frankfurter was then laboring to destroy, through his
contributions to what became the Norris–LaGuardia Act of 1932.

In New York Hiss met Pressman again through an association of *Harvard Law Review* veterans and their friends who were
publishing a law review of their own modeled after the campus
original, though with a different and quite specialized set of interests. Jerry Hellerstein, of the class of 1931, introduced him to the
group, which included Shad Polier, a classmate of Hiss's in 1929,
as well as Pressman and some other people Hiss had never met
before, one of whom was Nathan Witt. They called themselves the
International Juridical Association (IJA), which seemed rather
pompous to Hiss, since there was nothing international about it.
The review dealt with the legal problems of the union organizer,
the striking worker, the unemployed, the hunger marcher, the
dispossessed farmer, and the rioters who turned back the sheriff
when he came to foreclose the mortgage. The labor unions interested Pressman; Hiss got the farm cases, being the only one of the
group who had ever been on a farm.

The *IJA Review*, like others of its kind, contained reports
of current cases in which the writer analyzed the points of law
involved in the judge's decisions, the precedents and citations,
and the likelihood of reversal on appeal. The object was to present
the details that lawyers dealing with similar cases in the future

would want to know. And there were plenty of such cases, though the more established law reviews took less interest in them than did the young liberals in IJA.

These were the days when many dairy farmers were dumping their milk on the ground rather than sending it to market, because the price it would fetch was less than their cost of production. The idea was to raise the price by creating a scarcity, or at least getting rid of the surplus that people couldn't buy. The economic theory of supply and demand was the same then as now, and in 1933 it became one of the cardinal principles of Henry Wallace's AAA, when cotton was plowed under and little pigs butchered by government order. But such devices only work if everybody in the group agrees to do the same thing; and the dairy farmers who dumped their own milk in 1932 quickly realized it would do them no good unless their competitors' milk was dumped as well. When some of the farmers began to stop milk trucks on the highways and empty them into the ditches, there was trouble. People got hurt, and the sheriffs and police moved in, and people found themselves in jail and in courtrooms, arguing about who had done what and whose fault it was.

Then there was the tricky problem of farm mortgages, which were being foreclosed all over the heartland of America because the farmers couldn't sell their products, didn't have any money, and couldn't keep up their payments. A bank can foreclose one or two mortgages in a community without too much difficulty; but when practically every farmer is in the same trouble it's only natural for them to gang up on the sheriff as he goes from farm to farm, and keep him out by sheer force of numbers. And even if the bank succeeded in dispossessing the farmer, who would buy the farm from the bank and pay off the loan? Nobody in 1932 had any money to buy farms, and farming was obviously a poor investment; especially the small family farms in the corn, wheat, and dairy regions.

The solution was to put the farms up for auction, but in a community where nearly everybody was being dispossessed, the farmers had an answer to that too. Somebody would bid two dollars, and nobody else would bid; if anybody tried, there were plenty in the crowd to silence him. The successful bidder would then deed the farm to its original owner, who would do the same favor for him when his farm came up for auction. All perfectly legal, or so the farmers thought. Some judges thought it wasn't; there were arrests, threats, violence, actions for assault, people jailed for contempt of court, and tough legal questions raised by situations the existing laws had never been intended to cope with. The farmers and the banks were equally in trouble; it is not surprising that the banks were all closed by Inauguration Day.

These were the cases Hiss studied as a member of IJA, working evenings and weekends in his office at Cotton, Franklin. It was volunteer work that he found much more exciting than the antitrust cases that paid his salary; it made him feel part of "The Movement." He was doing something about the nation's crisis; he was involved. He fancied that the legal research he was doing would be useful to the hard-pressed farmers and to government lawyers looking out for the rights of the weakest classes of society, the people who were suffering most from the Depression, not because they had the most to lose, but because they were losing all they had. Until he joined the government, this was his way of trying to help; once he joined he found the *IJA Review* was no help to him at all; in any case, he thought best to sever his connections with the group to avoid any question of conflict of interest.

Whether Jerome Frank or Felix Frankfurter knew anything about these activities Hiss never asked. Frankfurter had a way of keeping an eye on what his former students were doing, and Hiss was quite proud of his IJA work, so it's possible; or Pressman may have mentioned it to Frank at some point. It didn't have anything in particular to do with Hiss's job in the AAA; but it expressed an interest in defending the underdog against the establishment that was to cause trouble for Hiss later, and to involve him in one of the first big battles that took place within the New Deal.

Roosevelt and his brain trust were doing everything at once in those first Hundred Days: drawing up legislation to reorganize the banks, abandon the gold standard, provide relief for the unemployed and jobs through the Civilian Conservation Corps

(CCC); to refinance farm mortgages and provide fresh credit to help the farmers keep going; to set up the Tennessee Valley Authority (TVA) and launch the National Industrial Recovery Act, soon to become the NRA with its famous Blue Eagle. All this, and the Agricultural Adjustment Administration (AAA), of which Hiss was a part—this was Roosevelt's first experiment in what became known as the "planned economy."

It was a program with three big objectives, all necessary and urgent, all requiring drastic action, and all more or less in conflict with each other. One was recovery from the Depression, measures to get business moving again, to put people to work, to put money in people's pockets, and to restore confidence in the business system. Another was relief for the victims of the Depression, and to the extent that this involved putting money in people's pockets, relief helped spur recovery. But since the money had to be provided by the government and involved such things as deficit spending, government handouts, and ultimately inflation and higher taxes, it tended to undermine business confidence and was blamed for hampering recovery.

The third objective was reform of the economic system to ensure that no such disastrous Depression could happen again, and to get rid of some of the abuses that were getting national attention for the first time. This was a long-range objective, which sometimes only seemed to be delaying recovery and adding to the burdens of relief; and since reform always meant improving the position of some people by taking advantages away from others, those who were hurt by it invariably protested. Indeed, because their loss was immediate and obvious, their protests came louder and sooner than did any appreciatory comments from those who were helped, while the gains that might result for the nation as a whole were uncertain and took time to develop.

This was the kind of problem facing AAA, although it wasn't defined that way at first. The main goal was to raise the price of farm products so the farmers could make a living, keep up their mortgage payments, and buy the products of industry. The farmer who got only a nickel a pound for cotton or a nickel a gallon for milk couldn't pay a dollar for a cotton shirt; but when textile companies couldn't sell their shirts they stopped buying cotton, and their employees who lost their jobs couldn't buy milk, so the problems of the cotton and dairy farmers only got worse.

The AAA attacked this vicious circle by paying the farmers to reduce production, which sounded crazy and somehow immoral, but it worked. With a smaller cotton crop, the farmer's price went from a nickel to a dime on what he grew and sold, while the government paid him almost a nickel for each pound he didn't grow. The farmer could live, and the effect on the dollar cotton shirt was to add only a couple of cents to its cost, since a shirt used less than half a pound of raw cotton. So the farmers could start buying them again.

From the standpoint of relief and recovery the system worked beautifully, but it ran head-on into problems of reform. The cotton plantations in particular were run on an old-fashioned paternalistic basis which had developed in the Reconstruction days after the Civil War, when slavery had been suddenly outlawed and new relationships had to be worked out between plantation owners and farm workers. It was a complex structure; at the top were cash tenants, only slightly less independent than the mortgaged farm owners of the corn and wheat country, and at the bottom were sharecroppers, only slightly better off than slaves, and in some respects even worse. In between were endless variations of tenant arrangements, depending on local custom and the needs of individual plantations and working families.

In the cotton South it was always the plantation owner who provided the land, while the tenant and his wife and children tilled the soil; the variations depended on who built and maintained the tenant's house (and how primitive a shack it might be); who provided the mules, plows, seed, fertilizer, and other necessities; and who made such managerial decisions as what to plant and where and when. It also made a difference whether the tenant paid rent in cash or a share of the crop, and how large a share; and whether he paid cash for his family's food, clothing, and other needs, or bought them on credit from the plantation owner's commissary, settling his debts once a year when the crop was sold and the shares distributed.

In this situation, how were the benefits and burdens of the AAA to be shared? There was nothing in the local customs to cover the new arrangements. If the acreage planted to cotton on a certain plantation was to be cut 40 percent—or 40 percent of the crop plowed under, as happened in 1933 because the act wasn't passed until the planting had been done—which tenants should take the loss, and how much of the benefit payments should they receive? If an owner in 1933 faced the necessity of cutting back his output 40 percent for the next two years, could he simply get rid of 40 percent of his tenants? If so, who would take care of them, what would they do for a living? If not, who would pay the plantation owner for the rent these surplus tenants would owe on their shacks and the bills they would be running up at his commissary?

These were essentially questions of policy with which Alger Hiss was not concerned. His responsibility was limited to the legal aspects—making sure that everything was done according to law, that the AAA law was constitutional and the contracts drawn up under it legal and enforceable. But questions of policy aren't always easy to separate from questions of law; the two are inescapably connected, and when fights over policy erupted within the AAA Hiss was inevitably involved.

The first year the tenant problem was simply ignored; the benefit program had to be launched in a hurry, and it had to be made attractive to the plantation owners. It was a voluntary program, and unless all or most of the owners agreed to take part it wouldn't work. A simple form of contract was drawn up by which plantation owners agreed to reduce production, and the government paid them for it according to a clearly defined formula. The owner was left to make whatever arrangements he wanted with his tenants. As the principal attorney in the crop contract field in the AAA's Legal Division, working under Jerome Frank as General Counsel, Hiss provided legal counsel to the policymakers who drew up the standard contract.

When the money started flowing it soon became clear that while the owners benefited from this arrangement, many tenants did not. The owners had debts of their own to pay, and debts from their tenants to collect; quite naturally they took care of these matters first, and the tenants wound up with smaller crops, smaller shares, and little, if any, of the government money. Though their debts were reduced, this was a cash benefit to the creditors rather than the debtors. Tenants were squeezed off the land, like the mortgaged family farmers of the year before, and became part of the mass of jobless, helpless, and landless who were streaming to the new Federal Emergency Relief Administration (FERA) for Support.

Before the summer was over the AAA was redrafting its cotton contracts for the 1934 and 1935 seasons, adding some general instructions to guide the owners in dealing with their tenants. The decision was made that owners could not meet their obligations simply by getting rid of tenants; the acreage reduction had to be shared proportionately among existing tenants, and the same number of tenants and employees should be maintained as usual, at least "insofar as possible." Tenants with no cotton to grow should be allowed to remain in their homes, rent free, and have access to woodlots and be allowed to grow food for themselves and their families and animals on the owner's land, and to use the owner's mules and plows in exchange for their labor—but all this was to be done in such "reasonable" and "adequate" ways as the owner should designate. And it wasn't to be done at all for any tenant who might "so conduct himself as to become a nuisance or a menace" to the owner.

Thus the contract offered some protection for tenants in general, and placed some limitations on the owner's freedom to deal with them in the usual way; but it also left the administration of the new provisions wholly in the hands of the owners themselves, who were not exactly disinterested observers. In the early planning sessions Hiss objected that the tenants needed better protection than that, but he was overruled. So he wrote a legal opinion on the matter for his boss Jerome Frank, who approved it and passed it on to the Production Division, then headed by Chester Davis.

Apart from the policy question, Hiss argued that a contract which required people to do things "insofar as possible" and allowed landlords to decide for themselves when they thought a particular tenant was being a "nuisance" or a "menace" was unenforceable; in case of dispute, how could a judge determine what was *possible* or what was a *nuisance* or a *menace* unless these terms were more clearly defined? Moreover, the proposed new contract would still require the government to make the benefit payments directly to the landlords, and require them to make a "proper distribution thereof" to their tenants. Hiss argued that it was improper, if not illegal, for the government to let interested private individuals make their own distribution of government funds to others.

After many conferences most of Hiss's ideas were rejected, but AAA Administrator George Peek accepted his recommendation that the tenants be given an avenue of appeal from their landlords' decisions, with the Secretary of Agriculture as the final arbiter. This was in line with the answer Secretary Wallace had given the Senate Agriculture Committee when the AAA bill was working its way through Congress—sticky problems like landlord–tenant relationships would be handled as a matter of administrative regulations. But this was no solution; it simply postponed the fight for another year.

The difficulty was that the only way the AAA could punish a landlord for cheating his tenants was to withold payment of the government benefits. But if the landlord didn't get the government money, he couldn't give it to the tenants, so they would be no better off. The Legal Division tried to get around this problem by proposing that payment be made directly to the tenants, but that idea was unacceptable.

Hiss still remembers the day this proposal came to the ears of Cotton Ed Smith—Sen. Ellison D. Smith of South Carolina, chairman of the Senate Agriculture Committee and a plantation owner himself, with a record of twenty-four years as Washington's most redoubtable champion of the cotton growers. He had been a senator since Hiss was four years old.

"Cotton Ed came to my office," Hiss recalls, "and it was pretty heady for a kid like me, to have senators come in to see you. He was furious at me, he said, 'You'll upset everything, what do you think you're doing, you young fellows? You say I've got to allow checks to be sent to my niggers, or I've got to pay them and give you receipts?' Nothing like that had ever been done, and Cotton Ed wasn't going to let it happen.

"After all, many of those tenants were illiterate, and the average landowner dealt with the outside world for them, and ran their plantations just like a feudal manor. Cotton Ed thought that was right; he thought he was taking care of his people. But we felt an integral principle of the New Deal was involved. We didn't think that sharecroppers and tenants had been treated very well in the past when they relied simply on the goodwill of planters taking care of their interests. So we wrote into the contracts all sorts of prescriptions, which we had no doubt were authorized. It meant giving these more or less subculture people status and standing; the government was reaching out and taking an interest in them.

"Cotton Ed was furious at me, and he was a good shouter. But I was absolutely unhorrified; I thought he was on the losing team, but he was an important member of the Committee. I wasn't rude to him, I sort of humored him, and I did my best to persuade him that this was part of the Administration's plan. I said, 'You should speak to Mr. Wallace if you think this is wrong. It's not my personal doing.' "

Hiss thought the venerable Senator was using him to bring pressure on Secretary Wallace, trying to scare a junior into bringing about a change of policy rather than facing the top man and making the quarrel public. But Hiss refused to be used that way. He didn't care if he got fired, he had a good job waiting for him back in New York; he felt he was volunteering his services in an emergency, and if some people didn't want his services, so much the worse for them. And he was young and enthusiastic enough to think he and his like-minded friends represented the "wave of the future"; he wasn't about to be scared by old fogies like Cotton Ed Smith. He was thinking of reform rather than relief or recovery, and he didn't know that the southern system wasn't going to be reformed that way.

What Hiss hadn't recognized was that he wasn't riding the crest of that wave, he was getting ahead of it and was in danger of being capsized from behind. The idea of making direct payments to tenants who had no contracts was never accepted; some tenants were allowed to sign their own benefit contracts for 1934–1935, but this affected only the small minority who paid cash rentals or at least furnished their own supplies and equipment and made their own planting decisions. Indeed, the problem of distinguishing between different categories of tenants created new opportunities for landlords to downgrade their tenants into lower categories, so again the landlord often gained where the tenant lost.

In the summer of 1934, as the price of cotton rose and the economic condition of the plantation owners improved, the plight of the tenants and sharecroppers got worse. Pushed off the land and deprived of their livelihood like millions of other jobless and landless throughout the nation, they wandered about the countryside, living on charity when they could get it and by stealing when they couldn't. There were no jobs for them in the cities, and they were not exactly welcomed by relief administrators of the new FERA. It was little wonder that some of them soon began organizing against the landlords, with the eager backing of Norman Thomas's Socialist Party, and a lot of attention from Communist organizers, agitators, and propagandists. Suddenly Washington began hearing about the Southern Tenant Farmers Union (STFU), organized on the then unheard of principle of racial integration, which was causing a lot of trouble, especially in Arkansas.

A Saint Louis attorney, Hiram Norcross, had bought a 4500-acre plantation in northeastern Arkansas, and was making it pay. He was systematically dismissing tenants who let their commissary credit run too high, holding out on the benefit payments due his sharecroppers, and otherwise taking advantage of every opportunity he could find in the AAA program. This caused a lot of protest and made Norcross a special target of the STFU; he retaliated by evicting tenants who adhered to that organization on the grounds that they were "nuisances" and "menaces." His actions were probably the most egregious abuses coming under the jurisdiction of the AAA, and they led to endless conferences in Washington, field investigations by AAA emissaries, occasional riots, and sensational newspaper stories. Ultimately there was such a widespread outburst of violence in Arkansas that it became known as the Arkansas "reign of terror" in January and February of 1935.

By that time the case had also precipitated the famous "purge" of the Agriculture Department, the first great confrontation between the liberal and conservative wings of the New Deal, the radical reformers versus the practical exponents of relief and recovery. The radicals lost and were dropped from the Department; while they found other jobs within the New Deal, they never again had the same power, and the ideal of a "planned economy" represented by the AAA began giving way to the return of more traditional free enterprise ideas.

In all of this Alger Hiss played a somewhat catalytic and quite significant role. His important contribution to the AAA program had been completed and his greatest battles for tenant farmers and sharecroppers lost by mid-1934, when the program of benefit contracts and acreage reduction was fully launched. The enforcement battles were waged by a young woman on his staff, Margaret Bennett, whom Hiss describes as "a beautiful firebrand, bright and sexy." She was a lawyer, which was unusual enough for a woman in those days, with the kind of attractiveness that was disturbing to young men and made enemies, as well as admirers, for ambitious career girls in a male-run world. She was also zealous in carrying out her ideas, and she made herself unpopular with the Cotton Section and lost on almost every issue. Meanwhile Hiss had been loaned to the Nye Committee, which, with a slender budget, was embarking on a battle against big business and the munitions makers, a cause that appealed to radical New Dealers like Hiss and his mentors Jerome Frank, Rex Tugwell, and Felix Frankfurter. But when the battle over the Hiram Norcross case erupted, the AAA Legal Division asked Hiss to interrupt his Nye Committee work long enough to develop a formal opinion on the matter.

The issue that dominated the case was the same one he had raised when the cotton contract was first written: what was meant by all that vague language protecting the tenants' interests "insofar as possible"? Specifically, the Cotton Section had been telling plantation owners that so long as they maintained the same number of tenants and employees after signing the benefit contracts, they were free to make any other changes they liked; they didn't have to keep the same tenants from one year to the next, or even the same categories of tenants. If they preferred to get rid of cash tenants and replace them with sharecroppers or day laborers, they could do so; and if they thought membership in STFU was grounds for dismissing a tenant as a "nuisance," they could do that too.

Jerome Frank took the opposite view, and since the question involved the interpretation of the law, he thought it should be decided by the Legal Division, not the Cotton Section. But he didn't know about the Cotton Section's interpretation until he learned of it in the course of the Norcross investigation in January 1935. Then he hit the ceiling. Chester Davis, who had replaced Peek as AAA Administrator, was out of town, so Frank persuaded his assistant, W. E. Byrd, to telegraph Arkansas to hold up action on the Norcross case; then Frank drafted a memorandum scolding the Cotton Section for usurping the Legal Division's functions, and called on his Opinions Section, under Hiss, to work up the necessary legal papers.

Hiss promptly delivered a formal opinion stating that membership in STFU did not make a tenant a "nuisance" or a "menace," and Frank notified Byrd that the Legal Division was instituting action against Norcross on this basis. Then Hiss put his assistant Telford Taylor in charge of the research and drafting of a much longer opinion dealing with the larger issues.

When completed and approved by Hiss in early February, the thirty-six-page opinion argued that a tenant could not be dismissed except for cause, and if a tenant chose to leave, he must be replaced by another in the same category "if possible." Trading down from cash tenant to sharecropper to day laborer wasn't legal. The opinion said that although this requirement was not specifically stated in the contract, it should be inferred from the provisions that "all tenants" were to "continue in the occupancy of their houses" and enjoy the other stipulated benefits, and that the acreage reductions were to be carried out in such a manner as to cause "the least possible amount of labor, economic, and social disturbance." Discharging tenants for the convenience of the landlord, according to the opinion, violated both these requirements and made various other provisions of the contract impossible to carry out.

Jerome Frank approved this opinion, and sent it to Chester Davis, along with a memorandum from Hiss suggesting that the law as thus defined would be difficult to enforce, since landlords could always fall back on the claim that the tenants they evicted were nuisances or menaces. Hiss thus conceded the practical difficulty while insisting on the legal principle, but so far as the battle between the STFU and Norcross was concerned he had already taken the STFU's side in his earlier opinion. And the planters were siding with Norcross; when Davis got back to his office from a Western field trip, he found his desk piled high with angry telegrams protesting the actions which Jerome Frank had taken. The planters liked the way the Cotton Section had been interpreting the contract, and didn't want it changed. Besides, it was too late to do so, for it would be fatal to punish landowners now for what they had done in good faith, relying on what the Cotton Section had told them.

Davis was furious. His first reaction was to call Hiss into his office, and demand what the hell he was doing. Hiss bridled; so far as he was concerned he had defined the law as he saw it, and if Davis found it unenforceable, that was Davis's problem. It was the same point Hiss had raised and been overruled on when the contracts were being drafted.

That only made Davis angrier. "Alger," he said, "this is a dishonest opinion."

Hiss was shocked. "Chester," he retorted. "I'm no longer on your staff. If you think that I would write a dishonest opinion, and you challenge my reputation, I hereby submit my resignation."

It was a discussion that led nowhere. Davis apologized, and the hothead withdrew his resignation. Hiss felt he had only done what Jerome Frank wanted, as any good lawyer does for his client, and he thought it was what Henry Wallace wanted too. Davis didn't agree, but it was obviously a matter that had to go to Wallace for decision.

When that decision was made a few days later, Hiss was astonished to find that Henry Wallace, the future apostle of the "Common Man," sided with Chester Davis and the rights of property against Jerome Frank and the needs of little people. But it was a decision Wallace had to make, as Hiss recognized in later years. To do otherwise would have produced rebellion in the Cotton Section and forced Wallace to resign, since Roosevelt couldn't let the whole cotton program be wrecked. And if Wallace resigned, what could his successor do? It was a lesson in practical politics which Alger Hiss, the young lawyer, didn't notice at the time.

It was also an occasion for Wallace to make a crucial decision about where his department was headed. The crisis over the cotton contracts ended not only with a decision in Davis's favor, but with a complete shake-up of the AAA. Jerome Frank was fired, and his Legal Division abolished; his ally Frederick C. Howe, head of the Consumer Council, was demoted and his agency reduced to a mere statistical service. Gardner (Pat) Jackson, Howe's assistant, who had used the Council in crusades for consumerism before the word was invented, resigned in protest; with him went Francis Shea, who had signed the objectionable cotton opinion under Hiss's direction, and Lee Pressman, the most radical of the lawyers in Frank's now abolished division. Jackson urged Hiss to resign as well, but he had already been through that with Davis and had reconsidered, and since he was practically out of the Agriculture Department already and devoting himself to the Nye Committee,* he didn't think it was necessary.

This was the famous purge, which ended a long struggle between the radical reformers, led by Jerome Frank and Rex Tugwell, and the practical-minded officials of the old-line Agriculture Department. A year earlier Frank and Tugwell had won the first round with the ouster of George Peek and his replace-

* See Chapter 6.

ment by Chester Davis; this time Davis won and Frank lost. Tugwell was in Florida and President Roosevelt made no move to intervene; it was an internal matter for Wallace to handle, he said. Raymond Clapper, writing in the *Washington Post*, said the effect was "the clipping of Dr. Rex Tugwell's left wing." The days of the AAA as the spearhead of New Deal idealism and radical reform were over.

The fracas over the cotton contracts was not mentioned in the announcement of the firings, nor in the press conference held the following day, when Davis and Wallace explained what had happened. They limited themselves to more general statements; Wallace talked about "harmony" in the Department and going "down the middle of the road." Davis talked about his "difficulty in getting things done." It was a matter of streamlining the organization, they explained, and ridding it of troublemakers.

Hiss returned to the Nye Committee, and though he and Secretary Wallace exchanged some courteous letters a few months later, he never returned to the Agriculture Department. He had made some friends in Agriculture, but he had lost some battles and made some enemies too. He had no reason to go back.

3

BALTIMORE AND THE FARM

I T was while Alger Hiss was working for the Nye Committee that he made the acquaintance of the young Communist who was to have such a devastating effect on his future, destroying his reputation and sending him to jail some fifteen years later. The meeting made no particular impression on him at the time, though it led to further contacts and a friendship of sorts, which was to give rise to many disputes. He didn't realize that his visitor was a Communist, for in those days Hiss knew virtually nothing about Communism or Communists; he had heard about them through his dealings with the International Juridical Association (IJA) and the Southern Tenant Farmers Union (STFU), but he regarded them as "energetic fighters for the rights of labor, doing God's work to help the jobless and landless poor." It was the same kind of political naïveté that had brought his battles in the Agriculture Department to such vainglorious defeats. His mind was focused on goals and ideals all his own, his view of life was shaped by his education, upbringing, childhood, and family background. At thirty he was in society's top drawer; a golden boy with a brilliant mind, the best Baltimore and Ivy League connections, and no real experience of the outside world.

Alger was born on November 11, 1904, fourteen years before that anniversary took on memorial significance with the signing of the Armistice that ended World War I. His family had been in Baltimore since the city's beginnings in the mid-eighteenth century; his great-great-great-grandfather, Valentine Hesse, born in 1729, was one of the German immigrants of that period who developed the rural lands around the newly organized seaport. Valentine Hesse married a French settler, Christine Arnault, who lived to be ninety-two, surviving her husband by thirty-two years. He became a successful farmer and landowner, and they raised a large family, changing their family name from Hesse to Hiss.

In succeeding generations the Hisses prospered, joining in marriage with other well-known Baltimore families. Alger's great-great-grandparents were Jacob Hiss and Elizabeth Gatch, and the site of their country estate off the old Harford Road is now marked by Hiss Avenue in suburban King's Ridge. His great-grandparents were Jesse Lee Hiss and Eliza Millemon, the daughter of the architect who designed the Maryland University Law School; they inherited little of Jacob's fortune, most of which he left to educational and religious endowments, but according to family tradition, Eliza counted herself happier than her sisters, who married money. George Millemon Hiss, Alger's grandfather, married Mary Ann Bosley, whose family boasted ancestors who had come to America with Lord Baltimore in the Ark and Dove Expedition of 1634. Largely self-educated, George read law, did some newspaper writing, and ultimately became owner and operator of two large paper mills.

Alger's father was Charles Alger Hiss, so named because of grandfather George Hiss's admiration, not for the fictional Horatio Alger, but for his old friend Russell Alexander Alger, who became Secretary of War under President McKinley. Evidently Charles Alger was sufficiently impressed with the name to pass it on to his son, though he didn't use it much himself. Charles was born during the Civil War, in 1864, the last of six children, and was educated in Baltimore public schools. After high school he became a salesman for the Troxell Carriage and Harness Company, and soon afterwards an apprentice in a cotton textile mill, before becoming a salesman for a Baltimore wholesale dry goods store. Charles was twenty-two when his father died, and two years later he married Mary Lavinia Hughes, the daughter of a respected middle-class Baltimore family, known to her friends and later to her children as "Minnie." Of English ancestry, she claimed direct descent from the Earl of Leicester, and on her mother's side from the Grundys, who were early settlers on the Eastern Shore and in Baltimore, and whose home, Bolton Place, became the site of the Fifth Regiment Armory off Baltimore's Park Avenue, which had once been known as Grundy Street. Minnie was three years younger than Charles Alger, and had been educated at the Maryland State Teachers College.

Soon after his marriage Charles joined Daniel Miller and Company, one of Baltimore's major dry goods importers and jobbers. This was to be his career and his road to business success; he soon became an executive, and by 1902, was a voting stockholder, an important position as responsible part-owner of a closely held firm. But before he achieved that dignity a family tragedy occurred that became a more important influence on his life and that of his children: in 1895 Charles's older brother, John, died of a sudden heart attack at the age of thirty-three. He left a widow and six children, the youngest only four months old.

From then on Charles became both the financial and emotional mainstay of his brother's family, caring for them devotedly, helping his sister-in-law with financial problems and treating her children almost as if they were his own. Charles had two children at the time, Anna, who was two, and Mary Ann, an infant. It was five years later that Charles's first son, Bosley, was born, and another five before the birth of Alger; then after two more years his last child, Alger's younger brother Donald, was born in December 1906. That made five of Charles's children and six of John's; they grew up together, not exactly as one family, because they lived six blocks apart; but they shared Sunday dinner together at Uncle Charlie's house most Sundays, went to church together, played and roughhoused together, and taught each other what they knew.

Charles was also helpful to his brother-in-law Albert Hughes, Minnie's favorite younger brother. He introduced him to the Daniel Miller Company, of which Albert soon became treasurer. Then something happened—nobody knows exactly what—but it seems to have involved some unsuccessful investments of the company's funds for which Albert was responsible, but which Charles made good. He raised the money by selling his stock in the company to the other owners, and that meant the end of his job as well. Albert remained with the company but offered to pay nothing, nor did he offer further financial help to his sister and her family.

Charles was forty-two at this time, and the year was 1907—the year of the famous Panic, the worst financial disaster in America before the Great Depression of the 1930s, though it didn't last as long. He couldn't get a job, his health was poor, his wife had just had another baby; in addition, his brother-in-law had let him down, and he was burdened with responsibility for John's six children. It was too much.

His elder brother George offered to take him into partnership to run a successful cotton mill in North Carolina, and for a while Charles's melancholy mood lifted. But when he went to North Carolina to visit the mill he realized he couldn't move his family away from Baltimore, and take his children from their six cousins, and his wife from the friends she had grown up with. And Minnie certainly didn't want to leave. Minnie was an energetic, active woman, who valued her place in Baltimore society. The Hisses were not wealthy by any means, but they were prominent, respected people. They kept their own horse and carriage, and on occasion Charles would hire a private railroad car for a family outing. They were seen at concerts and art galleries, they cultivated a life of good taste and literary interests, they knew everyone they wanted to know in Baltimore, they belonged to the best clubs, and they were recognized wherever they went. The simple life of a North Carolina mill town was not what Charles was accustomed to or what Minnie had been brought up to believe in.

So Charles's depression returned and grew deeper, and he worried more about his health. Only five days after his return from North Carolina, he sent Minnie to call the doctor, then lay down on his bed and cut his throat with his razor. It was Minnie who found him, when she went up to the bedroom to tell him the doctor was on the way and that it was time for breakfast.

34

Alger was two and a half when this happened. It was a disaster totally unexpected by family and friends, and although the circumstances were reported in discreet detail in the Baltimore *Sun* the next day, they were never mentioned in front of the children. Not until Alger was a teen-ager did he learn the manner of his father's death; all he knew in his early years was that his father was dead, and that was enough.

Minnie, left suddenly widowed with five children, one an infant, was a strong-minded woman, and the family rallied to her support. Charles's oldest sister, known to Alger as Aunt Lila, moved into Minnie's three-story house at 1427 Linden Avenue to help care for the children, and Aunt Lucy, who was doing the same for Uncle John's family, was a frequent visitor. The six cousins whom Charles had helped in his lifetime, all older than Alger by more than ten years, became an important source of emotional support. As he grew up Alger learned to depend a good deal on his cousins John and Charlie, as well as on his older brother Bosley.

Minnie faced her problems with energy and determination. She was up late at night and early in the morning, overseeing the management of the house, making most of her own clothes and mending and darning the children's. She kept a maid to do the cooking and housework, and left her daily detailed instructions; if the maid didn't always do everything she was told, Minnie didn't always notice. For she was out of the house a good deal of the time, busy with her club life. She helped organize a Mother's Club and became its first president; at various times she held office in the Arundel Club, Women's Civic League, League of Women Voters, District Federation of Women's Clubs, and the local Unitarian church. As she grew older her interest in such things did not flag; she worked for the Red Cross and USO during World War II, when she was in her seventies, and still belonged to seven or eight organizations when she died in 1958 at ninety-one.

Minnie liked to be well informed, and believed in self-improvement and winning advancement. She collected the advice of lecturers and experts on such matters as medicine and child care, and treated her children to endless exhortation and inspirational lectures. As Alger grew up he found his mother's aggressiveness a burden, and considered it to be in bad taste; his own instincts were more restrained. He admired his Aunt Lila, whose interests ran more to music, art, and the literary classics, and who liked to read aloud to the children. Minnie had no time for such things; she approved of them for her children, but preferred to further her own knowledge from the lectures and club meetings she attended.

In their different ways these influences of family tradition, social position, and early exposure to literature and the arts helped shape the man Alger was to become: one who was fond of reading, especially reading aloud; who identified himself as a member of an old Baltimore family with nothing to fear from any one else's social pretensions; yet he was oddly European in his sense of noblesse oblige, the aristocrat who considers it part of his role in life to be generous even when he has nothing to be generous with, to accept positions of public responsibility, to develop and exercise his intelligence without regard to the capacity of those around him to understand, to "show off" his knowledge without being aware of it as a "putdown" to others, to be arrogant without intending any offense, or even recognizing it when offense is taken. But there were many others besides Charles, Minnie, and Aunt Lila who helped to produce this result.

Minnie recognized that the children needed a man's influence, such as Charles had supplied for John's children; Uncle George now played this role, and for a time supplied Alger with his ideas of what a man should be. But Uncle George was the "rich uncle in North Carolina," and while he supplied regular financial help and was always excitedly welcomed when he came to Baltimore, he was not often there. A more frequent visitor was Charles Mann, a patent lawyer and a member of the Episcopal church Minnie attended in the early days, before she transferred to the Presbyterian and later to the Unitarian Church. He came often to dinner and found ways to organize treats for the boys. The thrill Alger remembers best is going to Mr.

Mann's office in downtown Baltimore to follow the World Series games—before radio and television, the play-by-play description was flashed by telegraph to newspaper offices, and the Baltimore *Sun* had a huge electric play-board that faced Mr. Mann's office windows across the street. As the game proceeded the lights would move around the board, each light representing a player, and if you knew how to follow it, the effect was the next best thing to being in the ballpark.

Yet Alger's childhood was mainly ruled by women, Minnie and Aunt Lila, and shaped by the children he played with, especially the older boys. He was forever being exhorted by his mother to be a brave little boy just as she was being a brave widow. Like other boys of his generation he was brought up on the stories of Horatius at the bridge, the little Dutch boy who stuck his finger in the dike, and the Spartan who hid a fox in his shirt and let it gnaw him to death rather than cry out, just to show how brave he was. More than most such little boys he learned to suppress his fears by pretending they didn't exist, persuading himself there was nothing to fear. It was a habit that made him admired by his childhood peers, but got him into trouble when he had to fight the more difficult and dangerous battles of adult life. By that time, it was such a habit that he wasn't aware of doing it.

Minnie and her large family weren't left destitute by Charles's death; with his insurance and investments, they had a capital of about $100,000, which was comfortable enough in 1907. Minnie had to give up Charles's horse and carriage, but that wasn't a great sacrifice because few of their friends had them, and the streetcar that went past their door on Linden Avenue was a highly suitable conveyance for fashionable middle-class ladies. All the children took music lessons on the old piano in the front parlor, and, by the time he was ten, Alger was taking German lessons every Saturday morning.

Bosley, Alger, and Donald always had chores to do; the most arduous one was bringing coal up from the cellar coal bin to supply the kitchen range and keep the Franklin stoves going in the

37

parlor and dining room, and, in later years, tending the coal furnace that was installed for central heating when Alger was about twelve.

He earned a weekly allowance of twenty-five cents, which he supplemented with the kind of enterprise popular among Baltimore boys in those days. One of his jobs was the spring water route, which in later years Whittaker Chambers remembered him talking about. In those days much of the German population of Baltimore, fresh from Europe and distrusting tap water, were happy to pay small boys fifteen cents a quart, or $2.50 for a five-gallon demijohn, of fresh, cold spring water that came out of a public spigot in Druid Hill Park. Alger and a school friend, Fritz Geyer, thought this a more attractive way to earn a living than a newspaper route, so they built themselves a long wagon with metal-rimmed wheels, which held a bottle rack big enough for two rows of a dozen quart bottles, and one huge demijohn at the end. They had to keep a double supply of bottles, so they could pick up the empties when they delivered the replacements, and some extras in case of breakage, which they stored on Alger's back porch.

Three or four days a week the boys would get up at 5:30 A.M. and pull their wagon up Linden Avenue and Eutaw Place the fifteen blocks to Druid Hill Park, and then up the hill beyond the reservoir to the spring at the top, where they would likely as not find others in the same trade ahead of them and have to wait their turn in line. Then they'd wash the empties, letting the water trickle in and sloshing it around, upending the bottles and methodically circling them so the water would pour out with a gurgle instead of a plop, since every spring water boy knows it goes faster that way. A boy could get his feet wet if he wasn't careful, but that didn't matter, because when the bottles were all filled and loaded in the wagon there was just room for Alger and Fritz to climb up beside the demijohn in back, and go careening lickety-split down the hill with no brakes, with a precious $6.10 worth of cargo, not to mention the bottles, to be lost if the wagon should crash. And the most beautiful memory of all was the cold winter mornings, when from a small shack at the park entrance, a man sold fried oysters. Oh, what a delicious snack at 8:00 in the morning for two boys who had been up since 5:30 working on nothing more than a glass of milk! It cost a nickel for two oysters on a roll, and that was a lot of money if the boys ate two apiece every morning, for they were eating up their profits.

Even with the oysters it was a lucrative business, and though the loaded wagon was heavy to pull, it got lighter at each stop as they made their deliveries on the way home. This was a more successful venture than Alger's partnership with his brothers in the pigeon business, which came a little later. By that time Alger was entering his teens, and Bosley, five years older, had some fancy homing pigeons he kept outside his bedroom window on the roof of the kitchen porch. Somebody had the idea of building a proper pigeon house and buying some of the big red birds that could be fattened and sold as squabs. Bosley, who as the oldest had the most money, put up the necessary capital, but soon lost interest in the project. Alger learned to keep the pigeon house clean, shoveling out the filth and putting tobacco stems in the nests to keep down lice, and he also got the job of killing the birds, and plucking and dressing them. Donald did most of the selling, mainly to Aunt Lucy and friends of the family who liked squab, and all three boys contributed from their allowances to buy feed. From their three initials, in descending order of age, they coined the name BAD Hiss Boys Pigeon Company, which they thought was so funny that they painted it on the wall behind the house.

It was fun, but it was also a lot of work, and the boys ran into unanticipated business problems. They sold and delivered the birds for thirty-five cents apiece, which was less than Aunt Lucy would have paid in a meat market, but the pigeons took eight or nine weeks to raise, and that meant a lot of feed as well as work. Besides, the rats got their share of the feed and some of the pigeons. And there was trouble with the homing pigeons, the pretty "blue bars" that had first attracted Bosley's interest, but weren't good to eat.

Donald remembers buying one from Carter's, the feed store where the boys bought their feed and breeding stock, but every time he let it loose the bird flew back to the store, and Donald bought it back, not once but five times. Alger remembers an opposite experience; the boys decided to sell Bosley's original blue bar because it wasn't laying any eggs, and when Alger took it down to Carter's it flew right back to the BAD Hiss Boys Pigeon Company. Alger took the bird back to Carter, who said it wasn't his loss, he'd already sold the bird to someone else who should have taken better care of it. So Carter bought the bird a second time, with the same result; the third time the bird met some other fate, and Alger never saw it again. But whether these are two separate experiences or two misremembered versions of the same one, neither Hiss brother could say today for certain.

Alger and Donald shared a lot of childhood experiences, since they were the youngest, separated by only two years. Bosley was the man of the house, with a bedroom of his own on the third floor, while Alger and Donald shared the room next door. Bosley was handsome, romantic, fun-loving—everything Alger wanted to be when he grew up. Sometimes Bosley would lead the family prayers on Wednesday evenings and Sunday mornings before the children went to Sunday school. But usually that was done by Minnie or Aunt Lucy or Aunt Lila, especially in the earlier years.

There was a lot of Bible reading and churchgoing in the Hiss household, and the religious training must have had a big influence on Alger's life, though he stopped going to church when he left home. Years later a television interviewer asked him what was the source of confidence that had sustained him through the trials, imprisonment, and struggle for vindication, and he answered, "Well, I'm a religious man, that helps a great deal."

"I was born and raised an Episcopalian," he continued, "and the Episcopal Church is very liberal. You don't have to believe in all the Thirty-Nine Articles, but I find my belief in the moral values I grew up with is very sustaining." It's an appraisal that might not be accepted in every Episcopal church, but the one Alger attended as a child was a breakaway group that considered itself Reformed Episcopal, and whatever its attitude toward theology, it certainly required many long hours of attendance.

There were services both morning and afternoon, one for the

children's Sunday school and one for the grown-ups, though in trying to recall those days Alger and his cousins disagree about which was which. Anyhow Sunday dinner came in between, and the eleven cousins and the two aunts would gather to eat at Minnie's house, and all the children had to report on what they had learned during the week, taking turns as they did for classroom recitations.

After dinner they had a little time to play before going to church again, the older cousins reading aloud to the little ones in the big armchair in the parlor, or roughhousing with them outdoors, or setting up the electric trains—quite an engineering job in those days, because they were powered by big storage batteries. When Alger and Donald were very small, they didn't have to sit through the sermon at the grown-ups' service; that would have been too distracting to their elders. But once they were confirmed, they were expected to listen and pay attention, and Minnie sat between them to make sure they did. Although she wasn't always successful.

Alger remembers a trick he used to play to make Donald giggle during the sermon, and it never failed to earn Donald a scolding from his mother. Donald never blamed him, because the fun was worth the scolding, and both boys enjoyed teasing their mother as well as each other. Minnie wore long hatpins in those days, as did all fashionable ladies, and there was usually some grown-up's fat bottom overflowing the pew in front, just waiting for a hatpin to be deliciously jabbed into it. Of course, Alger couldn't really pull out his mother's hatpin and use it for such a naughty joke, but he could pretend to do so. All it took was a silent gesture behind Minnie's back, which only Donald could see. Donald would burst into smothered giggles while Alger folded his hands and looked saintly. Then there would be the whispered scolding, and both boys would compose themselves, content with their Sunday adventure. Alger, having lost the thread of the preacher's discourse, would amuse himself for the rest of the sermon by listening for unfamiliar words and writing them down on a scrap of paper, so he could look them up in the big dictionary when he got home.

41

Alger was like that as a child; he loved reading, or being read to, or reading aloud when his turn came. He was bookish and he was bright, but he wasn't very big. By the time they were teen-agers Donald had outgrown him, though he was two years younger. Even when they were very young, Donald remembers that "he was my big brother, but he wasn't quite big enough—he couldn't dominate me physically, but he sure could intellectually." They both played in the neighborhood football and baseball games, but Donald was better at it, and sometimes Alger preferred to stay home and read a book. So Donald went on to be a college athlete, while Alger made Phi Beta Kappa easily but barely made the track team as a quarter-mile runner. He had gained his full height by then, an even six feet to Donald's six-two or three.

From his books, the Bible reading, the family prayers, and the sermons he didn't really listen to, Alger absorbed some of the principles of the Episcopal Church, which fitted in with his own experience of life. One of them was Saint Paul's famous admonition, "The love of money is the root of all evil"; Hiss now thinks that the fact that his father's death was associated with financial troubles accounts for what he calls his "neurotic attitude toward money." Another was Paul's "And now abideth faith, hope, charity, these three; but the greatest of these is charity." Modern translations substitute "love" for "charity," but in Hiss's childhood the distinction might not have meant much to him. People who loved his widowed mother and her family gave them things they needed, just as his late father had given to others and earned the title "Uncle Charlie the generous." He was taught to give and accept charity as a matter of course when occasions for it arose; and he has been sustained by faith, hope, and love because those are things he was taught to believe in.

There wasn't much discussion of such things in Alger's childhood; with so much Bible reading and churchgoing, who needed discussion? Alger left the reformed church after a while because he wanted to be a Boy Scout, and it didn't have a Scout troop; so he attended another Episcopal church a few blocks away that did. Minnie left it soon after and went to a Presbyterian church that had a more eloquent minister. Minnie liked good sermons, and Alger liked scouting: he became an Eagle Scout and a counselor, and one summer led a troop of scouts on a camping trip. But that came later.

Hiss's happiest memories of childhood are the summers he spent at Aunt Tege's farm near Saint Michaels on the Eastern Shore of Maryland. Aunt Tege was a remote cousin of Minnie's, with two boys, one Donald's age and one younger, and a younger daughter. The Hiss family would move to the farm every spring as soon as the school term ended, or sometimes sooner. In late summer the mothers would can the pears and apples and tomatoes for the winter, while the girls did the housekeeping and the boys did light work in the fields, and all the children learned to sail, swim, and catch crabs, and went on hay rides and did all the other things done on a farm besides work. Alger was the oldest of the four young boys, since Bosley was in a different generation altogether, and Alger enjoyed that.

There was plenty of work, too. The boys earned five cents a bushel for picking tomatoes, and were happy to get it, but what pleased Alger most was growing up as a farm boy and "eating lunch in the field with the real men." He helped with milking the cows and shearing the sheep and hoeing the corn to keep the weeds down, and joined the excitement of harvesting the wheat. All the hands from the neighboring farms would gather at one farm after another, bringing an old steam locomotive with huge wheels that could trundle across the fields, with a belt on it to drive the threshing machine. Into this great contraption, the sheaves of wheat were thrown, and straw was blown out through a spout into a great straw stack, while the kernels of wheat came pouring from a funnel. When he was only six or seven he was allowed to hold the bags under the funnel, and after they were filled, an older man would lift the now heavy bags onto the cart which carried them into the barn.

As he grew older Alger could do the lifting himself, and later he graduated to driving the cart; at fourteen or fifteen he went out into the fields with the men to help "set up" the wheat. The reaper would come along and cut the stalks, bind them into sheaves tied with twine, and throw them on the ground; then someone had to follow behind and pick up the sheaves in bundles of eight or ten, standing them with the cut ends on the ground and the heads leaning against each other to form a little hut. A sort of roof was made for it by half-breaking some sheaves and laying them on top, with the heads of the wheat dangling down on one side and the cut ends on the other. This allowed the rain to run down both sides and the roof wouldn't fall off.

Part of the joy of threshing was that it couldn't be done when it was raining but only in good weather. At lunch time huge trestle tables were set up under the shade trees on the lawn near the house, and all the farm wives remained in the kitchen while the men and boys ate their lunch in the open. For the rest of the summer Alger saw little of the neighbors from the other farms, but the men who worked Aunt Tege's farm were his heroes.

There was Cap'n Ned Dawson, the overseer, who skippered the little power launch, called the *Reba*—a child's nickname for Rebecca. On Sundays the *Reba* took all hands out on the Miles River with sandwiches and homemade ice cream, and the kids learned to catch crabs with a trot line. Cap'n Ned drank too much and came to an untimely end when he was gored by a bull, though he handled the animals well enough when he was sober. After his death the boys decided that the ghost of Cap'n Ned was haunting the attic, a dark and wasp-infested storeroom, where they were occasionally sent over their protests to fetch down heavy burdens. Bill Wrightson, the older of Aunt Tege's two boys, once dramatized this theory by covering himself with a sheet and materializing in front of his younger brother Jack at the top of the attic stairs, and Jack was so terrified that the grown-ups put an end to the ghost story after that.

Then there was Uncle Josh, Tege's husband, another heavy drinker and not much of a farmer, but a good waterman and an excellent shot with a bird gun. He used to show off his skill on a summer evening, when the air was full of insects and the long-winged bullbats, a local variety of nighthawk, were swooping after them like monstrous swallows, catching them on the wing, soar-

44

ing and diving but never flying in a straight line. Uncle Josh would get a bead on a bullbat, the most difficult of all birds to shoot, and stand on the lawn, weaving around and waving his gun as though he was too drunk to know what he was doing, and when it went off, he would fall flat on his back; but he usually hit the bullbat.

Cyrenius Caldwell was black and is remembered by Hiss as "one of the finest men I've ever known." On the long summer evenings, after a full day's work in the field, he would stand out behind the kitchen where there was a flat expanse of grass, not as neat as the lawn in front of the house but good enough for playing ball, and bat out flies for the kids to catch until it got too dark. Cyrenius's brother Sylvester was also nice to the boys, and let them drive the horses. These were not riding horses, though sometimes there would be a fox hunt and the men and boys would try to chase foxes on farm horses. There was a really difficult horse named Jim that fell down in the shafts one day when he was pulling a two-wheeled cart, and one of Alger's favorites, Frank Ellis, a salty-tongued farmhand, was thrown from the cart and pinned beneath the shaft next to the fallen horse. If Jim had tried to get up, it would have been the end of Frank, but Frank and the horse had a marvelous relationship. Frank said, "Whoa, Jim, whoa!" and the horse turned his head and looked at him, realizing his friend Frank was in trouble. So Jim lay quietly while Frank hollered for help, and pretty soon somebody came along and eased the shaft up enough so Frank could slide out, after which they helped Jim to his feet.

It was from these men, black and white working and eating their lunches together in the shade of a bush at the edge of the fields, that the future Agriculture Department lawyer got some of his first ideas about farm labor and race relationships. Sometimes there would be a tension that the kids didn't understand, and though blacks and whites would still work together in the field, they would separate for lunch. It was as though a cloud had blotted out the sun; something was wrong, and at first the kids wouldn't know which group to eat with. Then that night at dinner, when the two families were sitting around the big dining

45

room table, perhaps with some friends, the grown-ups would be talking about a lynching somewhere along the shore, or a rape. There were lots of such stories, sometimes exaggerated, and sometimes about things that hadn't really happened, but the tension was always there. Young Hiss found it very hard to understand.

And it wasn't just the times of tension; there was always an undercurrent, certain rules to be observed but not mentioned. Like the grandson of Corie the cook, son of her daughter Blanche and Sylvester Caldwell. He played with the white boys on the farm when he was little, for all the children on the farm played together. But after he was eight or nine years old, he was no longer permitted to do so. People didn't talk about "racial integration" in the South in those days; it was all right for small children, but they were supposed to grow out of it. Hiss never quite realized that, and his childhood attitude toward race stayed with him in later years.

4

THE EDUCATION OF A
HARVARD MAN

THE summer that Alger Hiss was thirteen, his mother decided he was ready for a more elegant environment than the farmhands of the Eastern Shore and the ducks and geese and oysters of the Miles River and Chesapeake Bay. So in 1918 and 1919, he was sent for the months of July and August to Camp Wildwood, Maine, on the banks of Moosehead Lake and the Allagash River, where he would meet boys from the best New England prep schools and counselors from such colleges as Harvard, Dartmouth, Yale, and Princeton.

Camp Wildwood was directed by Sumner R. Hooper, a conscientious improver of the minds of the young, who chose for the camp's motto a line from Virgil's *Aeneid*—"*Frondes silvestres puerique in fluctibus acres*," which he translated as "Wildwood leaves, and boys keenly fond of swimming." The camp published a weekly newspaper, printed on quality stock, called *Frondes Silvestres*, which carried inspirational messages about good manners and unselfishness, along with imaginative accounts of camp activities written by the boys. In due course, Hiss was elected to the board of editors.

He seems to have had a good time at Camp Wildwood and been a successful, if not particularly distinguished, member of the group. He played second base and won a bronze medal at the end-of-season track meet; he was one of the camp's two buglers, and had his turn as flag orderly, which meant raising and lowering the camp flag each day for a week, an honor for which two boys were chosen each Sunday "for their conduct and manner at meals." He joined the "Wildwood Army" for close order drill and study of the manual of arms under the instruction of four counselors who were veterans of World War I, which ended before his second year. He went on canoe trips with Indian guides and caught trout and landlocked salmon, and learned about Indian lore, nature study, and bird-watching from Ernest Thompson Seton, who visited the camp each year.

The famous naturalist and storyteller taught the boys that the Indians were noble savages, and that they should imitate the Indians' nobility and avoid their savagery. Accordingly, Camp Wildwood was organized in Indian tribes, and Hiss became head chief of the Black Feet tribe.

A major activity at Camp Wildwood was bird-watching, and the weekly *Frondes Silvestres* kept track of the boys' progress. By the end of August 1919, 110 different varieties had been seen and their identification verified, 62 of them by Henry Hill Collins III of Bryn Mawr, Pennsylvania, who won the prize. There was a lot of bug and butterfly collecting, too; forty boys caught more than 500 of them, representing 155 different species, to be displayed in bottles or pinned to cork or cardboard.

As a boy Hiss was only mildly interested in these pursuits; they were something everybody did at camp and afforded a certain competitive pleasure and the lure of being a collector. Later, when he was practicing law in Boston, he spent a weekend at Ipswich with a friend, who was interested in birds, and suddenly a goldfinch hopped into the room through a sunny window. His friend handed him a pair of binoculars and said, "Look at it through these." They brought the bird so close he could see the sparkle in its eye, and from then on he was hooked.

"I think they're beautiful," he says. "The complexity of the warblers' brilliant markings, the fact that they live in South America or Mexico and fly to our northern woods—the golden plover flies nonstop from Alaska, where he breeds, to an island like Hawaii, by dead reckoning—perhaps some die—think of what that means in terms of navigation! Then they head for the coast of South America, practically in the Antarctic—the precision engineering of the little creature, with a body no bigger than my hand, flying over a waste of water. Something tells him to do it every year, and he comes back a different way.

"Also bird watchers are nice people. They are not competitive in a hostile sense, they'll show you what they've discovered. They boast, but they're not monopolists, they're delighted if someone sees a new bird. It's a new life when you see a new bird— very exciting. We used to do it regularly in Washington. It's hard to describe why bird watchers like it so much; I suppose it's like trying to tell somebody who's never tasted steak what the taste of steak is. Any enthusiastic bird watcher will carry on the same way."

Minnie Hiss must have approved of the impression New England made on Alger, because she sent him back there to attend Powder Point Academy in Duxbury, Massachusetts, where his older sister Mary Ann, who had graduated from Smith College and married a wealthy Bostonian stockbroker, had a summer place. By this time he had graduated from high school at the age of sixteen, which Minnie thought was too young for college. He had made a better impression on his classmates than on his teachers; his grade average at graduation was only 79, but the class yearbook described him as "one of the best-liked fellows in our merry crew," and a "witty, happy, optimistical person," whose high school career had been "far more successful than that of the average fellow."

In order to save money while at Powder Point, he lived with his sister Mary Ann in Duxbury. He played end and quarterback, made the varsity baseball team as a second baseman, and was a mediocre guard in basketball, but doesn't seem to have done much studying or got much out of the experience. At the end of the fall term he came home to Baltimore, where he studied at the Maryland Institute of Art during the winter, and then went back to Powder Point for the spring term.

There was never any question that Johns Hopkins would be Alger's college. His brother Bosley had just graduated from there; he could save money by living at home; and Johns Hopkins offered scholarships. He had to get good grades to obtain and keep his scholarship, and he had to make a name for himself so he wouldn't always be regarded as "Bosley's little brother." Without much difficulty, he succeeded in doing both; by the time he was graduated from Hopkins he was a Big-Man-On-Campus of quite remarkable proportions. He was president of the student council, cadet commander of the ROTC unit, and a member of every honorary fraternity on campus except the engineering students' honorary, Tau Beta Pi, for which he wasn't eligible. He was voted the most popular man in his class, the best all-around man, biggest and best handshaker, and one of the eight men who had done the most for their alma mater; and he ran a close second for the most prominent person in student activities and the most perfect gentleman. The class votes he didn't win are equally interesting—he wasn't the best student, best athlete, best-dressed man, or leading politician, and he wasn't the biggest snake, most collegiate specimen, or leading "barn hound." (The "barn" was the favorite campus lounging place.)

The yearbook editor's description of him was a more than usually effusive tribute, even allowing for the hyperbole student editors sometimes employ. "And what shall we say of Alger?" it began. "Well, there is this to be said: when a man with a name like that can make a shining success on campus, such as he has made, he has the real stuff, nothing else can block him. Alger is the epitome of success, yet he is not the proverbial rah, rah lad, he is not a Hopkins Babbitt. Rather not. He goes in for culture, and activities are his sideline. Judging solely by the extent of his sideline, Alger must be the most-cultured, learned bozo around this neck of the woods. Many are the discussions that we have had with Alger, many and various. The topics ranged from Soviets to styles, from liberty to liquor, from Guelphs to Goodnow. [Dr. Frank Johnson Goodnow was president of Johns Hopkins.] And, like Socrates, we admit our ignorance in the face of his irresistible logic and rhetoric. To all of this we add the usual pat on the back, but this time it does not nauseate us to give it; Alger is a nice chappie, in spite of his attainments."

The "culture" Alger went in for in his college days was

mainly the theater, for which he had a passion. He had discovered the fun of acting at Camp Wildwood, and in his freshman year at Hopkins he joined a dramatic club, The Barnstormers, which specialized in farce. That was the year Walter B. (Pop) Swindell took over as dramatics coach, and the boys would have Sunday suppers at his home, talking theater and learning the difference between good acting and just showing off. They put on the kind of shows where the girls' parts were acted by boys, and made their own scenery and props, relying on their audiences to be sympathetic and not to take them too seriously.

One of Hiss's friends in The Barnstormers was Charles Ford Reese, whose family owned Ford's Theater in Baltimore, and in an earlier generation had owned the Ford's Theater in Washington, where Lincoln was shot. Charlie was also a fraternity brother of Alger's in Alpha Delta Phi, one of the oldest and most fashionable fraternities on the campus, and the two of them saw every play that came to Baltimore from the Ford family's box. During Christmas vacations Hiss would spend a week in New York at the Alpha Delt clubhouse on 44th Street with J. Hudson Huffard, another fraternity brother who shared his enthusiasm for the theater, and they would sit in the top balcony for Theatre Guild productions of the avant-garde drama of the period—George Bernard Shaw (*Saint Joan*), Ferenc Molnar (*The Play's the Thing*), Luigi Pirandello (*Six Characters in Search of an Author*), and Eugene O'Neill (*All God's Chillun Got Wings* and *Desire Under the Elms*).

There was an antiestablishment tone about this fare which Alger absorbed happily, in spite of his popularity with the campus establishment at Johns Hopkins. College boys are more or less irreverent in every generation, especially the bright ones, so he was not aware of any conflict between them. There was no real discussion of "Soviets" on the campus, in spite of the yearbook editor's alliteration. There were a few boys who listed themselves as Socialists, but Alger wasn't one of them; he himself was a Democrat. One of his favorite teachers, Broadus Mitchell, was a Socialist, but his views were regarded on campus as being harmlessly eccentric.

In later years Hiss wrote that Mitchell "owed the popularity of his course to his charm and wit, to his cultivated familiarity with English literature and to his reputation for being lenient in giving out grades. We were so thoroughly inoculated by prevailing social and economic views against his mildly Socialistic opinions that they made no impression on us. His examples of the shortcomings of business practices and philosophy did tend to fortify the moral and esthetic distaste for business some of us had developed, but none of us was led to consider the possibility of structural defects in our industrial society."

Nevertheless, young Hiss was picking up a lot of antibusiness ideas that he would be acting upon later as a New Dealer, and they weren't all coming from Broadus Mitchell. He was a fan of H. L. Mencken, that "scourge of middle-class values," who was then a resident celebrity in Baltimore. He revered Shaw, the apostle of Fabian Socialism, and he read Sinclair Lewis's *Main Street* and *Babbitt*, as well as works by Maxwell Anderson, James Joyce, and Theodore Dreiser. He was moved by *What Price Glory*, which confirmed his antiwar views and his distrust of militarism, in spite of his prominence in the ROTC. (After all, he explained, the Army paid him a modest stipend in the third and fourth years, and provided the uniform to wear once a week for drills and marching, which saved him money on his other clothes.) But at this stage he had learned nothing of Marx or Lenin; such subjects weren't taught at Johns Hopkins.

Nor were his interests in such intellectual matters very strong at the time. He was proud to be a member of the Tudor and Stuart Club, which sponsored readings by Robert Frost and Alfred Noyes, and which was endowed with the most valuable collection of Spenser's writings in the country. He wrote a wisecracking column for the Johns Hopkins *News Letter*, was president of the farcical Barnstormers, dramatic editor for the satirical *Black and Blue Jay*, and a member of the Cotillion Club, which organized the campus dances. He was also a stalwart of the Cane Club, a Prohibition era drinking society whose members carried canes and wore white carnations on festive occasions, and whose "conviviums" were described in the yearbook as "unexcelled for their gaiety, wit, and good fellowship."

It was frivolity of this kind that cost Hiss an award at Johns Hopkins that he didn't particularly want, although a lot of people expected him to win it. It happened in the spring of his senior year, the last night of a Barnstormers' performance of *His Majesty Bunker Bean*, in which Hiss played the title role, Charlie Reese played "a very young minister" and another close friend and fraternity brother, Jesse Slingluff, played "Cassidy (a janitor)."

In the final scene Bunker Bean was portrayed as taking the first drink of his young life, a tumbler full of gin thrust on him by his fun-loving fellows. It was a Barnstormers' tradition that, on the last night of a show, real booze had to be used on stage instead of the water and cold tea that were the usual substitutes, but since this was such an impressive quantity of gin to be put down in a single gulp, Hiss persuaded the club to let him drink water as usual, so the ensuing paroxysms of sudden drunkenness wouldn't be too real. The others agreed, but Charlie Reese got to thinking about it afterwards and decided that it wouldn't hurt to pour out half the water in the tumbler anyhow, and replace it with that much gin. And it probably wouldn't have, except that after he had secretly done so Jesse Slingluff had the same idea, and did it again. So Hiss's stage drink, which he expected to be water, was three-fourths gin.

An experienced actor and member of the Johns Hopkins Cane Club wasn't going to be thrown by a misadventure of that kind, so Hiss finished the play successfully and his slapstick climax brought down the house. After that the whole cast celebrated in the usual way, with more drink, and for reasons nobody could ever explain, they ended up on the steps of Gilman Hall, where they were puzzled to find a collection of whitewashed stones, gathered there for some purpose of which they were unaware. Hiss decided to build a pyramid with them, which would have looked nice, only before he had finished the structure came crashing down and cracked one of the marble steps of Johns Hopkins' most elegant building. Small matter, perhaps, but as President of the Student Council, Hiss was smitten with guilt.

The next morning, after a night at the fraternity house, where Charlie Reese held the housekeeper's dishpan for him while he got rid of the cause of his trouble, Hiss turned himself in. The punishment for the crime must have been something minor, because nobody remembers it; but it marred an otherwise exemplary record, and took him out of the running for the Alexander K. Barton Cup, which, as described by Professor George Boas, was awarded annually to the student who best exemplified "the virtues of Sir Galahad or somebody." The cup instead went to Robert Heyn, captain of the track team, which Hiss thought eminently suitable.

The big event of his college days, however, took place in 1924, the summer after his sophomore year, when he went to Europe on one of the first cheap student tours organized in the 1920s by the steamship lines. It was the beginning of what became known as "tourist third class," a new category of accommodations for young people who didn't mind being crowded into tiny cabins. There was plenty of space for deck sports in the open air, plenty of decent food without first class trimmings, and a bar, a good band and a dance floor. This was the way all the "Bright Young Things" went to Europe in the Twenties and Thirties, when nobody needed to be told that "getting there is half the fun," and shipboard romances flowered but didn't often last.

On this trip Hiss met Priscilla Fansler, daughter of an insurance agent in Philadelphia and a graduate of Bryn Mawr. He decided that she was that rarest of the rare and most sought-after by college boys, a combination of beauty and brains. She was almost a head shorter than Alger, a dainty woman with long blond hair and great hazel eyes, and her oval face showed the delicate and elegantly formed bone structure that catches a sculptor's eye. She was twenty and Alger nineteen; he thought she seemed fresh and helpless, and in need of his protection. He detoured to London to see her safely installed in a Kensington boarding house, and took a room there to look after her until the arrival of the Bryn Mawr friends with whom she was to tour England. Then Hiss went off to France, where he "did" the cathedrals and art galleries, the opera, the theater, and the cafés of Montparnasse and Montmartre, and bicycled through Normandy with Jesse Slingluff, the two of them singing and sampling the country wines and hoping to be taken for natives—or at least Europeans. Before the summer was over, Hiss was back in London to see Priscilla off to New York, after which he made his own quick tour of the Lake Country and the cathedral towns. And there were friends of Bosley's to look up in London. Then he, too, returned home.

Alger and Priscilla had not sworn to be true to each other that summer, because with two more years of college ahead of him and no money in his pocket, Hiss hadn't even begun to think about whom he might marry. Besides, his attentiveness apparently hadn't impressed Priscilla very much; remembering it years later, she denied that she had needed any "protection," or that she had been in any sense Alger's "girlfriend" that summer. She remembered her feelings toward him at the time as "brotherly but not emotional," and said she had regarded him simply as an attractive youngster.

They kept in touch, and it was only a few months later that Priscilla came down to Baltimore to visit friends for the holidays, and they were going to dances together again. Only by this time Priscilla was engaged—to somebody else. She was a graduate student at Yale now, where she had met Thayer Hobson, a handsome gallant who had been married before and could afford it again, and he apparently swept her off her feet.

The news came as something of a shock to Hiss, particularly in the manner of its telling. As he remembers it, they were crowded into a car with a gang of friends on the way to a dance, and Priscilla was sitting on his lap, which she had never done before. She seemed less fragile and defenseless, more mature and desirable than he had realized. He was just beginning to contemplate the possibility of taking Priscilla more seriously when she announced to all in the car that she was going to marry Hobson. He remembers it as a cruel blow; she doesn't remember the incident at all.

He reacted the way any normal, healthy young American

would react in such circumstances; he found another girl. She was one of the few woman graduate students at Johns Hopkins, a serious-minded blonde like Priscilla. She came from New Orleans, she was available, and she was the only girl Hiss ever wrote a poem about. For a while they were engaged, but when Hiss went to New Orleans to visit her family things weren't the same as they had been at Hopkins. New Orleans wasn't Baltimore, and he didn't want to be "beholden to her folks." So, in his first year in law school, he told her he didn't think they were suited for each other. He still wasn't ready for marriage; he had neither job nor money.

Law school was mainly hard work and Hiss was a serious-minded young man preparing for a career. He hadn't really intended to be a lawyer at first; his childhood ambition was to be a medical missionary, in emulation of some romantic hero of fiction or history he admired, but he gave that up when he found he wasn't interested in studying medicine. At Johns Hopkins he decided the diplomatic service looked attractive, a decision no doubt influenced by the good times he'd had in France and England. So he went to a friend of the family who knew about such things, Manley O. Hudson, and asked him what was the best way to prepare for a diplomatic career. Hudson, who was then professor of international law at Harvard Law School, naturally pointed out the virtues of studying law. Not until much later did Hiss realize that if he had really wanted to train for the Foreign Service, the place to do it would be at a Foreign Service school like the one at Georgetown University. But he took Hudson's advice, and with letters of recommendation from Hudson and Jesse Slingluff's cousin Bill Marbury, a Harvard graduate already practicing law, he was admitted to Harvard in the fall of 1926, winning a scholarship in December.

There he became absorbed in the law itself, and his interest in foreign affairs was laid aside, though not forgotten. He was fascinated by Professor Felix Frankfurter, whom he soon was calling by his first name and visiting at his home on Sunday afternoons. Frankfurter had been with the War Labor Board in World War I and had some experience of strikes and labor disputes; he was helping to draft the Norris–LaGuardia Act and writing about the Sacco–Vanzetti case, and he talked as much about these projects as about his classroom material. His wife Marion was a steadying influence for the young Hiss; she seemed to him typical of the "women of spirit and intelligence who were less likely to be corroded as time went on by the pressures of the marketplace and the outside world." Not that Felix Frankfurter seemed "corroded"; but Marion was a "pure spirit" and a lovely woman.

Marion was editing the Sacco–Vanzetti letters, along with Gardner (Pat) Jackson, the consumer advocate, who later would work with Hiss in the Agricultural Adjustment Administration (AAA) and be forced out in the purge; in the late twenties he was a young Boston newspaperman and a friend of Hiss's sister Mary Ann Emerson. He had inherited some money, and was devoting it to the defense of Sacco and Vanzetti. In the eyes of the Frankfurters, Jackson, Hiss, and liberals generally, in Massachusetts and throughout the world, the Sacco–Vanzetti case was a notorious miscarriage of justice, the worst in living memory or longer. The two Italian immigrants, hardly able to speak English, had been found with anarchistic literature in their possession shortly after the murder of two men in a payroll holdup at South Braintree, and though the evidence that seemed to connect them with the crime was flimsy and highly dubious, they had been convicted and sentenced to death in 1921.

For six years, the arguments went on in the press, at public meetings, and in the courts, over the weakness of the evidence and the prejudice of the judge. These were the years immediately after the Bolshevik Revolution, the murder of the Romanoffs, the exile of the Russian aristocrats, and the unsuccessful military intervention against the Bolsheviks. Given such circumstances, the popular hysteria against foreign radicals of all sorts was too much for the liberals to overcome. In August 1927, the summer after Hiss's first year at Cambridge, Nicola Sacco the shoe factory worker and Bartolomeo Vanzetti the fish peddler were executed at Charlestown. It was an event that those who had been associated with the case were never to forget, and to such writers as

57

Edna St. Vincent Millay, Upton Sinclair, Robert Morss Lovett, and John Dos Passos it was disillusioning and embittering in the extreme.

Another formative influence for Alger Hiss at the time was James M. Landis, later Dean of the Harvard Law School, who brought Harvard its first course in labor law in 1928. Hiss remembers it as not being particularly exciting or informative, but it was at least an introduction to the subject. Landis would sometimes sit up all night playing poker, and then go to work the next day, which Hiss found more than he could do, but he got to know the older man very well.

Beyond all these, the man who most influenced Hiss's thinking in these years was Oliver Wendell Holmes, then a Justice of the Supreme Court, and the man whom Hiss served as secretary for a year after obtaining his law degree. It was a Supreme Court tradition for each Justice to take a secretary (or clerk, as it is called today) from the graduating class of his own law school every year, selecting one of the best and the brightest to give him a broader insight into the law than he would get from spending that first year with a private law firm as he read for his bar exam. At Harvard the selection was done for Justice Holmes by his old and intimate friend Felix Frankfurter, who, after Holmes's death, was to be appointed to the Supreme Court by Franklin Roosevelt. Frankfurter didn't always choose the man who ranked number one in academic standing, but he had to be one of the top ten who edited the *Law Review*, and he had to be a gentleman of urbane taste and manners, who would get along well with the Justice. Alger Hiss was chosen in 1929, and by no coincidence his brother Donald won the same honor three years later.

Hiss remembers Justice Holmes as a skeptic of the first order, a man who believed in moral ultimates even though he denied the existence of God, and who agreed with the Old Testament Ecclesiastes that man's highest good is to do his own work well and enjoy the doing of it. Holmes was eighty-eight that year, which seemed impossibly old to the young man of twenty-five, and he seemed to Hiss almost an embodiment of the nation's history. When Holmes was a boy his grandmother had told him of watching the British enter Boston. His family home on Beacon Hill had been Lord Howe's headquarters for a time during the Revolutionary War; Holmes had a Queen Anne mirror that had been in that house, and according to Hiss, he "liked to think he could see in the murky glass the faint image of Howe's wigged face." Hiss admired the mirror, and when the Justice died it was left to him in his will, becoming one of Hiss's most treasured possessions.

Holmes had fought in the Civil War and had been wounded three times. So had Cousin Billy Lowe, one of the Wrightsons at the farm on the Eastern Shore where Hiss had learned so much; Cousin Billy had only been a drummer boy in Pickett's Brigade, but it was a point of contact. In a mystical way, Hiss identified the stories Holmes told him of the past with similar stories he had heard as a child on the farm, about Colonel Tench Tilghman who had brought the news of Cornwallis's surrender on his way up the shore from Yorktown to Philadelphia; about Royal Oak, the hamlet where a British cannon ball had lodged in a tree that was still standing; about Robert E. Lee, whom Aunt Tege claimed to have seen riding a white horse through a cornfield when she was a child, although nobody really believed she could be that old.

Hiss didn't entirely accept the Justice's skeptical views, for he was a romantic at heart, and was content to know that Holmes, too, had been more of a romantic when he was younger. Holmes had been disillusioned by the abolitionists in Civil War days; they had been the idealistic "movement" of his generation, not unlike the labor movement of Hiss's generation and the civil rights issues of more recent times. But at the time Hiss knew him, the Justice regarded the abolitionists as a silly bunch of propagandists, and argued in general terms that it was idle to try to solve the problems of the world through movements of any kind. Indeed, Hiss recalls, "He didn't think the problems would ever be solved. One just had to deal with them as they came along—you do the best you can, you have a humanistic outlook, but you don't think it's going to be the answer. I thought this was too skeptical—defeatist, cynical."

In this respect Hiss was more willing to follow the lead of Justice Louis Brandeis, an even more powerful patron of the New Deal, whom Roosevelt used to refer to as Isaiah. Brandeis was a champion of Zionism, a movement far too romantic for Holmes to approve; he was also a liberal and a supporter of labor unions and one who believed that great things really could be accomplished by cooperative effort. He was a frequent visitor to the Holmes household, and he made a point of inviting bright young men and their wives to occasional teas and dinners of his own, so Alger and Priscilla came to know him quite well.

Holmes was not in any sense antilabor; he had written a dissenting opinion in a Massachusetts case supporting the right of unions to organize and strike, in the days when most judges regarded them as simply illegal conspiracies threatening the rights of property. He was a humanist, if not an idealist; he would do his best, and he liked to help people, even if he didn't think much could be done for them.

Hiss loved the old gentleman, seeing in him the father he never had. One of his greatest pleasures was to read aloud to him, when the day's work was done. The Justice's tastes were remarkably varied; one day Hiss would be reading Hooker's *Ecclesiastical Polity*, and on another occasion, a new best-selling novel—Willa Cather's *My Ántonia* or Axel Munthe's *The Story of San Michele*. He read most of Augustine Birrell's *Obiter Dicta*, an English essayist's collection of anecdotes about the law, which both Hiss and Holmes found delightful; and Trotsky's autobiography, a work which the Justice detested but read because his friend Harold J. Laski, author, teacher, and one of the leaders of the British Labour Party, insisted on it. The book made no impression on Hiss of any kind; years later he was surprised to find it mentioned in one of Holmes's letters to Laski, of which he was preparing an abridged edition.

Trotsky's doctrines of Communism and world revolution reminded Holmes of the abolitionists; he thought Karl Marx's *Capital*, the bible of Communist theory, "showed chasms of unconscious error and sophistries that might be conscious." He added, "I think that the wisest men from Confucius and Aristotle to Lincoln (if he is entitled to the superlative) have believed in the *via media*. Of course that is unpopular in times of excitement and once in a thousand times it is the extremists who get there. But I have not had a very high opinion of the intellectual powers of such extremists as I have known or known about."

In the same letter (July 10, 1930) Holmes made a comment on the Sacco–Vanzetti case, which Hiss was to remember in a different context years later. "So far as I can judge without having read the trial," he wrote, "I doubt if those two suffered anything more from the conduct of the judge than would be a matter of course in England. It was their misfortune to be tried in a community that was stirred up, if not frightened by manifestations the import of which was exaggerated, and, without knowing anything about it, I presume that the jury felt like the community."

5

BOSLEY, MARY ANN, PRISCILLA, AND TIMOTHY

ALGER HISS had been secretary to Justice Holmes less than three months when he got married, which is not what the Justice's secretary was supposed to do, but Hiss didn't know that. Some years before, one of the Justice's secretaries had married, and the young man's bliss so interfered with the performance of his duties and the Justice's convenience that Professor Frankfurter was instructed not to let it happen again. Somehow Frankfurter forgot to mention it to Hiss; perhaps after seeing the boy break up with the blonde from New Orleans, he didn't expect him to marry someone else so soon. But then Frankfurter didn't know about Priscilla Fansler.

A great deal had happened to Priscilla since she blithely announced that she was going to marry Thayer Hobson. Hiss hadn't gone to the wedding; indeed, he lost touch with her altogether and was surprised to learn, in the spring of 1929, that she was divorced. He hastened to New York to see what the chances were of picking up where they had left off four years before, and it turned out the chances were very good. Yet they had both changed a great deal, more than either of them realized, and in different ways. They had had profound emotional experiences which they never discussed, for they both suppressed their emotions, concealing them from each other and even from themselves. Because of this habit, neither of them noticed how great the changes were. They seemed to each other the same as the day they'd first met on shipboard, and it was wonderful to be together again, almost as if nothing had ever happened.

Priscilla's marriage to Thayer lasted less than four years, for reasons she prefers not to discuss. They went for their honeymoon to England and stayed there a few weeks, then traveled to Paris and Savoy in the French Alps, and soon Priscilla became pregnant. They returned to New York on the French liner *De Grasse,* and Priscilla was thrilled when their son Timothy was born on September 19, 1926, just over a year after their wedding.

Priscilla got a job at a new magazine called *Time,* as office manager for its editors Henry Luce and Britton Haddon. Luce was a friend of Thayer Hobson's. Tim had a German governess named Heidi, a "great, big, fat, pretty person with pink cheeks," as Priscilla remembers her. In January 1929, Thayer got a Mexican divorce; meanwhile the job at *Time* had ended, and Priscilla was a graduate student again, this time at Columbia, earning the M.A. in literature she had not completed at Yale.

Hiss's emotional life in those years was shaped less by his brief romance with the girl from New Orleans than by the long illness and death of his older brother Bosley. All his life he had admired Bosley and tried to emulate him; when their father died Bosley had been the one Alger had first turned to for protection and leadership, since Bosley was a school boy of almost seven at the time, and Alger a baby of two and a half. As they grew older, Alger had tried to cultivate his brother's charm and wit, his literary interests and skills, his spontaneity and warmth, and his ability to make friends and relate to people. Bosley was a romantic, like Alger, and more of a nonconformist than Alger dared to be; indeed, Alger rather disapproved of his casual attitudes toward sex and his "undisciplined habits of sleep, diet, and drink." Bosley was a bit of a rake, but he was also brilliant, popular, and charming, and in many ways, Alger's ideal and his idol.

For a young man of such talents and proclivities, newspaper work was the obvious career, and Bosley became a reporter on the Baltimore *Sun,* as soon as he graduated from Johns Hopkins in 1922. But the long hours, the night work, and the temptations to eat and drink too much and go without sleep were more than he could take, and the following winter he contracted a severe kidney infection. It seemed to respond to treatment at first but then worsened; by the spring of 1924 he was an invalid with chronic, malignant Bright's disease.

To be bedridden at home was intolerable for the ebullient, gregarious Bosley, and after a quarrel with his mother he went to New York to live with Margaret Owen, a woman in her forties, nearly twice his age, with whom he had been in love since before his illness began. She cared for him with extraordinary compassion; she took him to Florida, where he got no better, and then to her home in Rye, New York, where he grew worse, in time becoming physically helpless. Under these circumstances and knowing his death was near, Margaret married him.

By June of 1926, when Alger graduated from Johns Hopkins, Bosley had been ill for three and a half years, and had not much longer to live. Margaret, a professional interior decorator, had to be in New York every day, and Alger moved to Rye to help out during the summer. Devoted to Bosley as he was, Alger thought of his last services to his brother as a kind of family duty; he regarded himself as "the family's deputed representative," and took the responsibility seriously. He ran the house as a steward or manager, driving Margaret's car to shop for groceries and taking Bosley to Presbyterian Hospital in New York for treatment. He read to him as he lay in bed, played phonograph records for him, and gave him the care that could not arrest his steady decline but could lessen his distress. Bosley's mind and spirit, Alger reported in his regular letters to the family, remained as vital and dynamic as ever.

In mid-September Alger had to leave his brother's bedside to enter Harvard Law School; barely a month later Margaret telephoned him, saying that Bosley's condition had worsened. Alger hurried to Rye with his sister Mary Ann, while Donald and Minnie arrived from Baltimore. Anna was in Texas, too far away to arrive before Bosley died on November 3.

The long hours of devoted service he had given Bosley in his final illness no doubt helped Alger absorb the shock of his brother's death and the impact of his own grief. Mary Ann seems to have been more deeply upset, for she had other troubles at the same time. Her husband, Eliot Emerson, had lost all his money in the postwar depression of the early twenties, and only the generosity of their two families had enabled him to pay off his debts and avoid bankruptcy. All the Hiss children had contributed something from their inheritance; Alger's share was $2,500, which was treated at the time as a loan because Alger was then only eighteen and a minor. But when Eliot's sister Ruth tried to repay the loan some years later, Alger refused to accept it, saying he would have made it a gift if he had been of legal age to do so. Ruth suggested then that the money be put into a fund for the education of the Emerson children, and this was done.

The sudden experience of poverty was more than either Eliot and Mary Ann could easily endure and led to continual quarrels between them. Eliot tried to recoup his losses by investing his remaining funds in Warner Brothers, pioneers in the new technique of adding sound to movies and turning them into "talkies." But before Warners had achieved success in this venture, there was another dip in the market and Eliot, who had bought heavily on margin, was wiped out again.

He was unable to change the extravagant habits of a lifetime. His idea of cheering Mary Ann, when she was depressed about money worries, was to buy her an enormous bouquet. There were fierce quarrels, many separations and reconciliations, and brief periods when Mary Ann was a patient at a sanitarium. Finally, on May 1, 1929, two and a half years after Bosley's death, Mary Ann climaxed a midnight quarrel with her husband by swallowing a bottle of caustic household cleanser. Like her father, she died at her own hand.

This was a month before Alger was to graduate from Harvard, and the news came to him as a shock for which he was totally unprepared. He had known nothing of the emotional stresses of Mary Ann's life, and her suicide seemed to him a sudden, irrational act which he was unable to comprehend. At twenty-four, having lost his father, his older brother, and now his closest sister, he was a very lonely young man. His renewed contact with Priscilla, which had begun only a few weeks before, suddenly took on extra importance.

That summer Alger had planned another trip to Europe with Donald, to celebrate graduation from law school and to revisit some of Bosley's old haunts and literary and bibulous friends before settling down as a sober clerk to a Supreme Court Justice. Before leaving he spent a good deal of time with Priscilla, without being quite sure what was to come of it. He remembers visiting her apartment and finding another man there, who seemed to be coming in and out as if he owned it, and Alger wondered if maybe he owned Priscilla too. She was ambiguous about that, as he recalls it; she doesn't recall the occasion at all. Alger went off to Europe feeling lonely for Priscilla, worried about the competition but hoping for the best.

About the first thing he did on his return that fall was to telephone Priscilla and learn that she was about to go into the hospital for surgery. Would he come and see her when it was over? Indeed he would; he went to her right away. She didn't tell him much about the nature of the operation, and he didn't inquire; forty-five years later she refused to discuss it for publication. Whatever it was, Alger concluded that the doctors would be able to help her, and he comforted and encouraged her with his bedside manner. Priscilla, it seemed, was ready to marry again, and now that Alger was about to start his new job, and a fabulously good job at that, he was ready to entertain the idea. Even the great stock market crash of 1929, which happened the same month, didn't deter him.

Priscilla was a lot like Alger in some ways. She had the same eager, intellectual curiosity, the same cultivated interest in music and the theater, the same adventurous taste for new ideas and a belief that the world's problems could be solved. Like Alger, she came from pioneer stock, and on her mother's side her Spruill and deRespass ancestors had been in America as long or longer than the Hisses. On her father's side her forebears were Dutch; grandfather Fansler had traveled down the Ohio River on a raft with his wife and children, from Tennessee to Cairo, Illinois, where the Ohio meets the Mississippi, and then the raft was towed up the Mississippi as far as Alton, Illinois, where the family went ashore and built a log cabin to live in. It was there that Priscilla's father, Thomas Fansler, was born in the 1850s; he grew up to become a trustee of Illinois College and a general agent of the Northwestern Mutual Life Insurance Company.

Priscilla was the youngest of six children, eighteen years younger than her oldest brother, Dean Fansler, who as a young man had gone to the Philippines, before returning to the United States to become a professor of English literature at Columbia. Later he would return to the Philippines to become a dean at the Philippine University in Manila, and to be interned by the Japanese for four years during the war. He was wasted and ill when he was released in 1945 to return home, and died soon after.

Priscilla's other brothers were Ralph, a bank examiner in Detroit; Henry, who had been wounded in World War I and was to become one of the top advertising men on the *New York Herald Tribune*; and Thomas, a teacher of English literature, the one closest in age and affection to Priscilla. Her sister Daisy was a music librarian at the Philadelphia Public Library.

Soon after Priscilla was born, the family had moved from Illinois to Saint Davids and then to Frazer in the Main Line suburbs of Philadelphia. Priscilla went to the Phoebe Ann Thorne School, a model school conducted by Bryn Mawr College, and was not quite seventeen when she entered Bryn Mawr.

While Alger was in Europe that summer she was teaching English in a summer school for women in industry at Bryn Mawr. The dean of the summer school was Hilda Smith, dean of women at the college and sister of J. Kellogg–Smith, who operated a camp on the Eastern Shore, where Timmy spent several summers in later years, and who became a good friend of the Hisses. Bryn Mawr was full of do-gooders, who took themselves seriously, and Priscilla was one of them. Alger regarded them as "blue stockings," a male term for female intellectuals in those days. But he didn't mind that; he thought it made her a more exciting person.

Alger's mother disapproved, however. She had heard some uncharitable observations about Priscilla from the mother of one of the boys who had known her at Yale, which Priscilla thought highly unfair. Whether or not this was the reason, Alger's mother didn't come to the wedding. She was in Texas at the time with his sister Anna, and she sent Alger a telegram which read, "Do not take this fatal step." It arrived on their wedding day, and Alger was naïve enough to show it to Priscilla. She never forgave her mother-in-law for that; and she is still angry at Alger about it today.

Alger was living in Washington at the time in a bachelor apartment on Connecticut Avenue that he shared with Charlie Willard, a Harvard classmate, who with remarkable generosity agreed to move out of the apartment after the wedding and let Priscilla and three-year-old Timothy take his place. The wedding was arranged for Wednesday evening, December 11, in the apartment; a Presbyterian minister performed the ceremony, and Priscilla remembers it as a charming little wedding, even though Justice Holmes couldn't come. A few of Alger's friends were invited—Charlie Reese, Jesse Slingluff, Bill Marbury and Ridgely Howard from Baltimore, and Dick Field from Harvard. Donald was there to represent the Hiss family, and Priscilla's parents were there for the Fanslers.

It was on the morning of the wedding day that Dick Field happened to mention to Alger that Justice Holmes's secretary wasn't supposed to marry during his term of office. Horrified at the idea of offending the Justice, Alger hurried to him and broke the news, apologizing profusely but explaining that it was really too late for him to back out now. Holmes graciously accepted the apology, there being nothing else he could do, and forgave the transgression. He told him to take two weeks off for a honeymoon.

Heavens, no, said young Hiss; he hadn't anything like that in mind, and couldn't afford it. But he would like to leave early on Friday afternoon so that he could take his bride to Aunt Tege's farm on the Eastern Shore for the weekend. The Justice agreed, and told Hiss to fetch his checkbook, so he could give him a wedding present. Again, Hiss demurred; he wanted no money. What would he like instead? A copy of Holmes's collected speeches.

The Justice agreed, and Hiss went to the bookshelves and

68

found a copy of the slim volume, which he brought to the Justice to inscribe. Holmes wrote in it: "To Alger Hiss."

"Oh, that's not enough!" Hiss protested. "Write something more."

So Holmes dipped his pen in the inkwell again and added, "Et ux." No name, no comment; just "and wife" in abbreviated Latin.

Priscilla was well pleased with all this, though it took her as long to get used to her new name as it does most brides. On her first visit to the Justice's home she announced herself to the maid as "Mrs. Hobson." She and the Justice got along very well after that, and he seemed to admire her intelligence. She enjoyed having tea and an occasional lunch with him at his home from time to time. Hiss concluded that it was all very successful.

Priscilla made quite a hit with Alger's cousin Elizabeth, a tough-minded, independent, intellectual woman; Charlie Reese's wife Laurie liked her too, admiring her alertness of mind and liberal views. There were others among Alger's friends who thought her too radical and too intellectual; some adhered to the older tradition that well-brought-up young ladies went to finishing schools and became debutantes instead of going to college, much less graduate school. Priscilla didn't care much for Alger's Baltimore friends; she regarded them as part of his "undergraduate" experience, which he grew out of once he was a married man. Alger never felt that way about it; but one of his bachelor friends is said to have observed that, after his marriage, Alger seemed to lose his sense of humor and take on "the air of one dedicated to a cause." Alger doesn't recall feeling that way either.

One evening soon after Alger and Priscilla were married they drove to Baltimore to have dinner with the Marburys, and other old friends of Alger's were there. Priscilla had met Bill Marbury for the first time at the wedding; the others were new to her. Alger remembers that on the way home that night Priscilla complained that he had left her to shift for herself among a lot of strangers while he had a good time talking to his friends. She thought that was "disloyal," and Alger was shocked at the word. If there was one thing he prided himself on it was his loyalty. Thereafter, whenever they were in such a large gathering he stayed at Priscilla's side. Priscilla doesn't remember ever seeing Marbury again.

Alger took his new responsibilities as a stepfather seriously, lavishing on Timothy the care and attention he wished he had had from a father of his own. But it seems to have been a conscientious effort rather than a spontaneous reaction; he and Priscilla read books on child psychology, which she regards as wise and sensible, and reasoned with the child when he would rather have been scolded or spanked. As Timothy grew older he came to think of his stepfather as a "walking beatitude"; it was like living with a Presbyterian minister, and he found it a burden.

As a child, Tim called his parents Alger and Prossy instead of Dad and Mummy, which pleased Priscilla. This was considered quite modern in those days, and it dodged the question of whether Tim could accept his stepfather as the father he wanted to be. Visitors sometimes had the impression that Prossy never said no to the child and let him ask too many questions; she remembers giving him "lots of nurture and maybe some curbing." Every effort seems to have been made to avoid open displays of emotion, on the part of either the child or his parents. When Alger and Priscilla had a dispute, they would reason with each other, which usually meant that Alger would offer a compromise, and if Priscilla didn't accept it, he would say, "Well, I think we're making too much of this. Let's not discuss it any further." Whatever it was they had been arguing about, in the end it would be done Priscilla's way, and Alger would go out for a walk around the block to get rid of his anger. He had a temper, and those who knew him well could see it at work inside him, but from the time he was quite small and for nearly thirty years of married life, he never allowed himself to show it.

Alger wanted children of his own, brothers and sisters for Timothy, and so did Priscilla, but for a long time she was afraid she couldn't have any more children. In the course of their discussions of the subject over the years, Alger learned a lot of things about Priscilla that he hadn't known before, including the fact that she had once had an abortion, which was illegal in those days.

Priscilla naturally wanted no one else to know about it, and Alger kept her secret for thirty-five years or more—over forty-five, according to Priscilla, who says she told him about it when they were first married; as Alger recalls it she didn't tell him until they had been married at least ten years. In any case, many things that happened at Hiss's perjury trials were influenced by Hiss's knowledge of this secret and the way he protected it.

The long years of waiting for another child finally ended, and on August 5, 1941, Anthony Hiss was born, to his parents' supreme delight. His mother was then thirty-seven, his father thirty-six, and his stepbrother Tim not quite fifteen.

None of these considerations were in the young couple's minds in the early days, of course. Alger devoted himself to the Justice, while Priscilla went house-hunting, finding a place on Thirtieth Street recently vacated by Drew Pearson, into which they were able to move from Charlie Willard's bachelor "digs." She became an assistant librarian for the Wickersham Commission, which was studying proposals for judicial reform, and among other things, was finding much to criticize in the way the Sacco–Vanzetti case had been handled.

When summer came, and the Justice went to his country home in Beverly Farms, Massachusetts, Hiss volunteered to go with him, although traditionally the Justice's secretary had the summer free. But Holmes's wife had just died, and the old gentleman was desolate. Hiss thought he could be of use, and the Justice agreed, so he and Priscilla and Timmy went with him and rented a summer place of their own at nearby Montserrat. They used to picnic on the beach, and one day Timmy made a great impression on Felix Frankfurter, who had come up from Cambridge to visit Holmes, by asking him, "Oh, do you know Justice too?" Out of the mouths of babes and sucklings, thought the professor; for to him, as to Alger Hiss, Mr. Justice Holmes was the very embodiment of the whole idea.

By the time that summer was over Hiss had a job with Choate, Hall & Stewart in Boston, and an apartment in Cambridge, where he looked forward to a contented life practicing law in the company of old friends from Harvard. But within a year Priscilla decided to go to New York to collaborate with her old friend and sister-in-law Roberta Fansler on a book about fine arts for the Carnegie Foundation. Alger got a job with the New York law firm of Cotton, Franklin, Wright & Gordon, but he couldn't leave Boston until some litigation he was working on for Choate, Hall & Stewart was completed.

Priscilla went to New York in the fall of 1931, and settled into an apartment on Claremont Avenue in the same building as Roberta and her husband, Priscilla's brother Tom Fansler. Her apartment was on the same floor as the Fanslers', so Timmy could play with their children, and it was all very convenient. Alger came down from Boston on weekends during the winter to visit.

This was the winter of 1931–1932, the first really bad one of the Depression, and the hardships of the unemployed were a lot more obvious in New York than in Boston. Along Riverside Drive, not far from Priscilla's apartment, was a vast and shabby array of tarpaper shacks and empty crates and packing cases, where the homeless and jobless huddled for shelter on public land from which the city dared not evict them. They filled the park from the Drive down to the river, where cars now travel the Henry Hudson Parkway. This was a "Hooverville," one of many around New York City and in other major cities throughout the nation, so called in contempt of the President, who was exhorting businessmen to solve their own problems and put the unemployed back to work so that the government wouldn't have to support them or make jobs for them.

Hiss had watched Hoover's efforts at first with complacent hope and then growing disillusionment, coming gradually to the conviction that the business leaders on whom Hoover relied could not or would not solve the problem; that the private charities in which Hoover placed his faith would never be adequate to do the job; and that those who argued that the basic economic problem was not "overproduction" but "underconsumption," caused by too many working people being paid too little for the work they did, were probably right. From his liberal friends in academic Cambridge, he had absorbed the idea that it made sense for working

72

people to band together in labor unions and force the managers of industry to give them what they would not give freely. He had read some of the publications of A. J. Muste's Brookwood Labor College, and talked to some of the men who had lectured there. He had begun to study the history of labor and social reform, and had finally discovered Karl Marx, Robert Owen, and Sidney Webb.

Hiss was appalled at the sight of the apple vendors who stood on every downtown street corner in their threadbare overcoats that winter, marketing the orchards' surplus at five cents apiece, a high price for those days and one that gave the purchaser a sense of doing charity, but gave the ex-businessmen who sold them a pitifully poor living. These were self-respecting middle-class executives, salesmen, teachers, and clerks, who had lost their jobs through no fault of their own and were in danger of losing their dignity as well, for it was hard to escape the idea that somehow it must be their fault that the axe had fallen on them instead of others. And the apple vendors were the lucky ones; they at least had enough money to buy the apples they sold, and a little money left at the end of the day, or apples to eat if they couldn't sell them.

In more desperate condition were the penniless men in the Hoovervilles, who came every day to the soup kitchens and bread-lines along upper Broadway for the pathetic handouts that the Salvation Army and other smaller, newer missions could afford to give. There was one near Priscilla's apartment that she discovered soon after she moved in, operated by the local branch of the Socialist Party, and Priscilla decided "in a burst of sympathy or altruism" to help by making sandwiches. This led to a lot of argument at Hiss's perjury trials, when Priscilla admitted that she had worked in the Socialist "feeding station," contributed small sums of money, gone to some party meetings, and identified herself as a Socialist when she registered to vote in 1932. But she insisted then and still does that she never joined the Socialist Party.

Hiss had no objection to all this; he thought it quite right and proper, and he attended some of the meetings with his wife to hear about the Socialists' proposals for relief of the poor and reform of the economic system. Tom Fansler, who was then out of a job, went with them on one occasion, but once was enough for him. The talk that evening was being given by a rather bedraggled seaman, who addressed his audience as "Comrades," in the Communist fashion. Fansler shot up from his seat and shouted, "Don't you call me 'Comrade'!" and Hiss remembers Priscilla pulling him down in evident embarrassment.

The Hisses' interest in Socialism caused some dismay among their more conservative friends and relatives, though Priscilla says she was unaware of it. One of Alger's bachelor friends remembered commenting mildly that it was a nice day, only to be told by Priscilla that "It might be a nice day for people with homes and servants, but it wasn't a very nice day for the sharecroppers in Oklahoma!" Priscilla denies that she would ever have said such a thing, and Alger doesn't remember being present at the time, but he says it would have been perfectly in character for her, and in those days he might have said the same thing. He was already reading up about sharecroppers for the International Juridical Association (IJA), though it wasn't until he joined the AAA in 1933 that he was in a position to try to help them.

When spring came Hiss was ready to settle in New York, and he moved Priscilla from Claremont Avenue to more agreeable premises on Central Park West. The Claremont Avenue apartment was of the "railroad" type, one room wide with a narrow hall running from the front of the building to the back. Alger remembers it as a roach-ridden walk-up; Priscilla says there was an elevator and no roaches. In any case, now that Alger was back with her, they were no longer obliged to rent separate establishments and could afford to live more comfortably. But they still didn't have a great deal of time to spend together. Alger established the habit of working evenings and weekends, as became an eager young lawyer on the way up; while Priscilla was busy with her sister-in-law writing their book. They no longer went to the Socialist meetings on Claremont Avenue, but the IJA that kept Hiss so busy was working on the same kind of problems.

The move to Washington and the Department of Agriculture

the following year was a further improvement in their living standard. They found a comfortable house in Georgetown at 3411 O Street, with extra rooms on the top floor that were made into an apartment for Alger's brother Donald, who was Justice Holmes's secretary that year. After she and Roberta had finished their book, Priscilla took a volunteer job in a subsistence home-steads project, organized in the Interior Department by Eleanor Roosevelt and run by Clarence Pickett, a Quaker who later became famous as head of the American Friends Service Committee.

Now Hiss was working longer hours than ever, staying late at the office almost every night, spending his Saturdays and Sundays in work sessions with the other men at Jerome Frank's big house on P Street, or at Rex Tugwell's, or at the homes of his New Deal bachelor friends. It was very much of a man's world, in which Priscilla saw herself as a good wife and Georgetown matron, devoted to her husband and his career. Even the summer picnics in Rock Creek Park or at Dean Acheson's country place in Ashton were working sessions; Priscilla went along with the other wives and girlfriends, and the women prepared and served the food, while the men talked shop. She didn't play tennis or ride horseback with Alger; she had been thrown by a horse when she was about twelve, and, while it did her no permanent harm, she never enjoyed riding after that. But they belonged to a skating club and went there together in winter.

Priscilla had some lonely meals at home, but there were also times when suddenly five or six people would drop in, and she'd feed them with whatever was available. They didn't do much formal entertaining until a few years later, when Hiss was in the State Department, and it had become part of the job.

He used to take the streetcars to work, as most people in Washington did then. They were some of the nation's best—numerous, fast, clean, comfortable, the fare was only a dime. They came out of Georgetown on O and M Streets and along Wisconsin Avenue, meeting cars from other parts of the city and passing down Pennsylvania Avenue past the White House in a solid phalanx, bumper to bumper but moving. Sometimes around 8:00 or 8:30 in the evening Priscilla would run down to Alger's office in their little Ford roadster to pick him up for dinner, and usually it meant a lot of waiting when she got there. It wasn't until he'd been in Washington several months that Hiss happened to be out on the street going somewhere at 5:00 o'clock, when the government offices were closing and all the clerks were pouring out on to the street. He'd never seen anything like it and couldn't imagine what was happening; at first he thought there must be a fire.

Timothy attended a series of private schools, which in Priscilla's words were "of uneven merit, but all with considerable individual supervision and little formal schooling." By the time he was ten, in 1936, he could read well and enjoyed it, but was poor at spelling and writing; fond of arithmetic, but without satisfactory grounding in the fundamentals, for which his mother thought he would "require special help." He enjoyed music, had a naturally good ear and sense of rhythm, and liked to sing.

In the summers he went to a camp on the Eastern Shore called Rigs O'Marlow, operated by the Hisses' friend J. Kellogg–Smith and his wife Peggy. The camp was near Chestertown, where for some years the Hisses rented an apartment in the summer in order to be near Tim. At camp Tim enjoyed the swimming and riding, but wasn't good at organized sports and was often tense and overexcited. But the Kellogg–Smiths were very fond of him.

Under the terms of Priscilla's divorce settlement, Thayer Hobson undertook to pay for Tim's education, so he always went to private schools. His performance at the early progressive schools was disappointing, and when he was nine he was transferred to the Sidwell Friends School but did no better there. After a year he was withdrawn and placed in the Landon School, off Connecticut Avenue, which seemed more promising although it was more expensive. As a teen-ager he went to George School, a Quaker boarding school near Doylestown, Pennsylvania. This was more than Thayer Hobson could afford, so Hiss paid part of the cost.

From time to time over the years, Tim visited his father, who gave him rather more presents than Priscilla thought wise. She would find "traces of strain" on his return, which she attributed to the "lavish" presents and the "absence of familiar routine." For his part, Tim remembers enjoying those visits. He doesn't recall much about his father's third wife, but he grew to love the fourth. She let him spend the day collecting frogs on their farm in upstate New York for a frogs' legs dinner, and only thought it was funny when he upset the bucket and the frogs went jumping and slippy-sliding all over the kitchen floor, and had to be caught all over again.

After her year of volunteer work on subsistence homesteads, Priscilla devoted herself to the Bryn Mawr Alumnae Association of Washington, of which she was president in 1936–1937, and then to premedical studies, which she was obliged to give up when she found she didn't have enough time for them. In 1940–1941 she worked in the Library of Congress on the staff of Julian Levitt, then head of the Catalogue Division. She had been his assistant before, when the Hisses were first in Washington in 1930, and Levitt was librarian of the Wickersham Commission. After the Commission's work was finished Levitt went through a period of very hard times; he was out of work in the depths of the Depression and lived for a while in a tiny shack in Norwalk, Connecticut, where the Hisses used to visit him when they were living in New York. They would bring him crates of canned goods to live on; nothing fancy, but solid food that he needed, and they even managed to scrape together a little money to lend him. He repaid it all later, a couple of hundred dollars altogether, after he got the Library of Congress appointment.

That was the way a lot of people did things during the Depression, if they could. Hiss thought everybody did, but as he was to find out later, he was wrong about that.

6

THE NYE COMMITTEE

IN the Spring of 1934, after Donald had finished his year with Justice Holmes and moved into his own place, the Hisses moved from O Street to 2831 Twenty-eighth Street, near the Wardman Park Hotel. Their apartment was another walk-up, on the top floor of a four-story building of square, solid masonry that looked out of place at the end of a row of neat little houses that climbed side-by-side up the hill. The Hisses were at the rear with a fire escape and a view of the neighbors' laundry. The place was less expensive, but Priscilla didn't like it as much as Georgetown. Timmy was eight by now, and Alger was spending most of his time on Capitol Hill with the Special Senate Committee to Investigate the Munitions Industry, of which Sen. Gerald P. Nye of North Dakota was chairman.

The Committee was established in the spring of 1934, in response to a vague feeling among the public that there ought to be some better way of handling the threat of another war than the endless disarmament conferences that had been going on in Europe ever since the end of World War I. Of course, it was not called World War I in those days; it had been talked about as the "war to end wars," and it had been the most devastating experience of mass murder the mind of man had so far achieved. Millions of people in America devoutly hoped there would never be another war like it, but, already in 1934, it was becoming clear that there would indeed be another and probably worse conflict unless something was done to prevent it. Nobody knew how to do that, and most people simply hoped for peace, but there were others who argued for it, clamoring that something had to be done to prevent another war. The biggest clamor was raised by the isolationists, who had kept the United States from joining the League of Nations in 1920. The League was the only peacekeeping institution that had been devised so far, and it wasn't working; those who opposed it wanted something else instead.

This was the year that Paul von Hindenburg died, the dignified old gentleman who had been President of Germany since 1925, who anxious people in Germany and the rest of the world had hoped would keep the upstart Adolf Hitler under control. Hitler was a terror to contemplate, even from the other side of the Atlantic. His bands of toughs in brown shirts had already begun the campaign of expropriation, exile, and murder against the Jews of Germany, which, in barely a decade, would climax in gas chamber and firing squad genocide.

Hitler had vowed vengeance against the Western nations for Germany's defeat in the war, and had denounced the Versailles Treaty on which the organization of the postwar world had been built. That treaty had decreed the disarmament of Germany; other nations were supposed to disarm by agreement, but they were having trouble agreeing upon a formula. For a time there were allied occupation troops in the Ruhr Valley on Germany's western frontier, but by 1934 the troops had been withdrawn, and Hitler was rearming Germany quite openly in defiance of the treaty. He made no secret of his plans to regain by force the territory Germany had lost and to conquer more if he could; they were described all too plainly in his book, *Mein Kampf*. And he had most of an angry and embittered nation behind him.

This was the man who headed the National Sozialistische Deutsche Arbeiterpartei ("National Socialist German Workers Party"), known as the Nazi party. This was Germany's answer to Russian Communism—autocratic, totalitarian, and militaristic like the Russians' version, but a Socialism as different from Marx

79

and Lenin as it was from Shaw and Laski. It was modeled on the Fascism of Benito Mussolini's Italy, but it was a Fascism of a far more violent and dangerous sort.

Hitler was already the German Chancellor, the nation's head of government, and had been so since January 30, 1933. Upon Hindenburg's death he fused the offices of President (the head of state) and Chancellor (the head of government) into one, calling himself "Der Führer" ("The Leader"), which was simply a German version of Mussolini's "Il Duce." A plebiscite, in which only Yes votes were counted, endorsed Hitler's action, and established the technique by which he won formal approval of subsequent moves. His Brown Shirts in the meantime had assassinated the Chancellor of Austria, Engelbert Dollfuss, in the first step toward Nazi control and eventual German annexation of that nation.

And there was fighting in other parts of the world, too. The Japanese had been in Manchuria since 1931, and were enlarging what they called their "greater East Asia co-prosperity sphere" by systematically pushing their invading forces farther into China. In the Western Hemisphere, Bolivia and Paraguay were at war over the Gran Chaco; and in Africa, Italian troops were clashing with Ethiopians on the borders of Italian Somaliland. For those who wanted to keep America out of all future wars, there was plenty to be concerned about.

Senator Nye's inquiry into the profits of munitions makers was, at best, a peripheral approach to the problem, but it attracted a lot of attention. Many thought that if you could take the profit out of war, you could put an end to war, since under the American system everything worth doing had to be profitable; if it wasn't profitable it wasn't worth doing. This was a variation on a theme dear to the Communists, who taught that war was caused only by the greed of profiteering capitalists, and therefore the way to end war was to abolish capitalism. The Communists in America were quite interested in the Nye Committee's revelations, and found them useful for their own propaganda purposes.

To New Deal Democrats like Alger Hiss, the Committee was a useful stick for attacking big business, which was mainly

Republican and getting most of the blame for the Depression. If big business was responsible for the Depression, why not the war too? But Hiss was not starry-eyed about preventing war; he was more concerned about stopping Hitler, and as the Nye Committee's investigations proceeded, he turned up some dismaying evidence that big business was on Hitler's side, or at least the evidence indicated that some American companies were giving him a lot of help.

There was United Aircraft, for example, which was selling airplane engines to Germany that were manufactured for commercial use but which were being used by the Germans in bombers and fighter planes, the beginning of the Luftwaffe that was to dominate the early phase of World War II. And United Aircraft was entering into patent-licensing arrangements with Bayerische Motor Werke so that its engines could be made in Germany for military use and United Aircraft's profit.

The company's president testified that no engine had been shipped to Germany without the knowledge and consent of the U.S. government, although the government found it had not been given quite as much detailed information about the transactions as the Nye Committee subsequently developed. Nevertheless, there was nothing the government could do about it now. Secretary of State Cordell Hull made public a letter to aircraft manufacturers, which noted, "This government would view the export of military planes from this country to Germany with grave disapproval." But that was all; Hull was not empowered to take further action.

By the summer of 1935 Congress was ready to take action of its own, in the form of the Neutrality Act. Based on the Nye Committee's idea that it was business profits that got the U.S. entangled in other countries' wars, the Act provided, among other things, that Americans must not do business with customers in warring nations. This meant an embargo against nations which the President should find were at war and a restraint on Roosevelt's policy of trying to help those who were resisting Hitler. One result of this legislation was to split American public opinion between the isolationists, who didn't care what Hitler did so long as America stayed out of war, and the anti-Fascists, who feared Hitler would bring about another war if he were not stopped.

Senator Nye and his Committee were leading isolationists; Hiss took the anti-Fascist position, which was consistent with President Wilson's concept of the League of Nations and "collective security." Thus, because Hiss was at odds with the Committee on the major issue, he didn't stay with them long. Later, when Hitler opened World War II by invading Poland in 1939, the Neutrality Act was repealed, and in due course the ideal of collective security was revived and embodied in the United Nations; and Hiss, supporting the UN, found himself again at odds with the isolationists who opposed it.

Hiss had not been assigned to the Nye Committee because of his ideas about collective security, however, but because the Committee had friends in the Agriculture Department and needed help. The Committee's budget was small, and, having hired Stephen Raushenbush as their chief investigator, they had no money for his staff. Two of the Committee members, Sens. Homer T. Bone of Washington and James P. Pope of Idaho, were also on the Agriculture Committee, and the Department was always happy to do them a favor. And Sen. Arthur H. Vandenberg of Michigan, another Nye Committee member, was a powerful voice on the Appropriations Committee, which was also important to the Department. So when Jerome Frank was asked to lend one of his bright young lawyers to the Committee, to help with the investigative work but to remain on the Agriculture Department's payroll, he chose Hiss as the brightest available man. Hiss was well known to the senators, since he had done a lot of the legislative work on the bill creating the Agricultural Adjustment Administration (AAA). He had never met Steve Raushenbush before, but his friend Pat Jackson knew him well from their days at Amherst, and had recommended Raushenbush to Senator Nye.

Hiss was excited by the thought of tangling with such powerful people—Irénée and Pierre Du Pont, heads of one of the nation's biggest corporations at the time; Bernard Baruch, the highly respected "adviser of Presidents," who had been chairman of the War Industries Board during World War I; and the presidents and board members of big companies such as Curtiss-Wright and United Aircraft. He recognized that in trying to tame big business he was to some extent tilting at windmills, yet he regarded it as a part of the New Deal that tied in with his work at the Agriculture Department. If the government was to regulate milk prices and meat packers, not to mention the codes of industry conduct in the National Recovery Administration (NRA), it would be helpful to deflate some of the power and public impact of the big outfits and make them more responsible to the public interest.

He spent weeks in preparation for the hearings, going through the files of the Du Pont Company in Wilmington, Delaware, armed with a subpoena that entitled him to look at almost anything he wanted. He accumulated an enormous stack of documents, which dazzled the press, and some sensational facts and figures to ensure front-page headlines. Among other things, he found that Du Pont had made a profit of almost $2 million on its operation of the Old Hickory powder plant, which was built by the government at a cost of $90 million, while Du Pont's investement was stated on the company's books as only $5,000. Hiss calculated that this represented a profit on investment of 39,231 percent, and Irénée Du Pont angrily retorted that it wasn't a profit at all, but a management fee for the company's services to the government. "Abracadabra," said Hiss; his point being that the company had "gone on strike against the government" to get its way, and forced the payment of huge profits, while the compay had assumed none of the risk. It was a cover-up, a fraud on the public, and Bernard Baruch and the War Industries Board had been part of it, in Hiss's view.

Hiss had a lot of tough questions for Baruch, who had first popularized the slogan about "taking the profits out of war" and never ceased to boast that that was what he had done. Hiss didn't agree, and he wanted to throw the slogan back in Baruch's teeth. He reasoned that while Baruch might have obliged some war contractors to reduce their charges, he had allowed too many others to charge too much; and that Baruch's way of running wartime industry had produced profits as high or higher than usual, while labor and consumers had been asked to make patriotic sacrifices. It was a charge that had been made often before by many people, and had been denied just as often. After all, it was a matter of which side you were on, industry or labor; but never before had the issue received so much publicity.

The questioning of Baruch was begun by the senators, who were respectful and polite, enjoying the press coverage they were getting. The touchy points were left for Hiss to cover when the senators were through, and he made no effort to hide his point of view. In later years he would look back and concede that he must have been "an arrogant young squirt," but at the time he looked on Baruch as an "old buzzard, and the very fact that he was a tin god annoyed me, because I didn't think he deserved to be."

Hiss went into Baruch's personal finances, to show what his financial interests were during the war, and implied that far from the unselfish dollar-a-year-man he pretended to be, he had been making profits from investments of his own in companies that were benefiting from his policies. Baruch didn't like it, and he made no secret of his opinion of Hiss, either. Anybody who would ask questions like that had to be a Communist, in Baruch's view, and in later years he didn't hesitate to say so. Hiss found that out in 1948, when he was under attack, and it hurt.

The Du Ponts didn't think of Hiss as a Communist, or at least never said so publicly. At one point in the hearings a Du Pont executive offered him a job, telling him that whatever he was being paid by the government he could do much better by working for them. Hiss thought that rather transparent and disregarded the offer. During the Nye Committee hearings two other Du Pont directors, R. M. Carpenter and John J. Raskob, had an exchange of correspondence that defined rather neatly the point of view that Hiss was up against.

Carpenter was taking Raskob to task for saying something at a directors' meeting that supported Franklin D. Roosevelt, and he presented a string of grievances against the President prefaced with the observation that "through some method unknown, the President has strangled free speech both over the radio and by the daily papers." He urged Raskob, as a friend of the President, to take up the matter with him, and ask him, among other things, why he was carrying on "a campaign of labor against capital, and a campaign to eliminate wealth."

"Who can possibly give employment to labor if wealthy men and capital are eliminated?" Carpenter wrote. "Why should he lend his assistance to legislation publishing salaries of employees of corporations which can possibly have no effect except to pre-judice certain classes?" (That struck a responsive note, when Hiss found the letter in the Du Pont files. A week before it was released to the public by the Nye Committee, in December 1934, the Committee made public a list of 181 men who had made incomes of over $1 million in one or more of the war years.)

Raskob replied that he hadn't intended to support Roosevelt, but that he simply had said it was no use attacking him without knowing the facts. He then suggested that an organization of some kind be formed to educate the public so that everybody would know the facts. As he had written to Carpenter:

"You haven't much to do and I know of no one that could better take the lead in trying to induce the Du Pont and General Motors groups, followed by other big industries, to definitely organize to protect society from the suffering which it is bound to endure if we allow communistic elements to lead the people to believe that all businessmen are crooks, not to be trusted, and that no one should be allowed to get rich.

"There should be some very definite organization that would come out openly with some plan for educating the people to the value of encouraging people to work; encouraging people to get rich; showing the fallacy of Communism in its effort to tear down our capital structure, etc. . . . If you undertake this job in a really big way, you will find tremendous support and will be able to do one of the finest jobs that could be done for the nation and the future of society everywhere."

Thus was born the Liberty League, which for the rest of the Roosevelt Administration labored to crystallize anti-Roosevelt feeling in both parties and to defend the rights of capital and wealth. It never was very effective, and it enjoyed more prestige than popularity, since the number of people wealthy enough to feel the same way was not great in those days. Many people, including Hiss, didn't take it seriously. He thought the reference to "communistic elements" was simply funny, and it never occurred to him to apply the term to himself or to what he was doing.

These stories were front-page news in the fall of 1934 and the spring of 1935, and day after day, while the hearings were being held, the big Senate caucus room was filled with spectators. Newspaper and magazine writers and radio commentators from all over the world crowded into the front rows and besieged Hiss and Raushenbush for copies of the documents they were putting into the record. Hiss occasionally was mentioned in the papers, which he didn't particularly mind. Sir Wilmott Lewis, who covered the hearings for *The Times* of London, one day tapped Hiss on the shoulder and said, "Young man, you're wasting your time. These people control the world, you're not going to take it away from them." At the other end of the political spectrum was Dorothy Detzer, Washington Director of the Women's International League for Peace and Freedom, who was tilting against the established order with the "Merchants of Death" theme as her lance.

It was in this period that Whittaker Chambers, the Communist who had talked about "barricades in the streets" on the weekend of Roosevelt's Inauguration, came into Hiss's life, though under a different name. It would be more than thirteen years before Hiss found out his real name and what kind of a man he was, and by then it would be too late. Chambers the Communist, the former editor of the *Daily Worker* and *New Masses*, would become Chambers the anti-Communist, a senior editor at *Time*, who would call Hiss a Communist and make the charge stick. But their first meeting, sometime in 1934 or 1935, did not impress Hiss as being particularly important, which was unfortunate for him, because Chambers considered it very important.

In later years the two couldn't agree upon what name Chambers had used on that occasion, or the exact date and circumstances of their first meeting; for like so many of the stories Chambers told about his relationship with Hiss, the facts have remained in dispute. Other details of Hiss's life can be checked and often have been; his other friends and enemies knew one another, and what they and his relatives have said about him all fits together into a consistent picture, however much their opinions may differ. Only Whittaker Chambers was unknown to anyone else who knew Hiss, until the sensational day in 1948, when Chambers denounced him in public. Only Whittaker Chambers said things about Hiss which Hiss denied, and which nobody could corroborate—except Chambers's wife, who backed him up on some extraneous details, but said she didn't know anything about the alleged Communist spy plot.

Chambers, in 1934–1935, according to the stories he told later, was a dedicated member of the Communist underground, engaged in setting up an "apparatus" in Washington of promising young men in the government. Their functions at first would be to use their governmental positions to give secret help to the Communist Party and the Soviet Union, by whatever means opportunity might afford or the Russians might demand. Then there would be an espionage ring, and Chambers would assign an important role in it to Hiss, or so he would say in later years.

Chambers was a man of brilliant imagination and extraordinary fantasies, which three psychiatrists, who later made separate studies of his record, would eventually describe as psychopathic, although his friends considered him a man of sound mind whose only abnormality was a kind of literary genius, a phenomenal capacity for using words to create drama, excitement, fantastic imagery, and vivid illusions of reality. To the psychiatrists, these were too often illusions where reality didn't exist, products of a mind deranged by tragic and destructive experiences throughout his early life (see Chapter 17). Chambers loved secrecy, mystery, conspiracy, and using false names; in later years he could not be certain what name he had used when he first met Hiss, because he had used so many. Hiss remembered it as George Crosley; Chambers said it was simply "Carl," his code name as a secret agent (although later in the trial, while under cross-examination, he would say that it might have been George Crosley after all). Hiss said he knew nothing about secret agents nor of Chambers's involvement with them; he had simply met a man who said he was George Crosley, a free-lance writer, and Hiss had taken his word for it.

As Hiss recalled it, Crosley was a down-at-the-heels young man who turned up at the Nye Committee office in the Senate Office Building one day in late 1934 or early 1935, after the hearings on aircraft sales and the Du Pont profits. He told Hiss that he was writing some articles on the subject, which he hoped to sell to *The American Magazine.* He wanted to look at the transcript of the hearings, which had not yet been printed, to ask Hiss some questions about them. These were perfectly legitimate requests from a free-lance writer, and it was part of Hiss's job to comply with such requests as much as he could. They met several times in Hiss's office, and he occasionally took the writer to lunch.

Crosley impressed Hiss as being well read and he talked knowingly of the publishing business and literary matters and about other articles he had written. He was about three years older than Hiss, and said he had traveled widely in Europe and knew a lot about German literature. Hiss found him rather entertaining, although he thought some of his recollections were tall stories, particularly one about helping to lay the tracks for the first streetcars in Washington when he was a teen-ager. Crosley talked about his sexual exploits in a way that Hiss remembered as "boastful" and didn't encourage. He judged Crosley to be rather vain but didn't find his appearance particularly striking, remembering him as short, with lightish hair and ordinary features except for his teeth, which had been notably neglected. There was a gap in front, where a broken tooth seemed to have decayed and never been replaced.

In some respects the writer reminded Hiss of his brother Bosley, who would have been about the same age if he'd lived, and who had talked in the same romantic way when he worked for the Baltimore *Sun.* Hiss decided Crosley fancied himself a combination of Jim Tully, a popular novelist of the 1930s (*Blood on the Moon*; *A Hollywood Decameron*) and Jack London, a novelist of his boyhood days, who specialized in adventure, violence, wildlife, and gloomy prophecies of world revolution (*The Call of the Wild*; *The Iron Heel*). Like so many others, Hiss was mainly impressed with the young man's apparent literary gifts.

In the spring of 1935, according to Hiss, Crosley told him he'd need to spend several months in Washington to finish his articles, and was looking for a place to stay, where he could bring his wife and baby. It was about the time that Hiss was moving from the Twenty-eighth Street apartment to a much handsomer home at 2905 P Street, a three-story semidetached house with a guest suite on the top floor, which he expected his brother Donald to live in, as he had when they were on O Street.

The house was owned by a Navy officer, who was going to be away for a year or so and had left all his furniture behind. The Hisses wouldn't need most of their furniture, except for a few favorite things, and the Twenty-eighth Street apartment would be empty for the two or three months remaining in the Hisses' lease, for which the rent had already been paid. Maybe Hiss's new friend would like to use the apartment, and if he could pay back the sixty-dollars-a-month rent, all the better. But there was no hurry; he obviously didn't have any money now, and they could wait until he sold his articles.

The suggestion was accepted with alacrity, but the result was not quite the simple arrangement Hiss had expected. As Hiss recalls it, Crosley arrived a few days later with his wife and daughter, but they didn't go to Twenty-eighth Street; they turned up on Hiss's doorstep on P Street instead. Crosley said his moving van hadn't arrived from New York, and there were things in it he would need to supplement the furniture the Hisses had left at Twenty-eighth Street. So the Crosleys stayed at 2905 P Street for a few days as house guests.

It was all rather inconvenient, and the guests were not popular with Priscilla. However, there was room for them on the top floor, since Donald wasn't using it after all, and the Crosleys made themselves comfortable there. Eventually, Hiss recalls, the missing moving van arrived and the Crosleys moved to Twenty-eighth Street. The incident was of no importance to the Hisses at the time, but it was to prove damaging to him years later when he tried to explain it to the House Un-American Activities Committee.

Throughout the year Hiss saw Crosley occasionally to talk about Nye Committee business, and sometimes lent him the Ford roadster, just as he occasionally lent it to other people. Hiss vaguely recalled giving Crosley a lift to New York, sometime in the spring of 1935. He also made some small loans to him of a dollar or two, maybe as much as five dollars at a time, which were rarely repaid, and that got to be a nuisance.

In the summer of 1935 Hiss bought a new Plymouth, a dealer's demonstration car, which he drove on the dealer's plates for a while before registering it in his own name. The dealer offered him twenty-five dollars to trade in the old Ford, but Hiss turned it down. He liked the old car; he'd had it since he was first married, and he was sure it had more than twenty-five dollars' worth of life left in it.

Hiss remembers the Ford standing on the street in the snow that winter, occasionally having to be moved or collecting a parking ticket, and not getting much use. Eventually, he got rid of it, under circumstances which he didn't particularly note at the time, but which were to count heavily against him years later when his reputation and career were at stake.

As reconstructed by Hiss, when he was able to consult the few records that had been kept, he had told Crosley he could have the old Ford and had given him the title certificate, but he hadn't thought to sign the assignment of title on the back of the certificate or to register the transfer. Then one day somebody brought the certificate to his office in the Justice Department (he doesn't remember who), asking him to sign it, have his signature notarized, and put in the name of the Cherner Motor Company as purchaser. This Hiss did, taking the certificate down the hall to his friend W. Marvin Smith to have it notarized. Presumably this happened on July 23, 1936, the date typed on the certificate above Marvin Smith's signature, but neither of them could remember anything about it.

In late 1935, Hiss doesn't remember exactly when, Crosley gave him an Oriental rug which he said "some wealthy patron" had given him. Hiss didn't particularly like the rug, which was bright red and too loud for his taste, but he accepted it as part payment for the rent of the apartment, the Ford, and the small unpaid loans. He put it on the floor in Timmy's bedroom in the P Street house. After that Hiss remembered Crosley again asking him for a small loan in 1936, but this time Hiss turned him down. He was no longer working for the Nye Committee, and had no further obligation to the free-lance writer; the articles Crosley talked about had never been sold or published, and it didn't look as if they ever would be. Hiss had concluded by this time that Crosley was "some kind of a deadbeat," and, having received the rug, he was willing to call it quits. He didn't want anything more to do with Crosley and let him know this in a polite but unmistakable way. It seemed to have been effective, for Crosley never bothered him again, and Hiss forgot all about him until he reentered his life some twelve years later, using the name Whittaker Chambers.

When Chambers appeared before the House Un-American Activities Committee in 1948, he told a very different story. He said he had first met Hiss early in 1934, for the purpose of giving him new orders. For, according to Chambers, Hiss was then a secret Communist too, and operated under Communist "discipline." Chambers said he had ordered Hiss to guard this secret by behaving as though he were not a Communist, and by having nothing to do with other Communists in public. He was to keep his record clean and advance in the government to as high a position as he could, so that he could influence policy in the future.

Chambers said he had never written any articles for *The American Magazine*, and had never intended to pay rent for Hiss's old apartment. He had simply accepted it as the kind of help one Communist gives another. After all, there had been other occasions when Chambers had occupied rent-free premises supplied by Communist friends, and his arrangement with the underground was that the Party was supposed to supply the wherewithal for "bourgeois" accommodations, over and above his salary.

All this sounded very plausible in 1948, because Chambers told his story with such bland confidence, and Hiss, when he denied it, had no way of proving it wasn't true. Indeed he had let Chambers use his apartment, and collected no rent, whether he was a Communist or not; and indeed he had kept his record clean and advanced in the government, doing nothing a Communist would do and having nothing to do with Communists. This is what loyal government employees were supposed to do, and only Chambers made it seem sinister by saying that it was all pretense, that Hiss was really a Communist all the time.

Chambers testified that he had moved to Twenty-eighth Street directly from Baltimore where he had been living at 903 Saint Paul's Street, and that Hiss drove over in his Ford roadster to pick up the baby's collapsible bathtub and high chair and one or two other things for them. Apart from the furniture the Hisses left in the Twenty-eighth Street apartment, that was all they had. The "rather meager furnishings" of the Saint Paul's Street apartment they gave to their landlady, since they were not worth moving to Washington.

At the trial, Chambers's wife Esther recalled going to New York, or at least to the Long Island suburb of Lynbrook, to stay with her mother-in-law between the time she left Saint Paul's Street and the move to Washington. But she also supported her husband's story about Hiss coming to St. Paul's Street to pick up the baby's furniture in the Ford, and she was never able to straighten out exactly how the two recollections fitted together. Both Whittaker and Esther Chambers remembered staying at the Hisses' P Street home for a few days, but they didn't think it was because they were waiting for their moving van before moving into Twenty-eighth Street. They thought it was some other time. Esther remembered it as a rather unsuccessful visit. It hadn't worked out well, she said, and she sounded disappointed.

Whatever the facts behind these distant recollections, there was no dispute that Chambers and his wife and baby had lived, without paying rent, in the Hisses' apartment on Twenty-eighth Street for a couple of months in the spring of 1935, and that they also stayed for a few days on the top floor of 2905 P Street, while the Hisses lived there. When the lease on the Twenty-eighth Street apartment expired at the end of June, the Chambers family moved to New York and lived briefly on Fourth Street, in the home of Professor Meyer Schapiro, a friend from Columbia University. But they found it uncomfortable and soon moved to a summer cottage on the Delaware River at Long Eddy, New York.

Chambers remembered driving Hiss's Ford roadster, but denied that Hiss had ever given or sold it to him. He said Hiss had insisted on giving it to the Communist Party for the use of some poor organizer, and the Party had agreed to accept it, although it was against the rules. The Cherner Motor Company was an innocent intermediary in the transaction, according to Chambers; they didn't know one of their employees was using their name to cover up the conspiracy. Nor, said Hiss, did he; the whole Chambers version was new to him.

As for the rug, Chambers said it was a gift to Hiss from the Soviet people in recognition of his services as a Communist secret agent; it was one of four such rugs Chambers said were purchased with Communist Party funds and given to Communist agents in Washington early in 1937. Acting on this information, the FBI turned up records showing that four Oriental rugs had indeed been purchased by Chambers's friend Meyer Schapiro, for a total of $876.71, on December 29, 1936, and Schapiro said he had bought them at Chambers's request, with money supplied by Chambers. Whether the rug on Timmy's floor was indeed one of these four rugs, and whether the gift was explained to Hiss at the time in the way Chambers later described, remained in dispute.

Chambers said he had never gone to any office where Hiss worked, but met him often at Hiss's home and sometimes at his own home, and that sometimes they went to various places on trips together. Hiss denied all this, except for the one ride to New York, and he could not recall any details of that trip.

When Chambers enlarged his story to include the stealing of government documents and passing them on to the Communist underground to be photographed for transmission to the Soviet Union, he said the first experiment in this technique had been undertaken at Hiss's suggestion, while he was working for the Nye Committee. According to Chambers, the head of the underground, identified as J. Peters, had approved the idea until he saw the documents. The Soviet agent to whom he had shown them wasn't interested. But the idea was revived later, according to Chambers, and successfully carried out when Hiss was in the State Department in 1937–1938. Hiss denied all of this; according to his testimony, he had given no secret documents to Crosley or to any other unauthorized person, and had had nothing to do with Chambers, under any name, when he was in the State Department.

As a matter of fact, there was trouble about confidential State Department documents finding their way into the hands of the Nye Committee, but there was nothing secret about it, and it involved neither Hiss nor the Soviet Union. Secretary Hull describes in his memoirs how, almost from the beginning of the hearings in September 1934, he had received protests from other nations regarding the publicity given heretofore confidential documents. At first they concerned letters from aircraft salesmen to their home offices about bribery of high government officials in Latin America and "rumored charges concerning King George V," which brought a sharp protest from the British Acting Foreign Secretary, Sir Robert Vansittart. Then the Committee began publishing details of communications from other governments to the State Department, which caused enormous embarrassment and kept Hull busy explaining and apologizing to aggrieved ambassadors.

Hull protested to Nye, who expressed his regrets; nevertheless, he subpoenaed the records of the New York City banks that had loaned money to the British and French governments during the war. The British Ambassador, Sir Ronald Lindsay, told Hull this would be considered an act of "grave discourtesy" by his government, and Hull urged President Roosevelt to call the whole Nye Committee to the White House and tell them to end their harassment. Roosevelt did speak to the Committee, but not as strongly as Hull had wished. Hull was concerned about the "wave of anti-British and anti-French feeling" that the Committee was engendering, at a time when he wanted the American public to back Anglo–French efforts to stop German rearmament and to dissuade Mussolini from invading Ethiopia. "The spectacle of bitter quarreling between Britain and France on the one side and the United States on the other over documents two decades old," as Hull wrote in his memoirs, was not much help.

Then came what Hull called "the worst example of carelessness by the Nye Committee." It concerned a confidential memorandum from British Foreign Secretary Arthur Balfour to Secretary of State Robert Lansing, dated May 18, 1917, in which Balfour referred to Britain's "secret agreements with other Allied Governments." Nye argued that this proved Lansing and President Wilson had lied when they said they had no knowledge of British secret commitments before the Paris peace conference of 1919.

Hull hit the roof at that. He demanded that the Committee return all their copies of the memorandum, and called a press conference to announce that, from now on, the State Department would not cooperate with congressional committees that took such liberties with confidential documents. And he added a personal tribute to the "patriotism and scrupulous honesty" of President Wilson, under whom he had served.

Hiss had left the Nye Committee by this time, because he shared Hull's admiration for President Wilson and didn't like the way the Committee was attacking Wilsonian idealism and America's Allies in the war. By the spring of 1935 the Committee was spearheading the isolationists' fight for the neutrality bill, and spreading the idea that it was the Wall Street bankers who had got America into the war, and American boys had been sent overseas to die for the bankers and their loans. Hiss wanted no part of that, and by July 1935 had found job in the Justice Department. But the Committee, nearing the end of its life, didn't replace him, and he continued to do occasional services for them as legal counsel until well into 1936.

It was at about this time, when his work for the Nye Committee ended, that Hiss saw the last of George Crosley, according to his recollection. Chambers, who said in 1948 that Hiss had known him only as Carl, insisted that their relationship continued for another two years, until after Chambers broke with the Communist Party. He said he called on Hiss just before Christmas 1938 and urged him to break with the Party too, but Hiss refused. Hiss, when he heard that story, said Chambers was a liar, and to prove it, he sued Chambers for libel. That was when Chambers decided to produce his documents and microfilms, and began his sensational reminiscences about espionage.

What actually happened between the two men in those years, 1936–1938, remains in dispute. It was this conflict that provided the drama of the House Un-American Activities Committee hearings in 1948 and the trials of 1949–1950, which will be described in later chapters. But first it will be helpful to look at some of the other things that were happening between 1936 and 1948 to Alger Hiss and the rest of the world at large.

7

THE CRUCIAL YEARS

WHILE Hiss was having second thoughts about the Nye Committee's isolationism, more trouble was brewing for the Agricultural Adjustment Administration (AAA), the agency which had first brought him to Washington. Having survived the efforts of radicals to turn it into an agency of land reform, AAA was now being challenged by conservatives on constitutional grounds. Stanley Reed, then Solicitor General, was preparing to defend the case before the Supreme Court. Hiss, who was looking for another job, was the obvious choice for his assistant.

The constitutional question was one that Hiss had dealt with in the AAA Legal Division, from the time the act was framed. Did the government really have the power under the Constitution to pay farmers to reduce their output, to enter into agreements with farmers and processors to carry out the reductions in an orderly way, or to finance the program by a special tax on the processors? Nobody really knew, because the question had never been raised before. President Roosevelt and Secretary Wallace had decided to take a chance and go ahead with the program, because in the emergency of 1933 something had to be done, and this was the best plan their experts could devise. It had been part of Hiss's job to make sure the AAA programs had a sound basis in the law and could be defended against constitutional attack.

Hiss was the man best qualified to write the government's

brief on the subject, and as Special Assistant to the Solicitor General, he began work on it in August 1935. It was to his advantage in this assignment that he had been secretary to Justice Holmes, which had familiarized him with the procedures and personalities of the Supreme Court. Holmes had retired in 1932, but Hiss knew and admired his successor Justice Benjamin Cardozo as well as his old friend, Justice Louis Brandeis. As it turned out, Cardozo and Brandeis agreed with the government's view of the case, as did Justice Harlan Stone, who wrote the opinion. But theirs was the dissenting opinion; the majority of the Court, in a decision read by Justice Owen J. Roberts on January 6, 1936, found the AAA to be unconstitutional.

This was not the first New Deal program to be struck down by the Court in this way, nor was it the last. Already, on May 27, 1935, the Court had shaken the foundations of the New Deal by finding the National Recovery Administration (NRA) unconstitutional. After the AAA case a series of anti-New Deal decisions put the Court in direct conflict with President Roosevelt, who turned it into a personal and political battle, which resulted in one of his greatest defeats. These wider issues, however, were not part of Hiss's concern; he was concentrating on the constitutional questions raised in *United States* v. *Butler*, in which the government sought to collect the AAA processing tax from a reluctant cotton mill.

The government's case rested on Article 1, Section 8, of the Constitution, which gives the Congress power to "lay and collect taxes [to] provide for . . . the general welfare of the United States," among other purposes. The cotton contracts and similar AAA crop-control programs and subsidies to farmers clearly served the general welfare, according to Hiss's argument, because they were the means of reviving the depressed farming industry and thereby helping to revive the economy as a whole, putting food in people's mouths and clothes on their backs. The processing tax was defended as a suitable, effective, and legal means of financing these programs.

Perhaps it was effective, Justice Roberts reasoned, but not legal. Because the AAA programs imposed contractual obligations on the farmers who accepted the money, he found that they were a means of coercing farmers into accepting a federal system for regulating agricultural production. But under the Tenth Amendment, in his view, the right to do such things was reserved to the states. If Congress could usurp states' rights in this way, Justice Roberts foresaw "the independence of individual states obliterated, and the United States converted into a central government exercising uncontrolled police power in every state of the Union."

Justice Stone, dissenting, called this "a tortured construction of the Constitution," which, he said, "is not to be justified by recourse to extreme examples." From a farm relief program of the kind conducted by AAA, he found it too long a jump to the police state envisioned by Roberts. Nevertheless, Roberts's decision was supported by the majority of the Court, and the AAA was overthrown by a 6–3 vote.

The decision was a blow to the New Deal, and the issues of governmental philosophy it raised were fought out in other cases for years thereafter; but the effect of the decision on the farm program was by no means fatal. A new system was devised to get around the Court's objections; the AAA was abolished and replaced by the Soil Conservation Service, which gave farmers essentially the same benefits and ensured the same kind of crop control, but avoided the processing tax of the AAA. It was, in any case, a more suitable program for long-term use, and became a permanent successor to the emergency programs of AAA.

After the *Butler* case was over, Hiss continued in the Solicitor General's office to work on another New Deal program that was under attack in the courts, the foreign trade agreements then being negotiated by Secretary of State Cordell Hull. This was the Democrats' answer to the high-tariff policies of previous Republican administrations, culminating in the Smoot–Hawley tariffs of 1930, which had earned their share of blame for the Depression. Hull was systematically taking the tariff structure apart by negotiating separate trade agreements with individual countries on a reciprocal basis—you give a little here and we'll give a little there. The new agreements normally contained a "most favored nation" clause, which meant that any concession granted to one nation would automatically be extended to all others with similar agreements. This was a powerful incentive to other nations to join the group, and it had the desirable effect of gradually lowering tariffs on a growing number of products from a growing number of nations. Hull was extremely proud of this program, and it was popular among most exporters and importers, because it was good for the business of both.

The agreements were naturally unpopular, however, among domestic producers, who relied on the protection of high tariffs. Their tariff shelters gradually were being taken away, and their competition from foreign producers was growing. They made repeated efforts to upset the trade agreements in the courts and to get new legislation introduced against them. When so many other New Deal innovations were being thrown out by the Supreme Court, there was anxiety in the State Department that the trade agreements program might go the same way. Consequently, Hiss was put to work building up their legal defense.

The trade agreements rested on stronger grounds than had the AAA, in terms of both constitutional law and contemporary politics. It was difficult for anyone to show he had been damaged by the government's act; at worst, a manufacturer could show only that a special privilege had been taken away from him. If tariff cuts meant lower prices, the manufacturers who suffered were outnumbered by their customers who benefited. If some people were losing their jobs to foreign competition, there were far more new jobs opening up as the export trade expanded. On the whole, the program was working well.

Nevertheless, it was under constant attack, and its legal defenses had to be constantly guarded. Hiss's work brought him into frequent contact with Secretary Hull and the State Department people who were working on trade agreements, especially Francis B. Sayre, Assistant Secretary for Economic Affairs, who had general supervision, and John S. Dickey, his assistant. Thus when, in the summer of 1936, Dickey left the Department to return to private practice (ultimately to become President of Dartmouth), it was natural for Sayre to ask Hiss to take his place.

This was an invitation Hiss couldn't turn down, for it meant entering the world of foreign affairs, the diplomatic service he had dreamed of as a boy. He remembered a line from James M. Barrie to the effect that life never gives you a second chance, you can't go back to a fork in your life and take the other road. Yet, this was exactly what was happening to him; he'd been in law and now he'd be in diplomacy. He was going to have the best of both worlds.

His acceptance was also motivated by a conviction that the world was drifting toward another major war, and Hiss, with his sense of mission, wanted to do what he could for the side he believed in. For some time, he had been a member of one of the study groups on foreign affairs that were popular among Washington intellectuals, meeting once a month or so to talk about such things as the rise of Hitler and the Italian aggression in Ethiopia, and what could be done about them. There were seven or eight men, all members of the Foreign Policy Association (FPA), and their wives—Charles Yost, Roy Veatch, John S. Dickey, Leroy Stinebower, Larry Duggan, Noel Field, all State Department employees, and one or two others. Occasionally, the FPA would hold larger meetings in the Department of Agriculture cafeteria, featuring journalists returning from abroad, or visiting dignitaries such as Herbert Morrison, former leader of the British Labour Party, and subsequently a member of the Cabinet.

By the time Hiss joined the State Department he had concluded that the postwar period, through which the world had struggled since 1918, was over, and a new prewar period had begun. Many New Dealers and anti-Fascists felt the same way, but this was not the popular view. Most of the State Department disagreed, as did the isolationists and probably the majority of Americans. The State Department was not yet committed to an anti-Fascist or anti-Nazi policy, or even an anti-Communist policy. Roosevelt wanted to aid our wartime allies Britain and France in their efforts to stop German rearmament and to forestall Hitler's threats of aggression, but in other respects the State Department tended simply to deal with whoever was in power.

Hiss looked upon the trade agreements program as an instrument for peace; trade draws nations together just as war divides them, and anything that promoted trade between nations was expected to strengthen the hands of those in foreign governments who counseled moderation, so that the threat of war would not disturb the prosperity of peace. As late as 1939, until the outbreak of the general European war made such things impossible, the State Department was seriously considering the possibility of a trade agreement with Hitler's Germany. It was a country to trade with, regardless of its ideology.

In July 1936, however, a struggle began in Europe that was to make the position of ideological neutrality increasingly difficult to maintain. This was the Spanish Civil War, in which the rebels under General Franco were supported with arms, planes, and troops from Fascist Italy and Nazi Germany, while the established government was aided by Communist Russia. At first the war commanded little attention in America, since it was all so far away and seemed remote from domestic concerns. But it was reported in the press and on radio by some of the most brilliant and best-known writers of the day, people like Ernest Hemingway and John Dos Passos, and as it dragged on from year to year it became a center of attention for intellectual idealists, as well as interested pressure groups. It compelled the partisanship of people in America as well as in Europe, people who had no personal reasons to care who governed Spain but who believed that issues of faith and philosophy were involved that transcended life itself.

This was the first time that Fascism and Communism, the new ideologies of the twentieth century, had met on the battlefield, and the fighting was as bitter and destructive as in the religious wars of earlier centuries. It was a cruel, horrifying war, with ferocious acts of massacre and atrocity on both sides. Between the warring ideologies believers in Democracy found themselves obliged to choose sides, depending on which side they hated and feared the most.

Some, like Alger Hiss, were mainly afraid of Fascism. They regarded Franco and his supporters as rebels against a democratically elected government, and they sided with the government against the rebels. Even Senator Nye, the isolationist who had done so much to get the Neutrality Act passed, didn't want its embargo applied against Spain, because that would work in Franco's favor.

Others, who were more afraid of Communism than Fascism, regarded the Spanish government as a danger to the world, because the Communist Party and its allies had won the elections. The anti-Communists felt that such an election result was a corruption of the democratic process, one more dangerous to democracy then armed rebellion, so that they sided with Franco and the rebels. This was the view of many organized religious groups, particularly the Catholics, because the Communists were aggressively anti-religious while Franco supported Spain's vast and powerful Catholic institutions. Polish–Americans, who were generally Catholics, also hated Russia because Poland and Russia had been enemies for generations; Italian–Americans tended to side with the Catholic Church and the Italian alliance with Franco.

The anti-Communists had the votes in America in 1936, because Communism had been hated and feared since the Russian Revolution, which had occurred nineteen years before, while Fascism was a newer phenomenon, one which many people were only beginning to discover. Accordingly, Roosevelt invoked the Neutrality Act, imposed the embargo, and cooperated with the Non-Intervention Committee that had been set up in London to keep the war from spreading.

For it was not only a civil war, it was an international war, with Germany and Italy united against Russia, though it was fought on Spanish soil with mainly Spanish fighters and victims on both sides. It was all too clearly a dress rehearsal for a bigger war to come later, for which neither the United States, Britain, France, nor their lesser allies were prepared. But they were impressed by the danger and by the demonstration of Fascist and Communist military strength. They began building up their own defenses and striking power, first slowly and then at a panic rate; the United States began last but eventually mounted the biggest effort, with the greatest resources.

Though the democratic governments stayed out of the war,

some of their impatient citizens got into it, a few on Franco's side and more in an International Brigade of volunteers to help the Loyalists, as those loyal to the Republican government that Franco sought to overthrow were called. The American recruits styled themselves the Abraham Lincoln Brigade and were denounced by Franco supporters as Communists, which some of them were. Many others were not, or certainly didn't consider themselves to be; they were fighting not for love of Communism, but for Democracy against Fascism.

The Communist Party in America got a lot of mileage out of its support for the Spanish Loyalists, gaining new sympathizers in this country, who might otherwise never have been interested. They made more enemies, too, among people who feared Communism more than Fascism and who believed the growing number of Communist sympathizers meant there was a danger that the Communists would take over America. As the war helped shape Hiss's thinking, it also stimulated the anti-Communist passions he would later have to contend with. But he wasn't aware of that at the time.

Indeed, there were times when Hiss himself was tempted to join the International Brigade, although he never considered the possibility very seriously. His duties in the State Department were his contribution to the cause of better international relations, even if it was less romantic than fighting in Spain. He was getting a little old for such things—thirty-two in November 1936. And he had family responsibilities to keep him home.

There was, for example, the problem of Tim's schooling. Relations with the faculty of the Sidwell Friends School had reached the breaking point, and after many consultations, the decision was made in June 1936, to transfer Tim to the more expensive Landon School. The results were promising, but the following February Tim was knocked off his bicycle by a car, and spent a week in Georgetown Hospital. Then he was at home in bed for the whole month of March, his leg in a cast and suffering a severe reaction from an antitetanus injection. In April he was able to come downstairs on crutches, and the school sent his work home to him everyday. Only in the last few weeks of the term, at the end of May, was Tim able to attend school, and it wasn't until late in August that he was able to discard the crutches.

Meanwhile, the Hisses had moved out of 2905 P Street, which had lost a lot of its charm for them when the furnace broke down in the middle of winter, when Alger was in bed with pneumonia and the pipes in the second-floor bathroom had frozen. In any case, the house was too large without Donald on the top floor, and when, at the end of June 1936, its owner returned from abroad, the Hisses moved to 1245 Thirtieth Street, two doors from the house they had lived in when they were first married.

It was a much smaller house, having only two stories and a basement, with a living room occupying the entire first floor and with two bedrooms on the second, a small one in front for Tim and a larger one in back for Alger and Priscilla. The basement contained a small kitchen, maid's room, and a dining room at the back with French doors opening on to a small garden. But the kitchen was modern, and the house had just been completely renovated; in fact, the work wasn't quite finished when the Hisses moved from P Street, so that they stayed a few days at the Hotel Martinique before moving in.

This was the house where Tim was bed-ridden for a month, and spent several more months on crutches. The experience of caring for him aroused Priscilla's interest in medicine, and she thought it would be useful to study some of the fundamentals, and perhaps get a job as a therapist or medical aide of some sort. She wrote to the University of Maryland for information, and when Tim was able to go back to school, she enrolled in a summer course in inorganic chemistry at the School of Dentistry and Pharmacy. The course lasted until the end of July, and she got a B in it; then she applied for admission to George Washington University's pre-medical course.

At the beginning of June Tim went to camp as usual at Rigs O'Marlow, and Alger and Priscilla rented an apartment for the summer at nearby Chestertown, Maryland, so they could keep an eye on his progress. They had also undertaken to look after Priscilla's niece, Ruth Fansler, who was at Rigs O'Marlow for the summer, while her parents were in Europe. Alger's vacation ran from July 14 to August 14; the rest of the summer he was at Chestertown on weekends, and Priscilla was a weekend visitor until she finished her chemistry course. It was a difficult summer; Ruth caught pneumonia and was in Delaware Hospital in Wilmington from July 15 to 26, for, in the days before penicillin, pneumonia was a serious and dangerous disease. Priscilla and Alger visited her there several times and brought her back to Rigs O'Marlow when she was well enough. Tim was on crutches through July and much of August, but was able to ride in the Children's Horse Show in September. Tom Fansler, Ruth's father, returned from Europe at the beginning of August and came to Chestertown the next weekend to see her, staying with the Hisses.

When the Hisses came home from Chestertown in the fall, they decided the Thirtieth Street house was too small. Alger's job as an assistant to an Assistant Secretary of State called for a certain amount of formal entertaining, and there wasn't room for it. Sayre had occasionally dropped in for tea with the Hisses, for a sociable chat and friendly inquiries about Tim, and these visits made Priscilla acutely conscious of the house's very limited amenities.

It was the middle one of a row of three almost-identical houses, which had been created by the remodeling of an old wooden building formerly used as a nurses' residence during the Civil War. The three had a common roof and clapboard facade, each painted a different color in order to distinguish one house from another; the Hisses' was bright yellow. The houses were so narrow and close together that the windows of one overlooked the front steps of another, and the walls that divided them were so thin that every sound in a neighbor's house could be heard. It was a clubby neighborhood; the Mays on one side and the Robbs on the other were good friends of the Hisses, and so were the Horskys, who lived a little farther down the hill at number 1239. Charlie Horsky played the piano with Priscilla and tennis with Alger. They were forever dropping in on each other, sometimes unannounced.

By November Priscilla had found something much better, though they wouldn't be able to move in until after Christmas. It was a three-story house just off Thirty-fourth Street, on Volta Place, which was separated by an open stretch of untended grass from the imposing Victorian Renaissance structure that houses the Volta Institute for the Deaf on Thirty-fifth Street. There was a formal dining room and a long living room with two fireplaces on the first floor; an open staircase leading up to the second floor, with master bedroom, guest room and bath; and an attic bedroom on the third floor, for Tim. The kitchen was in the front of the house, with windows overlooking Volta Place and the front door, so it was easy for the maid to see who was coming and to answer the door. The doorbell didn't work, but there was a big brass knocker that everybody used.

Outside the front door was a huge maple tree, which towered over the house, growing out of an embankment held by a retaining wall. It was one of the most striking and attractive features of the house in the Hisses' mind; in 1943, after they were gone, the tree was cut down to make room for an addition to the house on that side and other alterations were made that would cause a good deal of confusion at Hiss's trial.

This was a suitable home for a diplomat, and getting it properly furnished and decorated took so much of Priscilla's time that in December she withdrew from the premedical course she was taking. They moved in on December 29, and began paying back their social obligations with cocktail parties, dinners for six or eight, overnight guests, and the kind of entertaining that the State Department expects of its higher-echelon staff. By this time the Hisses knew a great many people in the embassies, and Alger was no longer expected to work at the office until 8:00 P.M. or later; he was usually free around 6:00, and devoted the extra time to the social affairs that were part of his job.

Alger and Priscilla also belonged to square dancing and ice skating clubs that kept them busy, and Priscilla was involved with chamber music groups. She was an experienced pianist and always had a piano in her house; the old-fashioned upright at P Street had been turned in for a more modern spinet piano, which didn't take up so much room. She used to play two-piano arrangements of Schumann, Brahms, and Haydn with Katherine Stanley–Brown, a friend whose living room was large enough to contain two grand pianos placed back to back. Priscilla and Alger subscribed to the National Symphony, and regularly attended the string quartet concerts at the Library of Congress.

It was through the Stanley–Browns that the Hisses met Don Tilghman, one of the Tilghmans whose family farm on the Eastern Shore was not far from the Wrightson farm, where Alger had spent so much of his childhood. They had not known each other then, but when Tilghman came to Washington in 1938 to work in the Agriculture Department, he looked up the Stanley–Browns, who were old friends. Katherine said to him, "It's strange you don't know Alger," and took him around to Volta Place. Tilghman and Hiss hit it off immediately.

Like many others who knew him in those days, Tilghman admired Hiss's intellect and found him generous, kind, friendly, interesting to talk to, fun to joke with, always polite and calm, and very warm but in a rather superficial way. It was difficult to get below the surface of his feelings, and Tilghman concluded that he bottled up his emotions inside but could probably tear the hide off people if he ever lost his temper. But the two grew very fond of each other, and in later years when Tim was having difficulties, it was Don Tilghman who had Tim's confidence, and was able to serve as a link between the young man and his stepfather. After Alger and Priscilla separated in 1959, he was for some years one of the few people who continued to see them both.

Meanwhile Hiss was getting along very well with Francis Sayre, who had been one of his professors at Harvard Law School. He had never been as close to him as to Felix Frankfurter or Jim Landis, but he knew and liked him. In his capacity as Assistant Secretary for Economic Affairs, Sayre was becoming increasingly involved in the preparations for granting full independence to the Philippine Commonwealth. Hiss had a personal interest in Philippine affairs because of the years his brother-in-law, Dean Fansler, had spent there, teaching at the University of the Philippines in Manila. It was one of those connections that sometimes smooth the path of diplomacy, and Hiss took occasion to mention it the first time he met Manuel Quezon, the President of the Philippine Commonwealth. Quezon was delighted; he whipped out his watch fob, from which dangled an enormous medal that he had won as a member of the University debating team, and told Hiss how it was Dean Fansler himself who had given it to him.

The problem of Philippine independence was complicated in those days by tariff problems. The Philippines had been under various forms of American administration since the Spanish–American War in 1898, and enjoyed special tariff preferences on their sugar, tobacco, and other products in the American market. They wanted political freedom, but not at the cost of losing this economic advantage. Independence became a matter of endless negotiations and postponements, and when Sayre was appointed High Commissioner for the Philippines, in September 1939, matters were still dragging on. Two years later the Japanese invasion stopped the process until after the war, when independence was finally achieved in 1946.

While Hiss worked for Sayre, he was involved in these matters as well as in trade negotiations with other countries, along with his defense of the trade agreements program in Congress and the courts. The law that authorized the program was temporary and had to be renewed in 1937, which meant further congressional hearings and the drafting of new legislation. It also meant writing speeches for Sayre to deliver around the country in an attempt to build popular support for the program and put pressure on the Congress. Hiss soon learned that he could work endlessly trying to develop new material for a speech, and then Sayre would say, "This is very good, but it isn't quite my style. Would you mind getting out that speech I made last week? I think there's a paragraph or two in it we could use again." Soon Hiss realized that the best thing to do was to get ten old speeches Sayre liked and had confidence in, and pick out familiar paragraphs. Since it was always pretty much the same message given before a different audience, all that was needed was updating and a local touch. That way the work went faster.

Hiss also found satisfaction in working on the termination of an economic treaty with Japan, when the Japanese incursions in China reached the stage of open warfare in the summer of 1937. There was pressure from isolationist groups to invoke the Neutrality Act and impose embargoes on both nations, but Secretary Hull and President Roosevelt were reluctant to do so because it would have hurt China more than Japan. When Roosevelt announced that government vessels would not carry munitions to the war zone, but that private vessels could do so at their own risk, China complained to the League of Nations that even this partial embargo was unfair. It was possible, however, to terminate a long-standing commercial treaty between the United States and Japan, and restrictions could then be imposed on the shipment of such strategic materials as scrap iron and oil.

Bigger things were happening meanwhile in Europe, which were soon to lead to another worldwide war, and the United States was going to be involved in it despite all that the isolationists or anybody else could do. The Spanish Civil War ended on March 29, 1939, when the last of the Loyalists surrendered to Franco. This was a defeat not only for Communist arms and policies, but for the hopes and idealism of non-Communists, who had supported the Left in democratic countries. Earlier that month Hitler, having annexed Austria the previous year, seized most of Czechoslovakia and turned the rest of that country over to Hungary. And on August 24 Joachim von Ribbentrop and Vyacheslav Molotov, the Foreign Ministers of Nazi Germany and Communist Russia, respectively, astonished the world by signing a nonaggression pact between their two countries in Moscow, which was promptly ratified by their principals, Hitler and Stalin. Before dawn on September 1 Hitler's troops smashed into Poland in defiance of warnings from England. For although the British had been powerless to help Austria or Czechoslovakia and had no way of defending Poland's borders, they were determined at last to draw the line and fight back, ready or not.

On September 3 England and France declared war on Germany, and were promptly joined by Australia, New Zealand,

South Africa, and Canada. Russian troops occupied eastern Poland, moving up to an agreed demarcation line, where they faced the Germans without hostility, at least for the next twenty-one months. The three little Baltic states of Latvia, Lithuania, and Estonia, Russian provinces before World War I, were occupied and soon incorporated into the Soviet Union, and in November the Russians invaded Finland. Italy, bound to Germany by a military alliance, waited until the following June to enter the war; Japan, bound to Italy and Germany by an alliance against Russia and world Communism, known as the Anti-Comintern Pact, continued her incursions in China, while the United States watched uneasily, unable or unwilling to do anything about it.

It was in September that Sayre went to the Philippines, and Hiss became assistant to Stanley Hornbeck, State Department Adviser on Political Relations. One of his first assignments of his new post was to find a basis in international law for American aid to the Allies against Germany, without involving the United States as a participant in the war. President Roosevelt declared a state of "limited national emergency" on September 8, and the Neutrality Act was repealed at the beginning of October, but that did not signify that the President or Congress wanted the nation to join the war. Practically everybody in America wanted to stay out of it, if that could be done.

But most Americans wanted to see the Germans defeated, too. Now that the Germans and Russians appeared to be making common cause, the dispute between the anti-Fascists and anti-Communists in America seemed to lose its importance. Catholics and Polish–Americans no longer saw Germany as a bulwark against Russian Communism, and Americans from Finland and the Baltic states, as well as those from Austria and Czechoslovakia joined in their calls for aid to the Allies. Only the American Communists and some German–Americans (though by no means all of them, for many were passionately anti-Nazi, including the refugees from Hitler's Germany) had reason for opposing it. The Communists found themselves in unexpected partnership with the pro-Nazis and diehard isolationists, many of whom were largely motivated by a feeling that America's destiny lay across the Pacific rather than the Atlantic, and wanted to save America's strength for the coming struggle against Japan.

It was a confusing time, and, for many people, a passionate time. Hiss, in his cold, intellectual way, concentrated on narrow issues of international law. He argued that there was no law to prohibit the United States from aiding one warring nation against another without becoming a military partner in the war; it would merely mean that America would have no legal claim to compensation if Germany retaliated, say, by attacking American vessels carrying arms to England. The chance of collecting on such claims would be slim in any case; but acceptance of this doctrine meant accepting the idea that the United States need not be drawn into war by a repetition of the *Lusitania* incident, which had had such powerful effect on American opinion in World War I.

Hiss's argument was endorsed by Hornbeck and passed on to Secretary Hull, who found it useful support for the position he and President Roosevelt were taking—that the United States should and would aid the allies by every possible means short of war. This was the theme of Roosevelt's policies, actions, and speeches from then until Pearl Harbor, although with each passing week the distance by which they were "short of war" grew less. Hiss's memorandum became the basis for an article written by Professor Clyde Eagleton of New York University in the *Journal of International Law*. It also led to his cooperation with a national citizens' committee formed to support Roosevelt's aid-the-Allies policy, under the chairmanship of William Allen White, editor of the *Emporia* (Kansas) *Gazette*, which was one of the nation's most distinguished newspapers of its day, although it spoke for a rather small farming town.

The opposite view—keep America out of the war no matter what—was championed by a group called the America First Committee, enjoying the oddly assorted support of Communists and isolationists. It was an alliance of opposites with no hope of survival; it cracked apart when the Russians and Germans abandoned their pretense of friendship and Germany invaded Russia on June 22, 1941, and it lost all meaning when the Japanese attacked

Pearl Harbor less than six months later. America was in the war now, like it or not, and the big question was how to divide her still unready strength between the European and Pacific battle-fronts. The quarrel between anti-Fascists and anti-Communists was revived as a kind of undercurrent, and Roosevelt's policy decisions became complicated by the embarrassment of having such an unpopular and unexpectedly powerful ally as the Soviet Union.

8

UNITED NATIONS,
DIVIDED NATION

THE war brought no immediate change in Hiss's way of life, except that like everybody else he had to work harder. As an ROTC lieutenant he tried to volunteer for active duty immediately after Pearl Harbor, but quickly learned that the Army didn't want thirty-seven-year-old lieutenants; they wanted officers of either higher rank or lower age. Nor had the State Department wanted him to leave, insisting that their contribution to the war effort was at least as important as the Army's. Hiss's job as assistant to political adviser Stanley Hornbeck involved him in the complex problems of getting military aid to Chiang Kai-shek, who was battling the Japanese on the mainland, while American forces were painfully fighting their way from island to island across the Pacific.

From the work standpoint it was a return to the habits of early New Deal days, when Hiss was at his office, on nights and weekends, and every after-hours social contact was another working session. But now, as a fairly senior officer in the State Department, the requirements were a little different, and in many ways easier. The working social events were the endless round of diplomatic functions and informal teas and cocktail parties with co-workers and representatives of foreign nations, and these tended to become less frequent and less elaborate. Rationing made them more difficult, and the austerities of wartime behavior reduced the entertainment schedules of even the neutral embassies.

Still, there was always something planned for at least two or three evenings a week and always work to take home as well.

Priscilla became a Civil Defense warden, which meant going to meetings in the evening after Tony was in bed and patrolling the streets during air raid drills to make sure the blackout rules were obeyed. Tim was at boarding school, and Tony was a baby, born four months before Pearl Harbor; Priscilla was doing the bottles-and-diapers routine again after fifteen years, and Alger was learning it for the first time. He loved the experience of being a father, and tried to do all the things young husbands do. At least a few times a week, he managed to get home early enough to help put the baby to bed, and before Tony was old enough to talk more than a few words, his father was telling him bedtime stories. Alger made up his own nonstop serial story, based on *Alice in Wonderland*, but gave the White Rabbit a much bigger role than Lewis Carroll had. (After all, Tony was a boy and would be much more interested in a White Rabbit than in a little girl called Alice.)

These were good years for Alger and Priscilla, in spite of the war. It was a period of calm domestic pleasures; Hiss was very happy in his new role as a father and felt he was performing it well. He liked having people in the house, enjoyed hosting small, informal parties for his diplomatic colleagues and putting up guests overnight, when hotel rooms were impossible to find in wartime Washington. He found the small talk of the formal diplomatic dinners boring, as did Priscilla; but she usually found someone among the guests who was interesting. In spite of gasoline rationing they were occasionally able to get over to the Eastern Shore, where the farm products and the fresh fish, oysters and crabs were a welcome supplement to their food rations. They rented a summer cottage each year at Peacham, Vermont, although getting there by train was an ordeal, because the trains were always crowded, uncomfortable, undependable, and generally late. But Tony was a good traveler, even as a baby, always placid and cooperative, and never bored, especially with his father along to keep him amused with games, tricks, and stories.

The cultural life in Washington was as active as ever; they

often attended chamber music concerts at Dumbarton Oaks, the former home of Mr. and Mrs. Robert Woods Bliss, a baronial mansion and twenty-seven-acre park just across Wisconsin Avenue from the Hisses' home on Volta Place. In 1940 the Blisses had given it to Harvard University as a museum and research center for the study of Byzantine and medieval humanities, and a close friend of the Hisses, Mrs. Barbara Sessions, was on the staff there.

In the fall of 1943 the Hisses had to move because their house on Volta Place, which they had been renting, was sold over their heads. It was impossible to find another place to rent in war-time Washington, and with some misgivings Hiss bought a home, for the first and only time in his life. It was an attractive little house at 3210 P Street, only three blocks from where he had lived in 1935–1936, and practically around the corner from Dumbarton Oaks. It was much smaller than their first P Street home, with three tiny bedrooms, a tiny parlor and study, and kitchen and dining room in the basement. Hiss paid $13,000 for it, mostly mortgage, and thought it a frighteningly high price, but he found he liked being a homeowner, and enjoyed caring for the place and fixing it up to his own taste. Four years later, when the time came to move to New York, he would hate to leave it.

If Hiss's domestic life was peaceful in these years, his work in the State Department was hectic. Chiang Kai-shek's part of the war in the Far East, which Hiss was engaged in supporting, wasn't going well, and part of the trouble came from what the Communists were doing. It was embarrassing enough from the political standpoint to have Russian Communists as our allies in the European war; in China the Communists were both allies against the Japanese and enemies of Chiang Kai-shek, engaged in a civil war which had been going on long before the Japanese war started. What could be done about allies that were fighting each other? Which of Chiang's two wars was more important to the United States, in the immediate crisis and in the long run? There was no agreement on such questions among different factions in the State Department or the public at large.

The official policy, which Hiss and his boss, Stanley Hornbeck, supported, was to give maximum aid to Chiang and let the Communists get what help they could from the Russians, with whom they had direct communications, since they held much of the interior of China, along the Mongolian and Siberian borders. Some of the younger China service officers argued that too many of the supplies sent to Chiang were simply captured by the Communists and used against him, and they wanted to impose conditions on aid to Chiang, which Hiss and Hornbeck found unrealistic. Whether Chiang was losing battles against the Communists or the Japanese, he had to be kept in the war, and he needed all the help we could give him, in Hiss's view. To hold out on Chiang for the sake of hurting the Communists would benefit Japan in the long run, and our men in the Pacific would be the losers.

Others wanted to go all out with aid to the Communists, arguing that they were fighting more successfully against the Japanese anyway, but this idea was opposed by Hiss and Hornbeck. It was their hope and purpose to preserve Chiang's regime as the future government of China after the war; it was a policy that failed in the end, and Hiss's efforts to defend it only earned him the enmity of those who blamed him—and the Roosevelt and Truman administrations generally—for its failure.

From this narrow concentration on a local and intractable issue, Hiss was rescued, to his great satisfaction in April 1944, when he was appointed deputy director of the newly formed Office of Special Political Affairs. From then on, his job was to work on President Roosevelt's plan for the coming postwar world, the dream of a new world organization to keep peace among nations, one that might succeed where Woodrow Wilson's League of Nations had failed.

Over the mantelpiece in the Cabinet Room of the White House during the years Franklin Roosevelt was President hung a portrait of Wilson, the last Democrat to be President before him and the man who led the nation through World War I. Wilson had set the precedents which Roosevelt must either follow or depart from in this second great war; as Robert Sherwood, one of his intimates, described it, the "ghost of Woodrow Wilson" was never far from his shoulder.

Wilson's dream had been to put an end to all great wars, and he had failed; but Roosevelt had to try again. Wilson had sought to reconcile the warring nations by offering "peace without victory," but it hadn't worked; the defeated Germans had felt betrayed by the Versailles Treaty, and the new war was their revenge. Wilson had created the League of Nations as an international institution for settling disputes by peaceful means, but his own nation had refused to join for fear of losing some of its sovereign independence and being drawn into other nations' quarrels.

Wilson had pushed his ideas stubbornly, having too little regard for domestic and international political realities, but Roosevelt was determined above all to avoid that mistake. For "peace without victory," he substituted "unconditional surrender," and for the League of Nations he substituted a new design for international cooperation, which came to be called the United Nations Organization, and then simply the United Nations. He was more careful than Wilson to bring his political opponents into the planning at every stage, and to gain at least *pro forma* cooperation from Republican leaders and isolationists within both parties. This time the United States was a founding, and in some respects, the dominant member from the beginning. But not everybody in America liked the idea; from its inception the nation was divided, and the divisions became deeper as time went on.

Alger Hiss was one who believed in the United Nations idea from the beginning and wanted to be a part of it. He was a Wilsonian idealist from way back; one of his professors at Johns Hopkins had been Dr. John H. Latané, who had served under President Wilson during World War I and was so proud of the association he never missed a chance to remind his students of it. They used to make book on how many times in a single lecture he would say, "As I said to Woodrow," or "As Woodrow said to me." It was Wilsonian idealism that had first aroused Hiss's interest in the Nye Committee's campaign against warmongers in 1934, and driven him away from the Committee when it turned isolationist in 1935. Francis Sayre, Hiss's first boss in the State Department, was Wilson's son-in-law; everything in Hiss's experience assured him Wilson had been right about the League of Nations, and the isolationists wrong. To help build a new League, under the new political conditions, was to Hiss the kind of honor and privilege he would have aspired to if he had thought it possible. Now it was.

The first steps toward forming a new international organization had been taken even before Pearl Harbor. A declaration issued by the foreign ministers of Britain and her allies in London in June 194_ defined their war aims in terms of establishing a world free from the "menace of aggression"; Roosevelt and British Prime Minister Winston Churchill carried the idea a step further in their Atlantic Charter of August 14, 1941. The Charter looked forward to a "wider and permanent system of world security" after the war, and the idea was endorsed within a month by all fifteen nations then at war with Germany and Italy. After Pearl Harbor, there were suddenly twenty-six nations allied against Germany, Italy, and Japan, and their representatives met in Washington to sign a manifesto, the "Declaration of the United Nations," on January 1, 1942. Thus, a name was given to the coalition of nations now working together to win the war, who hoped to continue their cooperation in the future postwar world.

So far the United Nations idea was primarily British and American, and largely shaped by the need for ensuring the support of American opinion. Roosevelt decided from the beginning that, if it were to succeed, the Soviet Union must also be a founding member; one of the reasons the League had failed was that the Russians had been excluded until 1933, and one of the last acts of the dying League had been to expel them in 1940 because of their invasion of Finland. Roosevelt foresaw that the Soviet Union would be a major world power after Germany's defeat, and a potentially dangerous one; it was better to make her a responsible partner in the new world order, if that could be done, than to leave her outside to become its enemy.

To this end, a conference of the foreign ministers of the

United States, Britain, and the Soviet Union met in Moscow, in
October 1943, to coordinate plans for the war effort and the future
peace settlement. The Moscow Declaration, which they issued at
the end of their meeting, promised the establishment of "a general international organization" open to membership of all nations
on a basis of "sovereign equality" and devoted to "the maintenance
of international peace and security." A month later the work of
the foreign ministers was ratified and carried a step further by the
Big Three themselves, Roosevelt, Churchill, and Stalin, at Te-
heran, the capital of Iran, which was conveniently close to Russia
but under British protection at the time. There the Big Three
agreed to proceed at once with preliminary plans for the new
organization.

At this point, there was no great hurry, of course, since the
war must first be won, but all agreed that the organization was
more likely to succeed if the basic plans were laid before that
happened, and while all concerned were united in a common
purpose. Secretary of State Cordell Hull assigned his assistant,
Leo Pasvolsky, to set up the necessary office for this purpose
within the State Department, and to recruit staff for it. By April
1944, the Office of Special Political Affairs was at work, making
arrangements for a three-power conference on the subject, and
preparing draft proposals for the conference to consider.

Edward Stettinius, Undersecretary and soon to be Secretary
of State, was appointed U.S. delegate, and his first suggestion
was that the conference be held at Montauk Point on the extreme
eastern tip of Long Island. Privacy and the security of the foreign
delegations could be assured there, and a comfortable hotel and
surrounding cottages could be used as accommodations. The conference was to meet toward the end of August, a beautiful season
at Montauk.

Hiss demurred, pointing out that while the remoteness of
the location might simplify security problems, it would also make
communications, transportation, and everything else more difficult. He proposed the more convenient estate of Dumbarton Oaks;
there was a high brick wall surrounding the grounds, which would
ease the security problem, the mansion was only a few blocks from

the Russian and British embassies, where the visiting delegations could stay very conveniently at their own nations' expense. Its great hall, furnished with paintings and tapestries of medieval Europe, was ideal for plenary sessions, and the surrounding ante-rooms and galleries provided ample space for delegation meetings and committee work. Hiss knew whom to approach to arrange for the government's use of the estate; Harvard University and the Blisses were only too pleased to consent.

Before the conference met, Hiss and his chief Edwin R. Wilson worked with their staff on drafting the "Tentative Proposals for a General International Organization," which were to form the starting point of the delegates' discussions. They had the Covenant of the League of Nations as their own starting point, but there were many changes to be made. The Security Council of the new United Nations was to have more clearly defined powers than the old League Council had, with authority to impose economic sanctions and to apply armed force against nations found to be in violation of a UN decision. There were to be many more members of the United Nations than there had been in the League; and the whole problem of former colonies and dependent territories of various kinds had to be reviewed. At the end of World War I, the colonies of defeated Germany had become "mandates" of the League, assigned to the care of interested member nations—Britain, France, Italy, South Africa, and Australia. Now these countries were to be given their freedom, or at least were promised their eventual freedom, and all members of the United Nations were to be required to give or to promise the same freedom to any other dependent territories under their administration. It was an idea fraught with opportunities for dispute and possible conflict; at Dumbarton Oaks it was agreed to substitute the term *trusteeship* for the League's *mandate*, but the delegates carefully avoided coming to grips with the political difficulties involved.

It was in connection with the trusteeship problem that Pasvolsky recruited Ralph Bunche, head of the political science department at Howard University and a specialist in such matters, for Stettinius's staff. Bunche was later to become a distinguished member of the U.S. delegation to the United Nations,

121

and afterwards Director of the UN Trusteeship Division, UN mediator in Palestine after the 1967 Arab–Israeli War, and Undersecretary General of the UN. But in 1944 he was the first and only black officer in the State Department, and as such his appointment had to be specially cleared with the Senate Foreign Relations Committee. Sen. Tom Connally of Texas, then chairman of the Committee, accepted it with some surprise, when Cordell Hull telephoned him to break the news, assuring him that Bunche was "the best man for the job." He worked well with his white associates in the State Department, and the only difficulty Hiss was aware of was that Bunche always had some excuse for not joining the others for lunch at the Hay–Adams House. It was some time before Hiss understood why; the color bar was never mentioned.

At the conference Bunche was a member of the U.S. delegation, but Hiss was not; his job as executive secretary of the conference, put him in charge of such matters as the physical arrangements, communications, transportation, the recording of the minutes of the sessions, and providing for the translation and distribution of working papers. They were similar to the functions he would exercise on a larger scale the following April at the San Francisco conference, when the Dumbarton Oaks proposals were developed into a Charter for the United Nations by agreement of all the founding members. Hiss was also an adviser to the U.S. delegation at both conferences, attending delegation meetings as Pasvolsky's chief staff aide.

The Dumbarton Oaks conference was a success, because all three participating powers wanted it to be. Agreement was reached on the main outlines of the new organization's structure, and the thorny questions that would require more work were identified. Besides the complex problems raised by the trusteeship question, two others were particularly difficult.

One related to the use of the veto within the Security Council. All three powers at Dumbarton Oaks agreed that they would become "permanent members" of the Council, and that smaller nations would be entitled to Council representation on a rotating basis, and would be elected to serve there by a periodic vote of the General Assembly. They also agreed that each of the permanent members would be entitled to veto any action proposed by the Council which they objected to. But Andrei Gromyko, Soviet Ambassador to Washington and chief delegate for the Soviet Union, said his government wanted power to veto even the discussion of such matters. Stettinius and Sir Alexander Cadogan, British Undersecretary for Foreign Affairs, thought this was going too far, and the dispute remained unresolved until the San Francisco conference.

The other dispute concerned the makeup of the General Assembly, in which every member nation was to enjoy equal representation. Gromyko argued that, since the votes of the British Commonwealth nations—Canada, Australia, New Zealand, South Africa, and India—could always be counted on to support the official British position, and the United States could count on the support of the twenty Latin American nations, Canada and the Philippine Commonwealth, the Soviet Union should be entitled to a similar bloc of supporters among the smaller member nations. He proposed that the three largest of the sixteen constituent republics of the Soviet Union—the Ukraine, Byelorussia, and Lithuania—should be admitted to membership and vote in the Assembly as separate nations. Stettinius and Cadogan rejected the idea, and it was left for President Roosevelt to resolve the argument with Stalin and Churchill at their conference in Yalta, a Soviet resort on the Black Sea, the following February.

Hiss was attached to the U.S. delegation at Yalta for the same kind of administrative functions he had handled at Dumbarton Oaks, although now he was serving only the delegation, rather than the conference as a whole. He maintained a liaison between the delegation at Yalta and the naval support vessels in the Black Sea, seeing to the transmission of cables to and from Washington, as well as providing such American comforts and conveniences as the delegation might require. They were quartered in the Livadia Palace, one of the royal residences of Czarist days, which had been transformed into a resort hotel for Soviet workers before the war, until it again was transformed into something of its old elegance for the needs of the conference. It had been used as a military headquarters by first one side and then the other during the fighting in the Crimea in 1942–1943, and its furnishings had been looted thoroughly by the retreating Germans. The Russians had completely equipped it as a first-class hotel, with elegant linens and silverware as well as furniture, and were lavish in their vodka-and-caviar hospitality. Hiss grew tired of eating caviar three times a day, and ordered peanut butter from the Navy communications ship, but the only thanks he got for that from his associates was a contemptuous: "You peasant!"

Hiss also advised the delegation on matters of UN procedure, and plans for the San Francisco conference, based on his Dumbarton Oaks experience. Thorny problems, such as how many votes the Soviet delegation would be allowed in the Assembly, were argued first at meetings of Stettinius and his opposite numbers, Anthony Eden of Britain and Vyacheslav Molotov of the Soviet Union, and Hiss attended these meetings and participated in drafting the minutes. Then the recommendations of the three Foreign Ministers were submitted to their chiefs, Roosevelt, Churchill, and Stalin, who reached their decisions at plenary sessions, where no official minutes were kept. Each participant made his own notes; these were essentially personal meetings between three men who trusted each other about some things but not others and wanted no official record to show where their trust began and ended.

The secretarial staffs of the three delegations alternated in typing and translating the Foreign Ministers' minutes, and on the day they took up the matter of Soviet voting strength the typing was done by the British. The meeting had reached a compromise of sorts; Molotov had agreed to leave Lithuania out of the General Assembly and reduce the demand from three extra votes to two—the Ukraine and Byelorussia; Eden had agreed to support both republics for admission to the General Assembly; and Stettinius had reserved the U.S. position, saying in effect that the United States would neither support nor oppose the resolution but would accept the decision of the other member nations. That meant that Russia would get her way, but Roosevelt wouldn't have to accept the responsibility for the decision or explain it to the American public.

The issue was not, after all, very important; in an Assembly that would begin with fifty members and quickly grow much larger, there didn't seem much harm in the Soviet proposal. Besides, Britain wanted Russia's support for giving membership to India, which as yet did not enjoy the independence of the other Commonwealth nations, but would have caused trouble for Britain if she had been excluded. And the United States wanted Russia to enter the war against Japan, which she hadn't done yet, pleading the necessity of using all her forces against Germany. The U.S. Joint Chiefs of Staff had calculated that Russian participation could shorten the war against Japan by a year or more, and save a million American lives. Stettinius knew nothing about the plans for the atom bomb, and even Roosevelt didn't know yet if it would work. It hadn't been tested yet, and he wasn't taking chances of prolonging the war.

India and Japan weren't mentioned in the Foreign Ministers' discussion of the Soviet republics, but they didn't have to be. It was a question of yielding on one issue in order to gain on another. And in any case, the U.S. position had not been announced, or at least that's the way the meeting went according to Hiss's minutes. When he received his copy of the minutes from the British typists immediately before the plenary session that day, he was astonished to find that they had been altered; the decision was presented as unanimous, with the United States agreeing with Britain and Russia that the Ukraine and Byelorussia should be independent members of the General Assembly. Hiss rushed up to Eden and pointed out the change. "Oh, that's all right," Eden told him. "You don't know what's happened since then. Go talk to Stettinius."

Hiss did, and Stettinius described for him one of those incidents that are the despair of staff assistants at meetings of Great Men, even when the staff assistants involved are of the high rank of Secretary of State. Apparently, Stettinius had gone to report privately to Roosevelt after the Foreign Ministers' meeting, and told him what a marvelous meeting it had been and how they had all "agreed on everything but—"; and before he could get the "but" out of his mouth and add "the extra Soviet votes," Stalin burst into the room with another of Roosevelt's staff for a social call before the plenary meeting. Roosevelt called to him, "Come in, Marshal, our Foreign Secretary has just been telling me they had a marvelous meeting, they agreed on everything."

Stettinius tugged vainly at Roosevelt's sleeve without getting his attention, and Stalin said, "And the two republics too?"

Roosevelt answered happily, "Oh, yes, everything!"

And so, as Hiss remembered Stettinius telling him, we were hooked, and the minutes had to be changed to reflect the new agreement. At the time it seemed like a monumental gaffe, but in retrospect Hiss recognized that the incident could not have occurred if Roosevelt had not already made up his mind to approve the Soviet demand, whatever the Foreign Ministers might recommend. But there was more trouble to come over the way the decision was made known to the public.

James F. Byrnes, then the President's number two man in the White House (head of the Office of War Mobilization, who subsequently became Secretary of State under Truman), was present at the Yalta conference in a somewhat honorary capacity to attend the plenary meetings. His chief role there was what Hiss calls "a hostage of the Senate"; he was a former Senator, highly regarded by his Senate colleagues, and a political conservative on whom Roosevelt relied to persuade conservative politicians and voters to accept his foreign policy ideas. It was part of Roosevelt's plan for avoiding Wilson's mistakes—he made certain that a prominent conservative was involved in setting up the United Nations, so that he would be committed to supporting it when the time came, bringing his followers into line. However, in this case it didn't work.

Byrnes was not only surprised to learn of the three Soviet votes, he was horrified. It seemed to him a sudden switch and a sellout to the Russians, of whom he was highly suspicious, and he immediately flared up and began protesting. He carried the news to his friend Ed Flynn, a powerful Democratic Party leader from the Bronx, who was also at Yalta with no other function than to bring his people into line behind whatever was decided there, and who also operated from a conservative and highly anti-Soviet viewpoint. Flynn didn't attend the official sessions of the conference; he and his wife had a room in the Livadia Palace and were expected simply to enjoy themselves. Sometimes Roosevelt would say to someone on his staff, "Go on up and tell Ed Flynn what's been happening; he must be very lonely up there."

There wasn't anything Byrnes and Flynn could do about the three-vote decision at Yalta, but they could and did talk about it when they got home. Roosevelt's decision had been to avoid publicizing the matter until it came up for a vote at the San Francisco conference; then the United States would quietly do nothing, and the two extra Soviet republics would be accepted as members, along with a lot of other last-minute signers of the United Nations Declaration. But it turned out to be a secret that couldn't be kept for long.

The basic plan for the San Francisco conference was one of the key accomplishments at Yalta. The conference was called for April 25, 1945, and all nations that had declared war on Germany and signed the United Nations Declaration were invited to send delegates. Their mission would be to study the Dumbarton Oaks recommendations and draw up a charter for the proposed new international organization. One of the first things Roosevelt did on his return to Washington was to appoint the U.S. delegation, including among others, Sen. Tom Connally, Sen. Arthur Vandenberg, Rep. Sol Bloom, and Rep. Charles A. Eaton. Prompted again by "the ghost of Woodrow Wilson," Roosevelt wanted to make sure both Houses of Congress and both political parties were involved in drafting the UN Charter; Vandenberg and Eaton were Republicans, and Vandenberg was a former isolationist, while Connally had a strongly conservative following.

The U.S. delegation had to be briefed on the decisions made at Yalta, including the three Soviet votes, and President Roosevelt told them about it in strictest confidence at a White House meeting on March 23, a month after his return from Yalta. He added that Stalin had agreed to give the United States two extra votes too, if we wanted them, to be used by Alaska and Hawaii. These territories were not yet states, nor were they independent nations;

and when that suggestion became known, most people found it ridiculous and offensive.

Six days later, on the morning of March 29, the whole story appeared in the *New York Herald Tribune* under the by-line of Bert Andrews, the paper's Washington Bureau chief. He didn't reveal who had leaked the story to him or why, but the theme that Andrews and other newspaper writers hammered at in the following days and weeks was that, regardless of whether the extra Soviet votes made a difference or not, the agreement shouldn't have been kept secret. What other secret deals were made at Yalta, people wondered? The story caused a fearful hullabaloo, and marked the beginning of a campaign by hard-line anti-Communists to denounce the whole Yalta agreement as a sellout to the Russians.

Hiss was horrified at Andrews's story, not that it was any surprise that members of Congress couldn't keep a secret, but that Andrews had reported it without first checking with the State Department. Hiss knew Andrews and respected him as a good newspaperman, one who had often come to him for background information about Dumbarton Oaks and other matters. He called him to ask what the hell had happened, and tried to explain the reasons for the agreement and why it wasn't anything to make such a fuss over. But he got nowhere. Andrews wouldn't say where he had got the story, but Hiss assumed the source was Byrnes, who had protested so much previously and who was now doing so publicly. He was sure it wasn't Vandenberg, whose reaction had been that it was too bad, but there was no use bringing Alaska and Hawaii into it. Byrnes, on the other hand, was saying that it was one of the mistakes of Yalta, and if they'd listened to him, it would never have happened.

This was the first time Hiss ever crossed swords with Andrews, and the relationship between the two men was never the same again. Andrews was not a man to take a rebuke kindly, especially if it came from someone in the government with whom he didn't agree. The next time they would find themselves on opposite sides of an issue would be three years later, when Chambers would denounce Hiss as a Communist, and Andrews again would ignore Hiss's side of the story.

After Yalta, Hiss succeeded Edwin R. Wilson as director of the Office of Special Political Affairs, and devoted himself to preparations for the San Francisco conference. It was to be a repetition of Dumbarton Oaks but on a larger scale: delegations from fifty nations instead of three, headed by foreign ministers and prime ministers instead of undersecretaries and ambassadors; five official languages into which documents must be translated, although only French and English were generally used in the debates. Supporting services, including transportation, communications, and security, were vastly greater, and would be handled as before by the armed services. Hiss was Secretary General of the conference; and again was in close touch with the U.S. delegation and attended most of its meetings. At the plenary sessions he sat on the rostrum beside the president of the day, a function which was rotated among the four nations that were sponsoring the conference. These were the Big Three plus China, making the ruling group now a Big Four.

There were moments of tension and comedy, such as occur at all elaborate conferences. On one occasion Hiss was checking the arrangements at the head of the table before a session of heads of delegations, on a day when Molotov was to preside; and, without giving the matter any thought, he happened to pour himself a glass of water from the thermos provided for Molotov's use. Into his glass plopped what looked like cracked ice, which shouldn't have been in the thermos; Hiss looked again and found it was not ice, but broken glass. Apparently, the enlisted man who had set up the table had somehow cracked the glass lining of the thermos, and it didn't take a trained civil servant to imagine what might have happened had Molotov poured out that broken glass for himself.

On another occasion, a security guard came up to Hiss during a plenary session and pointed out to him a man scrambling in the rafters high above the stage of the vast auditorium, aiming what looked like a rifle with telescopic sights directly at the chair in which Molotov was to sit. The guard was about to raise the alarm, but Hiss restrained him; the man was an authorized photographer for *Life* Magazine, and his apparatus only a camera with its telephoto lens extended.

Molotov was a source of special anxiety in the political climate of San Francisco, where the old atmosphere of wary cooperation between Roosevelt and Stalin had suddenly been replaced by Truman's much more suspicious and hard-nosed attitude. Two days before the conference opened, Molotov had stopped off in Washington on his way to San Francisco from Moscow, paying a courtesy visit to Truman that had turned into an angry confrontation. Hiss heard about it from Stettinius, who told him Truman had complained that Russia's activities in Poland were a breach of the Yalta agreement. It was only eleven days after Roosevelt's death, and the new President had not had time to master the subtleties of the long discussions over Poland at Yalta, and the agreements, which had been couched in deliberately ambiguous language to avoid open disagreement. Molotov, according to what Hiss learned from Stettinius, had become very excited, saying, "You're accusing us of violations. . . . I've never been talked to like this in my life!" Truman answered, "You keep your agreements, and you won't be talked to like this."

Hiss remembered that Stettinius's usually ruddy face was pale, as he told the story the next morning. "My God, I didn't think we were going to have the conference," he said. "I really thought the whole thing was going to blow up."

The Polish issue became a major source of conflict at San Francisco, and so did the more far-reaching question of the Security Council veto. Molotov continued to insist that the Big Powers should have the right to veto, not only actions of the Security Council, but even the discussion of matters they didn't want discussed. To the United States and Britain, and to the smaller nations as well, this was too much to ask. In early May, less than a week after the German surrender had ended the war in Europe, Molotov and Eden went home, and it looked as though the San Francisco conference would be a failure. Anti-Soviet feelings, which had been confined to a relatively small part of the American press for so long as the Soviet Union was our wartime ally, began to be expressed more widely, openly, and bitterly. The war that for nearly four years had suppressed the arguments between anti-Communists and anti-Fascists was suddenly over, and the old hostilities began to reappear in a new guise with new slogans and to grow more passionate.

At this point Truman sent Roosevelt's old friend and trusted emissary, Harry Hopkins, to Moscow to talk with Stalin. Hopkins knew Stalin well and got along with him; he had been at Yalta with Molotov and knew what the agreements made there about Poland and the veto question were intended to mean. It took five meetings with Stalin to reach an agreement on the Polish question; at the sixth meeting they quickly disposed of the veto matter. Molotov explained the issue to Stalin, who according to Hopkins hadn't fully understood it before, and Stalin said it was an insignificant matter, and he would accept the American position. The San Francisco conference was saved.

It took another month for the delegates to settle all the other disputes, large and small, and to agree upon the wording of the United Nations Charter, but by June 26 it was ready for signing. The ceremony took eight hours; for by now there were fifty delegations, including Argentina and Denmark as well as Ukraine and Byelorussia, and four members of each delegation were required to sign the historic document. President Truman attended to witness the signature of the U.S. delegation, and to speak at the closing ceremonies which followed.

Since the signing of the Charter was a solemn event to be recorded for motion picture and radio use in every member nation, and in many others too, it occurred to Oliver Lundquist, chief of the Presentations Division, which had charge of such things, that it might be a good idea to give the principal delegates an opportunity to rehearse backstage before going before the klieg lights in the Veterans Memorial Auditorium, where the ceremony took place. So he set up a table with a choice of pens for the delegates' use, and laid out a sheet of "treaty paper," the high-quality parchment on which formal documents are engrossed, that had the position of each delegate's name indicated on it, as previously decided by agreement of the Big Four. As sponsors of the conference, the Big Four nations headed the list, then came France, which at San Francisco was admitted to big power status as a permanent member of the Security Council, making five instead of four; followed by the other forty-five members, arranged in columns according to English alphabetical order. The order of signatures had been circulated in advance, so that each delegate would know where to sign; still, it was a good idea to refresh his recollection before going on stage, and to let him make sure his hand wasn't going to shake.

Everyone seemed pleased with the idea, but Lundquist had a special purpose in mind. As one of its final acts, the Steering Committee of the Conference had unanimously adopted a resolution praising Hiss for the efficient way he had presided over all the arrangements and supporting services that had made the conference run so smoothly. While this sort of courtesy is fairly routine on such occasions, Lundquist felt that, from the language of the resolution, the delegates really meant it. Also, he had achieved a considerable personal admiration for Hiss, who was his boss, and had become a sort of "culture hero" to him. Lundquist planned to have the text of the resolution engrossed on another sheet of treaty paper and have it framed alongside the rehearsal signatures of the fifty principal delegates, as a souvenir for Hiss. But when he mentioned the plan, Hiss demurred.

Lundquist was a little hurt by Hiss's refusal, but felt better when Hiss explained that he had no love for symbols of power and achievement, or for souvenirs of those occasions at which he rubbed shoulders with the Great Men who ruled the world. Lundquist thought it a commendable example of Hiss's humility, yet it also expressed Hiss's feeling of disappointment that the conference hadn't really been the brilliant success it appeared. He feared that the United Nations wasn't going to turn out as well as he had hoped, and that Truman's foreign policy wasn't going to be the same as Roosevelt's. He didn't think the change of policy would be an improvement.

A trivial incident occurred that day, which Hiss still remembers. Truman was on stage at the closing plenary session, while Stettinius acted as president of the day, and each of the principal delegates from the member nations came up to the rostrum to make a final speech in his own language. The meeting was held in the Opera House, but didn't last long, for the delegates were tired and their speeches were short. As each delegate approached the podium, he was to pause in front of President Truman and give him a deferential bow, like an after-dinner speaker's bow to the toastmaster. No words need be exchanged, but Truman was supposed to acknowledge each delegate's greeting with a nod, before he mounted the rostrum to begin his speech.

One after another, the delegates accomplished this simple ceremony to everyone's satisfaction, until the delegate from Brazil, a distinguished gentleman with an impressively large and shiny bald head, approached. As he arrived at the rostrum, a naval aide at Truman's elbow leaned over and whispered something in the presidential ear, and Truman smiled, ignoring the presence of Pedro Leão Velloso, Brazilian Acting Minister for Foreign Affairs and Chairman of the Brazilian delegation. Velloso again bowed to Truman, a little more deeply, and began to flush. A deliberate affront appeared to be in the making, a diplomatic embarrassment of potentially dangerous proportions. Hiss nudged Truman, and the President, turning suddenly, noticed the Brazilian and gave the required nod. Hiss relaxed; a small thing, but part of his job.

He might not have given it another thought if the matter hadn't come up again a few days later, when Hiss arrived in Washington with the precious United Nations Charter for its formal delivery to the President. This was a big occasion, for Hiss and many others. His photograph was featured as "Picture of the Week" in *Life* Magazine; he was shown disembarking from a special Army plane with the Charter, which had its own parachute and forwarding address in case anything happened to Hiss or the plane on the way. Hiss carried the Charter to the White House, as he had been instructed, but was met there without ceremony and told to go upstairs, where the President was expecting him.

Not being a White House habitué, Hiss didn't know where

to look when he arrived there, but he finally found the President in a large room with several friends, all in their shirtsleeves drinking bourbon, with half-unpacked suitcases and dirty linen overflowing the nearby chairs and tables. It was a hot day, before air-conditioning, and the windows were open. The President was very relaxed. "Give the young man a drink," he said to the tailcoated waiter, who poured a glass of Old Muehlenbach and offered it on a silver tray, half bowing. Hiss thought it rather incongruous.

He turned over the Charter to the President, and that started reminiscences about Truman's day at San Francisco. "You remember when that baldheaded man came up the aisle?" said the naval aide, who had been at Truman's elbow, and everybody roared with laughter. The President turned to Hiss and said, "You know what he said to me? He said, 'Pipe the Simonize job!'"

The President guffawed at the recollection, but Hiss didn't think it was funny. He had dedicated himself to the service of an international organization, which he hoped would bring a new era of peace to the world, and he didn't think the new President's light-hearted approach to international ceremony was going to help. Nor did he think Truman's hard-nosed attitude toward the Russians was the way to preserve and carry forward what Roosevelt had started in a spirit of accommodation. The arguments at San Francisco that Hiss had witnessed seemed to him an uneasy portent of a difficult future, and he wasn't happy at the prospect.

9

THE COLD WAR

Aﬀter the San Francisco conference Alger Hiss decided it was time for him to leave the government and return to the private practice of law. He had enlisted in the New Deal "for the duration of the emergency," in 1933; the emergency of Depression had turned into the emergency of war and postwar planning, but now, after twelve years, it seemed to be over. The United Nations was launched, and Hiss's work for it was done. His old friend, Thurlow Gordon, wanted him back at Cotton, Franklin, Wright & Gordon, as did Choate, Hall & Stewart in Boston. He had received offers of teaching positions at Yale and Harvard, but they hadn't particularly appealed to him.

Leaving the government wasn't as easy as that, however. Edward Stettinius, now replaced as Secretary of State by James F. Byrnes, was soon to become the U.S. representative to the UN Preparatory Commission, and he wanted Hiss to stay on, at least until the new organization was in full operation. There was a lot to be done to bring that about; first, the Preparatory Commission was to meet in London to draw up temporary rules of procedure for the Security Council and the General Assembly and its committees; then these bodies were to have their first organization meeting to adopt permanent rules, to elect officers, to establish permanent agencies of the UN such as the Trusteeship Council and the Economic and Social Council, as well as to establish a permanent Secretariat and to appoint a Secretary-General.

Lord Halifax, the British Ambassador in Washington, had been so impressed by Hiss's handling of the San Francisco conference that he proposed him for the same position at the Preparatory Commission meeting. Hiss declined, pointing out that the job depended, among other things, upon the ability to mobilize the resources of the host country to get things done—transportation, housing, communications, and supporting services of all kinds. This would be more difficult in London, where vast areas of the city had been reduced to rubble by German bombs and rockets, and food was even more scarce than it had been during the war. Truman had stopped the flow of lend-lease aid after the Japanese surrender in August, and the Marshall Plan had not yet been devised to take its place. Meanwhile, Britain had not the resources to feed herself and rebuild what the Germans had destroyed. Supplying the needs of delegations from fifty nations and their staffs under these circumstances was not going to be easy; certainly the man who directed the work would have to be part of the British government. Hiss proposed Gladwyn Jebb, a member of the British delegation at Yalta and San Francisco, who had headed that delegation's administrative and staff work.

The proposal was accepted, and Jebb became Executive Secretary of the Commission, beginning a long and brilliant career, which brought him first a knighthood and then a peerage as Britain's UN representative. Hiss, under pressure from Stettinius, agreed to stay on long enough to help with the preparations in Washington for the Preparatory Commission and to serve as principal adviser to the U.S. delegation, when the General Assembly met for its organization meeting in London the following January.

Hiss wasn't eager for the London assignment, which came up just at a time when he was preoccupied with a family problem involving his stepson Timothy. He didn't want to go away for five or six months and leave it all to Priscilla or to leave her alone again in Georgetown with Tony, now five years old. It had been hard enough for her when he was in San Francisco for two months, although she hadn't complained, and as wartime separations went, theirs had been short and relatively easy. Still, she hadn't been used to their being separated and hadn't liked it, and he hadn't grown used to it either. Once when he had tried to cheer her up with a telephone call, he had confused the time zones, placing the call at midnight San Francisco time, thinking it would be 9:00 P.M. in Georgetown. It had been 3:00 A.M., and he hadn't understood at first why she sounded so sleepy.

There was plenty to be done in Washington during the Preparatory Commission's work. Stettinius needed a man at headquarters to coordinate the messages that went back and forth and to see that they were properly cleared within the State Department with everyone who needed to be consulted. Hiss took over this responsibility, while Adlai Stevenson went to London as Stettinius's alternate to the Preparatory Commission. But in January, when the full delegation went to London for the first session of the General Assembly, Hiss, as principal adviser, accompanied them for a session that lasted three months.

His duties then had to do with the niceties of procedure, such things as finding a way to define the use of the Security Council veto that would cover all possible contingencies and mean the same thing to all delegations. For example, an agreement had been reached at San Francisco that the veto could be used on substantive questions but not procedural ones, but how was it possible to tell which was which? And was that question itself subject to the veto? There were endless tangles of this kind, because procedural decisions unavoidably affected the course of debate about substantive issues. And there were some serious and dangerous issues to debate, even before the Security Council was ready with its rules of procedure: Iran complained of Soviet interference in its domestic affairs; the Soviet Union complained of British interference in Greece; and Lebanon and Syria complained about British and French troops on their soil.

As Hiss had learned at San Francisco, the powers were not going to use the UN as a kind of world government, a Senate or Parliament, in which to argue out their differences and settle them on a basis of mutual trust, accommodation, compromise, or give-and-take. This might be done on some issues, but not the really vital ones. There were many ways in which the UN could be useful in working out such issues, and it could keep what was soon to be called the *Cold War* from getting too hot; but it couldn't prevent it. Instead, the UN became the arena in which many of these confrontations would be staged.

In 1946 many could not see the necessity for such confrontations, and Hiss was one of them. The term *Cold War* hadn't been invented yet, and there was a respectable body of opinion that hoped for what was called "peaceful coexistence" between the democratic and Communist nations, despite their different economic and social systems. This was the idea on which the Dumbarton Oaks, Yalta, and San Francisco conferences had been based, but it didn't last long after the war ended. In June 1946 Winston Churchill, Britain's wartime Prime Minister who was out of office, came to the United States to give his famous "iron curtain" speech at Fulton, Missouri. He called for an anti-Communist coalition of Western democracies against the Soviet Union. The speech brought some protests in England, where the new Labour government of Clement Attlee was trying to build its foreign policy around the idea of peaceful coexistence; but Attlee would not repudiate Churchill, and Truman publicly supported him.

The heart of Churchill's argument was that the Soviet Union should not be left in control of the lands of Eastern Europe, which its armies had overrun when the Germans were driven out —Poland, the three Baltic republics, Hungary, Czechoslovakia, Bulgaria, Rumania, Yugoslavia, Albania, and East Germany. Naturally, the Western democracies wanted these nations to have democratic regimes, and the Russians wanted them to have Communist regimes. As a practical matter the Russian armies controlled these areas, and there was no way to prevent them from doing what they wanted, short of sending in troops and starting another war. But it became American policy to protest against everything the Russians were doing, and to use every means short of war to try to upset their plans. War itself was unthinkable now that the power of the atom bomb had been demonstrated.

The issue, as presented to the American public, was that if the Russians were allowed to get away with imposing their system on the lands under their control, they would soon spread Communism over the rest of Europe and Asia, and become a threat to democracy within the United States. Resisting the spread of Soviet power and Communist ideas thus became the cornerstone of American policy, and it remained so through the Korean and Vietnam wars and the shaky détente that began in the final Nixon years. In the late 1940s Hiss, and a dwindling number of believers in Roosevelt's policy of accommodation, thought the danger grossly exaggerated, and believed that if it became necessary to resist or "contain" the Russians, as Truman put it, there was no need to be so uncompromising or aggressive about it. As the Monroe Doctrine made Latin America an exclusive "sphere of interest" of the United States, the argument ran, Russia could safely be allowed her own influence over nations on her borders. And even if Socialists or Communists should gain strength in democratically elected governments of Western Europe, was that a threat to the United States? The Attlee government in Britain was Socialist, and Sweden had been Socialist for years, yet the United States was able to deal with them. That, at least, was the argument, though in retrospect Hiss finds it rather naïve.

In any case, Hiss felt that Truman's foreign policy was leading in directions he didn't want to go, and he no longer wanted to be a part of it. When Dean Acheson was making fiery anti-Communist speeches, Hiss complained to him that he was scaring the hell out of Congress, and making people think there was real danger of a Russian invasion of Western Europe, when the Russians were clearly too exhausted by the war to do anything of the sort. "This will scare the whole public," Hiss said, "it's hysterical."

"If you don't scare Congress, they'll go fishing," Acheson replied, as Hiss remembers it, and Hiss retorted: "If you do scare them, they'll go crazy."

Acheson didn't think that was funny; two years later, Hiss, while standing before the House Un-American Activities Committee (HUAC) and trying to convince them he was not and never had been a Communist, concluded it had been prophetic. That was a mistake on his part; the Committee members didn't think they were crazy, nor did the public. And they took offense at Hiss's attitude.

On his way to London, in January 1946, Hiss had already made up his mind he would leave the State Department as soon as the Department was willing to release him, and he listened with interest when John Foster Dulles, a Republican member of the delegation and a trustee of the Carnegie Endowment for International Peace, sounded him out about becoming President of that institution. When it came to Hiss's trial three years later, there was a lot of argument about exactly what Dulles and Hiss said to each other on this and several other occasions, which will be described in Chapter 20. Dulles appeared as a prosecution witness to impeach Hiss's credibility, and the jury apparently preferred Dulles's recollections to Hiss's. However, when Dulles's papers were opened to the inspection of scholars after his death, records were found which give Dulles's account of these conversations at the time they took place. An analysis of these documents, and the light they shed on the affair, was published in the spring 1973 issue of *University: A Princeton Quarterly*, by Richard D. Challener, then Chairman-designate of Princeton's Department of History.

According to Challener, Dulles had agreed, in 1945, to become Chairman of the Board of Trustees of the Carnegie Endowment on a part-time basis, provided that he could appoint a full-time President to take over the administrative responsibilities. He was interested in Hiss as a possible candidate, because he had met him at the San Francisco conference and had a high regard for him. He found an opportunity to talk to him about it on the *Queen Elizabeth*, while they were traveling with the rest of the delegation to the General Assembly meeting.

Dulles reported their conversation in a letter to John W. Davis, Chairman of the Endowment's Executive Committee, saying that Hiss "seemed quite interested in the idea of the Carnegie Endowment. Although he feels that he probably ought not to leave the State Department for three or four months, he wanted me to talk with Jim Byrnes to get the Secretary's ideas as to how soon he could leave the Department without embarrassment." Dulles made no commitment to Hiss regarding the appointment, since the decision would have to be made by the Board of Trustees, and his own election as Chairman was not to take place until May.

Hiss was interested, and he liked Dulles's idea of reforming the Endowment to concentrate its efforts in support of the UN, and to act as a liaison between the UN and such institutions as the Rockefeller Foundation and the Carnegie Corporation. Hiss, too, thought the Endowment could be useful in promoting public support for the UN and helping to make it a central element in American foreign policy. Dulles also wrote to Davis that he was "more and more convinced he [Hiss] was the right man for the job," and after talking with Byrnes, Dulles wrote again, saying, "I am inclined to think that he would become available."

But a hitch developed soon after Hiss returned from London with the delegation. Byrnes called him into his office and said some Congressmen were accusing him of being a Communist, and threatening to make speeches about it in the House. Hiss denied the charge with some astonishment; Byrnes told him he had better talk to the FBI, since the Congressmen had apparently got their information from a former FBI agent, who was then working for HUAC as an investigator.

Hiss promptly telephoned J. Edgar Hoover, Director of the FBI, but Hoover was away, and Hiss talked to his second in command D. M. Ladd instead. Ladd set up an appointment for him, and Hiss went down Pennsylvania Avenue to his office. Ladd did not reveal who was calling him a Communist or why; he merely asked Hiss if he wanted to make a statement. Hiss mentioned all the organizations he had ever belonged to that the FBI might be interested in, and the only one on their subversive list was the International Juridical Association (IJA), which had been taken over by the National Lawyers' Guild after Hiss left it. The Guild had some Communist members, and was regarded as a Communist "front." The FBI asked Hiss if he knew various people whom they named, but the only name he recognized was that of Lee Pressman. Hiss explained that he had met Pressman at Harvard, worked with him in the IJA, and known him in the Agriculture Department, in 1933–1934. So far as Hiss could remember later, he was not asked about Whittaker Chambers at that time; and when he was asked about Chambers by the FBI a year later, he didn't recognize the name. He had known a Tony Whittaker and a Bob Chambers, but had never known anyone calling himself Whittaker Chambers.

The incident was unsettling, because a great hue and cry was already being raised against Communists, and the succession of loyalty acts and executive orders on the subject that preoccupied the government for the following decade was already in the making. Hiss told Byrnes that, should the accusation against him cause the State Department any embarrassment, he was prepared to resign immediately, but he didn't want to resign under fire. Byrnes agreed with him, and there was no embarrassment to the Department yet; all kinds of people were being called Communists in those days who weren't, and it was a kind of political slander that hadn't yet become effective. In any case, nothing more was heard from the Congressmen who had raised the charge, and Hiss never even found out who they were. He heard nothing more from the FBI, and, concluding the matter had been dropped, he forgot about it.

But it had not been dropped; there was a great deal going on behind the scenes that Hiss knew nothing about. Chambers had started it in August 1939, just after the signing of the Nazi–Soviet pact that triggered the war in Europe. He approached Adolf Berle with a long list of people he accused of being involved in one way or another with the Communist underground. The last name on the list was Alger Hiss. Berle, who was then Assistant Secretary of State, did some checking on Hiss and on some of the others, and found nothing to support Chambers's story. But because he was worried about it, he began tightening up on State Department security and exchanging security information with the FBI on a regular basis. The FBI also began checking Chambers's story, and in the ensuing years, Hiss's record was periodically reviewed under the various security procedures that were developed during the war and after, as were the records of the others named by Chambers, and of all government employees in sensitive positions. Hiss's security files grew fatter and fatter, though he never saw them; and, so far as one can determine from the published record, no evidence had been found at this stage to support Chambers's charges. However, they had been repeated and elaborated often enough by Chambers and others, always without revealing the source of the rumor, so each repetition seemed like new evidence to those who wanted to believe it.*

There was a good deal of such repetition, and it was all the more damaging because the source of the information was never identified, so what actually originated from a single source was passed around as though it came from many sources. Among those who used Chambers's story in this way were Isaac Don Levine, for a time the editor of an anti-Communist magazine called *Plain Talk*, who had arranged for Chambers's original interview with Berle; Alfred Kohlberg, a wealthy importer of Chinese textiles, who helped Levine with financial backing, blaming Hiss, among others, for the loss of China to the Communists; and Benjamin Mandel, former FBI investigator and former Communist, who was on the State Department security staff in 1945–1946, and for the rest of the 1940s was an investigator for HUAC. Mandel was an old associate of Chambers, and was said to have

* In 1948 William Marbury, one of Hiss's lawyers, was told by an FBI agent that Hiss's phone had been tapped for years, and the FBI had three cabinets full of transcripts, but nothing derogatory or incriminating had been found. Apart from the evidence at the trials, the only outside support Chambers's story ever received was from Nathaniel Weyl, a free-lance writer, who told the Senate Internal Security Committee in 1952 that he had been a member of the same Communist "cell" as Hiss in Washington in 1934, but had concealed this fact when he was questioned by HUAC in 1943, and had said nothing about it during the Hiss trials. The cell, described by Weyl in 1952, consisted of the same persons whose names Chambers had supplied in 1948, except that Chambers had not mentioned Weyl as a member, and Weyl said he had not known Chambers at the time. Nothing was done to check Weyl's story; he was one of a number of ex-Communists who publicly recanted during the Korean War, and was the author of several books about treason and espionage then current, including *Treason: The Story of Disloyalty and Betrayal in American History*, and *The Battle Against Disloyalty*. His testimony, on February 19, 1952, came while Hiss was in jail and at the time his lawyers' efforts to gain him a new trial were receiving considerable publicity.

been the one who issued Chambers his Communist Party membership card in 1925; like Chambers, he was now as passionate an
anti-Communist as he had once been a passionate revolutionary.

Another important member of the group was the Reverend
John F. Cronin, an economics teacher at a Catholic school in
Baltimore, who was asked by the FBI in 1941 to gather information about Communist activities in labor unions in the Baltimore
area. He was glad to do so, and in return the FBI supplied him
with information about Communist infiltration within the government. Soon he was also getting similar information from HUAC
files, through the help of Ben Mandel. In the fall of 1944, Father
Cronin was asked by Archbishop Mooney of Detroit to prepare a
confidential report on the Communist problem in the United
States, which he completed and circulated to the American
Catholic hierarchy in November 1945.

Among other items, Father Cronin's report named Alger Hiss
as one of the leaders of a Communist organization within the
Agricultural Adjustment Administration (AAA) in the 1930s. The
source for this information was identified only as an editor of a
national magazine, a sufficiently blind description of Whittaker
Chambers, who, in 1945, was a senior editor of *Time* and didn't
want his name brought into the anti-Communist campaign.

Following this report, Father Cronin became Assistant Director of the Social Action Department of the National Catholic
Welfare Conference in Washington; he also carried out an assignment from the U.S. Chamber of Commerce to prepare a series of
anti-Communist pamphlets, which were widely circulated in
1946–1947. Though the report to the bishops was confidential, it
found its way into many hands, including those of a freshman
Congressman, Richard M. Nixon, who in early 1947 was looking
for someone to give him information about Communists.

Nixon in those days was an unknown from California, whose
political experience had begun less than eighteen months before,
when a committee of Los Angeles bankers and businessmen had
endorsed him to run for Congress against the popular Jerry
Voorhis, a moderately liberal Democrat, who had represented the
district for ten years. Nixon was a man of enormous ambition,

with a law degree from Duke University, who had given up a so far unrewarding career as a lawyer and Assistant City Attorney in Whittier, California, for a job in Washington with the Office of Price Administration (OPA) after Pearl Harbor. Subsequently, he had given up his Quaker training to obtain a commission in the Navy. He was still in the Navy, doing legal work in connection with the termination of Navy contracts, when the Los Angeles Republicans called him in September 1945, and asked him if he were a Republican and available.

"I guess I'm a Republican," he is said to have replied. "I voted for Dewey."

It was an uphill fight against Voorhis, and Nixon learned from Murray Chotiner, his first adviser in the art of politics, that the way to win is to be always on the attack. So Nixon attacked Voorhis as a Communist sympathizer, something he'd never been called before because it was untrue. Nixon, however, carried on his attack just as though it were true, getting so many voters to believe him that he trounced Voorhis in the election by 65,586 votes to 49,994. After that, it was natural for Nixon to look for ways to attack people as Communists.

He asked Rep. Charles Kersten, a colleague on the House Education and Labor Committee, for help, and Kersten introduced him to Father Cronin, who assured Nixon that Alger Hiss, among others, was a Communist.

Father Cronin recalls that his sources for this information were the FBI and Ben Mandel, both of whom had heard it from Chambers but from no other original source, so far as the record shows. But apparently Father Cronin was not aware of this point; his recollection is that he "told Mr. Nixon that Mr. Hiss was in fact a Communist and that, therefore, Mr. Chambers's story probably had some credibility."*

---

* The quotation is from a letter to the author from Father Cronin, written in September 1974; my request for more details has gone unanswered. Efforts of Professor Allen Weinstein and others to gain access to the FBI and HUAC files on Hiss have produced only limited results as of this writing, and the material so far released contains no previously undisclosed evidence against him.

Hiss knew nothing of all this at the time. He didn't see or hear of Father Cronin's report, and the FBI didn't tell him what information they had or where it came from. He stayed on at the State Department until December 1946, when the Board of Trustees of the Carnegie Endowment formally elected him President. He took on his new job in February 1947.

Meanwhile, Alfred Kohlberg, who was acquainted with Gen. David P. Barrows, one of the trustees of the Endowment, used this connection to gain an interview with Dulles in order to tell him of the reports that Hiss was a Communist. Dulles asked Kohlberg if he had any evidence to support the charge, and Kohlberg undertook to find it. Dulles telephoned Hiss about it some days later, according to Dulles's testimony; this was in January 1947, before Hiss had come to New York to take up his new duties. After that Hiss heard no more about it and assumed that the matter had been dropped. And so it had been, for the time being; Kohlberg wrote to Dulles on February 24, 1947, to say that the information was "uncorroborated except, I am informed, by the files of the FBI." Kohlberg later explained to another House committee that he had asked Isaac Don Levine if he could persuade Chambers to see Dulles and tell the story himself, and Levine had pointed out that Chambers had no documents or other proof, so it wouldn't be much use for him to do so.

Kohlberg didn't mention Chambers's name to Dulles, because Chambers wanted to be kept out of it. But Chambers had told his story to FBI agents, who came to interview him at his *Time* office in 1941, and on other occasions over the years, when the FBI came back to him for more detail. And in June 1947, after the Kohlberg letter to Dulles, the FBI sent two agents to Hiss's office at the Carnegie Endowment to find out what he could tell them. They asked him if he knew Whittaker Chambers, or if Chambers had ever visited his home; Hiss said he didn't know him, noting that "No individual by that name has ever visited my home on any occasion so far as I can recall." It was the first time Hiss had heard the name, and he didn't know it belonged to the man who was calling him a Communist. This circumstance caused great confusion later, and counted heavily against Hiss the following year, during his testimony to HUAC.

Chambers, meanwhile, was telling his story to other people as well, but always demanded that his name should be kept out of it. Barbara Kerr, a researcher for Time, Inc., in 1946, heard it when she was interviewing Chambers with Arthur M. Schlesinger, Jr., for a story in *Life* about the American Communist Party, and it made an indelible impression on her. As she recalls, Chambers insisted that no names be used in the story, so that when it appeared in July it identified neither Hiss nor his accuser, nor any of the others Chambers said were in the same "apparatus" with Hiss. Chambers had even implored Mrs. Kerr to remove her notes from the building, because he was afraid they might be stolen. She was particularly excited at the mention of Alger Hiss, because he had once interviewed her for a State Department job, which she didn't get, and he had struck her then as being a "rather uptight, pukka sahib type."

Mrs. Kerr was enormously impressed by Chambers's dramatic account of how he feared the Communists would kill him if he told all he knew, and how he had "made a deal with them that he would not turn them in if they would let him live, so to speak." She believed everything Chambers said, because she felt he was in fear for his life and had no reason to lie. And she promised to tell no one what she had heard.

Nearly two years later, in 1947, at a New Year's Eve party Mrs. Kerr momentarily forgot her promise, while under the influence, as she later explained, of more alcohol than she was then accustomed to drink. The conversation at the party had turned to the subject of loyalty oaths, which were a center of controversy that year, and Mrs. Kerr found herself saying, "I don't see the point of loyalty oaths, they don't catch the dangerous people like Alger Hiss." There was a sudden total silence, and the party of twenty people froze; Mrs. Kerr realized to her horror that the man she was talking to was Edward Miller, a State Department officer who knew Hiss very well.

"He told me to apologize immediately, or I'd be sued for

libel," Mrs. Kerr recalled. "I wouldn't retract it. I was in a great state of nerves—floods of tears—and had a severe row with my husband over it."

Miller reported the incident to Hiss, not directly but through Hiss's brother Donald, and when Miller called Mrs. Kerr again, she told him that "as far as I was concerned it was the truth, but I would guarantee not to repeat it, which I did not do. I didn't think it was my business to go around accusing people of being Communists." According to Mrs. Kerr, Miller told her Hiss wasn't going to sue her for libel after all, because he was a magnanimous person. Mrs. Kerr doesn't remember mentioning Chambers's name, because she was trying to protect him, but she must have said something about where she had heard the story, because Miller mentioned the name to Donald, and he mentioned it to Hiss.

This was the second time Hiss had heard the name, and he now knew that a man named Whittaker Chambers had called him a Communist. But he didn't remember that the FBI had asked him six months before if Whittaker Chambers had ever visited his home, and he didn't know that Whittaker Chambers was now the name of the man he had once known as George Crosley. So it meant nothing to him. And when Mrs. Kerr's promise to stop calling him a Communist was relayed back to Hiss through Miller and Donald, he thought it meant Chambers wouldn't be talking about him anymore. Wishful thinking perhaps; but nothing could have been farther from the truth.

This was in January 1948. In March, according to Professor Challener, Dulles got in touch with Rep. Walter Judd, a friend of Kohlberg's, to ask if there was any truth in Kohlberg's story that Judd had information suggesting Hiss was a former Communist. Judd apparently replied that he had; Dulles showed the letter to Hiss, who said the rumors no doubt stemmed from his acquaintance with Lee Pressman and other radicals in the Agriculture Department in the early 1930s, and Dulles dictated a note for his files recording this answer. Dulles also checked with a State Department security officer, who told him that whatever the FBI might have in its files about Hiss, the State Department

security officials were "convinced of his complete loyalty to the
United States and, in fact, thought of him as more conservative
than many in the State Department." Challener adds that the
security officer "also asked Dulles to tell Judd that he had never
intended to suggest to the Congressman that Hiss was disloyal."

It happened that the occasion on which Dulles showed
Judd's letter to Hiss and talked to him about it was immediately
after Hiss had testified before a federal grand jury, which was
investigating allegations of Communist subversion. Hiss had been
questioned about his statement to the FBI of the previous June,
and had confirmed everything in it; the questioning had cen-
tered around the connection with Pressman, who had recently
resigned as general counsel of the Congress of Industrial Organizations (CIO), under circumstances which led many people
to believe that he had been thrown out because of his pro-
Communist views.

After his grand jury testimony, according to Hiss's recollection, he went routinely to Dulles, who was his boss, to report on
it, and was surprised to learn about Dulles's correspondence with
Representative Judd. Apparently Hiss's report satisfied Dulles,
because in his reply to Judd he described Hiss as a strong supporter of American foreign policies, including the Marshall Plan,
which was, as Dulles described it, "the phase of our foreign policy
which the Communists are fighting most bitterly." Indeed, before
leaving the State Department, Hiss, with the Department's
approval, had been directly involved in the formation of the
Committee for the Marshall Plan to Aid European Recovery. It
was a nationwide organization working to generate popular support for official policy, much as William Allen White's Committee
to Defend America by Aiding the Allies had done with Hiss's
help in the years of the Nazi–Soviet pact, August 1939–June
1941, when American Communists were opposing the official
American foreign policy because they preferred that of the Soviet
Union.

With the Cold War underway, the Communists were again
supporting the Soviet Union against the United States, and losing
support in the United States as a consequence. But they weren't

losing it fast enough to suit the anti-Communists, including such people as Whittaker Chambers, Isaac Don Levine, Alfred Kohlberg, and Representatives Judd and Nixon, who for various reasons wanted the Communist Party outlawed altogether and denied the rights and privileges extended to other political parties. They regarded the Communists as a criminal conspiracy rather than a political party and bent their efforts toward persuading the rest of the nation to this conclusion.

Hiss was not particularly aware of this aspect of the developing ideological warfare in the United States, and he didn't attach any importance to his own involvement in it. He had been warned six times in two years—first, in early 1946, when Byrnes sent him to the FBI; then by Dulles's inquiry, in January 1947, which had been prompted by Kohlberg; next, by the visit from the FBI in June and the New Year's Eve incident at the end of that year; and finally by the grand jury inquiry in March 1948; and the conference with Dulles immediately after it. But all these inquiries seemed to revolve around the same incident in Hiss's life, his association with Pressman in the IJA and the AAA. That was long ago, and Hiss's record of faithfulness to the official policy, even when the Communists opposed it was clear. He didn't think he was a particularly vulnerable target for anti-Communist slanders; after all, he wasn't mentioned in Elizabeth Dilling's *Red Network*, that compendious volume of alleged Communist infiltrators, although a lot of his friends were. Hiss didn't realize that to be a friend of a man called a Communist was, in many people's eyes, proof enough that you were one as well.

There were other things on Hiss's mind in those days that seemed a greater cause for worry, because they involved his family. He wasn't happy about the way his son Tony was developing, and he blamed the problem on Priscilla's attitude, which he thought overprotective. Tony was now almost seven and in the Dalton School, where Priscilla was teaching. Alger remembers it produced an unpleasant strain in his relationship with Priscilla, but she denies it, and says Tony was doing marvelously at Dalton.

They had other anxieties about Timothy, who at twenty-one was not at all the kind of young man they had expected him to be. Tim had enlisted in the Navy V–12 officer training program right after high school, at a time when he was suffering from an emotional maladjustment that neither the Navy nor Alger and Priscilla had recognized. It became more apparent in 1945, when at eighteen Tim was found to have been involved in a homosexual experience, which was not tolerated by society in those days to the degree it is today. The Navy treated it as a breach of discipline; Tim was given an undesirable discharge after five days in the brig and fourteen days of solitary confinement. It took years after that for him to work his way through an emotional crisis and overcome the problems of his youth; but he did it. Today he is married, the father of four children, and successful in a professional career; but in 1948 his stepfather had no way of knowing that would ever happen. He could only hope.

Neither Alger nor Priscilla had any knowledge of homosexuality, and they didn't know how to help him. Tim refused most of their efforts; he was not yet ready for psychiatrists or change. For the time being, all they could do was use some of Alger's influence to bend the Navy's rules so that Tim was allowed reading matter in his cell and visits from his parents, while he was in solitary confinement.

After his discharge, Tim turned away from both sides of his family and most of the family friends. By August 1948, when Hiss was before HUAC, Tim was on the West Coast. Hiss didn't know exactly where, but he knew Tim could get in touch with him whenever he wanted to, and that was the way Hiss wanted it. As far as he was concerned, Hiss would allow nothing to interfere with Tim's chances of working his way back to a better life for himself.

10

BATTLE JOINED

WHEN Hiss started working for the Carnegie Endowment in February 1947, and moved with Priscilla and Tony to New York, they rented an apartment on East Eighth Street, just off Fifth Avenue, which was the nearest thing they could find to the kind of homes they had enjoyed in Georgetown. They sold the little house at 3210 P Street for a handsome profit, but it wasn't enough to buy anything in New York City. The money became a nest egg with which they hoped to purchase a summer home in Peacham, Vermont, where they had been renting a cottage every summer for almost ten years. In 1948 they found just the place they wanted, but by then it was too late; the money would be needed for legal fees.

Peacham is a quiet little mountain-top village in northern Vermont, commanding magnificent views on every side. It is seven miles from the main highway, and more than thirty-five from the railroad station at Montpelier, where the night train from New York arrived at dawn. In 1948 Peacham was approached mainly by dirt roads, and still is, on one side; the other road is blacktopped, and both wind through forests of spruce, cedar, pine and birch, with occasional sheep and dairy farms. The nearest phone to the Hisses' cottage was in the general store, and they didn't bother with newspapers. There was a town library of modest proportions, a small local academy, a clay tennis court for Alger, and a piano for Priscilla. There were a number of intellectuals among the summer visitors, who joined Priscilla in amateur chamber music and sophisticated parlor games of the kind popular in those days. Priscilla was rather good at them; she had a reputation for making "psychic" guesses. She usually spent the whole summer in Peacham, enjoying the long vacations of a teacher; in winter she taught at the Dalton School in New York. Alger joined her weekends in the summer and for his vacation, which in 1948 was the month of July. Tony was going on seven and took a lot of Priscilla's time. Tim was twenty-one and out of touch.

This was the summer that the Republicans nominated Gov. Thomas E. Dewey of New York to run against Harry Truman for President, with high hopes that he would win. There were problems of postwar inflation and economic readjustment to make Truman unpopular, and the Republicans had already, in the 1946 elections, won a majority in Congress for the first time in fourteen years. The Democrats were badly split; Strom Thurmond had fielded the States' Rights Party, champion of white supremacy and right-wing political conservatism, and it was destined to take the thirty-nine electoral votes of the Solid South away from Truman. On the left wing of the party Henry Wallace, Secretary of Agriculture in Hiss's days in the Agricultural Adjustment Administration (AAA) and later Secretary of Commerce and Vice President, was running for President on the Progressive Party ticket, with the open support of the Communists.

Wallace's platform was the exact opposite of Thurmond's; he demanded equal rights for Negroes, especially in the South, and peaceful coexistence with the Soviet Union. In addition to the Communist Party, which was still a legal political organization in the United States in 1948, he was supported by a host of left-wing groups which were commonly regarded by their opponents as "Communist fellow-travelers," "dupes," "fifth columnists," "transmission belts" (so called because they were thought to transmit orders from Moscow in obedience to Soviet policy), and other unflattering names. This was the last attempt of the Communists in the United States to organize a "popular front," as it was called. Many people were afraid of the Progressives and thought they would draw a lot of support, mainly from people who would otherwise vote for Democrats. As it turned out, Wallace drew very little support and won not a single electoral vote.

The political institution that provided focus and leadership for the campaigns of the anti-Communists was the House Un-American Activities Committee (HUAC), now ten years old and carrying on with unflagging determination the work that Rep. Martin Dies of Orange County, Texas, its famous (or notorious, depending on one's point of view) progenitor, had begun in 1938. The Dies Committee was a far cry from its predecessor of 1934, which, under the chairmanship of John W. McCormack of Massachusetts, had concentrated on the twin threats of Nazi infiltration and home-grown Fascism. Dies had made occasional token inquiries into the German–American Bund, William Dudley Pelley's anti-Semitic Silver Shirts, and the equally anti-Semitic Gerald L. K. Smith; but this was only to disarm the Committee's critics, who claimed that Dies was actually on the side of these malcontents, and chided him for not going after such rightist organizations as the Ku Klux Klan and Father Charles Coughlin's Christian Front. Indeed, the Dies Committee's few excursions into taking testimony from such people as Bundist Fritz Kuhn and Pelley were an embarrassment; the witnesses insisted on praising the Committee for its work instead of behaving like the Committee's enemies, as the Communists and their supporters did.

The idea of investigating subversive activities of every political stripe was a popular one in 1938, when Americans were divided in their fears of Fascism and Communism, but Dies found it politically more popular to attack the Communists and leave the Fascists alone. It was more to his personal liking too, as it was to such outstanding associates on the Committee as Rep. Joseph Starnes of Alabama, and later Rep. John Rankin of Mississippi.

By 1948 the foreign Fascists had been defeated in history's greatest war, and the Communists were virtually alone as targets of the Committee's interest. The then chairman, J. Parnell Thomas of New Jersey, was continuing and expanding the strategy developed by his predecessors before and during the war. This consisted in defining Communism as the one great threat to the nation's welfare, defining everyone the Committee didn't like as a Communist, and accusing them in public of Communist activities of one kind or another, while allowing them no opportunity to defend themselves. By this means Dies had attacked the New Deal as being riddled with Communism before the war, and harassed the Roosevelt Administration during the war by demanding the dismissal of government employees whom the Committee labeled Communists. By the same techniques he and his successors harassed the unions, particularly the Congress of Industrial Organizations (CIO), and grossly exaggerated the extent to which Communist organizers had found their way into positions of power in American unions during the period when the Soviet Union was welcomed as a wartime ally.

All this might have been accepted as legitimate right-wing politics if the Committee had observed the elementary rules of fairness in its activities, but such an approach had been abandoned from the start by Martin Dies, and in the climate of anti-Communist fears that were so strong in 1948, J. Parnell Thomas found no reason to depart from Dies's ways. These were the days when the United States had the atom bomb and the Russians didn't; the illusion that by keeping our bomb a "secret" we could prevent the Russians from making one of their own was almost universally cherished by the public, and it was easy to pretend that any attack on domestic Communists was a necessary part of preserving the "secrecy" of America's terrifying weapon. So the public, politicians, and even Federal judges condoned abuses on the part of HUAC that in calmer times might not have been so readily permitted.

Dies had made his position clear in his opening statement at the Committee's first hearing on August 12, 1938, using 1984 "newspeak" before the word was coined. The outstanding feature of his statement was that he promised not to do the things which he and his successors from then on never ceased from doing. The action was the exact opposite of the words, but the words well defined what was wrong with the action.

"This Committee will not permit any 'character assassination' or any 'smearing' of innocent people," he said. "It is the Chair's opinion that the usefulness or value of any investigation is measured by the fairness and impartiality of the committee conducting the investigation. Neither the public nor the Congress will have any confidence in the findings of a committee which adopts a partisan or preconceived attitude." (Here he was wrong, as no doubt he knew; for the Committee always managed to gain the confidence of enough voters and Congressmen to stay in business, under one name or another, until the beginning of 1975, when the first Congress after Nixon's departure let it die.)

"It is easy to 'smear' someone's name or reputation by unsupported charges or an unjustified attack, but it is difficult to repair the damage that has been done," Dies observed correctly. "When any individual or organization is involved in any charge or attack made in the course of the hearings," he added untruthfully, "that individual or organization will be accorded an opportunity to refute such charge or attack." The attacks were made, as Dies anticipated, and opportunities to appear before the Committee were granted to the accused upon request, but any attempt to refute the charges was uniformly frustrated by denying the accused the right to be represented by counsel, or to confront the accusing witnesses or cross-examine them. Committee members made a habit of bullying the accused unmercifully while he was on the stand, and citing him for contempt of Congress if he protested—which meant up to a year in jail and $1,000 fine.

Those who felt strongly about such matters, such as the famous Hollywood Ten in 1947,* often turned Committee sessions into spectacular shouting matches, and then served their time in jail. But most of the accused preferred to ignore the charges altogether, and if called to testify, simply "took the Fifth Amendment," as the saying goes—refusing to testify on the ground that they might incriminate themselves.

Many (though by no means all) of those accused by the

---

* Alvah Bessie, Herbert Biberman, Lester Cole, Edward Dmytryk, Ring Lardner, Jr., John Howard Lawson, Albert Maltz, Samuel Ornitz, Adrian Scott, and Dalton Trumbo. All were screenwriters.

Committee were indeed members of the Communist Party, or former members, or liberal nonmembers who believed the Communist Party had a right to exist in the United States and had no objection to accepting Communist support for political causes in which they were interested. The Communist Party was not, after all, illegal in those days, and a substantial number of Americans did not regard it as the terrible threat to American liberties that HUAC said it was. Many of them thought the Committee was a greater threat because it did such violence to traditional ideas of political freedom and freedom of speech, not to mention the lack of a fair trial for those accused of crimes. Moreover, the Committee represented entrenched political power, while the Communist Party was a small band of political nobodies.

But the Committee was determined to convince the American public that its own view was the right one, that the Communist Party should be illegal if it wasn't already, and that all Communists should be driven from the country. In time they were largely successful; but in 1948 this outcome was by no means assured, and it sometimes seemed that it was the Committee, rather than the liberals, who were in the minority.

The main strength of the anti-Communist feeling was within the Republican Party and among their allies the Southern Democrats. Accordingly, one of the main thrusts of the Republican election campaign against Truman in 1948 was an attempt to show that he was "soft on Communism"; and that, in spite of the radical changes he had already made in foreign policy, he wasn't being hard enough on the Russians. Roosevelt had been pro-Communist, the argument ran, and the New Deal had been rotten with Communist infiltration, just as the Dies Committee had said. Truman was said to be no better, a pawn of the Communists like his predecessor. Roosevelt had given away half of America's security at Yalta, the anti-Communists said, and Truman had given away the rest at San Francisco and Potsdam. (It was at Potsdam, a suburb of Berlin, that Truman had met with Stalin and Churchill, in July of 1945, to carve up the occupation zones of Germany and arrive at a deadlock over how the defeated nation was to be administered from then on. By the summer of 1948

American and British troops in West Berlin were surrounded by Russian troops enforcing a blockade which had begun that April; they were kept supplied by air, in a massive operation that first put the word "airlift" into common use, for the eighteen months until the blockade was lifted.)

The Berlin blockade was a matter of which Hiss was necessarily aware in his work for the Carnegie Endowment for International Peace. But, for the month of July, he could leave it to others to worry about. It didn't occur to him that the blockade and airlift were lending strength to the anti-Communist campaigns of the Republicans, and generating increasingly bitter attacks on the Roosevelt foreign policy and all who were involved in it. In the quiet of the Vermont mountains he didn't read the news' stories coming out of HUAC, which was preparing for a new series of hearings to dramatize what it called "Communist espionage in the federal government." He wasn't aware of it when on the last Saturday of his vacation, July 31, a woman named Elizabeth Bentley appeared before the committee and created a sensation by naming thirty-two government officials who she said had supplied her with secret documents to pass on to a Soviet spy ring. And he wasn't aware of the enormous excitement the subject of Communist espionage was arousing in some sections of the press and public, Hearst and Scripps–Howard vying with each other for the more sensational "scoops."

On Monday, August 2, Hiss returned to his office in New York, leaving his wife and son in Peacham, and began catching up on the news. He was rather surprised that evening when a reporter telephoned him to say he had heard that a man named Chambers was going to call him a Communist at the following day's hearings. Hiss didn't take it very seriously; he had heard such charges before and dismissed them, and didn't see why anyone should pay attention to them if they were made again.

The next day at Hiss's office the phone began ringing before noon, and this time he was even more surprised at the volume of inquiries from the press. He was told that Whittaker Chambers, a senior editor of *Time* magazine, had testified that Hiss had been "attached" to "an underground organization of the United States Communist Party" when he was employed by the government some years before. Hiss told all callers that it was completely untrue, that he didn't know anyone named Whittaker Chambers, and so far as he knew, had never even seen him.

At first Hiss thought the whole thing was simply a nuisance, but the more he considered it the more he felt something ought to be done about it. His friends at lunch that day, and his associates at the Endowment, advised him to do nothing; forget it, and the world would forget it too. Hundreds of people had been denounced as Communists before HUAC but the charge had never yet been proved against anyone. Some had denied it, some had taken the Fifth Amendment, and some had ignored it and never been called to testify. The Committee's reputation for bullying its witnesses and disregarding Constitutional freedoms was such that it was regarded with contempt and hostility, even ridicule, by most respectable liberals. Hiss was advised to have nothing to do with the Committee; it could be safely disregarded, he was told, and nothing but trouble could come from tangling with it.

To Hiss this advice seemed like the bureaucratic ideas he had encountered too often in government—if problems are too difficult, it's best to ignore them, and maybe they'll go away. Certainly his position in the Endowment would be in less jeopardy if he did nothing than if he invited publicity by denying the charge. If the Committee called him, he could plead the Fifth Amendment, as many others were doing, not because they had anything criminal to hide, but because once you started arguing with the Committee you were not only exposing yourself to privileged slander, but risking jail for contempt of Congress if not perjury.

The Committee members had their own ideas of who was a Communist and who wasn't, and of what was true and what wasn't. Any witness who took a different view did so at his peril. And if pleading the Fifth might place Hiss's job in jeopardy, so would the publicity of arguing with the Committee; either way he could return to the private practice of law—which had always been his intention. There were plenty of Fifth Amendment lawyers (who either had taken the Fifth themselves or had defended clients who had) around, making a good living with plenty of clients.

What bothered Hiss was the press inquiries. He had denied the charge when talking to reporters, but that wasn't quite the same as denying it under oath in front of the Committee, where the charge had been made. If he stopped short of that, how many would believe him? And the charge had been circulating for some time now; it was more than two years since Hiss had first heard of it from Secretary Byrnes. He had never known where the story came from, or who it was that had been slandering him behind his back. Now he could find out; he could face his accuser before the House Committee, find out who he was, and silence him once and for all. It was a temptation that he could not resist.

Accordingly, before the afternoon was over, Hiss sent a telegram to Rep. J. Parnell Thomas, of New Jersey, Chairman of the House Un-American Activities Committee, which read:

> My attention has been called by representatives of the press to statements made about me before your committee this morning by one Whittaker Chambers. I do not know Mr. Chambers and insofar as I am aware have never laid eyes on him. There is no basis for the statements made about me to your committee. I would appreciate it if you would make this telegram a part of your committee's record, and I would further appreciate the opportunity to appear before your committee to make these statements formally and under oath. I shall be in Washington on Thursday and hope that that will be a convenient time from the committee's point of view for me to appear.

It was then Tuesday afternoon; Hiss had suggested Thursday because he was going to be tied up on Wednesday with some appointments in Philadelphia. While he was there he telephoned his boss John Foster Dulles to let him know what he was doing, and Dulles counseled caution.

As Hiss recalls it, Dulles reminded him that many people of Hiss's generation had been rather radical when they were young, and probably got mixed up with Communists whether they realized it or not, and nobody would hold anything against Hiss if he said something like that had happened to him too, and that now he was older and wiser he knew better and wouldn't have anything to do with Communists. Hiss was rather offended by that. So far as he was concerned it didn't apply to him at all; he didn't think he had ever been a "parlor pink," as the phrase went, and he wasn't going to say he ever had been. But as it turned out he didn't have much opportunity to use this approach; his troubles with the Committee revolved around an entirely different issue.

After talking to Dulles, Hiss called his old friend William Marbury, the Baltimore corporation lawyer, who had helped him get into Harvard Law School and had been a guest at his wedding. Marbury agreed to go with him to the hearing the following morning, and to help him prepare a formal statement. Witnesses before the House Committee weren't allowed to be represented by counsel, as defendants are in a court of law, but they were allowed to consult with their counsel if they wanted to, and, being a lawyer, Hiss thought that would be a good idea.

Hiss and Marbury were at the Committee's office early Thursday morning, and obtained a copy of the transcript of the testimony Chambers had given on Tuesday. It didn't add much to what they had read in the newspapers, but there was some interesting material in it, and they studied it carefully.

Chambers had begun with a prepared statement, a rather flamboyant description of his years as a Communist revolutionary, his subsequent change of heart, and his new role as the defender of America against Communism. It is rather a remarkable document, worth reproducing here in full:

"Almost exactly nine years ago—that is, two days after Hitler and Stalin signed their pact—I went to Washington and reported to the authorities what I knew about the infiltration of the United States by Communists. For years international Communism, of which the United States Communist Party is an integral part, had been in a state of undeclared war with this Republic. With the Hitler–Stalin pact, that war reached a new stage. I regarded my action in going to the Government as a simple act of war, like the shooting of an armed enemy in combat.

"At that moment in history, I was one of the few men on this side of the battle who could perform this service.

"I had joined the Communist Party in 1924. No one recruited me. I had become convinced that the society in which we live, western civilization, had reached a crisis, of which the First World War was the military expression, and that it was doomed to collapse or revert to barbarism. I did not understand the causes of the crisis or know what to do about it. But I felt that, as an intelligent man, I must do something. In the writings of Karl Marx I thought that I had found the explanation of the historical and economic causes. In the writings of Lenin I thought I had found the answer to the question, what to do?

"In 1937 I repudiated Marx's doctrines and Lenin's tactics. Experience and the record had convinced me that Communism is a form of totalitarianism, that its triumph means slavery to men wherever they fall under its sway, and spiritual night to the human mind and soul. I resolved to break with the Communist Party at whatever risk to my life or other tragedy to myself or my family. Yet, so strong is the hold which the insidious evil of Communism secures on its disciples, that I could still say to someone at the time: 'I know that I am leaving the winning side for the losing side, but it is better to die on the losing side than to live under Communism.' "

This oracular sentence made a strong impression on Rep. Richard M. Nixon, the freshman Congressman from California, who was to play such an important part in the subsequent proceedings, although Hiss and Marbury couldn't know this at the time. Writing about Chambers fourteen years later in the first chapter of *Six Crises*, Nixon said that these words made him realize for the first time that "Chambers was a man of extraordinary intellectual gifts and one who had inner strength and depth. Here was no headline-seeker but rather a thoughtful, introspective man, careful with his words, speaking with what sounded like the ring of truth." The words had special meaning for Chambers, too; in later years he identified the "someone" to whom he had first spoken them as his wife, and he repeated them often, insisting for the rest of his life that Democracy was still losing to Communism in spite of all he had done to save it. This was a recurring theme in the letters and diaries that were published by his friends after his death.

Chambers's statement continued: "For a year I lived in hiding, sleeping by day and watching through the night with a gun or revolver within easy reach. That was what underground Communism could do to one man in the peaceful United States in the year 1938.

"I had sound reason for supposing that the Communists might try to kill me. For a number of years I had myself served in the underground, chiefly in Washington, D.C. The heart of my report to the United States Government consisted of a description of the apparatus to which I was attached. It was an underground organization of the United States Communist Party developed, to the best of my knowledge, by Harold Ware, one of the sons of the Communist leader known as 'Mother Bloor.' I knew it at its top level, a group of seven or so men, from among whom in later years certain members of Miss Bentley's organization were apparently recruited. The head of the underground group at the time I knew it was Nathan Witt, an attorney for the National Labor Relations Board. Later, John Abt became the leader. Lee Pressman was also a member of this group, as was Alger Hiss, who, as a member of the State Department, later organized the conferences at Dumbarton Oaks, San Francisco, and the United States side of the Yalta Conference.

"The purpose of this group at that time was not primarily espionage. Its original purpose was the Communist infiltration of the American Government. But espionage was certainly one of its eventual objectives. Let no one be surprised at this statement. Disloyalty is a matter of principle with every member of the Communist Party. The Communist Party exists for the specific purpose of overthrowing the Government, at the opportune time, by any and all means; and each of its members, by the fact that he is a member, is dedicated to this purpose.

"It is ten years since I broke away from the Communist

Party. During that decade I have sought to live an industrious and God-fearing life. At the same time I have fought Communism constantly by act and written word. I am proud to appear before this committee. The publicity inseparable from such testimony has darkened, and will continue to darken, my effort to integrate myself in the community of free men. But that is a small price to pay if my testimony helps to make Americans recognize at last that they are at grips with a secret, sinister, and enormously powerful force whose tireless purpose is their enslavement.

"At the same time, I should like thus publicly to call upon all ex-Communists who have not yet declared themselves, and all men within the Communist Party whose better instincts have not yet been corrupted and crushed by it, to aid in this struggle while there is still time to do so."

Robert Stripling, the Committee's chief investigator, then took Chambers through a long series of questions to bring out other names and details. Chambers added the names of Victor Perlo, Charles Kramer, and Hiss's brother Donald to the list of "cell leaders" in the Communist "apparatus" he had referred to, and said they met in the apartment of Henry Hill Collins III, who was treasurer of the group and collected their dues. He said Mrs. Alger Hiss was also a Communist, but Mrs. Donald Hiss was not. (Nixon was impressed by this distinction. He wrote in *Six Crises* that it showed Chambers "was not a man who was throwing his charges about loosely and recklessly.") Stripling was prepared with the employment records of Pressman, Abt, and the Hiss brothers, and with information about a man named J. Peters, whom Chambers identified as "the head of the whole underground United States Communist Party." Stripling said he had been trying to serve a subpoena on Peters for more than a year, but couldn't find him.

Much of the discussion concerned Harry Dexter White, Assistant Secretary of the Treasury, who had been called a Communist spy by Elizabeth Bentley the previous Saturday. Chambers said he didn't know positively whether White was "a registered member of the Communist Party, but he certainly was a fellow traveler." He was quite positive that neither White nor the others he had named were spies. Their job was to infiltrate, that is, to ˜get into positions where they could influence policy, according to Chambers.

"I should perhaps make the point," he said, "that these people were specifically not wanted to act as sources of information. These people were an elite group, an outstanding group, which it was believed would rise to positions—as, indeed, some of them did, notably Mr. White and Mr. Hiss—in the Government, and their position in the Government would be of very much more service to the Communist Party—"

Rep. F. Edward Hébert, of Louisiana, cut him short. "In other words," Hébert said, "White was being used as an unwitting dupe?"

"I would scarcely say 'unwitting,' " Chambers replied.

Rep. Karl E. Mundt, of South Dakota, and Rep. John E. Rankin, of Mississippi, followed their usual practice for such occasions. They were not so much interested in getting new information from the witness as in using him as a sounding-board while they aired their own views. The witness's function was to agree with them.

Mundt was intent on convincing the public that the Russians, who had been our allies in World War II, were every bit as dangerous as the Germans, who had been our enemies, if not worse, and that as far as he was concerned there was no difference between the German Fascism against which we had fought and the Russian Communism we had helped and been helped by. It was a point on which many people agreed with him, including Chambers, and it was the rationale on which the Cold War policy came to be based; but, in 1948, it was a bitter pill to swallow for Americans who had fought and suffered through the war with an entirely different set of beliefs, and there were many who didn't want to swallow it. Mundt missed no opportunity to ram it down the public's throat.

"It is pretty hard to find any basic distinction between Fascism and Communism as Communism is practiced by the Stalinists in Moscow and as they direct the activities of the American Communist Party," he observed at one point.

"I think you have raised a philosophical and intellectual point, which would require almost a book," said Chambers mildly. "It would require almost a book to develop and interpret that."

"Do you know of any vital distinction between Communism as practiced in Russia and Fascism as we generally understand it to be?" Mundt persisted. "I know the committee would be very glad to find that distinction because we have been unable to get it from any other witness."

"I don't feel qualified to emphasize the distinction," Chambers replied.

At that point Rankin undertook to help him with some leading questions of his own.

"Communism is atheistic, is it not?" Rankin asked.

"It is," said Chambers.

"One of the basic principles is the wiping out of the Christian church throughout the world?"

"Wiping out all religion. Every Communist is *ipso facto* an atheist."

"It is also dedicated to the destruction of this Government and to the wiping out of the American way of life; is that correct?"

"Yes; it can be said."

"And also the wiping out of what it calls the capitalist system?"

"Certainly."

"The right to own private property?"

"That is true."

"In other words, Communism would make a slave of every American man, woman and child excepting the commissars that dominated them; is that correct?"

"That is."

"And would close every Christian church in America?"

"Well, the Russian church seems to have some kind of unhappy existence."

"I understand, but you know that they closed every church in

Russia, and they were closed at the time you quit the Communist Party?"

"It can be said quite simply that Communism is completely atheistic and is the enemy of religion in every form."

"In other words, they would close all churches of all kinds?"

"Mohammedan mosques, Jewish synagogues, as well as Christian churches."

Rankin was satisfied. Mundt directed Stripling to go ahead with the next question.

In all of this there was relatively little that involved any direct reference to Alger Hiss. Chambers identified Hiss as one of the men whom the Communists regarded as "going places in the Government," and said he was very fond of him. He said that Hiss was the only one of his seven "cell leaders" whom he approached, after he had ended his connection with the Communist Party in 1937.

"I went to the Hiss home one evening, at what I considered considerable risk to myself, and found Mrs. Hiss at home," Chambers said. ". . . Mrs. Hiss attempted while I was there to make a call, which I can only presume was to other Communists, but I quickly went to the telephone and she hung up, and Mr. Hiss came in shortly afterward, and we talked, and I tried to break him away from the party.

"As a matter of fact, he cried when we separated; when I left him, but he absolutely refused to break."

"He cried?" Rep. John McDowell of Pennsylvania asked in surprise.

"Yes, he did," said Chambers. "I was very fond of Mr. Hiss."

"He must have given you some reason why he did not want to sever the relationship," said Mundt.

"His reasons were simply the party line," Chambers said.

A little later Mundt, accepting Chambers's story without question, returned to the subject of Alger Hiss, commenting that he had had occasion to check Hiss's activities in the State Department.

"There is reason to believe," Mundt said, "that he organized within that Department one of the Communist cells which endeavored to influence our Chinese policy and bring about the condemnation of Chiang Kai-shek, which put [Aldo] Marzani [a State Department employee] in an important position there, and I think it is important to know what happened to these people after they leave the Government. Do you know where Alger Hiss is employed now?"

"I believe Alger Hiss is now the head of the Carnegie Foundation for World Peace," said Chambers.

"That is the same information that came to me, and I am happy to have it confirmed," said Mundt. "Certainly, there is no hope for world peace under the leadership of men like Alger Hiss."

Rankin chimed in with the observation that the Carnegie organization was based in New York, and a man like Hiss could get away with that sort of thing in New York, but they wouldn't let him do it in Mississippi.

All this looked like ridiculous nonsense to Hiss and Marbury as they studied the transcript. Hiss knew nobody called Marzani and nothing of any "Communist cells" in the State Department; he had done his best for Chiang Kai-shek and nothing for the Communists, when he was in Hornbeck's office in the early 1940s. Hiss had never cried when he parted from a friend; nothing would be more unlike him. Nobody had ever asked him to "break away" from the Communist Party; he had never had anything to do with the party and knew nothing of its organization or membership. He had no idea who this Whittaker Chambers could be, or where he could have got such fanciful ideas. The pictures of Chambers he had seen in the newspapers looked vaguely familiar, but he couldn't guess who they reminded him of. Somebody he didn't like, no doubt; it's always easier to forget people you don't like.

Hiss wanted to retort in detail to Chambers's accusations, and tell the Committee what a fine man he thought Lee Pressman was, but Marbury counseled him to avoid the "histrionics" and stick to the facts. Joseph Johnston, an Alabama railroad lawyer, who was an old law school friend of Hiss's, happened to be in Washington on business. He had joined Hiss and Marbury in the hearing room and seconded Marbury's advice. So Hiss left that part out of his statement and resolved to conduct himself as conservatively as possible, like the correct and conscientious lawyer he was.

He had nothing but contempt for men like Mundt and Rankin, but they were Congressmen and he respected their office. He knew nothing about Nixon, whom he had never seen before. Like many others in those days, he thought of HUAC as a bunch of buffoons, more un-American in their way than most of the people they were attacking; but he had no desire to pick a fight with them or identify himself with the anti-HUAC campaign that was being mounted by the Committee's enemies. He saw his problem as a personal one: he would explain to the committee that Chambers had made up a lot of fanciful lies about him, and then they would drop the matter and that would be that.

The Committee had summoned him for 10:30 A.M., and he took his place in the front row of spectators in the caucus room of the Old House Office Building, the largest hearing room on Capitol Hill and the one normally used for occasions that would attract a great deal of press coverage. Chambers had been heard in the smaller Ways and Means Committee room, but his sensational statements, and Hiss's immediate denial had already created a cause célèbre. The huge caucus room was filled to capacity, the press section was crowded, and the air of excitement was greater than anything Hiss had seen in his Nye Committee days, or at any other Congressional hearings he had attended.

But Hiss had to wait his turn. The hearing opened with a proposal from Rankin that Henry Wallace, the Progressive Party candidate and former Secretary of Agriculture, be subpoenaed, since so many people accused by Chambers had worked for him at one time or another, including, of course, Alger Hiss. (Stripling had mentioned on Tuesday that two of them, Pressman and Abt, were working in Wallace's campaign for the presidency.) For the next half-hour or so, the Committee took testimony from Rep. Fred E. Busbey, of Illinois, who accused the Civil Service Commission of failure to root out Communists from government employment, and described the Agriculture Department under Henry Wallace as "the spawning ground of all Communists in Government, because from this little group in AAA they fanned out into all branches of Government."

With this introduction, Hiss was sworn in as a witness and permitted to read his prepared statement. It was shorter than the one Chambers had read, and went as follows:

"I am here at my own request to deny unqualifiedly various statements about me which were made before this committee by one Whittaker Chambers the day before yesterday. I appreciate the committee's having promptly granted my request. I welcome the opportunity to answer to the best of my ability any inquiries the members of this committee may wish to ask me.

"I am not and have never been a member of the Communist Party. I do not and never have adhered to the tenets of the Communist Party. I am not and never have been a member of any Communist-front organization. I have never followed the Communist Party line, directly or indirectly. To the best of my knowledge, none of my friends is a Communist.

"As a State Department official, I have had contacts with representatives of foreign governments, some of whom have undoubtedly been members of the Communist Party, as, for example, representatives of the Soviet Government. My contacts with any foreign representative who could possibly have been a Communist have been strictly official.

"To the best of my knowledge, I never heard of Whittaker Chambers until in 1947, when two representatives of the Federal Bureau of Investigation asked me if I knew him and various other people, some of whom I knew and some of whom I did not know. I said I did not know Chambers. So far as I know, I have never laid eyes on him, and I should like to have the opportunity to do so.

"I have known Henry Collins since we were boys in camp together. I knew him again while he was at the Harvard Business School while I was at the Harvard Law School, and I have seen him from time to time since I came to Washington in 1933.

"Lee Pressman was in my class at the Harvard Law School and

we were both on the Harvard *Law Review* at the same time. We were also both assistants to Judge Jerome Frank on the legal staff of the Agricultural Adjustment Administration. Since I left the Department of Agriculture I have seen him only occasionally and infrequently. I left the Department, according to my recollection, in 1935.

"Witt and Abt were both members of the legal staff of the AAA. I knew them both in that capacity. I believe I met Witt in New York a year or so before I came to Washington. I came to Washington in 1933. We were both practicing law in New York at the time I think I met Witt.

"Kramer was in another office of the AAA, and I met him in that connection.

"I have seen none of these last three men I have mentioned except most infrequently since I left the Department of Agriculture.

"I don't believe I ever knew Victor Perlo.

"Except as I have indicated, the statements made about me by Mr. Chambers are complete fabrications. I think my record in the Government service speaks for itself."

That concluded his statement, and Stripling proceeded to routine questions about Hiss's educational background and his career in Federal employment. He hadn't got far with them when Hiss, forgetting that he had been advised not to tangle with the Committee, began to bridle. It happened when Nixon interrupted to ask him for the names of the Government officials who had asked him to come to Washington in 1933. Hiss mentioned Jerome Frank, his first boss in AAA, who by 1948 was a judge of the U.S. Circuit Court. Nixon replied:

"You said it in the plural. Was he the only one then?"

"There were some others," said Hiss. "Is it necessary? There are so many witnesses who use names rather loosely before your committee, and I would rather limit myself."

"You made the statement—" Nixon began.

"The statement is correct," Hiss interrupted.

This was Nixon's first intervention in Hiss's testimony, and it came only a minute or two after Hiss had finished reading his statement. Hiss had no idea what Nixon was after; in fact, he knew nothing about Nixon except the bare fact that he was a freshman Congressman from California. Nixon, on the other hand, had heard about Hiss more than a year before from Father Cronin, and while he says nothing about this phase of his research in *Six Crises*, Nixon also had access to the files on Hiss prepared in advance of the hearings by Stripling, Father Cronin's friend Ben Mandel, and others on the Committee staff. Having been assured by Father Cronin that Hiss was in fact a Communist, Nixon was prepared to cross-examine him as a hostile witness.

Hiss knew nothing about all this, and expected his testimony to be believed without question; but as long as he was being tarred with the guilt-by-association brush, he didn't want to spread the tar around to anyone else. It was bad enough being called a Communist because he knew Lee Pressman; he didn't want other people being called Communists because they knew Alger Hiss.

Nixon, however, persisted. "I don't question its correctness," he said, "but you indicated that several Government officials requested you to come here and you have issued a categorical denial to certain statements that were made by Mr. Chambers concerning people that you were associated with in Government. I think it would make your case stronger if you would indicate what Government officials."

"Mr. Nixon," Hiss answered, "regardless of whether it strengthens my case or not, I would prefer, unless you insist, not to mention any names in my testimony that I don't feel are absolutely necessary. If you insist on a direct answer to your questions, I will comply."

"I would like a direct answer to the question," said Nixon.

Hiss gave in. "Another official of the Government of the United States, who strongly urged me to come to Washington after I had told Judge Frank I did not think I could financially afford to do so—and I am answering this only because you ask it —was Justice Felix Frankfurter." (By 1948 Frankfurter was a Justice of the U.S. Supreme Court.)

"Is that all?" said Nixon.

"That is all I care to say now."

"There were other officials, however?"

"When I came to Washington for interviews with respect to my proposed appointment, I also talked naturally to the Administrator of the Agricultural Adjustment Administration, who would have been my main chief. His name was George Peek. The Co-Administrator was Charles Brand.* Both of them urged me to join the legal staff."

"That completes the group?"

"That completes it as far as I am concerned. I might think of a few others."

Stripling then resumed the questioning, and Hiss summarized his succession of jobs with the Nye Committee, the Justice Department, the State Department, and finally the Carnegie Endowment. Nixon commented in *Six Crises* that his career was "impressive to everyone in the room." Nixon added that "his manner was coolly courteous and, at times, almost condescending."

Indeed, the suppressed anger with which Hiss was wrestling after his brush with Nixon comes through clearly, even from the printed transcript. A page and a half later Mundt referred to Chambers as a man "whom you say you have never seen," and Hiss interrupted to correct him: "As far as I know, I have never seen him." In the next breath Mundt quoted Chambers as listing "a group of seven people," and then recited the list himself, inadvertently adding an extra name, and Hiss interrupted: "That is eight."

Mundt brushed the comment aside, and went on: "There seems to be no question about the subversive connections of the six, other than the Hiss brothers, and I wonder what possible motive a man who edits *Time* magazine would have for mentioning Donald Hiss and Alger Hiss in connection with those other six."

* The name is spelled "Bryan" in the official transcript of the hearings (page 644).

"So do I, Mr. Chairman," said Hiss in his precise, carefully controlled manner. "I have no possible understanding of what could have motivated him. There are many possible motives, I assume, but I am unable to understand it."

"You can appreciate the position of this committee when the name bobs up in connection with those associations," said Mundt.

"I hope the committee can appreciate my position, too," Hiss answered quietly.

"We surely can," said Mundt, "and that is why we responded with alacrity to your request to be heard."

"I appreciate that."

"All we are trying to do is find the facts."

"I wish I could have seen Mr. Chambers before he testified," said Hiss.

Stripling asked Hiss when he had first heard of Chambers's allegations, and Hiss replied that a reporter had called him the night before Chambers took the stand. "You say you have never seen Mr. Chambers?" Stripling asked.

"The name means absolutely nothing to me, Mr. Stripling," he answered.

Stripling showed him a picture of Chambers taken by the Associated Press on Monday, and asked Hiss if he had "ever known an individual who resembles the picture."

"I would much rather see the individual," Hiss answered. "I have looked at all the pictures I was able to get hold of in, I think it was, yesterday's paper which had the pictures. If this is a picture of Mr. Chambers, he is not particularly unusual looking. He looks like a lot of people. I might even mistake him for the chairman of this committee."

There was a burst of laughter from the audience, and Mundt, who was acting as chairman in the absence of Representative Thomas, said: "I hope you are wrong in that."

"I didn't mean to be facetious," Hiss said, "but very seriously, I would not want to take an oath that I have never seen that man. I would like to see him, and then I think I would be better able to tell whether I have ever seen him. Is he here today?"

"Not to my knowledge," said Mundt.

"I hoped he would be."

Mundt ignored the comment, and pushed on. "You realize that this man whose picture you have just looked at, under sworn testimony before this committee, where all the laws of perjury apply, testified that he called at your home, conferred at great length, saw your wife pick up the telephone and call somebody whom he said must have been a Communist, plead with you to divert yourself from Communist activities, and left you with tears in your eyes, saying 'I simply can't make the sacrifice.' "

"I do know that he said that," said Hiss, not realizing how Mundt had embellished Chambers's story. "I also know that I am testifying under the same laws to the direct contrary."

When Nixon wrote his account of the affair in *Six Crises*, he singled out this passage of the testimony as Hiss's first and fatal mistake. Had he simply denied being a Communist without denying that he had ever heard the name Whittaker Chambers, Nixon wrote, "he would have been home free. Hundreds of witnesses had denied such charges before the Committee in the past and nothing more had come of it because it was then simply their word against that of their accusers. In fact, this was one of the primary reasons the Committee itself was under such attack at the time."

But to deny that he even knew his accuser was something else again. Looking over his notes during the hearing, Nixon realized that Hiss had never exactly done that; he had simply said he didn't know the name and didn't recognize the picture. So Nixon told Ben Mandel to telephone Chambers in New York and find out if he had used some other name when he was a Communist. This was a significant point, although Nixon didn't explain it in *Six Crises*. Chambers had said nothing in his testimony on Tuesday about using false names, but Mandel, who had known Chambers in his Communist days, was in a position to know about it, and Nixon must have known too, or the idea wouldn't have occurred to him. In fact, as his later testimony was to show, Chambers had used a great many false names; but at this stage Hiss didn't know that.

It wasn't until after the hearing ended at 12:30 that Mandel got his answer from Chambers and passed it on to Nixon: Yes, Chambers had used the name "Carl" when he was dealing with Hiss in the 1930s; Hiss had never known him as Whittaker Chambers.

Some people might have concluded from this information that Hiss was, after all, telling the truth. Hiss had never known a man by the name of Whittaker Chambers, as he had told the FBI in 1947; the name did indeed mean nothing to him, as he had testified that morning. The picture was apparently vaguely familiar to him, since he would not swear he had never seen the man; but if he had not seen him in ten years or so, and had known him then under a different name, no wonder he didn't recognize the man from the picture.

Nixon took a different view. He now knew something about the relationship between Hiss and Chambers that Hiss didn't know, and it could be used against him. He now had another reason for believing Chambers's story that he had once known Hiss, in spite of Hiss's denials, and this could be used against Hiss too. And so it was.

11

TO CATCH A LIAR

THE hearing of August 5 ended in triumph for Alger Hiss, and acting Chairman Karl E. Mundt expressed the Committee's appreciation "for your very cooperative attitude, for your forthright statements, and for the fact that you were first among those whose names were mentioned by various witnesses to communicate with us, asking for an opportunity to deny the charges."

Even Representative Rankin congratulated Hiss because he "didn't refuse to answer the qestions on the ground that it might incriminate him, and he didn't bring a lawyer here to tell him what to say." Rankin came down from his seat to shake Hiss by the hand as he was leaving, a gesture that Hiss found embarrassing, but there was nothing he could do about it. He left with Bill Marbury and Joseph Johnston to look up other friends in Washington and have a celebratory luncheon.

At this point Hiss thought he had won his battle. He had denied the charges, and the Committee appeared to believe him, even if they had given him a rough time. He hadn't found out who Chambers was, or even been confronted with him yet, but he had Nixon's assurance that this would be arranged. As he said in a letter to John Foster Dulles, which he dictated at the Endowment's Washington office after lunch, he felt "a very definite sense of relief from the oppressive feeling of being completely unable to come to grips with the source of all the ugly rumors that have been floating around for months." It was now evident to Hiss that they all came from "the same single source," and he was looking forward to putting a stop to them.

On his return to New York on Friday, he found on his desk the first half-dozen of what was to be a long series of letters of encouragement, sympathy, and support from people who knew and admired him. These first letters were from friends who reacted to Chambers's charges without waiting to see how Hiss would reply to them; later, after Hiss's statement and testimony of August 5 appeared in the newspapers, the volume of letters was heavier, and they included congratulations on the stand he had taken, exhortations to carry on the battle, and many more offers of help.

The first group of letters contained one from Francis B. Sayre, Hiss's old boss in the State Department, who commented that "these unfair and totally unjust accusations [were] the price that all of us must be prepared to pay for offering ourselves and our lives in the public service." He added, "I stand ready to back you at every turn and I want you to know of my unfailing confidence and affection."

Robert P. Patterson, the former Secretary of War, wrote in a similar vein, and so did James F. Green, of the U.S. Mission, and Egon Ranshofen–Wertheimer, Chief of the Overseas Office Division of the United Nations, both of whom had served under Hiss in the State Department; Michael Carmichael, President of the Carnegie Foundation for the Advancement of Teaching; Devereux C. Josephs of the New York Life Insurance Company, who was a former president of the Carnegie Corporation; and Rabbi Morris Lazaron, who had known Hiss since his boyhood in Baltimore. "I am so accustomed to such misrepresentation that I know how you must feel," Rabbi Lazaron wrote. "Stand fast and be strong in the conviction that truth will prevail."

A note of caution was sounded in a letter from Charles Dollard, President of the Carnegie Corporation of New York, who was one of the friends who had advised Hiss not to send his telegram to HUAC upon first hearing of Chambers's attack on August 3. "Perhaps you were right about the telegram (I still lean the other way)," Dollard wrote on August 4, while Hiss was in Philadelphia preparing for his testimony the following day, "but, for Heaven's sake, don't lose your sense of proportion. Your peers have a confidence in you which is not to be undermined by the reckless charges of a hysterical renegade, and you must long since have discovered, as I have, that an honest man must chart his course in terms of the judgment of the few rather than the many. . . . I think you now have the Endowment on the high road and I should hate to see your attention distracted by a campaign against termites."

But Hiss was less concerned with the "termites" who were attacking him than with the defense of his own reputation for loyalty, honor, and integrity. And he was heartened by the letters that began coming in the following week, from such distinguished supporters as Herbert H. Lehman, former Governor of New York; Clarence E. Pickett, Executive Secretary of the American Friends Service Committee; Ralph Bunche, then number two man in the UN Trusteeship Department; and Cabot Coville, a foreign service officer who had escaped from Corregidor by submarine with Francis Sayre and General MacArthur after the Japanese attack of 1941, and who wrote to him from Tokyo that "The charge against no person has so clearly and fully indicated to me the absurdity of the whole proceedings [of the House Committee]."

Other such letters came from Mrs. Vincent Astor, who, as Mary Cushing, had been a close friend of Hiss in his law school days; Manley O. Hudson, the Harvard professor of international law who had first persuaded Hiss to go to law school; Anson Phelps Stokes, the canon of the Washington Cathedral; Harding Bancroft, then in the State Department's Office of UN Affairs, and later an executive of *The New York Times*; Stanley K. Hornbeck, who had been Hiss's boss after Sayre; Stanley M. Isaacs, former Borough President of Manhattan; and many others, including some total strangers who had read of Hiss's testimony in the newspapers and been impressed.

Altogether, Hiss had every reason to be pleased and confident. Most of the press were on his side; there were some scathing editorials about the Committee in the *Boston Herald*, the *Washington*

Post, the Baltimore *Sun*, and other papers. Hiss took the train to Peacham on Friday evening, prepared to reassure Priscilla that everything was all right. He had written to her, since there was no telephone in the cottage, but he didn't know until he reached Peacham that she'd read about Chambers's attack in one of the New York newspapers, which a friend had picked up Tuesday night on the way back to Peacham from a business trip. Priscilla had spent the week trying to recall who the picture reminded her of. "I remember a dreadful man named Crosley or something like that," she had said to her friend, but it wasn't a very clear recollection.

Hiss was also concerned about his mother and his elder sister Anna, who had been visiting him at his New York apartment when the news of Chambers's testimony broke. His mother was eighty-one, and had recently had a painful operation on her lower jawbone; Hiss commented in his letter to Dulles that it was "by happy fortune" that he was able to be with her "during the first very unpleasant hours following Chambers's testimony."

Meanwhile, in Washington other things were happening of which Hiss was unaware. The House Committee had met in executive session after lunch on Thursday, and as described by Nixon in *Six Crises*, it was "in a virtual state of shock." After Hiss finished testifying, news reporters had told Nixon that the Committee was going to be in trouble if it couldn't prove Chambers's story. President Truman had said at his press conference that morning that the Committee's whole spy investigation was a political "red herring," cooked up to distract the public from the failures of the Republican Congress. Committee members themselves were discouraged; Rep. F. Edward Hébert of Louisiana, who had taken little part in the morning's questioning, wanted to turn the Hiss–Chambers affair over to the Justice Department to let them decide who was lying. Nixon thought the majority of the Committee felt the same way.

"I was the only member of the Committee who expressed a contrary view," he wrote, "and Bob Stripling backed me up strongly and effectively."

Nixon reminded the Committee that Chambers had testified

that he told his story to Adolf Berle, as early as 1939, and repeated it to the FBI several times since. And, according to *Six Crises*, Nixon added that "No action had ever been taken to check the credibility of his charges." This was of course untrue, as Nixon must have known from his conversations with Father Cronin and Ben Mandel, but it was certainly true that nothing had yet been found to substantiate the charges. Thus, Nixon was stretching a point when he wrote that "judging from that record, we could only assume that if we turned the investigation over to the Department of Justice, the case would be dropped." In the absence of anything to support Chambers, an investigation of the conflicts of testimony between Hiss and Chambers might have led to an indictment of Chambers for perjury, which Nixon didn't want.

Moreover, Nixon pointed out, if the Committee backed out of the case, it would probably destroy its reputation for good. "It would be a public confession that we were incompetent and even reckless in our procedure," he wrote. "We would never be able to begin another investigation without having someone say, 'Why do you amateurs insist on getting into these cases? Why don't you leave the job where it belongs—to the experts in the Department of Justice?' "

Nixon then argued that, even if the Committee couldn't prove that Hiss was a Communist, it "should be able to establish by corroborative testimoney whether or not the two men knew each other." And it followed, according to Nixon, that if Hiss were shown to be lying about not knowing Chambers, then he might also be lying about whether he was a Communist. This was a plausible argument, consistent with the legal doctrine about perjury; a jury would be allowed to draw such an inference if it wanted to. Moreover, Nixon's chances of making Hiss look like a liar on this point looked pretty good—Nixon knew that Chambers had been using a different name at the time he met Hiss, but Hiss didn't know that. Apparently, Nixon hadn't mentioned this point to the Committee, either; at least there's nothing in *Six Crises* to show that he did.

The clincher, according to *Six Crises*, was Stripling's comment that he had heard rumors that Chambers was an alcoholic, that he had been in a mental institution, and that he was a paranoiac. These were typical Communist smear tactics, Stripling said, employed by Communists to destroy any witness who testified against them. If that didn't prove Hiss was a Communist, it at least contained a clear enough implication to satisfy the Committee.

"Finally my arguments prevailed," wrote Nixon, "and Karl Mundt, as acting Chairman, appointed me to head a subcommittee to question Chambers again—this time in executive session, with no spectators or press present. Stripling was directed to subpoena Chambers to a hearing in New York two days later, on August 7." That was the Saturday Hiss arrived in Peacham, by night train from New York.

Nixon went back to his office, elated over his success but aware that he had his work cut out for him. "I had put myself, a freshman Congressman," he wrote, "in the position of defending the reputation of the Un-American Activities Committee. And in so doing, I was opposing the President of the United States and the majority of press corps opinion, which is so important to the career of anyone in elective office. . . .

"I recognized that the future of the Committee on Un-American Activities was at stake. The Committee in 1948 was under constant and severe attack from many segments of both press and public. It had been widely condemned as a 'Red-baiting' group, habitually unfair and irresponsible, whose investigations had failed to lead to a single conviction of anyone against whom charges had been made at its hearings. . . .

"The Committee had survived many past attacks for its failure to prove the charges of witnesses appearing before it. But I was convinced that a failure in this case would prove to be fatal. The President of the United States himself, the great majority of the press corps, and even some of the Committee's own members were mounting an all-out attack on its alleged 'sloppy' procedures."

Nixon further reflected, looking back on the case in 1962, that at the time of the Hiss–Chambers affair his attack on Communism was regarded by his critics as "an attack on the free expression of ideas." Communism, he wrote, was then regarded in most intellectual circles as a political idea that was generally unpopular, but "one that any individual should have the right to express freely without running any risk of investigation or prosecution." The Hiss case and other developments of the period were to change all that, he reflected. As he described it, he correctly foresaw, in 1948, that to convince the nation that the Communists "had been able to enlist the active support of men like Alger Hiss" would make a great impression.

"More important than the fate of the Committee," Nixon wrote, "the national interest required that the investigation go forward." And he bent to the task.

Nixon's first step was to find out how much Chambers really knew about Hiss, and, for this purpose, Nixon sat up most of that night studying the transcript of the hearings and "making notes of literally scores of questions that I might ask Chambers." On Saturday he went with his subcommittee—Rep. F. Edward Hébert of Louisiana and Rep. John R. McDowell of Pennsylvania—to the U.S. Court House at Foley Square in New York. Stripling and Mandel accompanied them, along with three other Committee investigators, Louis Russell, Donald Appell, and Charles McKillips. After Chambers was sworn, Nixon wrote, "For almost three hours I bombarded him with questions covering every fact I could think of which one man should know about another if they were friends."

The transcript of this session was released on August 25, at Hiss's request, but it consists of less than twelve pages, totaling barely half an hour's conversation in the period between 10:30 A.M. and 1:10 P.M. Toward the end is a gap identified as "Discussion off the record," which must have taken up most of the morning. It began at Chambers's request, when he began to explain why he had gone to Adolf Berle with his story in 1939; what was said after that has never been disclosed.

Whatever the discussion was about, it evidently resulted in Chambers winning Nixon's confidence, and presumably added nothing significant to what Chambers had already said about Hiss. This wasn't much, and not all of it accurate, but it was enough for Nixon's purpose. The story Chambers told is summarized in the following paragraphs.

Hiss, he said, did not know him as Whittaker Chambers, but "by the party name of Carl," and never questioned this pseudonymous arrangement. The same was true of the entire group of men with whom Chambers worked at the time.

Chambers knew Hiss was a Communist because he was told as much by J. Peters, head of the Communist underground in the United States. Chambers had no evidence to support Peters's statement "beyond the fact that he (Hiss) submitted himself for the two or three years that I knew him as a dedicated and disciplined Communist." (Chambers was not asked to explain what that meant.)

Chambers collected party dues from Hiss once a month during those two or three years; Hiss would give him the money in an envelope, which Chambers assumed also contained Mrs. Hiss's dues but no one else's, and Chambers would give the envelope to Peters. (This differed somewhat from Chambers's account on August 3, when he had said that Henry Collins had collected the dues from the whole group and handed them over to Chambers. However, Nixon didn't pursue the point.) Chambers said Hiss was "rather pious about paying his dues promptly."

All the Communists in the group accepted Hiss as a member of the Communist Party, according to Chambers. It was not an "intellectual study group"; its function was "to infiltrate the Government in the interest of the Communist Party." None of the group had party membership cards.

Mr. Hiss had no children at the time; Mrs. Hiss's son, Timothy Hobson, was about ten years old. His father Thayer Hobson was a member of the publishing house of William Morrow in New York.

Mrs. Hiss usually called her husband "Hilly" instead of Alger; he called her "Dilly" or "Pross." They were commonly referred to by members of the group as "Hilly and Dilly."

Chambers said he had stayed overnight in the Hiss home for a number of days from time to time, and once for as long as a week. He made it "a kind of informal headquarters." There was no financial arrangement involved; it was "part of the Communist pattern."

The Hisses had "a maid who came in to clean, and a cook who came in to cook. In one of the houses they had a rather elderly Negro maid whom Mr. Hiss used to drive home in the evening." Chambers didn't recall the maid's name.

The Hisses had a cocker spaniel, which they boarded at a kennel on Wisconsin Avenue when they took vacation trips to the Eastern Shore of Maryland.

When Chambers first knew Hiss he was living in an apartment house on Twenty-eighth Street, one of a pair of identical buildings at the end of a dead-end street. The apartment was on the top floor, but Chambers couldn't remember the furniture in it.

The Hisses' library was "very nondescript," and they cared nothing about food. "Hiss is a man of great simplicity and a great gentleness and sweetness of character," said Chambers, "and they lived with extreme simplicity. I had the impression that the furniture in that house was kind of pulled together from here or there, maybe they got it from their mother or something like that, nothing lavish about it whatsoever, quite simple."

Both Mr. and Mrs. Hiss were "amateur ornithologists, bird observers." They used to get up early in the morning to observe the birds at Glen Echo, on the canal near the Potomac River. "I recall once they saw, to their great excitement, a prothonotary warbler," Chambers added.

Their car was a Ford roadster, black and very dilapidated. The windshield wipers had to be operated by hand; Chambers remembered driving it on a rainy day. About 1936 they got a new Plymouth sedan.

Up to this point Nixon had done all the questioning, but suddenly Mandel interrupted to ask, "What did he do with the old car?" Chambers replied, "The Communist Party had in Washington a service station—that is, the man in charge or owner of this station was a Communist—or it may have been a car lot. The owner was a Communist. I never knew who this was or where it was. It was against all the rules of underground organization for Hiss to do anything with his old car but trade it in, and I think this investigation has proved how right the Communists are in such matters, but Hiss insisted that he wanted that car turned over to the open party so it could be of use to some poor organizer in the West or somewhere. Much against my better judgment and much against Peters's better judgment, he finally got us to permit him to do this thing. Peters knew where this lot was and he either took Hiss there, or he gave Hiss the address and Hiss went there, and to the best of my recollection of his description of that happening, he left the car there and simply went away and the man in charge of the station took care of the rest of it for him. I should think the records of that transfer would be traceable."

The Hisses had no other hobbies. Chambers said he was reasonably sure they did not have a piano. The only "particular piece of furniture" that he could recall was "a small leather cigarette box, leather-covered cigarette box, with gold tooling on it. It seems to me that the box was red leather."

Chambers couldn't recall what their silver pattern was, or whether it was sterling; or what kind of chinaware they used. They did not drink; at least they didn't drink with Chambers. "For one thing," he said, "I was strictly forbidden by the Communist Party to taste liquor at any time." But Hiss "gave cocktail parties in Government service."

Chambers described Hiss as "about five feet eight or nine, slender. His eyes are wide apart and blue or gray." Nixon pressed the point, and he added, "Bluish gray, you could say. In his walk, if you watch him from behind, there is a slight mince sometimes."

He described Mrs. Hiss as "a short, highly nervous little woman. I don't at the moment recall the color of her eyes, but she has a habit of blushing red when she is excited or angry, fiery red."

At this point Mandel interrupted again to say that a picture of Hiss showed his hand cupped to his ear, and Chambers replied, "He is deaf in one ear." He didn't remember which.

Chambers didn't recall that Hiss ever told him how he had become deaf in one ear, but he added: "The only thing I recall he told me was as a small boy he used to take a little wagon—he was a Baltimore boy—and walk up to Druid Hill Park, which was up at that time way beyond the civilized center of the city, and fill up the bottles with spring water and bring them back and sell it."

Chambers described Timmy Hobson as "a puny little boy, also rather nervous." He said the boy's father was a cousin of Thornton Wilder's, and that he was paying for Timmy's education, but the Hisses were "diverting a large part of the money to the Communist Party. . . . They took him out of a more expensive school and put him in a less expensive school expressly for that purpose." This was probably about 1936, Chambers said, adding, "He was a slightly effeminate child. I think there was some worry about him."

Hiss had one sister, living with her mother in Baltimore, but Chambers didn't know her name and didn't know if she was interested in athletics. (He was asked about this point by Representative Hébert, who presumably knew that the sister Chambers was referring to was Anna Hiss, head of the Physical Education Department at the University of Texas, who didn't live in Baltimore but did occasionally visit her mother there.)

Chambers had never met the mother or the sister. "My impression was his relations with his mother were affectionate but not too happy," he said. "She was, perhaps, domineering. I simply pulled this out of the air in the conversation."

Hiss was forbidden to go to church, according to Chambers; his wife came from a Quaker family. Her maiden name was Priscilla Fansler, and she came from Great Valley, near Paoli, Pa. "She once showed me while we were driving beyond Paoli the road down which their farm lay."

Chambers never went on any overnight trips with Hiss, and

never stayed in his brother Donald's home; he thought Donald's wife was the daughter of "a Mr. Cotton, who is in the State Department." But "my relationship with Alger Hiss quickly transcended our formal relationship," he said. "We became close friends."

Chambers's recollection of the homes Hiss had lived in during the period he said he had known him was very vague. He said nothing to the Committee on this occasion about the two months he had lived in the Twenty-eighth Street apartment, after the Hisses had moved; he recalled that Hiss had moved at that time to "a house in Georgetown—but it seems it was on the corner of P Street." (Actually it was next door to the corner house.) Chambers remembered it as a three-story house, with "a kind of a porch in back." This was the house in which Chambers and his wife had spent a few days in the guest suite on the top floor, but he didn't mention that to the Committee at this time either. The house actually had four stories, including the basement dining room and kitchen. Chambers correctly recalled that from there Hiss had moved to a smaller house "on an up-and-down street, a street that would cross the lettered streets, probably just around the corner from the other house and very near to his brother Donald . . . the dining room was below the level of the ground, one of those basement dining rooms; it had a small yard in back." This was the house at 1245 Thirtieth Street where the Hisses lived from June 15, 1936 until December 29, 1937. Chambers said of it, "I think he was there when I broke with the Communist Party."

Chambers said that the last time he had seen Hiss was in 1938, when Hiss was living in another house "on the other side of Wisconsin Avenue," which would have been 3415 Volta Place, though Chambers didn't remember the address. He said he didn't remember any of the furniture, but he was reasonably sure Mr. and Mrs. Hiss didn't have twin beds. And he was willing to submit to a lie detector test to prove he was telling the truth.

That was it; not much, and not all of it accurate, but enough for Nixon's purpose. Nobody had ever called Priscilla "Dilly," and Chambers had never used any Hiss home as "a kind of informal headquarters" except for his brief tenancy of the

Twenty-eighth Street apartment, which he hadn't mentioned; the Hisses had never had both a maid and a cook at the same time, and Hiss had never made a habit of driving the maid home in the evening. Thayer Hobson was indeed employed by William Morrow, but he was no cousin of Thornton Wilder's, and Donald Hiss's wife was not the daughter of a man called Cotton. The Hisses did have other hobbies besides bird-watching; Priscilla was an inveterate pianist and always had a piano in her house. Neither their furniture nor their library could fairly be described as "nondescript"; Hiss was inordinately proud of the antique Queen Anne mirror that he had inherited from Justice Holmes, and of his volumes of Holmes's speeches and Holmes's personal record of the books he had read. Priscilla was indeed short, but hardly "nervous"; her habit was to suppress her anger and excitement, never to blush fiery red. Hiss was six feet tall, not five feet eight or nine, and there was no "mince" in his walk. Tim was neither puny nor effeminate when he was ten years old, but he had been laid up for months with a broken leg that Chambers seemed unaware of. Tim's father did pay for his schooling, but in 1936 he had been moved to a more expensive school, not a cheaper one. Hiss had no means of diverting Tim's educational funds to the Communist party, even had he wanted to; the tuition checks were sent directly to the school by Thayer Hobson. Indeed, when Tim later was sent to the George School the fees were more than Hobson was prepared to pay, and Hiss made up the difference. Hiss had never been deaf in either ear; Priscilla's family was Presbyterian, not Quaker, and had never lived on a farm; Hiss drank as much as anyone, and was a collector of vintage wines, though Priscilla didn't drink much; Twenty-eighth Street wasn't a dead-end, and Druid Hill Park was quite close to downtown Baltimore, even in 1914.

Nixon didn't know about these details, and didn't bother to check them. Instead, according to *Six Crises*, the Committee staff, under Stripling's direction, "worked round the clock in a search for documentary proof, if it existed, of Chambers's story." They questioned real estate agents to get the addresses of the homes where Hiss had lived, which Chambers had forgotten, and found the kennel where the Hisses had boarded their spaniel. But they couldn't find the motor vehicle records Chambers had spoken of to document his story about the old Ford.

Nixon's primary concern, as he makes clear in *Six Crises,* was whether Chambers's story would be believed. He put it to the test by calling Bert Andrews, the *New York Herald Tribune* reporter who had been rebuked by Hiss in 1945 for his story about the "secret deal" at Yalta and the extra Soviet votes in the UN General Assembly. According to Nixon, he thought Andrews would be "predisposed to believe Hiss rather than Chambers," because he had recently attacked the State Department loyalty program in a Pulitzer Prize-winning series of articles. "From my brief acquaintance with Andrews and from his reputation among his colleagues in the press corps," Nixon wrote, "I was convinced he would be objective." Andrews also enjoyed the reputation of being a go-getter who would do anything for a good story; he was chief of the *Herald Tribune*'s Washington Bureau, a strong position for a man on the way up. The *Herald Tribune* was then one of the nation's leading newspapers, staunchly Republican and committed as a matter of principle to putting Dewey in the White House. It represented the Eastern liberal Republican viewpoint, a far cry from Nixon's California conservatism; but its support could be useful to Nixon, whose own ambitions already looked beyond California.

Nixon showed Andrews the transcript of Chambers's testimony at the "secret" hearing in New York, "with the understanding," Nixon wrote, "that he would write nothing about it until it was released for publication to all papers." When Andrews had read it, according to Nixon, he exclaimed: " 'I wouldn't have believed it, after hearing Hiss the other day. But there's no doubt about it. Chambers knew Hiss.' "

The fact was obvious and uncontested; all Hiss had said in his testimony was that he didn't know the name and didn't recognize the picture. But in the context that had now been created, it was most damaging: Chambers said he had been a Communist when he knew Hiss, and people who allowed themselves to be known by Communists were not the kind of people that good Republicans in 1948 were willing to trust with such important jobs as assistant to an Assistant Secretary of State or President of the Carnegie Endowment for International Peace. And if Hiss wouldn't admit that everything Chambers said about him was true, it could be argued that he was lying to protect himself, whether Chambers had used the same name ten years ago or not.

Nixon then showed the transcript to William P. Rogers, chief counsel for the Senate Internal Security Subcommittee, who reached the same conclusion as Andrews. And he showed it to Rep. Charles Kersten, his friend who had introduced him to Father Cronin the year before, and Kersten suggested that Hiss's boss John Foster Dulles be given "the opportunity to read the testimony." This was important because Dulles, who was acting as foreign policy adviser to Tom Dewey, expected to be Secretary of State when Dewey was elected. Dulles had already been embarrassed by the calls from Alfred Kohlberg about Hiss's reputation for being a Communist, but so far he had taken Hiss's side.

The next day Nixon and Kersten took the train to New York and met Dulles at the Roosevelt Hotel, where he was working on the Dewey campaign. As Nixon described it, Dulles's brother Allen, later to become head of the Central Intelligence Agency (CIA), was also there. "Both men read the testimony. When they had finished, Foster Dulles paced the floor, his hands crossed behind him. . . . He stopped finally and said, 'There's no question about it. It's almost impossible to believe, but Chambers knows Hiss.' Allen Dulles reached the same conclusion."

Thus encouraged, though not yet satisfied, Nixon decided to see Chambers again, this time privately, to see "what kind of man he really was." To avoid publicity, as he wrote in *Six Crises*, Nixon made the two-hour trip by car from Washington to Chambers's farm in Westminster, Maryland. "We sat on some dilapidated rocking chairs on his front porch overlooking the Maryland countryside," Nixon wrote. "It was the first of many long and rewarding conversations I was to have with him during the period of the Hiss case, and through the years until his death in 1961." Nixon found him to be "a man of extraordinary intelligence, speaking from great depth of understanding; a sensitive, shy man who had turned from complete dedication to Communism to a new religious faith and a kind of fatalism about the future."

Nixon asked him what his motive was for "doing what he had to Hiss." Chambers's reply was evasive, but oddly characteristic; he said, according to Nixon, " 'Certainly I wouldn't have a motive which would involve destroying my own career.' " Later, when a *Washington Daily News* reporter asked him the same question, Chambers replied, according to the *News*, " 'I am a man who reluctantly, grudgingly, step-by-step, is destroying himself [so] that this country and the faith by which it lives may continue to exist.' " And this theme of self-destruction became one of the unifying threads that run all the way through Chambers's own account in *Witness*.

Nixon, however, was impressed by Chambers's eagerness to "warn his country of the scope, strength and danger of the Communist conspiracy in the United States." He was also impressed when Chambers remarked that Priscilla Hiss was a Quaker and "often used the plain speech in talking to Alger at home." Nixon, whose mother was a Quaker, knew that meant she said "thee" instead of "you," and the remark gave him "an intuitive feeling" that Chambers "was speaking from firsthand rather than secondhand knowledge."

Two days later Nixon took Bert Andrews out to the Westminster farm to meet Chambers, and this time another incident occurred, which Nixon found significant. Chambers brought out a book of Audubon bird pictures, saying that Hiss had given it to him; he pointed to a drawing of a hooded warbler and said that the Hisses had had the same picture hanging in their dining room.

Finally, on the Saturday of that week, Nixon took Stripling to the Chambers farm, because he thought Stripling had a "sixth sense" about such matters. Stripling commented, according to Nixon, " 'I don't think Chambers has yet told us the whole story. He is holding something back. He is trying to protect somebody.' "

Meanwhile, the Committee had summoned Hiss to appear

at another secret session on the following Monday, August 16; they had sent him a telegram to that effect on Friday, August 13. The session would be at the Committee's offices in Washington; they had journeyed to New York to interview Chambers, but extended no such courtesy to Hiss.

Hiss was beginning to be concerned about the stories he was reading in the newspapers concerning what Chambers had said in the secret session of August 7, and what he had told Andrews and Nixon on their visits to his farm. Nixon had only asked Andrews to hold up his story of the secret session until other reporters had it too, and soon many of them did. (It was an effective use of the "leak" technique that Nixon was to protest against so vigorously twenty-six years later, when it was used against him in the impeachment proceedings of the House Judiciary Committee.) Hiss was annoyed, but helpless.

When the leaks began to appear, Hiss decided it would be a good idea to look up Chambers in his office at *Time* magazine and find out who he really was. But Dulles told him not to do so; the Committee would arrange for him to see Chambers in due course, Dulles said, and it would be better to leave everything in the Committee's hands. This time Hiss took his boss's advice, not knowing about Dulles's previous conversation with Nixon, or how Dulles's attitude had changed. And when he got the telegram summoning him for a session on Monday, he assumed that Chambers would be there.

That, however, was not the way Nixon had planned it. For this major event, Rep. J. Parnell Thomas, the Committee Chairman, made one of his infrequent appearances, and Reps. McDowell and Hébert were there as well as Nixon. Stripling, Appell, Russell, and Mandel were on hand for the committee staff, strengthened by William A. Wheeler, an investigator; A. S. Poore, an editor; and Mrs. L. E. Howard, a member of the research staff. Only Chambers was absent.

Hiss began by asking if the proceedings were to be recorded, and if he could expect a copy of the transcript. Chairman Thomas said no. "This is an executive session, and that speaks for itself that everything is supposed to be right within these four walls.

Therefore we do not naturally give out the testimony taken in executive session," he explained.

The stenographer, however, was taking all that down, and Nixon intervened to say that in the event a transcript was made public, Hiss would receive a copy, but if it were not made public he wouldn't. Stripling then introduced everybody present, and Nixon made a brief statement to the effect that either Hiss or Chambers must have given the Committee some false testimony, and he wanted to straighten out the conflicts between them. Whoever has given false testimony, he said gently, "must, if possible, answer for that testimony."

There followed a series of questions and answers in which Hiss described his interviews with the FBI in 1946 and 1947, saying that the first time he ever heard the name Whittaker Chambers was in the 1947 interview. Nixon told him that Chambers now said he had used the name "Carl" in 1934–1937, and Hiss said he could not recall anybody by that name "that could remotely be connected with the kind of testimony Mr. Chambers had given," and that, in any case, everyone he ever knew by the name of Carl had a last name as well. Chambers had said that as "Carl" he had not used any last name. In answer to further questions, Hiss denied that he had ever known J. Peters, the reputed underground chief, or had ever attended the meeting of seven cell leaders in the apartment of Henry Collins that Chambers had described. Nixon then brought out another picture of Whittaker Chambers and pressed Hiss to identify it.

Hiss answered at some length that the face in the picture had "a certain familiarity," but he wasn't prepared to identify it without seeing the man.

Nixon asked if it would help him to know that the man in question had "stayed overnight in your home on several occasions." Hiss said a lot of people had done that over the years, but he found it difficult to believe that the man in the picture could have done so "and his face not be more familiar than it is." He added politely, but firmly, "I don't want to suggest any innovations in your procedure, but I do want to say specifically that I do hope I will have an opportunity actually to see the individual."

Nixon replied that that would be arranged. Then he added, in an oddly revealing statement, that there were two other things he wanted to do first. One was to clear up the question of mistaken identity—which could have been most easily done by arranging for Hiss to see Chambers, as Hiss had requested. Indeed, if HUAC had been following the procedures required by the Constitution in criminal prosecutions, this would have been a necessary first step. But HUAC was a committee of the Congress, not a court, so the constitutional safeguards didn't apply. And Nixon preferred to keep the accuser's identity a secret from the accused as long as possible. That way Nixon would be safe; he could drop the case if it turned out Chambers had made a mistake. Hiss, however, had no protection as long as he didn't know who Chambers was, or what Chambers might know about him to lend plausibility to his lies.

The other thing Nixon wanted to do before letting Hiss see Chambers was, Nixon said, to get some "clear conflict on certain pieces of testimony." That, he said with evident satisfaction, "we are getting now."

"Yes, sir," said Hiss.

There were further questions about Priscilla, Tony, and Timothy of a routine nature and some discussion of when it would be convenient for Priscilla to testify. Then Nixon asked for Timothy's address in New York, and suddenly the atmosphere changed. The idea that the Committee might question Tim and make a public display of his homosexual problems was something Hiss would not accept.

"Mr. Nixon," said Hiss, "you are asking me about a subject which is one of rather deep concern to me."

"I understand," said Nixon.

"My son served in the Navy, V–12," Hiss continued, choosing his words carefully. "He went in as a very young man. When he left the Navy, he did not wish to go on with college. I did wish him to go on. He had some college while in the Navy V–12 program. He feels the need of independence of his parents at the present time. He is being what people in Vermont call not only independent, but 'indegoddampendent.' That is a Vermontism.

"I have an address for my son which I am told is not his present address. He has not told me or his mother in the past few months what his present address is. I expect he will do so. This is not the first time in the last year when he has changed his address and told me after the event instead of before. I believe he tried to reach me by telephone the night before I testified here, because the phone call came in for me at the hotel from Los Angeles, and I couldn't figure who it was and didn't know he was in Los Angeles at the time. I have since learned he was in Los Angeles, and I believe he was calling me.

"I learned from the same person who knew he was in Los Angeles that he would be back in New York on the 16th. I don't know of my own knowledge. I can give you the address in New York. I don't think you can reach him there.

"I wonder if you would mind if I gave you instead the address of his doctor, because he has been consulting a psychiatrist in the last couple of years."

Nixon interrupted to ask if the doctor would know where Timothy was.

"He will get in touch with the doctor as soon as he returns," Hiss said. "The doctor has his other address, and I didn't think it appropriate to ask the doctor for his address. It is Dr. Abram Kardiner. You will understand why this is a very difficult subject to talk about because I love my stepson very deeply. Many people take an exaggerated view of what psychiatric assistance means."

"You can be sure, Mr. Hiss," said Nixon, "that there will be absolutely no statement whatever concerning these statements."

Hiss then gave the Committee Dr. Kardiner's address, and Nixon started to shift the questioning to the subject of Hiss's servants. But Hiss now had other things on his mind, and he interrupted: "Mr. Nixon, may I raise a question at this point?"

"Certainly," said Nixon.

"I have been angered and hurt by one thing in the course of this Committee testimony," Hiss said, "and that was by the attitude which I think Mr. Mundt took when I was testifying publicly and which, it seems to me, you have been taking today, that you have a conflict of testimony between two witnesses—I restrained myself with some difficulty from commenting on this at the public hearing, and I would like to say it on this occasion, which isn't a public hearing."

"Say anything you like," said Nixon.

"It seems there is no impropriety in saying it," Hiss went on. "You today and the acting chairman [Mundt] publicly have taken the attitude when you have two witnesses, one of whom is a confessed former Communist, the other is me, that you simply have two witnesses saying contradictory things as between whom you find it most difficult to decide on credibility.

"Mr. Nixon, I do not know what Mr. Whittaker Chambers testified to your committee last Saturday. It is necessarily my opinion of him from what he has already said that I do know he is not capable of telling the truth or does not desire to, and I honestly have the feeling that details of my personal life which I give honestly can be used to my disadvantage by Chambers then ex post facto knowing these facts.

"I would request that I hear Mr. Chambers's story of his alleged knowledge of me. I have seen newspaper accounts, Mr. Nixon, that you spent the weekend—whether correct or not, I do not know—at Mr. Chambers's farm in New Jersey."

"That is quite incorrect," said Nixon.

"It is incorrect?" said Hiss.

"Yes, sir," said Mr. Nixon. "I can say, as you did a moment ago, that I have never spent the night with Mr. Chambers."

It was a neat deception. Nixon could claim that he hadn't told a lie, since his three visits to Chambers's farm had not involved staying overnight, and Hiss was "incorrect" in describing the farm as being in New Jersey instead of Maryland. But to Hiss, unaware of Nixon's mental processes and still upset about Timothy, it sounded as though Nixon had repudiated the newspaper stories altogether. So he didn't press the point, and didn't bother to correct Nixon's misstatement of his own testimony. (He had not, after all, said that he had never spent the night with Chambers.) He let it pass and proceeded to his next point—the identity of Whittaker Chambers.

"Now, I have been cudgeling my brains," Hiss said, "particularly on the train coming down this morning, and I had three or four hours on the train between New York and Washington, as to who could have various details about my family. Many people could.

"Mr. Nixon, I do not wish to make it easier for anyone who, for whatever motive I cannot understand, is apparently endeavoring to destroy me, to make that man's endeavors any easier. I think in common fairness to my own self-protection and that of my family and my family's good name and my own, I should not be asked to give details which somehow he may hear and then may be able to use as if he knew them before. I would like him to say all he knows about me now. What I have done is public record, where I have lived is public record. Let him tell you all he knows, let that be made public, and then let my record be checked against those facts instead of my being asked, Mr. Nixon, to tell you personal facts about myself which, if they come to his ears, could sound very persuasive to other people that he had known me at some prior time."

Nixon replied that he was only looking for facts to corroborate the story, and protested against the "very serious implication" that his purpose was "to get information with which we can coach Mr. Chambers so that he can more or less build a web around you." There was a lot more argument on this point, and Stripling said that, on the basis of what Chambers had already testified, "he has either made a study of your life in great detail or he knows you, one or the other, or he is incorrect." Then he showed Hiss another picture of Chambers.

Hiss repeated his earlier comments that the face looked familiar but that he couldn't identify it. He protested that the issue wasn't whether he remembered the man or not but whether he was a Communist or not, "which he has said and which I have denied."

Chairman Thomas intervened at this point, brushing Hiss's protest aside, to ask if he would recall a person who had "positively been in your house three or four times, we will say, in the last ten years?" Stripling redefined him as a man who had spent a whole week in Hiss's house, while Hiss was there.

Hiss answered, "Mr. Chairman, I could not fail to recognize such a man if he were now in my presence." Thomas showed him the picture again, and Nixon asked if the man in it had spent a week in Hiss's house. Hiss replied, "I do not recognize him from the picture. I cannot say that man did, but I would like to see him."

The answer wasn't very helpful; in fact, Chambers never had spent a week in Hiss's house while Hiss was there, as he later admitted under cross-examination at the trial. But at this early stage the Committee didn't know that, and Hiss still didn't know who Chambers was. Under pressure from the Committee and after some more rather repetitious argument, however, he was prepared to make a guess.

On the train from New York, Hiss had gone over the problem with two of his old friends from Cotton, Franklin, Wright & Gordon, who had brought with them a full collection of the newspaper stories which had appeared over the weekend while Hiss was in Peacham. From the references to the Twenty-eighth Street apartment and the P Street house Hiss had come to the conclusion that Chambers might be the free-lance writer he remembered as George Crosley. But he wasn't sure, and while he remembered Crosley as rather a "creep," he didn't think he was "creepy" enough to call him a Communist. And if Chambers wasn't Crosley, he didn't want to get into more trouble by saying that he was. He hadn't seen the man in twelve years, and he saw no reason to bring his name into the affair until he was sure it was the right one. Hiss's friends agreed with this approach, but advised him to go ahead and use the name should it seem necessary.

With this advice in mind, Hiss worked out what he thought might be a way around the difficulty. He said to Nixon, "I have written a name on this pad in front of me of a person whom I knew in 1933 and 1934, who not only spent some time in my house but sublet my apartment. That man certainly spent more than a week, not while I was in the same apartment. I do not recognize the photographs as possibly being this man. If I hadn't seen the morning papers with an account of statements that he knew the inside of my house, I don't think I would even have thought of this name. I want to see Chambers face to face and see if he can be this individual. I do not want, and I don't think I ought to be asked to testify now [about] that man's name and everything I can remember about him. I have written the name on this piece of paper. I have given the name to two friends of mine before I came in this hearing. I can only repeat, and perhaps I am being overanxious about the possibility of unauthorized disclosure of testimony, that I don't think in my present frame of mind that it is fair to my position, my own protection, that I be asked to put down here of record personal facts which, if they came to the ears of someone who had for no reason I can understand a desire to injure me, would assist him in that endeavor."

This was pay dirt for the Committee, and Nixon moved in immediately to develop it. "Where were you living at the time?" he asked.

"Mr. Nixon," said Hiss, "if I give details of where I was, it is going to be very easy if this information gets out for someone to say then ex post facto, 'I saw Hiss in such and such a house.' Actually, all he has to do is look it up in the telephone directory and find where it is."

Thomas interrupted, "The Chairman wants to say this: Questions will be asked and the committee will expect to get very detailed answers to the questions. Let's not ramble around the lot here. You go ahead and ask questions and I want the witness to answer."

For a few minutes Hiss answered questions obediently, and then the argument began again, becoming nasty and angry. In the course of it Stripling said he had not known in advance what Chambers was going to say when he first appeared on August 3, which was as accurate and misleading as Nixon's remark about not spending the night on Chambers's farm. For while Stripling had not questioned Chambers in executive session for more than two minutes that day, he had read Chambers's prepared statement and was familiar enough with what Chambers had told the

FBI over the years to be ready with background information about the people named in his testimony.

Then Representative Hébert, who had not been involved in the preparations for Chambers's testimony and could speak more freely than Stripling and Nixon, launched into what he called a "man-to-man impression of the whole situation."

"We did not know anything Mr. Chambers was going to say," he said. "I did not hear your name mentioned until it was mentioned in open hearing."

"I didn't know that," Hiss commented.

"I will tell you right now, and I will tell you exactly what I told Mr. Chambers," Hébert went on. "Either you or Mr. Chambers is lying."

"That is certainly true," said Hiss.

"And whichever one of you is lying is the greatest actor that America has ever produced. . . . Up to a few moments ago you have been very open, very cooperative. Now you have hedged. You may be standing on what you consider your right, and I am not objecting to that. I am not pressing you to identify a picture, when you should be faced with the man. That is your right. . . .

"I recognize the fact that this is not an inquisitorial body to the extent of determining where the crime lies. We are not setting forth to determine ourselves which one of you two has perjured yourself. That is the duty of the United States attorney for the District of Columbia. . . .

"Now, if we can get the help from you and, as I say, if I were in your position I certainly would give all the help I could because it is the most fantastic story of unfounded—what motive would Chambers have had or what motive—one of you has to have a motive. You say you are in a bad position, but don't you think Chambers himself destroys himself if he is proven a liar? What motive would he have to pitch a $25,000 position as the respected senior editor of *Time* magazine out the window?"

If the question seems a little naïve at this point, it is because Hébert didn't know what Nixon, Stripling, and Mandel knew about Chambers's activities over the preceding nine years. It was in 1939 that he had first told Adolf Berle that Hiss was a Communist, and at that time Chambers was not a $25,000-a-year senior editor, he was a book reviewer, who was beginning to make his mark at *Time* by his showing of special knowledge about the Communist Party and people he said belonged to it. Hiss, in 1939, had been virtually unknown, a junior in the State Department, who could be safely attacked and had not yet made his name at Dumbarton Oaks and San Francisco. In the intervening years Chambers had repeated his story about Hiss many times to the FBI and other interested people, and had risen high in *Time* on the strength of his anti-Communist expertise. To preserve his $25,000-a-year job he had to make his stories stand up, and to get people to believe them by whatever means he could. It wasn't a question of pitching his job out the window, but of protecting it.

Hiss, however, knew even less about this than Hébert did. So he answered, "Apparently for Chambers to be a confessed former Communist and traitor to his country did not seem to him to be a blot on his record. He got his present job after he had told various agencies exactly that. I am sorry but I cannot but feel—to such an extent that it is difficult for me to control myself—that you can sit there, Mr. Hébert, and say to me casually that you have heard that man and you have heard me, and you just have no basis for judging which one is telling the truth. I don't think a judge determines the credibility of witnesses on that basis."

Hébert stammered rather awkwardly that, even if Chambers was "a self-confessed traitor—and I admit he is," that had no bearing on the matter.

"Has no bearing on his credibility?" Hiss interrupted.

"No," said Hébert. "Because, Mr. Hiss, I recognize the fact that maybe my background is a little different from yours, but I do know police methods and I know crime a great deal, and you show me a good police force and I will show you the stool pigeon who turned them in. . . . I am not giving Mr. Chambers any great credit for his previous life. I am trying to find out if he has reformed. Some of the greatest saints in history were pretty bad before they were saints. Are you going to take away their sainthood because of their previous lives? Are you not going to believe them after they have reformed?"

At this point Hiss was licked, though he didn't realize it. Hébert was the only friend he could have hoped for on the Committee; he was at least a Democrat, not so committed as Rankin to the Strom Thurmond reactionary wing of the party, and he was attending the meetings, which the other two Democrats on the Committee, John S. Wood of Georgia and J. Hardin Peterson of Florida, didn't bother to do. The rest of the committee—Thomas, the Chairman (who was soon to be convicted of accepting payroll kickbacks, sent to jail, and removed from office), Mundt, McDowell, Nixon, and Richard B. Vail of Illinois (who hardly ever appeared)—were all Republicans, standing to benefit in the 1948 election from showing that a prominent Democrat like Hiss was really a Communist. Now Hébert was telling him that his accuser was a saint, and therefore worthy of belief; it was a view that Hiss found obscene and contemptible, but when Hébert's comment was leaked to the press a day or two later it was accepted in vast sections of press and public as the gospel truth.

More argument followed. Hiss complained of reading in the New York *Daily News* that an unidentified member of the Committee had said the Committee believed "that Chambers had personally known Hiss," and he repeated his contention that this was not the issue before the committee. "I am not prepared to say on the basis of the photograph," he said, "that the man, that he is not the man whose name I have written down here. Were I to testify to that, what assurance have I that some member of this committee wouldn't say to the press that Hiss confessed knowing Chambers? . . . I have testified and repeated that I have never known anybody by the name of Whittaker Chambers. I am not prepared to testify I have never seen that man."

The committee gave him no such assurance; and, indeed, the story that Hiss confessed knowing Chambers was very soon in the newspapers. But the Committee wasn't through with him yet. A few minutes later, when the committee recessed to go into executive session, Hiss was asked to wait in the next room.

12

CROSLEY'S TEETH

W HY the Committee sent Hiss out of the room or what they discussed in his absence has never been made clear; it is part of the secret records which HUAC and its successor committees have refused to release. All Nixon said, when Hiss was brought back into the room, was that the Committee had decided there was no hurry about calling Mrs. Hiss to testify. "That is kind of you," said Hiss.

Hiss had used the intervening time to tell his two friends what had been happening so far, and they advised him that it was time to give the Committee Crosley's name. Even if the picture didn't look much like him, the lapse of time and the transformation of a down-at-the-heels free-lancer into a $25,000-a-year *Time* senior editor could account for the difference. Besides, holding back on the name was making a bad impression on the Committee.

If Hiss had any hesitation after that, it was resolved when he realized that the note pad with the words "George Crosley" written on it had been resting on the table in front of his chair during the time he was out of the room. He concluded that the Committee must have seen it, and there was no point in holding back any further. Consequently, he immediately gave the following statement:

"The name of the man I brought in—and he may have no relation to this whole nightmare—is a man named George Crosley. I met him when I was working for the Nye Committee. He was a writer. He hoped to sell articles to magazines about the munitions industry.

"I saw him, as I say, in my office over in the Senate Office Building—[along with] dozens of representatives of the press, students, people writing books, research people. It was our job to give them appropriate information out of the record, show them what had been put in the record. This fellow was writing a series of articles, according to my best recollection, free-lancing, which he hoped to sell to one of the magazines. He was pretty obviously not successful in financial terms, but as far as I know, wasn't actually hard up."

"What color was his hair?" asked Stripling.

"Rather blondish, blonder than any of us here."

"Was he married?"

"Yes, sir."

"Any children?"

"One little baby, as I remember it, and the way I know that was the subleasing point. After we had taken the house on P Street and had the apartment on our hands, he one day, in the course of casual conversation, said he was going to specialize all summer in getting his articles done here in Washington, didn't know what he was going to do, and was thinking of bringing his family.

"I said, 'You can have my apartment. It is not terribly cool, but it is up in the air near the Wardman Park.' [That is, the Wardman Park Hotel; it is now the Sheraton Park.] He said he had a wife and little baby. The apartment wasn't very expensive, and I think I let him have it at exact cost. My recollection is that he spent several nights in my house because his furniture van was delayed. We left several pieces of furniture behind.

"The P Street house belonged to a naval officer overseas and was partly furnished, so we didn't need all our furniture, particularly during the summer months, and my recollection is that definitely, as one does with a tenant trying to make him agreeable and comfortable, we left several pieces of furniture behind until the fall; his van was delayed, wasn't going to bring all the furniture because he was going to be there just during the summer, and we put them up two or three nights in a row, his wife and little baby."

Nixon interrupted at this point to ask, "His wife and he and little baby did spend several nights in the house with you?"

"This man Crosley; yes," said Hiss.

"Can you describe his wife?"

"Yes; she was a rather strikingly dark person, very strikingly dark. I don't know whether I would recognize her again because I didn't see much of her."

"How tall was this man, approximately?"

"Shortish."

"Heavy?"

"Not noticeably. That is why I don't believe it has any direct, but it could have an indirect, bearing." [Chambers in 1948 was very heavy; a round, pudgy, noticeably overweight figure.]

At this point Nixon asked a question that caused great excitement later, though it created no great stir at the time, and there is nothing in the record to show whether it was a shot in the dark or something Chambers had told him about in one of their conversations at the farm. After getting his answer he passed on to other matters; when he wrote *Six Crises* he left out this exchange altogether, as though there had been no preparation for the scene that occurred the following day.

The question was: "How about his teeth?"

"Very bad teeth," said Hiss. "That is one of the things I particularly want to see Chambers about. This man had very bad teeth, did not take care of his teeth." [There was nothing wrong with Chambers's teeth in 1948, at least not in the pictures Hiss had seen.]

"Did he have most of his teeth or just weren't [they] well cared for?" Stripling asked.

"I don't think he had gapped teeth, but they were badly taken care of. They were stained and, I would say, obviously not attended to."

Nixon changed the subject then, with a question about when Chambers rented the Twenty-eighth Street apartment. Hiss said he thought it was about June of 1935; later, when the records were found, it turned out Chambers had had the apartment from mid-April until the end of June in that year.

"What kind of automobile did that fellow have?" asked Stripling.

"No kind of automobile," said Hiss. "I sold him an automobile. I had an old Ford that I threw in with the apartment and had been trying to trade it in and get rid of it. I had an old, old Ford we had kept for sentimental reasons. We got it just before we were married in 1929."

"Was it Model A or Model T?"

"Early A model with a trunk on the back, a slightly collegiate model."

"What color?"

"Dark blue. It wasn't very fancy but it had a sassy little trunk on the back."

"You sold that car?" asked Nixon, remembering what Chambers had said about it the week before.

"I threw it in," said Hiss, who didn't know what Chambers had said, and whose memory of what had actually happened was rather vague after twelve years. "He wanted a way to get around and I said, 'Fine, I want to get rid of it. I have another car, and we kept it for sentimental reasons, not worth a damn.' I let him have it along with the rent."

This later turned out to be one of Hiss's more damaging mistakes, since the record when it was found showed that Hiss had signed the title transfer on July 23, 1936 (as described in Chapter 6). This was more than a year after Chambers had vacated the Twenty-eighth Street apartment, and the discrepancy convinced the Committee and most of the press and public that Hiss had not merely forgotten these details but was lying about them.

A little later Nixon returned to the subject. "You gave this Ford car to Crosley?" he asked.

"Threw it in along with the apartment and charged the rent and threw in the car at the same time," Hiss said.

"In other words, added a little to the rent to cover the car?"

"No," said Hiss, "I think I charged him exactly what I was

paying for the rent and threw the car in, in addition. I don't think I got any compensation."

"You just gave him the car?" Stripling persisted.

"I think the car just went right in with it. I don't remember whether we had settled on the terms of the rent before the car question came up, or whether it came up, and then on the basis of the car and the apartment I said, 'Well, you ought to pay the full rent.' "

Stripling changed the subject for a few minutes, then came back to it. "What kind of a bill of sale did you give Crosley?"

"I think I just turned it over," said Hiss. "In the District you get a certificate of title, I think it is. I think I just simply turned it over to him."

"Handed it to him?"

"Yes."

"No evidence of any transfer. Did he record the title?"

"That I haven't any idea," said Hiss, not remembering the day in 1936, when the title certificate had been brought to him in his office to sign. "This is a car which had been sitting on the streets in snows for a year or two. I once got a parking fine because I forgot where it was parked. We were using the other car." [He had bought a new Plymouth in the summer of 1935, but didn't remember the date.]

Nixon then questioned Hiss at some length on various details of his way of life that Chambers had mentioned on the previous Saturday, without, of course, letting Hiss know that that was what he was doing. Hiss confirmed some of the details and denied others (Priscilla often called him "Hill," sometimes "Hilly"; he called her "Prossy" but never "Dilly," and so on). To Nixon, comparing Hiss's answers with what Chambers had said, it was clear enough that Crosley and Chambers must be the same man, even if the details didn't all check. But Hiss was in a different position. The questions Nixon and Stripling were asking didn't give him any information about Chambers, and he knew nothing about the man except what he had read in the papers. So he still didn't know if his guess was right.

Oddly enough, the points that made the biggest impression

on the Committee were Hiss's statements that yes, he was interested in amateur ornithology ("I think anybody who knows me
would know that," he said), and yes, he had once seen a prothonotary warbler. Representative McDowell, who was also a bird
watcher, asked him the question, and was most impressed because
he had once seen one too. The bird is rare, and bird watchers
consider it a rare privilege to see one; those lucky enough to have
the experience commonly boast about it to all who will listen.
Somehow it became fixed in the minds of the Committee and
their supporters that Hiss had conferred a rare privilege on
Chambers, however, by mentioning it to him, and that this proved
positively that they were intimate friends. The point was tellingly
used against Hiss by Nixon and later, in arguments at the trials,
by Prosecutor Tom Murphy.

One other statement made by Hiss was to prove damaging,
and that was his remark that Crosley had once given him a rug.
It happened when Nixon asked him why he had gone on seeing
Chambers after he had moved out of the apartment without paying any rent. Up to that point Hiss had said nothing about
Chambers's nonpayment of the rent; Nixon was apparently relying on what Chambers had said.

Hiss, not realizing what was behind the question, answered,
"He was about to pay it and was going to sell his articles. He gave
me a payment on account once. He brought a rug over which he
said some wealthy patron had given him. I have still got the
damned thing." [Chambers, who had not mentioned the rug the
previous Saturday, had an explanation when he was asked about
it later: he said the rug was a gift from the Soviet people, as has
been described in Chapter 6.]

"Did you ever give him anything?" Nixon asked.

"Never anything but a couple of loans," said Hiss, "never got
paid back."

Nixon commented that the Committee still didn't know who
to believe, but Chambers had agreed to take a lie detector test,
and would Hiss also be willing to do so? Hiss said he had already
been asked about this by members of the press, and that he had
consulted some knowledgeable friends on the subject, who had

told him such tests were unreliable and unscientific, and measured emotional responses rather than veracity. Nixon pressed him, and Hiss agreed to make further inquiries and give the Committee his answer in a few days.

There the matter rested, and nothing was said about the real problem it created for Hiss: since Chambers had already agreed to take the test, it was clear that he was confident of passing it and thereby strengthening his own position. Having told the same story about Hiss many times in the past nine years, he had no hesitation about repeating it for a lie detector. If Hiss took the test and passed it, that would leave things as they were, and he would be no better off; but if the Committee chose to interpret Hiss's emotional responses as an indication that he was lying, he would be worse off. And Hiss was well aware that his responses during the hearing were highly emotional; if anyone asked him a question about Tim in the course of a lie detector test, the needle would go off the page. So he had everything to lose and nothing to gain. He couldn't afford to take the test, and that fact would later be used against him.

There was only a little more testimony after that. Hiss told the Committee that all Crosley had ever given him for the apartment rent, the car, and the small loans was fifteen or twenty dollars in cash and the rug, and that when they finally parted company Hiss had said, " 'Let's not talk any more about your ever paying back. I don't think you ever intend to, and I would rather forget all of this, and I think you have simply welshed from the beginning.' I didn't ask him to leave the house, but I practically did, and haven't seen him since," Hiss told the Committee. "I made it plain I wouldn't be a sucker."

Nixon asked if Hiss thought that this would be sufficient motive for Chambers to do what he had done, and Hiss replied, "No. That is why I say I can't believe it was the same man. I can't imagine a normal man holding a grudge because somebody had stopped being a sucker." (Later, when Hiss discovered that it was the same man, he concluded that Chambers couldn't be normal. He consulted a psychiatrist on the subject, Dr. Carl Binger, who, after studying the available records of Chambers's life, writings, and testimony, came to the same conclusion.)

After some more discussion, the Committee went off the record and sent Hiss out of the room again, and when he was called back the Chairman told him he would be given an opportunity to see Chambers in a public hearing the following Wednesday, August 25.

"I will be very glad of the chance to confront Mr. Chambers," said Hiss.

Nixon asked if he would rather have it done "informally," and Stripling asked if he wanted it in executive or open session. Hiss said it didn't matter to him. Nixon pointed out that "if you have a public session, it is a show." Hébert said he wanted it in public; Hiss said he had no preference. Stripling objected that it would be "ballyhooed into a circus," and that he preferred an executive session.

Hiss asked to be heard, and said: "I want to be clear that I am not asking for an executive session as opposed to public. As far as consideration to me after what has been done to my feelings and my reputation, I think it would be like sinking the Swiss Navy. No public show could embarrass me now. I am asking to see this man."

Nixon said Hiss should be given time to think it over, adding that, "We will also give Mr. Chambers an opportunity." The matter could be decided later.

Then Hiss said, "May I ask a question about the press?"

Chairman Thomas answered, "Yes. I want to tell you something. Every person in this room with the exception of yourself has stood up and raised his right hand and taken an oath that he will not divulge one single word of testimony given here this afternoon, questions asked, so I am going to ask you to take the same oath."

"No," said Nixon, "that is up to him."

"He can do what he wants to do," said Hébert.

"I have thought of this problem and wanted to raise it specifically," said Hiss. "I wanted to ask the committee's views as to what they preferred. I will be guided as far as I think I honestly can in terms of my own self-protection by what I now take to be the committee's view that this is executive."

"We are not going to divulge anything," said Chairman Thomas.

Nixon suggested that only two copies be made of the transcript, one to be delivered to Hiss and the other for the Committee clerk.

"We have sworn ourselves to secrecy," said Hébert.

Nixon then said he would like Mrs. Hiss to testify "before the public session on Wednesday," and Hiss agreed to arrange it. She would have to come down from Peacham, Vermont, a full day's journey each way. Stripling said there would be "absolutely no publicity" about her appearance, and Nixon added, "We don't want it here."

"Thank you for coming," Chairman Thomas said, "and we will see you August 25." The session ended at 5:30 P.M., three and a half hours after it had begun.

Hiss flew back to New York that evening, and was more angry than surprised to read in the newspapers the following morning that the Committee had asked him to submit to a lie detector test and to arrange for Mrs. Hiss to come and testify, as well as revealing other details of his testimony. So much for the Committee's oath of secrecy, he thought.

Later that day Hiss was shocked to read in the early afternoon editions that Harry Dexter White, the Assistant Secretary of the Treasury, whom Chambers had called a Communist fellow traveler, had died of a heart attack. White had been questioned by the Committee on Friday, and had told the Committee at the time that he was recovering from a severe heart attack, and would appreciate five or ten minutes rest after each hour of testimony. Chairman Thomas had made a sarcastic comment about it, and the spectators had applauded White. As the questioning continued, there had been a good deal more applause for White, and Thomas had admonished the audience to stop it. His sudden death was now an embarrassment to the Committee; columnist

Thomas L. Stokes called White a "victim of tyranny." In due course rumors were circulated that he hadn't really died from heart disease at all, but perhaps had been a suicide. The rumors were, of course, quite untrue; White's doctors attested to the genuineness of the heart disease and the final attack.

Meanwhile, Hiss received a telephone call from Donald Appell of the Committee's staff, who said Representative McDowell was going to be in New York late that afternoon and wanted to see him for ten or fifteen minutes. Hiss asked whether it was on Committee business or some other matter; McDowell was the only member of the Committee with whom Hiss on occasion had other business, and except for his interest in the prothonotary warbler McDowell had taken little part in the Committee's questioning of him. Appell said he didn't know what McDowell wanted. Hiss agreed to be available in his midtown office, at Fifth Avenue and Forty-fourth Street, during the afternoon.

A little before 5:30 that afternoon McDowell called Hiss and asked him to come to the Commodore Hotel, a few blocks away at Park Avenue and Forty-second Street, adding that Nixon and "one other" were with him. Hiss smelt a trap, and asked his friend Charles Dollard (who had originally urged him to have nothing to do with the Committee) to come with him. They went to the hotel room, and found Stripling, Wheeler, Russell, Appell, and Mandel there, as well as Nixon and McDowell and a stenographer. Chairman Thomas arrived later.

As quickly became apparent, this was to be the "confrontation" of Hiss and Chambers which had been discussed the day before, and it was to take place in executive session, as Stripling wanted, and immediately rather than on the following Wednesday, August 25, as the Committee had first decided. The events that had led to this change of plan were later described in quite different ways by Nixon in *Six Crises* and by Chambers in *Witness*.

According to Nixon, he and Stripling had spent several hours in Nixon's office after Hiss's testimony of the day before, comparing notes on their reactions. "We were convinced that Crosley and Chambers were the same man," Nixon wrote. "Chambers did know Hiss. But the key question remained: which man was telling the truth as to the character of that relationship?" Nixon and Stripling decided that the key to the problem was the old Ford roadster; every available member of the Committee staff was to concentrate on looking for records that would show what had happened to it.

Stripling left Nixon's office shortly before midnight, but Nixon went on thinking about his problem. He came to the conclusion that he would be playing into Hiss's hands by delaying the confrontation until August 25, "thus giving him nine more days to make his story fit the facts." So he decided not to delay.

"At two in the morning," Nixon wrote, "I called Stripling on the phone. I told him to summon Chambers and Hiss before the subcommittee in New York City that same afternoon. Desiring as much privacy as possible, we decided to have the meeting in a suite in the Commodore Hotel."

It was only after arranging the meeting, Nixon wrote, that he read about White's death in the newspapers, and he complained that "the Committee was subsequently to be accused of arranging the Hiss–Chambers confrontation on August 17 in order to divert attention from White's death. All I can say," he added, "is that this accusation—like so many others against the Committee—while plausible, is completely untrue. I myself had made the decision on the confrontation well before I learned of White's death."

Chambers meanwhile, not having heard what Hiss had said that previous afternoon, was "listless and undecided as to what I must do," according to his account in *Witness*. "Every venture into public had become an ordeal for me." Nevertheless, on the morning of August 17, he wrote, "I forced myself to leave the farm to go to New York. But by the time I reached Baltimore, I felt a curious need to go and see the Committee. . . . The impulse was so strong that, after buying a ticket for New York, I took the train for Washington."

At about noon he started up the steps of the Old House Office Building, using a back entrance to avoid newsmen, just as Mandel and Appell were coming out the door. "They were astonished to see me and greeted me with wild relief," Chambers wrote. "They had been frantically trying to reach me at home, in New York and Washington. . . . No one would tell me why I was wanted. Instead, the subcommittee bundled me into a car crammed with its staff. As we rolled to the Union Station, Appell wrested a newspaper out of his pocket and pointed to a headline: Harry Dexter White had died of a heart attack." After that Chambers asked no further questions, or at least none are recorded in *Witness*. He describes how he was taken to New York, still not knowing why, and how he stared out the train window wondering why other people's lives were so much more routine and uncomplicated than his.

The Committee had taken a two-room suite in the Commodore; Chambers waited in the bedroom, while Hiss was shown into the sitting room. He introduced Dollard to the Committee, and asked if someone could call the Harvard Club for him and cancel his 6:00 appointment, since it was clear the proceedings would last more than the ten or fifteen minutes he had been told. McDowell gave permission, and Dollard made the call.

Hiss then asked for permission to make a statement, and McDowell said, "Certainly." Hiss went on: "I would like the record to show that on my way downtown from my uptown office, I learned from the press of the death of Harry White, which came as a great shock to me, and I am not sure that I feel in the best possible mood for testimony. I do not for a moment want to miss the opportunity of seeing Mr. Chambers. I merely want the record to show that."

The Committee made no comment, and Hiss went on to his next point. He reminded the Committee of the oath of secrecy that had been described the previous day, complaining about the newspaper stories he had read about the lie detector test, the arrangements for his wife's testimony, and "other bits of my testimony which could only have come from the committee. They did not come from me," he added.

"I would like the record to show that is why I asked if I could bring Mr. Dollard, a personal friend, to be with me at this particular time," Hiss said.

Nixon brushed the protest aside and commented that Hiss

could find out about the newspaper story by asking the reporter who had written it—a staff member of the *New York Herald Tribune's* Washington Bureau who worked under Bert Andrews. Nixon asserted that neither he nor any member of the Committee had talked to that reporter. Hiss said he hadn't said anybody did, but somebody must have. McDowell, who was acting as chairman, interrupted to offer an apology.

"I, too, was greatly disturbed when I read the morning paper," he said. "Obviously, there was a leak, because the story that appeared in the various papers I read was part of the activities of yesterday afternoon. I have no idea how this story got out. In my own case, I very carefully guarded myself last night, saw and talked to no one except my wife in Pittsburgh. It is regrettable and unfortunate.

"Further than that, I don't know what else to say other than if it was an employee of the committee, and I should discover it, he will no longer be an employee of the committee. As a member of Congress, there is nothing I can do about that. It is a regrettable thing, and I join you in feeling rather rotten about the whole thing."

Hiss replied that he didn't mean to make any charges, just to state certain facts, which had a bearing on statements he had made before. McDowell then changed the subject by welcoming Dollard to the proceedings, and Nixon asked Russell to bring Chambers in. Chambers entered and sat down on a sofa next to Ben Mandel. Hiss was in a chair on the opposite side of the room, his back to the door through which Chambers entered.

There ensued a weird scene, in which Hiss, as so often before, dug himself into deeper trouble. It began when Nixon asked both men to stand and face each other, and said, "Mr. Hiss, the man standing here is Mr. Whittaker Chambers. I ask you now if you have ever known that man before?"

"May I ask him to speak?" said Hiss. "Will you ask him to say something?"

"Yes," said Nixon. "Mr. Chambers, will you tell us your name and your business."

"My name is Whittaker Chambers," he answered.

Hiss walked toward him, saying, "Would you mind opening your mouth wider?"

(As Hiss described the experience nine years later in his own book, *In the Court of Public Opinion*, he thought the short, plump figure in the rumpled suit was certainly familiar and might be George Crosley, but he wanted to hear his voice and see if he had Crosley's bad teeth to make sure.* "Chambers," he wrote, "did not meet my eye, but stared fixedly before him or up to the ceiling. He had given his name in a tight, rather high-pitched, constrained voice, barely opening his mouth. This seemed evidently not the man's normal voice, nor could I see if his front teeth were decayed.

"In response to my request that in speaking he open his mouth wider, he was able only to repeat his name, again in a strangled voice, through almost closed lips.")

Hiss repeated his request, "I said, would you open your mouth?" And in an aside, remembering the previous day's exchange, he added, "You know what I am referring to, Mr. Nixon." Then to Chambers: "Will you go on talking?"

"I am senior editor of *Time* magazine," said Chambers in the same tone as before.

Hiss turned to the Committee. "May I ask whether his voice, when he testified before, was comparable to this?"

"His voice?" asked Nixon.

"Or did he talk a little more in a lower key?"

"I would say it is about the same now as we have heard," said McDowell.

---

* Lionel Trilling, who knew Chambers at Columbia and used him as the source for one of the characters in his novel, *The Middle of the Journey*, commented in 1975 on the striking appearance of Chambers's teeth in his Communist period, and said he had not given the same appearance to his fictional character because "to do so would have been to go too far in explicitness of personal reference." In an article in *The New York Review of Books*, Trilling wrote, "When his [Chambers's] mouth opened, it never failed to shock by reason of the dental ruin it disclosed, a devastation of empty sockets and blackened stumps."

Hiss asked if Chambers could talk a little more, commenting that "I think he is George Crosley, but I would like to hear him talk a little longer." Then he turned to Chambers and asked him directly, "Are you George Crosley?"

"Not to my knowledge," said Chambers. "You are Alger Hiss, I believe."

"I certainly am," said Hiss.

"That was my recollection," said Chambers, and began reading aloud from a copy of *Newsweek* magazine that Nixon had given him.

Hiss was baffled by Chambers's "Not to my knowledge." As Nixon describes it, Chambers made the statement with "a quizzical smile," but its meaning was lost on Hiss. As before, when he had been misled by Nixon and Stripling, Hiss assumed that Chambers meant what he seemed to be saying—he wasn't Crosley after all. So Hiss had to check more carefully before making the identification in the face of this denial. (Later, of course, Chambers gave a fuller explanation under cross-examination at Hiss's perjury trial. He testified that he had "never been able to remember" what name he had used while living in Hiss's apartment on Twenty-eighth Street, and "it may have been" Crosley, though he wasn't sure. "It is a possibility," he said. Among other names he recalled using at various times were John Kelly, David Breen, Lloyd Cantwell, Charles Adams, Arthur Dwyer, Bob, Carl, Charles Whittaker, and David Chambers. His legal name, as shown on his birth certificate, was Jay Vivian Chambers.)

Nixon interrupted at this point to comment that "Some repartee is going on between these two people," and to suggest that Chambers be sworn. Hiss, who was already smarting under the impression that Chambers was being treated more as "part of the Committee's retinue" than as a witness, remarked with deliberate sarcasm, "That is a good idea." McDowell administered the oath, and Nixon followed it with a rebuke.

"Mr. Hiss, may I say something?" he asked with sarcasm of his own. "I suggested that he be sworn, and when I say something like that I want no interruptions from you."

Hiss lost his temper. "Mr. Nixon," he said, "in view of what happened yesterday, I think there is no occasion for you to use that tone of voice in speaking to me, and I hope the record will show what I have just said."

"The record shows everything that is being said here today," said Nixon.

Stripling told Chambers to go on with his reading, and after about thirty words Hiss interrupted.

"The voice sounds a little less resonant than the voice that I recall of the man I know as George Crosley," Hiss said. "The teeth look to me as though either they have been improved upon or that there has been considerable dental work done since I knew George Crosley, which was some years ago. I believe I am not prepared without further checking to take an absolute oath that he must be George Crosley."

Nixon then took over. "I will ask the questions at this time," he said. "Mr. Chambers, have you had any dental work since 1934 of a substantial nature?" Chambers said he had "a plate in place of some of the upper dentures."

Hiss said he wanted the dentist's name so that he could find out if this were true, "Because I am relying partly, one of my main recollections of Crosley was the poor condition of his teeth."

"Do you feel that you would have to have the dentist tell you just what he did to the teeth before you could tell anything about this man?" Nixon asked.

"I would like a few more questions asked," said Hiss. "I didn't intend to say anything about this, because I feel very strongly that he is Crosley, but he looks very different in girth and in other appearances—hair, forehead, and so on, especially the jowls."

Instead of letting Hiss ask the questions he wanted, Nixon cross-examined him on his testimony of the previous day about his meeting with Crosley and the arrangements about the apartment, the car, and the rug. When he finished, Stripling took over, making the point that, after knowing Crosley so well, Hiss ought to be able to remember him without examining his teeth.

"There is nothing else about this man's features which you could definitely say, 'This is the man I knew as George Crosley,' that you have to rely entirely on this denture," said Stripling. "Is that your position?"

Hiss answered at some length that this was not his position at all. "If this man had said he was George Crosley," he added, "I would have had no difficulty in identification. He denied it right here. I would like and asked earlier in this hearing if I could ask some further questions in identification. I was denied that."

Stripling interrupted, "I think you should be permitted—" but Hiss went angrily on.

"I was denied that right. I am not, therefore, able to take an oath that this man is George Crosley. I have been testifying about George Crosley. Whether he and this man are the same or whether he has means of getting information from George Crosley about my house, I do not know. He may have had his face lifted."

Stripling said he thought Hiss should be permitted to ask any questions he wanted, and McDowell, as acting Chairman, agreed.

"Do I have Mr. Nixon's permission?" Hiss asked.

"Yes," said Nixon. "The only suggestion I would make in fairness to Mr. Chambers is that he should also be given the opportunity to ask Mr. Hiss any questions."

Chambers had no objection, and Hiss proceeded with his questions. As before, they got him into more trouble.

"Did you ever go under the name of George Crosley?" He began.

"Not to my knowledge," said Chambers as before.

"Did you ever sublet an apartment on Twenty-ninth Street from me?" [Hiss had forgotten the address again; he should have said Twenty-eighth Street.]

"No, I did not."

"You did not?"

"No."

But the Committee had assured Hiss that Chambers had spent some time there. He rephrased the question:

"Did you ever spend any time with your wife and child in

an apartment on Twenty-ninth Street in Washington when I was not there because I and my family were living on P Street?"

"I most certainly did."

Then Chambers might be Crosley after all. But why was he contradicting himself? Hiss tried again, in the stilted language of a lawyer.

"Would you tell me how you reconcile your negative answers with this affirmative answer?"

"Very easily, Alger. I was a Communist and you were a Communist."

There it was; a repetition of the charge, made in a context that seemed to prove Chambers's point and made Hiss seem the liar. At first, Hiss didn't know what to make of it; he had never known before that Crosley was a Communist. As he described it in *In the Court of Public Opinion*, "This oracular statement revived my earlier sense of fantasy or dream." He temporized with another question, "Would you be responsive and continue with your answer?"

"I do not think it is needed," said Chambers.

Then the truth dawned on Hiss. "That is the answer," he said, more to himself than anyone else.

It was the answer to a lot of things. If Crosley had been a Communist and had thought Hiss was a Communist, it explained why Crosley had never bothered to pay Hiss the rent or the small loans. If Chambers was the man who had lived in the Twenty-eighth Street apartment, then Chambers was Crosley, whether he denied it or not. And if Crosley had been a Communist, it explained why he had changed his name. If Chambers was an ex-Communist turned anti-Communist, as he said, and still believed Hiss had been a Communist, that would explain why Chambers was attacking him now. For the first time, Hiss understood who Chambers was, and what he was doing and why. Now at last Hiss realized the trouble he was in. But he didn't yet understand how bad it was. He was only beginning to put the puzzle together.

Nixon intervened to ask Chambers some questions of his own, taking him again over his previous testimony about Hiss being a Communist and the friend who had offered the use of his apartment. Hiss interrupted to say, "Mr. Chairman, I don't need to ask Whittaker Chambers any more questions. I am now perfectly prepared to identify this man as George Crosley."

Stripling challenged him to produce three other people who could identify him as Crosley, and Hiss said he would see what he could do. It wasn't going to be easy; Hiss had not known Crosley well enough to introduce him to any of his friends, and the likelihood that anybody on the Nye Committee would remember the name after thirteen years was not great. There was no way of knowing whether Chambers had called himself Crosley in dealing with anyone else besides Hiss. As it turned out, the only person outside the Hiss household who ever came forward to identify Chambers as Crosley was Samuel Roth, a pornography publisher, who had done time in jail for obscenity. This was not the kind of person Hiss wanted to testify in his behalf at the perjury trial, and Roth's offer to do so was turned down, over his offended protests. Roth said he could have testified that Chambers had once sent him some poems under the name of George Crosley, but Roth hadn't published them. He had no documentary proof of this recollection, and by that time it was too late to help Hiss anyway; the question of Chambers's identity was not an issue at the trial. But in the Committee hearings it was an argument Nixon used to undermine Hiss's credibility.

Hiss was thoroughly angry by now, and his mood was not improved when Nixon said to him, "Mr. Hiss, another point that I want to be clear on. Mr. Chambers said he was a Communist and that you were a Communist."

"I heard him," said Hiss.

"Will you tell the committee whether or not during this period of time that you knew him, which included periods of three nights, or two or three nights, in which he stayed overnight and one trip to New York, from any conversation you ever had any idea that he might be a Communist?"

"I certainly didn't," said Hiss.

"You never discussed politics?"

"Oh, as far as I recall his conversations—and I may be confusing them with a lot of other conversations that went on in 1934 and 1935—politics were discussed frequently.

"May I just state for the record that it was not the habit in Washington in those days, when particularly if a member of the press called on you, to ask him before you had further conversation whether or not he was a Communist. It was a quite different atmosphere in Washington then than today. I had no reasons to suspect George Crosley of being a Communist. It never occurred to me that he might be or whether that was of any significance to me if he was." [By this statement, though Hiss didn't realize it, he was condemning himself out of his own mouth. What he said might be true enough, but as Dulles had warned him nearly two weeks before, it was the sort of attitude the Committee would expect him to apologize for and repudiate in 1948. To recall it in these defiant tones, as though it had been the right view to take in 1934–1935 and might still be the right view in similar circumstances, was only to persuade the Committee that he was still and always had been at least a Communist fellow traveler, if not a card-carrying party member. But Hiss didn't stop to think of these things; he hurried on with his statement.]

"He was a press representative and it was my duty to give him information, as I did any other member of the press. It was to the interest of the committee investigating the munitions industry, as its members and we of its staff saw it, to furnish guidance and information to people who were popularizing and writing about its work.

"I would like to say that to come here and discover that the ass under the lion's skin is Crosley, I don't know why your committee didn't pursue this careful method of interrogation at an earlier date before all the publicity. You told me yesterday that you didn't know he was going to mention my name, although a lot of people now tell me that the press did know it in advance. They were apparently more effective in getting information than the committee itself. That is all I have to say now."

"Well, now, Mr. Hiss," McDowell said, "you positively identify—"

"Positively on the basis of his own statement that he was in my apartment at the time I say he was there," Hiss interrupted. "I have no further questions at all. If he had lost both eyes and taken his nose off, I would be sure."

McDowell turned to Chambers, who was equally positive that Hiss was a member of the Communist Party at whose home he had stayed. Hiss got up from his chair and walked toward Chambers, saying:

"May I say for the record at this point that I would like to invite Mr. Whittaker Chambers to make those same statements out of the presence of this committee without their being privileged for suit for libel. I challenge you to do it, and I hope you will do it damned quickly."

This was a tactic Chambers had not expected, and until that moment it had not entered Hiss's head either. For the first time since the whole ordeal began he felt he was on solid ground; he now knew who Chambers was, knew Chambers was lying and libeling him, and had not the slightest doubt he could prove it. He acted in anger, without stopping to consider the consequences; only later did he find he had walked into a trap from which there was no way out.

Chambers, as he makes clear in *Witness*, was not happy about the prospect of being sued for libel, but it was too late for him to back down. The question was very soon put to him on Lawrence Spivak's "Meet the Press" radio program, and he answered flatly, "Alger Hiss was a Communist and may still be one." Hiss then brought suit, and in the examination before trial it became clear to Chambers and his lawyers that he couldn't hope to win the suit with the kind of testimony he had given so far. It might be good enough for HUAC, but it wouldn't stand up in court. So Chambers produced the documents which came to be called the "pumpkin papers," and made extensive changes in his testimony to account for them. And it was this changed testimony and these documents which led to Hiss's trial and conviction.

There were many lawyers who might have advised Hiss not to challenge Chambers to a libel suit, if he had asked for advice, since such suits are extremely difficult to win and generally do the plaintiff more harm than good. But Hiss had flung down the challenge in the heat of anger and never for a moment considered withdrawing it. He had by that time lost all hope of getting fair treatment from the Committee, and wanted the argument adjourned to a court, where he would have the protection of judicial procedure. He wanted to be able to cross-examine Chambers according to the rules of evidence, and to have the same rules applied to prevent the bullying he had received from the Committee. He was confident of his innocence, and wanted to prove it in court.

His anger was so obvious that Russell, one of the Committee investigators, intervened as he approached Chambers, apparently fearing that the quarrel would come to blows. In Nixon's description, Russell "walked up to" Hiss and "took him by the arm. Hiss recoiled as if he had been pricked with a hot needle."

"I am not going to touch him," Hiss said to Russell. "You are touching me."

"Please sit down, Mr. Hiss," said Russell.

"I will sit down when the chairman asks me. Mr. Russell, when the chairman asks me to sit down—"

"I want no disturbance," said Russell.

"I don't—" Hiss began.

And McDowell cut in, "Sit down, please."

"You know who started this," said Hiss.

McDowell called a short recess and left the room. When he returned, Hiss said, "Mr. Chairman, would you be good enough to ask Mr. Chambers, for the record, his response to the challenge that I have just made to him?"

But McDowell wouldn't do that, and a few minutes of argument on the point followed, and then a great deal more argument on a variety of other subjects. Hiss was cross-examined about his earlier testimony, and Chambers added a few details to his own. Hiss asked if the Committee intended to give any publicity to the afternoon's testimony; McDowell said he didn't know, and Nixon promised him an answer in five minutes, but didn't give it. The Committee decided to have their public session the following Wednesday, August 25, at which time both Hiss and Chambers would appear. Chairman Thomas, who had arrived a few minutes before and missed most of the testimony, insisted on issuing subpoenas to both, although Hiss said he would appear voluntarily and the subpoena was unnecessary. Hiss told the Committee that he had asked his wife to come to New York and testify, as the Committee had requested, and Nixon agreed to see her the following day.

At 7:15 P.M. the session was adjourned, an hour and forty minutes after it had begun. Chairman Thomas said to Hiss: "That is all. Thank you very much."

"I don't reciprocate," said Hiss angrily.

"Italicize that in the record," Thomas said to the stenographer.

"I wish you would," said Hiss. And so it was done.

13

THE DUMBWAITER SHAFT

HISS was a gone goose when he left the Commodore that evening but he was unaware of it. Priscilla was arriving on the slow day train from Vermont, and the hearing finished in time for him to meet her at Grand Central Terminal and have a late dinner before going back to the apartment. Then he tried to reach Nixon at the Commodore to fix a time for Priscilla's testimony the following day, but Nixon's phone was busy. He soon found out why —Nixon was calling the press.

The phone began ringing at Hiss's apartment, and it was a succession of newsmen reporting to him what Nixon had told them about the day's testimony. Hiss had confessed knowing Chambers, Nixon had said; Chambers had proved Hiss a Communist and a liar. Nixon believed in Chambers, and most of the press believed in Nixon.

"A great hurdle had been surmounted," Nixon wrote of the day's developments in *Six Crises*. "The inextricable chain of events that would ultimately send Alger Hiss to prison had been set in motion, and Hiss must have sensed this."

What Hiss sensed, as he told John Foster Dulles in a phone call that evening, was that he and the Committee were now at war. Dulles counseled caution as before, but Hiss was through taking Dulles's advice. He replied that he was going to fight back as best he could.

He started by calling a press conference of his own at midnight, and a large group of reporters showed up. But it did him no good; Nixon's story had been on the press wires for hours, and the early editions of the morning papers were already on the street with it. Nixon got the headlines in the afternoon papers too; Hiss's reply, when it was used at all, was buried as a brief and rather obvious rebuttal. Hardly anybody believed it; of course, if Nixon said Hiss was a liar, he would tell some more lies in his own defense. And the full transcript of the hearing was still secret, since it had been an executive session.

When Hiss finally reached Nixon on the phone that night they confined their discussion to arrangements for Priscilla's testimony, and the following morning she went to the Commodore at 11:00. Nixon was acting as a subcommittee of one, assisted by Donald Appell, an investigator. Before Priscilla arrived Nixon had brief interviews with Nelson Frank, a reporter on Scripps–Howard's *New York World–Telegram*, which was solidly committed to Nixon's anti-Communist crusade, and after she left he questioned Isaac Don Levine, editor of *Plain Talk*, the anti-Communist magazine published by Alfred Kohlberg.

Frank told Nixon he had been a part-time reporter on the Communist *Daily Worker* in 1928 and that he had known Chambers from then until 1932, after which he had not seen him again until late in 1944. He confirmed that Chambers had noticeably bad teeth in 1932, but had "got himself a nice set of teeth" by 1944. Frank had had no difficulty recognizing him at the time; at Nixon's request he promised to see if he could get some pictures of Chambers as he had looked in the 1930s.

Levine said he had known Chambers since 1939 and described the occasion when he had taken Chambers to see Adolf Berle in early September of that year. He said he had watched Chambers's career since then and had come to regard him as "a crystal honest person, dependable, sound, patriotic, intelligent, without malice toward anyone, with a high sense of justice and fair play." He was sure he could have recognized him from his current pictures, even if he had not seen him since 1939.

Between these two interviews Appell left the room, and

Nixon himself interviewed Priscilla for ten minutes, so far as the record shows. Apparently a stenographer was present, and Hiss and Dollard were also there. Dollard took no part in the proceedings; Hiss told his wife to stand while the oath was administered, and thanked Nixon for his courtesy at the end of the hearing, but otherwise said nothing. Mrs. Hiss asked if she had to swear to the oath, and Nixon, remembering that Chambers had said she was a Quaker, told her she could affirm instead, which she did.

Nixon asked her what she recalled about George Crosley, and it wasn't much. She couldn't remember when she had first met him, or what the occasion was; she had a "vague recollection of this man and his wife looking at the apartment which we sublet to them," and "a very distinct memory of their spending two or three days in our house before they moved into the sublet apartment." She had "a very dim impression of a small person, very smiling person—a little too smiley, perhaps. I don't recollect the face," she said, "but a short person."

"I am afraid the only impression I have was of being a little put out," she said.

"Put out about what?" asked Nixon.

"Well, I think the polite word for it is probably I think he was a sponger. I don't know whether you have ever had guests, unwelcome guests, guests that weren't guests, you know."

Nixon stopped questioning her after that, concluding, as he wrote later, that she was "nervous and frightened." He told Mrs. Hiss he appreciated her coming, and she replied; "I am glad it has been so quiet, because that was really what I had a strong distaste for. I would like to thank you for our just being together."

From that point on, Nixon and Hiss, in their different ways, prepared for the public hearing of August 25, then only a week off. Nixon drove the committee staff "at an even harder pace" to find corroborative evidence, and stepped up his own activity until he was "spending as much as eighteen to twenty hours a day" at his office, according to his own account. He couldn't find anyone who remembered knowing Chambers as George Crosley, but the Committee staff did find the 1936 Motor Vehicle Department record of the title transfer of the old Ford car. They were ahead of Hiss's investigators in this, and removed the document from the files, so that when Hiss's agent looked for it it wasn't there.

They found the lease on the Twenty-eighth Street apartment, which had expired on July 1, 1935, not September 1, as Hiss had thought (nor August 1, as Nixon wrote in *Six Crises*); and they found the title certificate to Hiss's Plymouth sedan, which was dated September 7, 1935, though Hiss remembered driving it earlier that summer, and concluded he must have used it for a while with the dealer's plates on it.* It was a demonstration car, and such accommodations were not unusual at that stage of the Depression. Better still, from the Committee's viewpoint, they found the name William Rosen on the title certificate of the Ford, with a false address; and they found a man of that name who was a known Communist and took the Fifth Amendment when he was asked to testify. All this could be used against Hiss in a public cross-examination.

Hiss, meanwhile, hired John F. Davis, a Washington lawyer, to make similar investigations, and consulted Max Lowenthal, a New York lawyer and close friend, who had been counsel to the Pecora Committee, on preparing a statement to read at the forthcoming hearing. Lowenthal wanted Hiss to strike back at the Committee in forceful language, appealing for public support over the Committee's head, since he had obviously lost all chance of changing the Committee's mind. Hiss thought that would be out of character for him; he didn't like to be bombastic. But he took his friend's advice, and signed his name to a statement, which he didn't like, and which ultimately did him no good.

Lowenthal and Hiss correctly guessed that the Committee wouldn't allow him to read the statement at the opening of the hearing, so they wrote it in the form of a letter to the Committee and released it to the press beforehand. It began by identifying the attack on Hiss with the political issues of the 1948 election, an approach which worried Hiss because he thought of his problem as an entirely personal affair. Lowenthal's instinct was sound,

* Chambers thought Hiss had the Plymouth as early as Easter 1935, according to his testimony in the second trial.

as later events proved, but the compromise he and Hiss reached was so woolly worded that it could hardly have enlisted much support.

The statement said, "This charge [that Hiss was a Communist] goes beyond the personal. Attempts will be made to use it, and the resulting publicity, to discredit recent great achievements of this country in which I was privileged to participate. [The reference was to the New Deal reforms, the Roosevelt foreign policy, and the establishment of the United Nations.] Certain members of your committee have already demonstrated that this use of your hearings and the ensuing publicity is not a mere possibility, it is a reality. Your acting chairman, Mr. Mundt himself, was trigger-quick to cast such discredit.

"Before I had a chance to testify, even before the press had a chance to reach me for comment, before you had sought one single fact to support the charge made by a self-confessed liar, spy and traitor, your acting chairman pronounced judgment that I am guilty as charged, by stating that the country should beware of the peace work with which I have been connected.

"I urge that these committee members abandon such verdict-first-and-testimony-later tactics, along with dramatic confrontations in secret sessions, and get down to business."

This was not the kind of thing the Committee wanted read in its presence, so Hiss was prevented from reading it as long as possible. Only after he had been cross-examined from 10:30 A.M. until past 5:00 P.M., on August 25, and every member of the Committee present—Thomas, Mundt, McDowell, Nixon, and even Vail—had had an opportunity to show why he thought Hiss was lying, was he allowed to read the statement. By that time newsmen and spectators were exhausted, as was Hiss, but he doggedly read it through to the end.

It continued with a summary of Hiss's public career, and a long list of personages in the Senate, the House, the Judiciary, the State Department, and in other aspects of public life, from Republican Sen. Arthur H. Vandenberg to Mrs. Eleanor Roosevelt, the late President's widow, with whom Hiss had been associated and who, he said, were in a position to know he wasn't a

Communist. "Ask them if they ever found in me anything except the highest adherence to duty and honor," Hiss said.

Then there was more criticism of the way the Committee had handled the inquiry, and a protest that Hiss couldn't be expected to answer the kind of questions the Committee had been asking, about where he had lived and when, and what he had done with his old car, until he could consult the records, which he hadn't been able to do. This was a fair point, and even more relevant at the end of the day's long hearing than at the beginning, because all through the hearing the Committee had been in possession of records that Hiss hadn't been able to find. Nothing was more damaging to him than the way Nixon used the motor vehicle records on the old Ford. It was made irresistibly and repetitiously clear that Hiss, in his earlier testimony, had been all wrong about what he had done with that car, and unaware of what had happened to it after he gave it to Crosley. Under Nixon's cross-examination it was useless for Hiss to say it was a case of mistaken recollection and misplaced confidence; in Nixon's view, and in the view of every other Committee member before the hearing ended, it was a case of Hiss deliberately telling lies.

Hiss concluded his statement with what he called, "One personal word. My action in being kind to Crosley years ago," he said, "was one of humaneness, with results which surely some members of the committee have experienced. You do a favor for a man, he comes for another, he gets a third favor from you. When you finally realize he is an inveterate repeater, you get rid of him. If your loss is only a loss of time and money, you are lucky. You may find yourself calumniated in a degree depending on whether the man is unbalanced or worse."

The Committee were unimpressed. They resumed their cross-examination of Hiss for nearly another hour, and then put Chambers on the stand to reassert some points that had been called in question during the day. The hearing ended at 8:00 P.M., after a session of nine and a half hours, including a 1½-hour lunch break. It had been exactly what Nixon and Stripling had said it would be: a show ballyhooed into a circus, with a sellout audience packed into the big caucus room, radio broadcasters, klieg lights, motion picture cameras for the movie newsreels, and that still new invention, television cameras. Nixon called it the first major congressional hearing ever to be televised, and regretted that so few Americans owned TV sets in 1948. The transcript of the hearing covers 131 closely printed pages; at the beginning of the day the Committee announced it was releasing at that time the transcripts of the executive sessions of August 7, 16, 17, and 18, which came to a total of 84 additional pages. But these were no longer news, since so much of the testimony had already been leaked to the newspapers.

Hiss's reputation was now thoroughly destroyed, so far as public opinion went, and he had become an embarrassment to the Carnegie Endowment. Dulles hinted rather strongly, if he didn't say it in so many words, that he thought Hiss ought to resign. Hiss, hoping to clear himself by winning his libel suit against Chambers, asked for more time; to resign at once would only damage his case and weaken his position. Dulles couldn't very well refuse, but he asked James T. Shotwell, a Columbia professor and long-time official of the Endowment, to take over "administrative direction" of the institution in the meantime. Evidently Dulles thought he was thereby relieving Hiss of his duties so that he could devote himself full time to his defense, but Shotwell and Hiss didn't see it that way. Hiss continued to do his Endowment job as usual, and Shotwell, who had full confidence in him, kept Dulles supplied with optimistic reports on the progress of Hiss's legal moves against Chambers, sending Dulles copies of the letters of support that were coming in.

Dulles was evidently more impressed by a letter he received in early September from Nixon. It was a four-page, single-spaced, typed letter summing up all the evidence against Hiss that Nixon found in the HUAC testimony, and focusing on the weak points in Hiss's positions.

"I have come to the conclusion," wrote Nixon, "that at the very least Hiss deliberately misled the committee in several important respects during his appearances before it. Whether he was guilty of technical perjury or whether it has been established definitely that he was a member of the Communist Party are issues which may still be open to debate, but there is no longer any doubt in my mind that for reasons only he can give, he was trying to keep the committee from learning the truth in regard to his relationship with Chambers."

This was apparently enough for Dulles, who was expecting to become Secretary of State when Dewey won the election, which every Republican then confidently expected him to do. It would only jeopardize his political position to be associated with any-one in the situation Nixon described. So he circulated copies of Nixon's letter to several of the trustees, and thanked Nixon for "setting out so carefully your conclusions." Then he went to Paris to attend a meeting of the UN General Assembly, leaving Vice Chairman John W. Davis in charge of the Endowment's affairs.

Chambers, meanwhile, had accepted Hiss's challenge to repeat his statements outside the HUAC hearing room, so he could be sued for libel. Two days after the August 25 hearing he had said on Lawrence Spivak's radio program, "Alger Hiss was a Communist and may still be one." The decision to do this had cost Chambers a good deal of anxiety, and after agreeing to appear on the program, he had wired Spivak to say that he had changed his mind. But by the time Spivak telephoned to protest, Chambers had thought about it some more, and realizing that he had no choice, he agreed to go through with it.

Hiss consulted with Edward C. McLean, an old friend and Harvard Law School classmate, who didn't like the idea of bring-ing the libel suit, but advised Hiss that it could be done on the basis of Chambers's statement, and that it should be brought in Maryland, where Chambers lived. Bill Marbury, Hiss's old friend from Baltimore, who had been with him at his first appearance before the House Committee on August 9, had already agreed to handle the case when the time came, but now he was in Europe. So Hiss waited until Marbury could come back and get the papers ready, and the suit was filed on September 27, a month after the offending statement had been made. Damages of $50,000 were claimed.

Chambers responded with a statement to the press, saying, "I welcome Alger Hiss's daring suit. I do not minimize the ferocity or the ingenuity of the forces that are working through him." By "the forces," as Chambers explained in *Witness*, he meant the Communist Party, and Marbury and Hiss regarded this statement as an additional libel. They duly amended the complaint and increased the damage claim to $75,000.

An entirely new situation had now been created; what had begun as a publicity campaign mounted by HUAC to charge that the Democratic Administration was riddled with Communism had now become an attempt to prove in court that Chambers was a liar and a fraud. Chambers, who had been supported so far by the Committee, was now obliged to defend himself on his own. But the future of the Committee and the whole politics of anti-Communism were involved. *Time* magazine was involved, because the credibility of one of its senior editors was at stake. The Republican Party, or at least the conservative wing that was using anti-Communism as a weapon against the Truman Administration, was also involved. And the investigative procedures of the Justice Department, which had been searching for evidence of Communist conspiracies and submitting it to a grand jury in New York ever since June 1947, more than a year before, were involved. So far the grand jury had not returned a single indictment, and its term was to expire on December 15.

The immediate political effect of the libel suit was to make it more difficult for the Republicans to use the Hiss–Chambers affair as an issue in the 1948 election campaign, since the matter was before the courts and still undecided. Nixon had no scruples about that; as one who had been involved in the Hiss case, he felt free to talk about it and, as he wrote later, "I found great interest in my audiences." But Dewey, according to Nixon, "felt it was not proper to give too much prominence to the issue." Whether this had any significant effect on the election or not, Nixon evidently thought it did. "The result on Election Day," he wrote, "was an unpleasant surprise for me and all Republicans." Dewey, the pollsters' favorite, received only 189 electoral votes, losing badly in spite of the 39 electoral votes which Strom Thurmond drew away from the Democrats. Truman received 303.

The effect on Chambers was different; his personal future

was at stake. In *Witness*, he brushed aside the $75,000 in damages
as unimportant; he was judgment-proof, he wrote, because his
property was in his wife's name, and he had no means of paying
any damages even if Hiss had won. *Time* volunteered to pay his
legal expenses, and later, when Chambers was obliged to leave
Time, the company gave him a financial settlement, which he
described as "so generous that, with what I had accumulated
over the years in its trust funds, I did not have to worry about
money again during the Case." (Chambers habitually spelled
this word with a capital C, when referring to his legal battles
with Hiss.)

But it was not the money that concerned Chambers, any more
than it concerned Hiss. As Chambers described it in a half dozen
pages of introspection and reminiscence in *Witness*, his compelling need was to convince the world that he was telling the truth
about his Communist conspiracy, even if he destroyed himself in
the process. He wrote that, for a long time, he tried to protect Hiss
from the consequences, and even attempted suicide in the hope
that he could somehow prove his point and destroy himself without
hurting anybody else. But that attempt failed, and, in any case,
it took place only after he had produced the documents that
would send Hiss to jail and put an end to his own career at *Time*.
That was the crucial decision, and it had taken him a long time
to arrive at it.

It was a dangerous decision, too, and he was made aware of
the danger soon after the libel suit was filed. The New York grand
jury, which had not called Chambers during his testimony before
the House Committee, suddenly summoned him to ask whether he
had any direct knowledge of Soviet espionage. He had talked
about espionage only in vague terms before the Committee; now
he would have to be specific, and submit to a more penetrating
examination than that which the Committee had given him. He
asked for time to think it over, and it was given to him; the following day he appeared before the grand jury again, and said his
answer was no. For the time being, at least, he was denying any
knowledge of espionage, or any part in it.

"My No to the grand jury stands for all men to condemn,"

Chambers wrote later in *Witness*. His explanation was that he remembered how his brother had committed suicide, and how the event had moved him to feel "an absolving pity" for "all humanity," and to believe in self-sacrifice to "perform a saving act for others." He wrote that it was necessary for him to "bear a witness of mercy for the Communists as men," and that "the source of what at last made it possible for me to bear witness against Communism, as a power of evil, lay close to the source of what made it necessary for me to bear [this] witness of mercy."

In any case, his denial before the grand jury was fairly consistent with what he had told the House Committee—the purpose of the "Communist apparatus" with which he said he and Hiss had been connected was "not primarily espionage . . . [but] the Communist infiltration of the American Government," he had said in his opening statement on August 3. But in the next sentence he had added that "espionage was certainly one of its eventual objectives." And his defense against the libel suit was soon to be an accusation that he and Hiss had indeed engaged in espionage and conspired together to do so. This was a defense, which would not only mean confessing to serious crimes, and to deliberately covering up those crimes for a period of nine years; it would now also mean admitting to perjury before the grand jury. This would be more serious than his perjury before the House Committee, because the Committee regarded him as a friendly witness and would be unlikely to prosecute. However, the Justice Department could not be expected to take the same attitude.

This was the dilemma that Chambers had to resolve on November 4, the first day of pretrial examination in the libel suit.* At the end of that day, after Chambers had added many details to his House Committee testimony but offered nothing

---

* The examination took place in Marbury's office in Baltimore, and the record of what was said and done is known as the "Baltimore depositions." (See Sources, Bibliography, and Notes.) Whittaker Chambers was questioned under oath on November 4, 5, and 17, 1948, and February 18 and March 25, 1949; Esther Chambers testified on November 16 and 17, 1948.

very significant to support his charges against Hiss, Marbury asked that Chambers produce, "if he has any, any correspondence, either typewritten or in handwriting, or anything of that sort, from any member of the Hiss family . . . any papers signed by Mr. Hiss which may be in his possession." One of Chambers's lawyers, William D. Macmillan, agreed, but the next morning at the opening of the session Macmillan said it would take a little time because Chambers "has not explored all of the sources where some conceivable data might be."

After the close of that day's questioning, Macmillan's partner, Richard F. Cleveland, warned Chambers that, if he did have anything of Hiss's he had better produce it. Up to that time Chambers's portrayal of Hiss as a Communist had not been very convincing; he had insisted that Hiss's assignment as a Communist had been "to keep himself as far removed from any Communist activity or suspicion of Communism as possible, and advance as far in the Government as possible." That, said Chambers, was Hiss's "principal function" for the Communist Party; and he continued, "It was hoped that when he arrived at certain positions, he would be able to influence policy." Meanwhile he was to have nothing to do with other Communists, at least in public; Chambers conceded that Hiss didn't live up to that part of his assignment very well, since it was part of Chambers's story that he often saw Hiss in public, and so did the others that he had named as Communists.

"I should not have stayed at his house as much as I did," Chambers said, "and he should not occasionally have eaten with me in public, and we should not have had occasion to take a trip together in the car, and he should not have driven me to New York."

Marbury spent much of the afternoon trying to get Chambers to describe specific instances of things Hiss had done that might show he was a Communist. Chambers repeated his story of giving the Ford car to the Communist Party, and declared for the first time that Hiss had obtained "certain special documents" from the State Department while he was on the Nye Committee. Chambers said the event had "caused a considerable stir," but he had not turned the documents over to the Communist Party; he had simply satisfied himself that Hiss could obtain such documents if he wanted to.

Chambers said that Hiss had sought the Communist Party's approval before accepting the State Department job under Assistant Secretary of State Francis B. Sayre, but Marbury ridiculed the idea and asked if there was anything else. Suddenly, and in a rather tentative way, Chambers introduced the idea of espionage. "He occasionally gave the Communist Party bits of information which he thought might be useful to them," he said.

"Just what information, and when?" asked Marbury.

The first two "bits" Chambers described were not particularly impressive and weren't followed up in the subsequent proceedings. He said Hiss had once warned him that a Communist "front" known as the Phantom Red Cosmetic Company in New York was under surveillance, and that a Bulgarian rug dealer in Milan had gone to Moscow to spy for the British. Marbury pressed for more details, and Chambers said Hiss had gained this information from some document he had seen in the course of his State Department duties, but he didn't know whether it was secret. Pressed further, Chambers said he had seen the document himself. Then he added, "I frequently read State Department documents in Mr. Hiss's house."

Again Marbury pressed for details, but Chambers didn't remember the document well enough to describe it. He said, "Mr. Hiss very often brought a briefcase with documents home, and I used to read those that were interesting. They were not very interesting, most of them. I think they were chiefly on trade agreements, and one thing and another. The most interesting ones were Mr. Messerschmidt's reports from Vienna, which were rather long and talky. . . .

"That was the period I would think either just before or after the German invasion of Austria, and the reports were fairly lively accounts of conditions in Vienna, and in the vicinity of Vienna."

"Were they of special interest?" Marbury asked.

"No," said Chambers. "They were not of special interest."

"Well, what documents that were of interest to the Communist Party or to the Soviet Government, if you please, did you ever obtain from Mr. Hiss other than this Phantom Red business?"

Chambers insisted that he had never "obtained" any documents from Hiss or transmitted them to the Communist Party. Of the documents he remembered seeing, the only ones he found of interest to the Communist Party had to do with "that Phantom Red business and the Bulgarian in Moscow." The others, he said, "were chiefly accounts of trade agreements, or commercial figures of one kind or another relating to exports and imports, and this and that. They were of no interest. I simply read most of them out of curiosity, to see what kind of things were written about in such places."

The curious thing about this testimony, though Marbury didn't know it at the time, was that it was a good description of most of the typewritten and microfilmed documents Chambers was to produce two weeks later, saying they were samples of documents he had "obtained" from Hiss and transmitted to the Communist Party and the Soviet Union. Included in the package were forty-eight pages of documents about negotiations for a trade agreement with Germany; sixteen pages of single-spaced typing about "commercial figures of one sort or another relating to exports and imports" in Manchukuo; and twenty-seven pages of cables from Europe and the Far East dating from immediately before or after the German invasion of Austria, many of which included "fairly lively accounts" of what was going on in and around Vienna. Among them were cables from Vienna, which weren't signed by Messerschmidt (there was no such State Department representative in Vienna at the time) but were marked to show they had been received in the Washington office of Assistant Secretary of State George S. Messersmith, and reported what a spokesman for the Austrian Foreign Minister named Schmidt had told U.S. Chargé d'Affaires John C. Wiley. From Schmidt and Messersmith to Messerschmidt was a confusion of names not unusual for Chambers.*

---

* If Chambers had seen Messersmith's copies of those cables, he hadn't got them from Hiss, who had different copies that didn't show Messersmith's name. This aspect is discussed more fully in Chapter 21.

Nevertheless Chambers, testifying under oath at the pretrial examination on November 5, swore that such documents were "of no interest" to the Communist Party and that he had never transmitted them or any other State Department documents from Hiss to the Communist Party. All he had done was to tell the Party about Phantom Red Cosmetics and the Bulgarian in Moscow. And when Marbury asked him if Hiss had engaged in "any other activities of this character," Chambers replied:

"No, I don't know that I can recall anything else that he did."

At the end of that day's testimony the examination was recessed for eleven days, until November 16, and during the interval Chambers experienced what he described in *Witness* as "the death of the will."

"A sense of the enormous futility of my effort, and my own inadequacy, drowned me," he wrote in the Foreword to his book. "I felt a physical cold creep through me, settle around my heart and freeze any pulse of hope." He was in the barn at his farm in Westminster, Maryland, milking the cows with his twelve-year-old son John. Then he went out into the orchard, alone under the stars. ("It was a very dark night. The stars were large and cold.") His son called to him, found him, and threw his arms around him, saying, as Chambers recalled it, " 'Papa, don't ever go away.' "

" 'No,' I said," the account continues, " 'no, I won't ever go away.' Both of us knew that the words 'go away' stood for something else, and that I had given my promise not to kill myself. Later on, as you will see, I was tempted, in my wretchedness, to break that promise."

At this point, as Chambers explained later in the book, he recognized that he might well lose the libel suit, but that wasn't what appalled him. He felt he was carrying on a struggle that involved the "life and death" of the whole nation, and that the public saw it as merely "a grudge fight or a scandal involving two men." This was indeed much the way Hiss felt about it, but the nation, as Chambers conceded in the next sentence, "did not feel that way to any such degree as I supposed. But I was sundered from the nation. In those days I felt incredibly alone.

"My sense of loneliness drove me to keep all the more to myself. My lethargy made any effort seem futile. The idea of making the long trip to New York to reclaim some scraps of paper that I had left there ten years before seemed an unendurable effort."

Cleveland, his lawyer, nevertheless persuaded Chambers that the effort must be made or he would lose the libel suit, so he contacted his wife's nephew, Nathan Levine, with whom he had left some papers in a sealed envelope for safekeeping in 1938. Chambers commented that what was in them "had seemed to me of so little importance that we had scarcely touched on it." (At the trials which followed he testified that he had forgotten what was in the envelope; he had recalled only "some handwritten specimens of Mr. Hiss" and "some typewritten notes."

The story of what happened after that was first told to the House Committee in a public hearing by Levine, on December 10, although the Committee had questioned Chambers in secret session a few evenings before, and Levine's testimony "corroborated" what he had said then, according to Rep. Karl Mundt. Levine described how Chambers had given him the envelope at a time when he was in fear of his life, and told him to turn it over to his wife, Levine's aunt, if anything ever happened to him; and should Mrs. Chambers be "liquidated" at the same time, Chambers had told Levine, "You would know what to do with it, you are an attorney."

Levine had hidden the envelope on top of a disused dumbwaiter shaft in his parents' home in Brooklyn, and had forgotten about it. When Chambers came for it on November 14, Levine said that when he had retrieved it for him, Chambers took it into the kitchen to open it. Levine wasn't in the kitchen when Chambers opened it, and didn't know what was in it. Nor had he ever known, because Chambers hadn't told him what the envelope contained, and he hadn't looked inside.

In *Witness*, and in his testimony at Hiss's perjury trial, Chambers identified the contents of the envelope as typewritten copies of State Department documents that he said Hiss had given him, of which there were sixty-five pages; four scraps of paper with notes scribbled on them in Hiss's handwriting; two strips of developed microfilm on which other State Department documents had been photographed; three rolls of undeveloped microfilm in metal canisters; eight pages of handwritten notes, which Chambers attributed to Harry Dexter White, the Assistant Secretary of the Treasury who had died on August 16; and "one or two smaller items of no particular importance" that were never publicly identified. This description passed unchallenged at the trials, since the defense had no contrary evidence for challenging it; only later, during proceedings on a motion for a new trial, was the defense allowed to submit the envelope and some of the papers to expert analysis. Daniel P. Norman, a specialist in physical and chemical analysis, found that the envelope wasn't big enough to hold all that Chambers had described, and that the sixty-five typewritten pages could not have been kept together in it for ten years, as he had claimed. The pages had not all aged in the same way, and the stains on them didn't match the stains on the inside of the envelope.

But Marbury had no way of knowing this when Chambers produced the typewritten pages and handwritten notes on the afternoon of Wednesday, November 17. Nor did he inquire where Chambers had found them, nor how he had arrived at the decision to produce them. He didn't ask whether these sixty-five pages and four scraps of notepaper were all the material Chambers had in his possession, and Chambers didn't tell him that he also had the microfilms and other items and was keeping them hidden. When Marbury saw Hiss's handwriting on the little scraps of notepaper he recognized it at once, and was so shocked he frankly didn't know what to do next. The last thing he had expected when he asked Chambers to produce documentary evidence was that he would be able to do it; and Chambers's long delay—almost two weeks since the question was first asked—had only strengthened that impression. Yet, here it was, in his friend's own handwriting, evidence of the most damaging kind.

There was nothing in Marbury's experience to prepare him for this day; he was a corporation lawyer who had never handled a libel suit before, never dealt with any kind of criminal activity except such business embarrassments as tax and antitrust problems, never even handled a case of burglary or embezzlement, much less espionage and stolen government documents. He had never tried a criminal case in court, and knew nothing of what guilty people in such cases do to protect themselves, or what innocent defendants are entitled to do or must do to escape conviction. All he could see was that his friend was likely to be a defendant in a criminal case very soon, and the thought appalled him.

Thus, it didn't occur to Marbury to insist on examining the documents that Chambers had produced; he left them in the hands of Chambers's lawyers, accepting photostats instead, all carefully numbered to correspond to the numbers that were being written on the originals. And it didn't occur to him to insist that the documents be kept in the same order as they appeared when Chambers produced them; he allowed Cleveland to reshuffle them so that they were numbered in the order of their dates. Marbury didn't know these things would make a difference later; but they did—they made a big difference.

After the numbering had been completed, Marbury listened almost without interruption to Chambers's story of where the documents had originated. It was a story he was to repeat many times thereafter, with many variations and embellishments to the House Committee, the grand jury, and two trial juries, not to mention in interviews with the press, a series of articles in the *Saturday Evening Post,* and ultimately his best-selling book, *Witness.* On this occasion, however, the account was brief and rather bare.

Chambers said that sometime in the middle of 1937* he had been introduced to a Russian whom he identified as Colonel Bykov (although he said the Russian called himself only Peter), who raised the question of procuring documents through Chambers's "apparatus" in Washington. Accordingly, Chambers arranged a meeting between Bykov and Alger Hiss in New York.

"I have forgotten where our rendezvous was held," Chambers

---

* In later testimony Chambers said this meeting took place in January 1937. See Chapter 15.

said, "but I believe it was somewhere near the Brooklyn Bridge. We then proceeded by the elevated train to a movie house quite a distance out in Brooklyn, which I cannot locate, but which I believe I could easily find. Alger and I waited on a bench on the mezzanine, and presently Bykov emerged from the body of the theater. I introduced them. We left the theater and went for a long walk, and by various conveyances we went back to New York City and had supper, the three of us together, at the Port Arthur Restaurant in Chinatown. Colonel Bykov spoke no English, or refused to speak English. He spoke German with a very bad Yiddish accent. He raised the question of procuring documents, and Mr. Hiss agreed."

"What?" said Marbury.

"Mr. Hiss agreed," Chambers repeated. "Colonel Bykov also raised the question of Donald Hiss procuring documents.* Alger Hiss said that he was not sure that his brother was sufficiently developed yet for that function—and perhaps I should say right here that Donald Hiss never at any time procured any documents. Nevertheless, he was a member of the apparatus which I headed.

"Following that meeting Alger Hiss began a fairly consistent flow of such material as we have before us here. The method was for him to bring home documents in his briefcase, which Mrs. Hiss usually typed. I am not sure that she typed all of them. Alger Hiss may have typed some of them himself. But it became a function for her and helped to solve the problem of Mrs. Hiss's longing for activity, that is, Communist activity.

"Nevertheless, there occasionally came to Mr. Hiss's knowledge, certain things, or he saw certain papers which he was not able to bring out of the Department for one reason or another, either because they merely passed through his hands quickly, or because he thought it inadvisable, but notations, in his handwriting are notes of such documents, such information, which he made and brought out in that form."

His explanation complete, Chambers then prodded Marbury. "Would you like to ask questions at that point?" he asked.

* Donald Hiss at the time was employed in the Solicitor's office in the Labor Department.

245

Marbury responded by asking for the dates when all this supposedly had happened, and Chambers was rather vague. Marbury asked why Chambers had never mentioned it before, and he replied with an emotional declaration that he had been trying to "shield such people as Alger Hiss from the most extreme consequences," and that while he wanted to "smash the conspiracy" he was also "not without compassion," and so far as he was concerned he was "perfectly satisfied as to what I have done."

Marbury tested that thought with a few more questions, and finding that Chambers would stick to it, he then changed the subject. The documents would have to be examined later, he decided; meanwhile he had prepared other questions in order to clarify some of Chambers's previous testimony, and these occupied the rest of the afternoon. The session was adjourned at 5:30 P.M., but no date was set for the next session. (It was three months before another session took place and by then the circumstances were very different.)

There was one point in all this that struck Marbury immediately, reinforcing the impression that he had gained from seeing Hiss's handwriting. That was Chambers's reference to Hiss's wife, Priscilla. Marbury didn't think Hiss had typed any of the documents; Hiss didn't know how to type. He had never faced a typewriter keyboard in his life, and wouldn't know how to operate one, even if he had to. Like other successful lawyers, including Marbury himself, he had stenographers, mainly female, to do his typing for him.

Chambers's comment that Priscilla had typed the documents was easier for Marbury to believe. He thought he knew Priscilla, and he regarded her as a domineering woman, who "held Alger in thrall." Whenever he called on the Hisses, it seemed to him that Priscilla did all the talking, and if he had something important to discuss with Alger, he would ask him to come out for a walk. Priscilla didn't seem to like this—she now denies it ever happened—and Alger's willingness to do it seemed to Marbury "the closest he ever got to disobeying Priscilla."

Marbury also recognized Chambers's description of Priscilla as "longing for activity," although he wouldn't have thought of

Alger Hiss's father Charles Alger Hiss died when Alger was two and a half.

The Hiss family in 1908: Alger on his mother's right, Mary Ann and Anna behind her, Bosley and Donald on her left.

Justice Oliver Wendell Holmes and his secretary at the Justice's summer home in Beverly Farms, Massachusetts, in 1930. (John Knox)

As Secretary General of the United Nations Conference on International Organization in San Francisco, Hiss sat next to Secretary of State Edward R. Stettinius at the speaker's rostrum when President Truman addressed the final plenary session on June 25, 1945. (United Nations)

A resolution praising Hiss and his staff for the smooth running of the conference was presented to him by the heads of the Big Four delegations: Lord Halifax of Great Britain, V. K. Wellington Koo of China, Edward R. Stettinius of the United States, and Andrei Gromyko of the Soviet Union. (UPI)

With the precious United Nations Charter at his feet, Hiss disembarks from a special Army plane in Washington to deliver the Charter to President Truman. It was strapped to its own parachute and marked with delivery instructions in case anything happened to Hiss or the plane on the way. (U.S. Army Air Force)

At his first appearance before the House Un-American Activities Committee (HUAC), on August 5, 1948, Hiss, when shown a news photo of Whittaker Chambers, said, "I would not like to take an oath that I have never seen that man. I would like to see him and then I think I would be better able to tell." (UPI)

On August 17, 1948, HUAC brought Chambers and Hiss together in a closed meeting, and Hiss identified Chambers as a man he had once known as George Crosley. The confrontation was repeated in public on August 25; Hiss is at left, with his back to the camera; Robert Stripling, HUAC Investigator, points to Chambers at far right. (UPI)

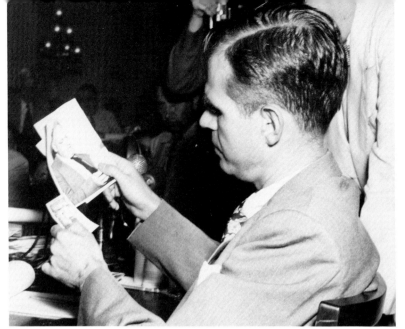

After the confrontation Hiss was shown two snapshots taken of Chambers in 1934 and another current news photo of him, and HUAC members argued that Hiss must be lying because he had not recognized Chambers from the news photo and would not identify Crosley from the snapshots. Hiss said he didn't remember what Crosley looked like except for his bad teeth, which didn't show in the snapshots. The news photo showed Chambers after his decayed upper teeth had been replaced. (UPI)

One of the news photos of Chambers testifying on August 3, 1948. (UPI)

The snapshots that were shown to Hiss. (UPI)

The next day Rep. Richard M. Nixon, Investigator Robert Stripling, and Chairman J. Parnell Thomas of HUAC posed for this news picture in which they displayed the "material gathered during the Committee hearings," on which they promised to issue a report a few days later. (UPI)

LEFT: *Henry Julian Wadleigh, former State Department economist, refused to tell HUAC whether he had turned over secret documents to Chambers but later admitted to the grand jury that he had done so and testified to that effect in Hiss's trials.* RIGHT: *Henry Collins, a boyhood friend of Hiss, who was accused by Chambers of being in the same Communist cell with Hiss in 1935, took the Fifth Amendment before HUAC but later denied the charge under oath before the grand jury. (UPI)*

When Chambers opened the pumpkin, Stripling and Bert Andrews of the New York Herald Tribune *radioed Nixon to cut short his Caribbean cruise on the SS* Panama *and come back to Washington. A Coast Guard plane picked him up at sea and flew him to Biscayne Bay, where he boarded the launch that brought him to waiting press photographers at Miami. (UPI)*

The microfilms that had been hidden in the pumpkin became Nixon's most jealously guarded prize. He unrolled them before the press cameras and grand jurors but would allow neither the grand jury, the Justice Department, nor anyone else outside HUAC and its staff to touch them. (UPI)

Reporter Bert Andrews, who worked closely with Nixon and Chambers from the time Nixon first approached him in early August 1948, interviews Chambers on a radio program after Hiss's conviction. (UPI)

Hiss and his brother Donald (left) arrive at the Federal Building in New York to testify before the grand jury in December 1948. (UPI)

When Hiss left the courthouse after pleading not guilty to the indictment, photographers followed him into the subway car. The headline in his neighbor's newspaper, "BARE 28 MORE SPY PAPERS," refers to the pumpkin papers, which were being made public in batches by HUAC. (UPI)

Judge, jury, and witnesses at the first trial of Alger Hiss had to run the gauntlet of Communist pickets outside the courthouse, protesting the trial of eleven Communist Party leaders on charges of criminal conspiracy. Though the pickets avoided any comment on the Hiss case, their presence helped confuse the issues. This picture was taken on June 6, 1949, when Chambers was testifying for his third day of cross-examination. (UPI)

Hiss and his attorney Lloyd Paul Stryker arrive at court for the opening of the first trial. (UPI)

Judge Samuel H. Kaufman presided at the first trial. (UPI)

LEFT: *Walter H. Anderson, chief of the State Department Records Branch, identified the government documents that were in evidence at the trials and explained the Department's procedures for handling them. (UPI)* RIGHT: *Francis B. Sayre, who as Assistant Secretary of State was Hiss's boss in 1937–1938, testified in his behalf. (UPI)*

Whittaker Chambers, the government's star witness, with his wife Esther, who corroborated some of his stories but knew nothing about the espionage her husband described or the documents he accused Hiss of giving him. (UPI)

*Assistant U.S. Attorney Thomas F. Murphy, the prosecutor in both trials,
receives the congratulations of U.S. Attorney Irving Saypol. (UPI)*

The house at 1245 Thirtieth Street, which Chambers said he visited "every week or ten days" during 1937 to pick up government documents from Hiss, is the middle one of this row of three. The window of the bedroom where ten-year-old Timothy Hobson, Hiss's stepson, was laid up for several months that year is above the front door (partly hidden by the tree). Photographed May 27, 1949. (Defendant's exhibit BB-1)

The house at 3415 Volta Place, where the Hiss family lived in 1938. The photograph was taken May 27, 1949, and shows the house essentially as Chambers described it at the trials. In 1938, however, the two street-level windows next to the gate did not exist, and there was no railing above the gate; the ivy-covered wall was a retaining wall, behind which grew a silver maple tree. Neither Chambers nor his wife remembered that. By the time of the trial further changes had been made on this side of the house, which further confused the jury. (Defendant's exhibit CC)

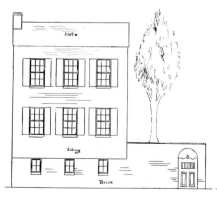

A sketch of the house, as it appeared in 1938, drawn by Teunis F. Collier, the Georgetown building contractor who made the alterations in 1943. (Defendant's exhibit CCCC, p. 4)

Claude B. Cross, Hiss's lawyer for the second trial, appeared in court with Hiss on October 10, 1949, to obtain an adjournment of the trial until November in order to have more time to familiarize himself with the case. (UPI)

OPPOSITE: *Alger and Priscilla Hiss on their way to court. (UPI)*

Between the two trials Alger and Priscilla Hiss rested in the quiet mountain-top village of Peacham, Vermont. *(Photo by author)*

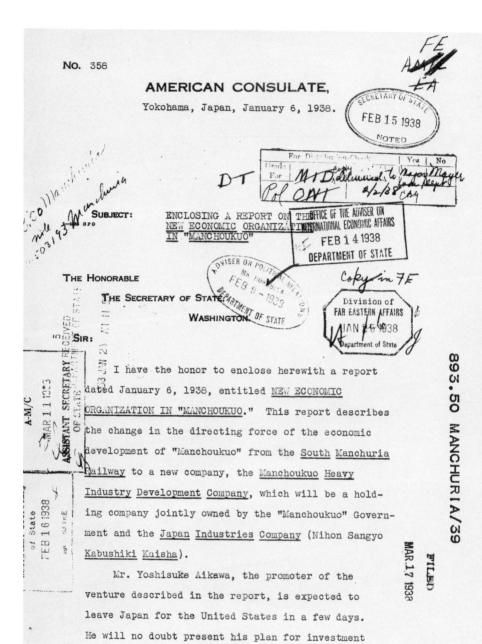

NO. 358

AMERICAN CONSULATE,

Yokohama, Japan, January 6, 1938.

SECRETARY OF STATE
FEB 15 1938
NOTED

SUBJECT: ENCLOSING A REPORT ON THE OFFICE OF THE ADVISER ON
NEW ECONOMIC ORGANIZATION INTERNATIONAL ECONOMIC AFFAIRS
IN "MANCHOUKUO"
FEB 14 1938
DEPARTMENT OF STATE

THE HONORABLE

THE SECRETARY OF STATE,

WASHINGTON.

Copy in 7E

Division of
FAR EASTERN AFFAIRS
JAN 1938
Department of State

SIR:

I have the honor to enclose herewith a report
dated January 6, 1938, entitled NEW ECONOMIC
ORGANIZATION IN "MANCHOUKUO." This report describes
the change in the directing force of the economic
development of "Manchoukuo" from the South Manchuria
Railway to a new company, the Manchoukuo Heavy
Industry Development Company, which will be a holding company jointly owned by the "Manchoukuo" Government and the Japan Industries Company (Nihon Sangyo
Kabushiki Kaisha).

Mr. Yoshisuke Aikawa, the promoter of the
venture described in the report, is expected to
leave Japan for the United States in a few days.
He will no doubt present his plan for investment

893.50 MANCHURIA/39

MAR.17 1938   FILED

with

The documentary evidence at the trials is reproduced in 8½- by 11-inch paperbound volumes of the Second Trial Record. ABOVE: The first page of Richard F. Boyce's dispatch, enclosing his report on "New Economic Organization of Manchoukuo," showing the date stamps of the offices to which it was circulated, and its file number. (Government's State Exhibit no. 5)

American Consulate
Yokohama, Japan, January 6, 1938.

Subject: ENCLOSING A REPORT ON THE
NEW ECONOMIC ORGANIZATION
IN "MANCHUKUO"

The Honorable
The Secretary of State
Washington
Sir:
I have the honor to enclose herewith a report dated January 6,
1938, entitled New Economic Organization in "Manchukuo". This report
describes the change in the directing force of the economic development of "Manchukuo" from the South Manchuria Railway to a new
company, the Manchukuo Heavy Industry Development Company, which will
be a holding company jointly owned by the "Manchukuo" Government and
the Japan Industries Company (Nihon Sangyo Kabushiki Kaisha).
Mr. Yoskisuke Aikawa, the promoter of the venture described in
the report, is expected to leave Japan for the United States in a
few days. He will no doubt present his plan for investment with
American capital in "Manchukuo" to possible American investors as
soon as he can arrange to meet them.

Respectfully yours,
Richard F. Boyce,
American Consul

The pumpkin paper copy of the document reproduced on the opposite page.
(Baltimore Exhibit no. 5)

INSET: *The old Woodstock typewriter N230099, now in the custody of Hiss's*
attorney. (Photo by author)

OPPOSITE: *Judge Henry W. Goddard, who presided at the second trial, is shown leaving the court after Hiss was found guilty on January 21, 1950. (UPI)* ABOVE: *Leaving the courthouse after the sentencing on January 25, Alger and Priscilla Hiss linked arms with two old friends, Mrs. Phelps Soule, a summer neighbor at Peacham, Vermont, and Mrs. John Alford, the former Roberta Fansler, who had been Priscilla's college roommate and sister-in-law. (UPI)*

On March 22, 1950, handcuffed to a fellow prisoner who hid behind his hat, Hiss climbed into a federal prison van to be taken to jail. (UPI)

Forty-four months later,
on November 27, 1954,
Hiss was released from jail,
and Priscilla and their son
Tony, then thirteen, met
him at the gate to bring
him home. (UPI)

Today Hiss is a salesman of office stationery and supplies, and Tony is on the staff of The New Yorker *and an author (with Rogers E. M. Whitaker) of* All Aboard With E. M. Frimbo *(New York: Grossman, 1974). At a publication party to launch the book in November 1974, Tony wore a locomotive engineer's cap for the occasion, and received his father's congratulations. (Michael Ginsberg)*

"Communist activity," because he knew nothing about Communism and didn't recognize the phrase. Still, he regarded Priscilla as a restless woman, forever taking up new projects and later abandoning them for others, and she had a reputation among Marbury's friends for being radical in her ideas and fanatic in her behavior. So her involvement in "Communist activity" didn't sound too unlikely; anyhow, Marbury was ready to believe that if Alger was in trouble, Priscilla was at the bottom of it. He thought of Alger as a romantic, almost like a "knight errant," devoted to his wife as Don Quixote to his Dulcinea. When Alger was a bachelor, Marbury and his friends had been afraid he'd get into trouble by "rescuing a damsel in distress," and his subsequent marriage to Priscilla had seemed exactly that.

These views were obviously not shared by Alger or Priscilla— she says now that Alger did think of her as romantic, but not domineering, radical, or fanatic. Nevertheless, they were views which influenced Marbury, and on that appalling day in November 1948, they helped undermine his confidence in his friend. Indeed, his friendship with Hiss was suddenly an embarrassment to him; and even twenty-six years later he has not been able to find a satisfactory explanation of the "enigma," as he calls it. The evidence given in the documents persuaded Marbury of Hiss's guilt, and a trial jury ultimately came to the same conclusion; yet Marbury has never been able to reconcile it with what he knows now and what he knew in 1948 of Hiss's character.

"I guess I didn't know Alger as well as I thought I did," he once said, "or perhaps I never knew him really well at all." It is a statement that cuts both ways, and is undoubtedly true; if he'd known Hiss better, he might have had the same confidence in Hiss as his other friends had. Indeed, Marbury's association with Hiss had never been particularly close; they had met at a party when Hiss was an undergraduate at Johns Hopkins and Marbury was already practicing law, and Marbury had been so impressed with the younger man's promise that he wrote letters of recommendation to help him get a scholarship at Harvard Law School, and later he had enlisted the endorsement of Maryland Sen. Millard Tydings for his Agricultural Adjustment Administration

(AAA) job. Over the years they saw each other on occasion, and exchanged letters about such matters as the literary style of Victor Hugo. Hiss was a man everybody admired in those days, and Marbury admired him too.

So it was natural enough that when Marbury read about Chambers's original accusations against Hiss in the Baltimore *Sun*, he had thought it a joke. He wrote to Hiss at the time, saying, "If you're a card-carrying Communist, send me a card!" And it was natural enough after that for Hiss to ask Marbury to accompany him to his first House Committee testimony in response to Chambers, on August 5, and later to ask him to represent him in the libel suit. Marbury had been glad to oblige, until he saw the documents; but they changed everything.

14

THE PUMPKIN

WHEN the session ended that day, Marbury's first act was to telephone Hiss in New York and tell him in great consternation what had happened. Hiss agreed he ought to look at Chambers's papers as soon as possible. Edward C. McLean had not been in Marbury's Baltimore office when the papers were produced, because he was in court on another case; but Harold Rosenwald, Hiss's old friend from Harvard and Washington days, who was acting as McLean's assistant, had been there. So Rosenwald returned to New York that night with the photostats, leaving the papers themselves in the hands of Chambers's lawyers.

Hiss recognized three of the handwritten notes at once as his own, though from the photostatic reproduction he wasn't sure about the fourth. He knew they must have been stolen, because he hadn't given them to Chambers, and he had no idea who else might have done so. The typewritten papers meant nothing to Hiss; he'd never seen anything like them before. But some of them were quite obviously copies of State Department documents that Chambers never should have seen, and some were apparently summaries of similar material. There was no question that Chambers had somehow gained unauthorized access to classified documents, so there was at least that much that was true about his story of an espionage conspiracy.

But Hiss saw nothing in the photostats to connect the Chambers papers to himself. It never occurred to him that they looked like the work of Priscilla's old Woodstock typewriter; he had hardly ever seen anything she typed on it, and had never used the machine himself, so that he didn't know what its work looked like. Anyhow, they had got rid of the machine years ago, and he had forgotten all about it.

It also didn't occur to Hiss to show the photostats to Priscilla, who was in Vermont. He was confident that she hadn't typed the papers, whatever Chambers said. (Or whatever Marbury believed, for that matter; but Marbury hadn't mentioned his suspicions yet.) This was unfortunate for Hiss, because although Priscilla wouldn't have recognized the typing as her own, she might have said, "That looks like the kind of type our old Woodstock used to have." Not likely, perhaps, but possible. And if that had happened, Hiss might have realized a little earlier the danger he was in and taken more effective steps to protect himself.

Hiss didn't realize the danger, however, and on that day when he first saw the photostats he made a number of decisions that weakened his position still further. Above all, he made the mistake of relying on his own judgment and that of an old friend instead of calling in some independent outside counsel. A lawyer who takes his own case has a fool for a client, the saying goes, and if he hires close friends to defend him, he is not much better off. His friends may be good lawyers, yet lack the particular kinds of experience required by the case; and they will be unable to see it with the objectivity which the situation requires.

After his indictment, Hiss did retain independent counsel, in the persons of Lloyd Paul Stryker and his assistant, Harold Shapero, at the first trial, and Claude Cross at the second. But he had to rely a great deal on the volunteer help of friends, too, simply because he didn't have enough money to do otherwise.

When Hiss so hotheadedly challenged Chambers to a libel suit on August 16, he hadn't counted the money cost. From his salary, his savings, and what was left of his small inheritance, he was able to spend about $20,000 in his own defense in the next few years; his salary lasted only until the beginning of the first trial in May 1949. But that was hardly enough to mount a good libel suit, win or lose; and the true cost of his legal defense to all concerned has been estimated at $500,000—in 1948–1950 prices, or well over a million dollars today.

Hiss borrowed another $20,000 from members of his family, and accepted almost $70,000 in voluntary contributions, but most of the cost had to be absorbed by the lawyers involved. McLean's firm absorbed a lot of it; after their expenses had been met out of the fees Hiss was able to pay there were only nominal amounts left to pay McLean and Robert von Mehren, who worked with him through both trials. John F. Davis, in Washington, was paid practically nothing; Marbury, in Baltimore, never sent a bill. Rosenwald, Stryker, and Cross accepted reduced fees, and paid some expenses out of their own pockets. Later, when the case was appealed and a new trial was sought without success, similar generosity was extended by Chester T. Lane, Walter E. Beer, Robert M. Benjamin, Helen L. Buttenwieser, and others. And much of the research work in all phases of the case was done by volunteers.

Hiss wanted no great fund-raising appeal, such as had been mounted for Sacco and Vanzetti and the Scottsboro Boys in the 1930s, and which were later to support Ellsberg, the Berrigans, and other defendants in political trials. Hiss wanted to keep his case on a personal, not political level, and he was necessarily anxious to avoid any suspicion of financial support from the Communist Party and its allies, who had been prominent in the Scottsboro case. He needn't have worried; the Communists in 1948–1950 were equally afraid of being identified with either Chambers or Hiss, not wanting any part of a story of espionage. But Hiss told Richard H. Field, another old Harvard friend, who acted as treasurer of the Hiss Defense Fund, that he "didn't want to be another Scottsboro Boy," and Field confined his letters of solicitation to people who had already sent in unsolicited contributions, and other friends whom he knew to be sympathetic and beyond reproach.

This decision gave Hiss no choice; with such limited resources he had to rely on friends, as he had been doing from the beginning. And Marbury's advice about the papers that Chambers had produced on November 17, 1948, was to have them turned over immediately to the Justice Department, so the matter could be investigated and the source of the papers traced. Hiss wholeheartedly agreed, seeing no danger in the proposal and regarding it as entirely correct. After all, it was up to the Justice Department to find the real culprit, and when they had, Hiss's name would be cleared. Having worked in the Solicitor General's office in 1935–1936, he had a high regard for the Department's abilities. So he didn't insist on examining the papers himself, or even ask that his lawyers do so.

On November 18 Marbury reported this decision to Chambers's lawyers and to Judge W. Calvin Chesnut, who was in charge of the libel suit, and they made no objection. Marbury notified the Justice Department, and Assistant Attorney General Alexander Campbell, the head of the Criminal Division, came to Baltimore the following day to take charge of the papers. After Hiss's indictment his attorneys applied for a court order to allow them to inspect the papers, but it was refused; the government argued that the defense had already had their opportuntiy in the libel suit proceedings. Thereafter, although the papers were occasionally shown to witnesses in the courtroom during the trial, the defense was not allowed to examine them until after Hiss was convicted; until then they had to rely on photographs or photostatic copies of them instead. It was a long time before the defense found out how much this circumstance had hurt them.

When Campbell took possession of the papers, he asked Judge Chesnut to postpone any further action on the libel suit for two weeks and to preserve utmost secrecy in the meantime, while the government would be making a thorough investigation. Judge Chesnut issued the necessary order, and by Friday, December 3, the last day of the two-week period, the Justice Department was ready with its announcement that new evidence had been produced and would be laid before the grand jury in New York. But two days before that, on Wednesday, December 1, the secrecy rule had broken down, and Nixon had found out what Chambers was doing. From then on it was Nixon who dominated the grand jury proceedings, as he had dominated the HUAC phase of the affair.

Two quite different newspaper stories appeared that day. The United Press (UP) reported that the Justice Department was about to drop its investigation of the Hiss–Chambers case unless new evidence was found, and *The Washington Post* reported without details that there had been a startling development in the libel suit in Baltimore.

According to Nixon's account in *Six Crises,* Nixon saw the UP story and called Stripling, who said he had heard rumors of new evidence. "Playing a long hunch," Nixon wrote, he went to see Chambers on his farm, taking Stripling with him, and Chambers said he had produced some documentary evidence at the Baltimore examination but wasn't allowed to talk about it. According to Nixon, Chambers said it was a "real bombshell."

"Stripling and I tried without success to get some inkling of the contents," Nixon wrote. "He smiled and said, . . . 'My attorney has photostatic copies, and also I didn't turn over everything I had. I have another bombshell in case they try to suppress this one.'

" 'You keep that second bombshell,' I [Nixon] said. 'Don't give it to anybody except the Committee.' Chambers did not respond but I was sure he got the point."

Chambers described the incident in a slightly different way in *Witness.* His version makes it clear that he understood what he had to do, though it doesn't say Nixon was there to tell him. Chambers wrote that Bert Andrews, the *New York Herald Tribune* bureau chief, telephoned him to ask about the *Post* story, and Chambers answered that he couldn't talk about it. "Andrews at once drew the proper journalistic inference that if nobody would talk about what had happened in the libel suit, something must have happened," Chambers wrote. "He got in touch with Robert Stripling."

Stripling appeared at the farm later that day, according to Chambers, and took occasion to compliment Chambers on his pumpkins. (It was now December, and the first killing frost in northern Maryland that year had been in October, followed by several others, so that healthy pumpkins on the vine must have looked remarkable.) Then, according to Chambers, Stripling asked about the *Post* story and said, " 'I hear that there has been a bombshell in the suit. What kind of a bombshell?' " Chambers repeated that he could not discuss the suit, and shook his head when Stripling asked if he had any more evidence that he had not presented yet. Ostensibly the gesture was a silent denial, but Chambers expected Stripling to know better.

"Stripling has been in the business of reading men's faces for many years," he wrote. "He never took his eyes off mine while he questioned me."*

What Chambers was hinting at was the microfilms he had, some of which were photographs of State Department documents, while others were still undeveloped and might show anything, he didn't know what. He had not given them to his lawyers along with the typewritten papers because of a complicated chain of what he called conscious and subconscious reasoning, which covers four pages in *Witness*. Consciously, he wrote, he wanted to develop the undeveloped film himself and see what was on it, and "there was also a possibility for the first day or so that I might destroy it and myself." Subconsciously, he explained, he was afraid of being indicted if the Justice Department got the microfilms, and he didn't think the Department would use them to indict Hiss. He had already decided to save them for the House Committee on Un-American Activities (HUAC), before Nixon asked him to do so.

"Congressman Nixon believed that the Government had already taken the preliminary steps necessary to indict me," he wrote. "A special night session of members of the House Committee on Un-American Activities was called to discuss ways to counteract the effort to indict me—not because the Committee felt any personal fondness for me or wished to save me from indictment as an individual man, but because my indictment must clearly smother the Hiss Case."

Here Chambers and Nixon were in agreement; Nixon made

* Stripling, in his account (*The Red Plot Against America*), says the original tip that Chambers had some documents came to him from one of Chambers's attorneys, Nicholas Vazzano. Stripling confirms that Nixon went to the farm with him, and quotes Nixon as asking the "bombshell" question.

the same point in *Six Crises*. And he knew what Chambers meant in the "bombshell" interview of December 1. He told Stripling that evening that "I had an intuitive feeling that Chambers was trying to tell us something," and on that basis he signed a subpoena directing Chambers to turn over to the Committee whatever documents he had. Stripling said that he would have it served on Chambers the next day, December 2.

Nixon, however, was scheduled to leave on his vacation the next day, sailing from New York on the *SS Panama* for a Caribbean cruise. He didn't want to postpone it ("I didn't have the heart to tell Pat the bad news"), so he told Stripling that he would be in Panama in four days and could fly back if necessary. Later he had a better idea, and arranged for a Coast Guard plane to pick him up at sea after three days. The plan added a touch of melodrama to what was to happen next.

While Nixon was on his way to his cruise ship in New York, Chambers was preparing to go to Washington. When he had his overcoat on, it occurred to him that the time had come to move the microfilms from the bedroom, where they had been for the past two weeks, to some "better hiding place." Hiss's investigators, he thought, might force their way in and ransack the house.

Chambers remembered a scene in a Soviet movie where underground Communists had hidden arms and ammunition in a pumpkin-shaped figure of a Chinese god, and it reminded him of Stripling's remark about his own pumpkin patch. He decided that a hollow pumpkin would be the perfect hiding place—"Investigators might tear the house apart; they would never think to look for anything in a pumpkin lying in a pumpkin patch." He broke off a pumpkin, took it to the kitchen and cut off the top. After scooping out the pulp he placed the microfilm, wrapped in waxed paper, inside. Replacing the top, which fit perfectly, he returned the pumpkin to its place on the vine where it had grown. "The whole art of the concealment," he wrote, "lay in its complete naturalness and complete unexpectedness."

Stripling meanwhile had telephoned Chambers to ask him to stop in at his office, and when Chambers got to Washington he did so and picked up his subpoena. Stripling said he would go back with him to the farm that evening to pick up the evidence, and Chambers concluded that "he had read my eyes correctly the night before."

Chambers returned to Stripling's office at 5:00 P.M. that evening, according to *Witness*, and went from there to the farm with two of Stripling's staff, Donald Appell and William A. Wheeler. They arrived at 10:00 P.M., having apparently stopped for a lengthy dinner on the way, since it was only a two-hour journey. Chambers led the investigators to the pumpkin, took the microfilms from their hiding place, and handed them over.

"I think this is what you are looking for," he told the investigators. It was; but they also wanted photostats of the typewritten papers that Chambers had produced in Baltimore, and though he didn't mention it in *Witness*, the record shows he turned those over too, in spite of Assistant Attorney General Campbell's request and Judge Chesnut's order. This gave the House Committee just the chance they needed to get the jump on the Justice Department in revealing this material to the press.

All this happened Thursday evening, December 2, while the SS *Panama* was steaming out of New York Harbor at the start of its cruise. Before Wheeler and Appell got back to Washington with the microfilms, Bert Andrews sent Nixon a radiogram that repeated what Nixon had already learned from his visit to the farm on Wednesday. As quoted in *Six Crises*, it read:

"Information here is that Hiss–Chambers case has produced new bombshell. Indications are that Chambers has offered new evidence. All concerned silent. However, Justice Department partially confirms by saying, 'It is too hot for comment.' "

Nixon received Andrews's message on Friday morning, and that evening another arrived from Stripling saying, "Second bombshell obtained by subpoena 1 A.M. Friday. Case clinched. Information amazing. Heat is on from press and other places. Immediate action appears necessary. Can you possibly get back?"

The following morning, which Nixon described as Sunday though he must have meant Saturday, he received another radiogram from Andrews, which he called "the clincher." He quoted part of it as follows:

"Documents incredibly hot. Link to Hiss seems certain. Link to others inevitable. Results should restore faith in need for committee if not in some members. New York jury meets Wednesday. Could you arrive Tuesday and get day's jump on grand jury. If not, holding hearing early Wednesday. My liberal friends don't love me no more. Nor you. But facts are facts and these facts are dynamite. Hiss's writing identified on three documents. Not proof he gave them to Chambers but highly significant. Stripling says can prove who gave them to Chambers. Love to Pat." And the signature was "Vacation-Wrecker Andrews."*

According to Nixon he promptly radioed Stripling to make arrangements to get him off the ship, and with the help of James V. Forrestal, then Secretary of Defense, a Coast Guard amphibious plane was sent to meet the SS *Panama* off the coast of Cuba and bring Nixon to Miami. The plane met the ship at 10:35 A.M. on Sunday, December 5, and Nixon was landed at Biscayne Bay at 2:10 P.M., but the orders recorded in the Coast Guard logs for that Saturday and Sunday do not support Nixon's version of how the operation was arranged, and from the timing of the movements of the plane and ship it appears that the necessary orders must have been issued well before December 4, and perhaps even before the ship left New York.

In any case, the press was ready with reporters and photographers to meet Nixon at Miami and again at Washington, and the melodrama of the air-sea rescue of the Congressman, following the midnight lanterns in the pumpkin patch, provided material for sensational and imaginative writing. The press had a field day. Their material was mainly secondhand, from Committee sources, but that circumstance only made the writing more vivid. The photostats of the secret documents made a stack four feet high, the story went; the stolen documents were of the most secret nature, and the damage done to the nation's security by the espionage ring was beyond belief. Nixon and Chambers were heroes

---

* Nixon quoted the word "Stop" after each sentence, a radiogram substitute for punctuation marks. Andrews didn't reveal in his stories for the *Herald Tribune* at the time how deeply he was involved in these events, and has been criticized on that account.

who saved the nation, a point Nixon was to make over and over again in the days and weeks that followed.

Nixon worked with Stripling that night "until dawn," going over the enlarged prints that had been made of the microfilms, and the photostats of the typewritten and handwritten papers. The Committee soon began releasing these materials to the press, and as a result they became associated in the public mind with the midnight opening of the pumpkin, and were thereafter all referred to as the "pumpkin papers." That style will be followed here for convenience, although there were never any papers in the pumpkin; only the microfilms, which had been hidden there for less than a day.

Nixon wanted to begin public Committee hearings on the pumpkin papers at once, but Chambers had been subpoenaed by the New York grand jury for the following day, and Nixon wanted to talk to him first. It was decided that Nixon would go to New York with Stripling and McDowell to question Chambers after he finished the day's grand jury testimony. But meanwhile something happened that momentarily shook Nixon's faith in his star witness, and had an even more depressing effect on Chambers.

Stripling had asked the Eastman Kodak Company to check the microfilms to make sure they were as old as Chambers had said they were and not something he had produced in a hurry to bolster his story. On Monday morning Stripling got a phone call from Kodak that seemed to confirm his worst fears—the film could not have been manufactured before 1945.

Again, there are separate accounts in *Six Crises* and *Witness* which record what happened next, each version revealing something of its author. First Nixon's account:

"The news jolted us into almost complete shock. We sat looking at each other without saying a word. This meant that Chambers was, after all, a liar. All the work, the long hours we had put into the investigation had been useless. We had been taken in by a diabolically clever maniac who had finally made a fatal mistake.

"I buzzed my secretary in the outer office and asked her to

get Chambers on the phone in New York. Before he had a chance to say anything, I asked him: 'Am I correct in understanding that these papers were put on microfilm in 1938?'

"He answered, 'Yes,'—obviously mystified by the question.

" 'We have just had a report from the Eastman Kodak Company that film of the type you turned over to us was not made by the company until after 1945,' I retorted. 'What is your answer to that?'

"There was a long silence at the other end of the wire. For a moment, I thought he must have hung up. Finally he answered in a voice full of despair and resignation, 'I can't understand it. God must be against me.'

"Then I took out on him all of the fury and frustration that had built up within me. 'You'd better have a better answer than that,' I said. 'The subcommittee's coming to New York tonight and we want to see you at the Commodore Hotel at 9:00 and you'd better be there!'

"I slammed the receiver down without giving him a chance to reply."

Chambers, whose account appeared five years before Nixon's, wrote that Nixon's phone call reached him while he was in consultation with Harold Medina, Jr., a lawyer who originally had been retained by Time, Inc., to help him in the libel suit. He could do so no longer because the pumpkin papers were more than the company had bargained for, and Chambers had been obliged to resign. He was asking Medina to recommend another lawyer, to help him in case he was indicted, when the phone rang and he heard Nixon's news about the date of the film. Chambers's account continues:

" 'It cannot be true,' I said, 'but I cannot explain it.'

" 'The subcommittee's going to be in New York tonight,' said Nixon, 'and we want to see you at the Commodore Hotel at nine o'clock. We're going to get to the bottom of this.'

" 'I will be there,' I said.

" 'You'd better be there,' said Nixon. His voice was harsh with the just anger of a man who has placed his confidence in another man who turns out to be an impostor.

"I had felt that Richard Nixon was one of the few friends who really understood what was going on. I put up the receiver slowly. As I did so, I saw Medina's eyes rest on me with a scrutinizing glance. He had learned from Nixon about the film. I knew what unpleasant thoughts must be hovering behind his eyes.

"I walked out of the broadloom and heavy oak hush of his office into the teeming Wall Street crowds. 'God is against me,' I thought."

For the next page and a half of *Witness*, Chambers describes how he walked about the streets of the financial district, meditating on what God's purpose might be, before he called Medina again. Meanwhile, according to *Six Crises*, Nixon had called a press conference, and made some notes for the statement he proposed to make. The news about the microfilms had shaken him so badly that he had "reminded Stripling that it was the Committee's responsibility not to prove Hiss guilty but to find out who was telling the truth." He put down some notes for a statement, and decided that "this would be the biggest crow-eating performance in the history of Capitol Hill, but I was ready to go through with it."

Five minutes before the press conference was to start, Stripling received a second call from Kodak, saying they had made a mistake; the film could have been manufactured in 1938 after all.* At that, Nixon wrote, "Stripling put the receiver down, let out a Texas rebel yell, grabbed me by the arms, and danced me around the room.

" 'Chambers's story has stood up again,' he exulted. 'Every time we check into something which sounds questionable, he comes through.' "

Nixon then gave this news to the reporters, without telling

* The truth of the matter has never been established; many researchers believe Kodak could have been right the first time. In response to a lawsuit under the Freedom of Information Act, the FBI agreed in July 1975 to permit the films to be examined under certain restrictions, and it is possible that some information may be obtained in this way. As of this writing HUAC and Justice Department records of what Nixon did with the microfilms and what he told the grand jury about them in December 1948 have not been made available.

them about the panic he had felt only a moment before. That part of the story did leak out to the *New York Herald Tribune* a few days later, but it was killed after the first edition.

By the time Chambers called Medina again, Nixon's secretary had called to give him the good news. But Chambers was not reassured. "An error so burlesque," he wrote in *Witness*, "a comedy so gross in the midst of such catastrophe was a degradation of the spirit. It continued to shake the soul." He walked around downtown New York until he found some stores that sold garden seeds and insecticides, and bought himself two cans of poison containing cyanide. He asked the clerk if it were dangerous, and was told that "if you breathe enough of it, it will kill you." Satisfied, he took his poison to the Pennsylvania Station and locked it in a luggage locker. This was the first tangible step toward carrying out the suicide plan he had thought of earlier, when he had first been asked to produce documentary evidence.

Nixon, McDowell, Stripling, and others of the Committee staff arrived at the Pennsylvania Station at 7:30 that evening, and the scene is described in *Witness* almost as though Chambers was there to meet them, though he says he wasn't. Representatives of the Justice Department were evidently there, however, though neither Nixon nor Chambers has identified them by name. They wanted custody of the microfilms to use as evidence in their investigation of who had committed what crimes, but Nixon said he "did not trust the Justice Department to prosecute the case with the vigor we thought it deserved. The five rolls of microfilm in our possession, plus the threat of a congressional public hearing, were our only weapons to assure such a prosecution." So Nixon refused; and a compromise was reached by which Nixon agreed to give the Justice Department full-size prints of the microfilms, and the Department allowed the Committee to question Chambers, although he was still under the Department's subpoena.

According to *Witness*, the agreement wasn't reached without a fight. "Battle was joined in the train shed of the Pennsylvania Station in New York," Chambers wrote. "When the Congressmen and their staff debouched from their coaches, representatives of the Justice Department were waiting for them. A strident scene followed on the platform. It was adjourned to a hotel room. It grew so shrilly invective at last, the air was so blue with shouts of meddling and bad faith, that at last Robert Stripling threw open a window. 'We might as well let them hear all about it on Fifth Avenue,' he said."

Chambers wrote that all this must have happened while he was shopping for his cyanide, and "I must have narrowly missed the warring factions when I left my parcels in the lock box in Pennsylvania Station." Following this, he walked toward the Commodore, and was met on the street before he got there by Appell, who put him in a taxi and took him to the ramp entrance of the hotel, so he wouldn't be seen by the newsmen in the lobby. Then, safe in the Committee's suite, he told them his story, which was thereafter leaked to the press instead of being kept secret as his grand jury testimony had to be.

"The hearing lasted for several hours, but my testimony was necessarily far from complete," Chambers wrote. [What he said is not fully known, either, since the transcript of this secret session has never been made public.] "I left the session late at night with the tired knowledge that I had to be at the Federal Building early next morning [for another grand jury session]. I took my two tins [of poison] out of the lock box and carried them to my mother's house on Long Island. I placed them in my bureau drawer under some shirts. I did not unwrap them, for I did not want my mother to see what was in them, and I knew that, if she found them wrapped, she would assume that they were Christmas presents. The scene that I had witnessed that night merely made me happier to have them."

One night soon after that—*Witness* doesn't say exactly when —Chambers wrote a series of suicide notes to his mother, his wife, his children, and two friends whom he had appointed guardians of his children in the event of his death, and another letter was addressed simply "To All." In it he wrote that while "my testimony against Alger Hiss was the truth . . . the world was not ready for my testimony. . . . My purpose had always been to disclose the conspiracy, never to injure any individual man or woman. . . . I could spare them the ultimate consequences of my actions and their own, by removing myself as a witness against them. My act was not suicide in the usual sense, for I had no desire to stop living. It was self-execution." [The quotations are from *Witness*, not from the letter, which has never been made public.]

Witness then describes how Chambers looked at the directions on the cans of poison, and found them difficult to read because "the letters were blurred," but concluded that he knew what to do. He poured some of the chemical in the cover of each can, rigged "a receptacle for my head," moistened the chemical as he thought the directions required, lay down with his head inside the "receptacle" (which is not further described), and draped "another damp towel" across the front to keep the fumes in. Then he went to sleep.

Once during the night, the account continues, "I half-awoke, as if I had been stabbed in the chest and my body had jack-knifed against the pain." In the early morning, he "awoke abruptly and painfully, [and] my first thought was sheer horror to find that I was still alive; my second, disgust that I had failed." He concluded that the towel had fallen off the receptacle when he jack-knifed in pain during the night, allowing the fumes to escape, and frustrating his purpose. His mother came in and rebuked him for what he had done, or tried to do; "perhaps with the memory of her other son in mind," Chambers wrote, "this possibility had tormented her since the Hiss Case began."

He quoted her as saying, " 'How could you, how could you? The world hates a quitter. They would never forgive you. . . .'

"I drank several cups of coffee, somehow made my way to the train and eventually to the Federal Building," the account continues. He sat alone for hours outside the grand jury room, but was not called to testify that day. But he felt that his act had "disciplined" him "for the public ordeal that I was to undergo in the two Hiss trials"; and he now had a new certainty about God.

A few days later, according to *Witness*, the grand jury asked him the question that he had been dreading: "Why had I said no when I was asked if I had direct knowledge of espionage?" He paused a moment, and then "the words came effortlessly and I listened to them as if someone else were speaking.

"I said: 'There are in general two kinds of men. One kind of man believes that God is a God of Justice. The other kind of man believes that God is a God of Mercy. I am so constituted that in any question I will always range myself on the side of mercy.' I said much more about my understanding of the difference of purpose of God and man in time and in eternity, but it is those words that I remembered. . . . I never doubted that the jurors understood exactly what I was talking about."

Nixon, meanwhile, was doing his best to help Chambers. On December 6, after his battle with the Justice Department representatives at the Pennsylvania Station and the Commodore Hotel, Nixon issued a statement attacking the Department for "trying frantically to find a method which will place the blame of possession of these documents on Mr. Chambers. . . . The real issue which concerns the committee," he said, "and should concern the Department of Justice, is to determine who in the State Department furnished this information to Mr. Chambers."

Two days later Nixon used a public hearing of the Committee as an occasion to make an even stronger statement, of which he gives a highly compressed and freely edited version in *Six Crises* (page 59), but the whole of it can be studied in the Committee transcript (pages 1419–1423). The gist of it was that the Department of Justice was threatening to indict Chambers for perjury, which, said Nixon, "he may be guilty of," but Nixon regarded Chambers's perjury as merely a "technical violation," and was quite satisfied with Chambers's explanation that he had simply been trying to protect Hiss and others. Chambers, Nixon added, had confessed and was no longer a danger to national security, but "the men who furnished this information to Mr. Chambers have not been brought to justice." It was these men, and specifically Alger Hiss, whom Nixon wanted prosecuted.

"They may not even be guilty of technical crimes due to the lapse of the statute of limitations," Nixon continued, "and in that case this committee has a solemn responsibility. . . . to continue its investigation and to call every witness before it until we find who was responsible for bringing this information to Mr. Chambers, and to see whether or not those people are still engaged in that kind of activity."

But if the Justice Department were to indict Chambers, Nixon asserted, they would be unable to indict "the other individuals involved, because the star witness against the other individuals will have been an indicted and convicted perjurer." It would appear from Nixon's careful avoidance of names that when he made this statement he wasn't sure he would be able to pin the documents on Hiss, but when he wrote *Six Crises* he had no such reservations, for he edited this same passage to read, "If Chambers is indicted first, Hiss and the others will go free because the witness against them will have been discredited as a perjurer."

As it happened, all "the others" named by Chambers did go free, because no effort was made to prosecute them. Only Henry Julian Wadleigh, a State Department economist, confessed that he had been part of Chambers's espionage ring, and earned freedom from prosecution by his testimony at Hiss's trial, and the significant role he played in the grand jury proceedings that produced Hiss's indictment.

Wadleigh was in New York for his first appearance before the grand jury on December 8, the same day that Nixon made the statement described above. The Committee was busy with public hearings all that week, getting headlines for its part of the story, while the grand jury sessions were going on behind closed doors. Chambers and Hiss were at the grand jury every day but Sunday until the indictment was brought in on December 15, the jury's last day. Chambers was given a private room to sit in while he waited his turn each day, at first with his door wide open, but later he kept it closed "all but a crack," so that he could see what was going on outside without being seen. Hiss waited each day in the general witness room with other witnesses, and that is how he learned of Wadleigh's involvement.

Hiss knew Wadleigh as an economist who had been in the Trade Agreements Section of the State Department in 1938, and whom Hiss had met before that, one summer on the Eastern Shore of Maryland, where they had mutual friends. The acquaintance had been useful to Wadleigh, and he had cultivated it; Hiss was not the kind of man to throw him out of his office, although he had found Wadleigh "a bit of a pest" in those days. He hadn't seen him in a good many years, when the two found themselves together in the grand jury witness room on Wednesday, December 8.

As Hiss recalled it when he dictated a memorandum for his lawyers' use later that day, Wadleigh said to him, " 'My lawyer tells me I am not supposed to recognize you because I am going to have to refuse to answer on grounds that it might incriminate me whether I know you or not.' "

Hiss said that was all right, but he pointed out that he had already told the grand jury he knew Wadleigh when they asked him the day before. So Wadleigh sat down on the opposite side of the room. Pretty soon Wadleigh got up and came over to Hiss and said it was silly for them not to talk to each other. He added, to Hiss's astonishment, " 'The FBI came to see me and I got sort of panicky and told them I had given some documents to Chambers. However, my lawyer tells me this may not be too bad to have said because I did not tell them whether the documents were restricted or not. Now my lawyer says I must not answer any questions or talk at all because one thing will lead to another and I will say too much.' "

This was shocking news to Hiss, who didn't know that Chambers had named Wadleigh as one of his "sources" when he was interviewed by Nixon on December 6, two days before.* Hiss warned Wadleigh that if the grand jury asked about their conversation together he would have to tell them, and it was Wadleigh's turn to be shocked.

" 'Couldn't you forget what I said so that it could be as if it hadn't been said?' " he asked, according to Hiss's notes. Hiss and

*Chambers had not mentioned Wadleigh in his public testimony before HUAC in August; but Wadleigh's name appeared in Adolf Berle's notes of his 1939 conversation with Chambers, and the FBI had reminded Chambers of him after the pumpkin papers were produced.

his brother Donald, who was also there to testify, said they could not; Wadleigh returned disconsolately to his seat, and when he was called into the grand jury room later that day, was there only briefly. On his return he said, according to Hiss, " 'Now they want to talk to my lawyer, but perhaps I shouldn't have told you even that. I don't know what to say and what not to say.' " He added that he was out of a job, so "there wasn't anything that the Committee could do to him."

What Wadleigh didn't tell Hiss at the time was that one of the Justice Department lawyers, Raymond Whearty, was pressing him to waive his Fifth Amendment privilege against self-incrimination, and to tell his whole story to the grand jury. That was what Whearty wanted to consult Wadleigh's lawyer about, as Wadleigh explained in a series of newspaper articles the following summer, between the first and second trials. Whearty, he wrote, told him he was sure the problem could be straightened out if only Wadleigh and his lawyers would talk to the Justice Department about it.

So Wadleigh went back to Washington, talked to Assistant Attorney General Campbell, changed lawyers, and agreed to stop claiming the Fifth Amendment. All this was brought out in testimony at the second trial, and the implication was clear enough. If Campbell hadn't exactly promised Wadleigh immunity from prosecution, he had at least given him enough reassurance so that Wadleigh was willing to talk about these activities in guarded terms, enough to prove that the conspiracy had taken place, but not enough to hurt the case against Hiss.

This was important, because without Wadleigh's testimony there was nothing but Chambers's word to show that the espionage conspiracy which he described so vividly had really existed. Chambers had some papers and microfilms that he shouldn't have had, but had he really obtained them from a Communist underground network controlled by the mysterious J. Peters, and turned others like them over to the even more mysterious Russian, Colonel Bykov? There was no Colonel Bykov to be found; he had either gone back to Russia or been assassinated or both, for all the Justice Department knew. J. Peters was the object of deportation proceedings as an alien Communist, and was refusing to answer questions. He was allowed to leave the country shortly before the trial started the following spring, for reasons never fully explained, and that made it impossible for either prosecution or defense to call him as a witness.

Hiss was arguing before the grand jury that Chambers was a psychiatric case and that his stories were made up of fantasy; and even Assistant Attorney General Campbell had moments when he wondered if Chambers was "unstable and abnormal." Two days before the indictment he said as much to McLean, Hiss's counsel, and added, according to the notes McLean made at the time, " 'I have expected for several days to pick up the paper in the morning and read that Mr. Chambers has jumped out the window.' "

In these circumstances confirmation of Chambers's story was badly needed, and to some extent Wadleigh could provide it. He could add the flesh and blood of human experience to the skeletal evidence of the microfilms, the typewritten papers, and the scraps of handwriting. He could drive home the point that there really had been a Communist spy ring in Washington in 1938. Not only the microfilms in the pumpkin and Chambers in the witness chair, the fat spellbinder who told such vividly detailed stories of delivering the films to Colonel Bykov; here was a diffident, spectacled, nervously thin, government employee who actually admitted giving secret documents to Chambers to be microfilmed and passed on. Whether or not this removed any of the blame from Hiss, Wadleigh was important because he made the spy plot seem real.

But Wadleigh still didn't tie Hiss into the plot; that had to be done by the evidence of the typewritten papers. There was nothing but Chambers's word to show that those papers had ever been part of a spy plot, but with the constant drumfire of argument coming from the House Committee, the number of people who still doubted Chambers's word was rapidly dwindling. In retrospect it may seem odd that a spy would sit at a typewriter copying out documents for hours at a time, risking errors as well as discovery, when photographing them on microfilm would be so much simpler, swifter, safer, and easier. No other example of it comes to mind from the history of espionage before or since.

But this aspect of the problem was not presented to the grand jury, except by Hiss, who offered the opinion that the pumpkin papers were some kind of forgery or frame-up, even though he was unable to say how or why it had been done. The government attorneys concentrated on persuading the jury that the papers had been typed on Priscilla Hiss's old Woodstock typewriter, and therefore Hiss was responsible for them. And there was expert testimony to back up this idea.

Hiss and Priscilla had searched out old letters typed on every machine they had ever owned, and turned them over to the FBI for comparison with Chambers's pumpkin papers. Hiss, of course, expected the comparison would prove that the pumpkin papers had not been typed on his wife's machine; it was quite a shock when the FBI said they had, and even more of a shock when document experts hired by Hiss's lawyers wouldn't dispute the FBI's conclusion. Only much later, after the trial was over and Hiss had been convicted and sent to jail, did the defense find evidence that the experts were wrong and the papers may not have been typed on Priscilla's old Woodstock after all.

Meanwhile, both sides were also hunting for the typewriter, and on December 13 a newspaper story reported that the FBI had found it. Nixon, in the first edition of Six Crises, wrote that the FBI did find the machine on that day, and that two days later, the final day of the grand jury's term, "an expert from the FBI typed exact copies of the incriminating documents on the old Woodstock machine and had them flown up to New York as exhibits for members of the grand jury to see." This was the clincher; the jury indicted Hiss that same day.

The evidence given at the trials, however, was that the typewriter had not been found at that time. When Nixon was challenged on the point after his book appeared, he said that it was a researcher's error, and deleted the passage from subsequent editions. The truth of the matter remains a mystery; since the grand jury records are still secret, it's impossible to know what the grand jury was told on December 15 or what typed copies the

FBI showed them. Whatever it was, it must have been persuasive if not wholly conclusive, for one of the jurors told Hiss's lawyers that they had split down the middle and voted to indict by a margin of "only one more than a bare majority." (Nixon claimed in *Six Crises* that "all nineteen members [of the grand jury] voted to indict Hiss," but never said where he had obtained that information.)

The jury also had the opportunity to hear Nixon's arguments in person, for on December 13 Nixon appeared to show them the microfilms himself, still refusing to turn them over to the Justice Department. On that occasion, as described by Nixon, Assistant Attorney General Campbell threatened to ask the judge to cite Nixon for contempt, but Nixon "warned him of the constitutional question that would be raised if a member of Congress, appearing voluntarily before a Grand Jury, were so cited while carrying out a mandate of the committee which he represented." It was a confrontation between the legislative and executive branches involving much the same issues as were to arise over the Watergate scandal a quarter of a century later, when the evidence in dispute was tape recordings instead of microfilms, and Nixon again refused to turn them over, taking the opposite position on the constitutional question.

In 1948 Campbell yielded, and "After a few anxious moments," wrote Nixon, "I was allowed to return to Washington with the microfilm still in my possession but with the understanding that, in the event Hiss was indicted, I would take the responsibility of seeing that the Committee would make the microfilm available as evidence in the trial."

The following day, according to the notes Hiss made at the time, Campbell came to him and "said in practically these words, 'The FBI has cracked the case. You are in it up to your eyes. Your wife's in it. Why don't you go in there and tell the truth?' " Hiss replied that "I had continuously told the truth and that I will continue to do so. Mr. Campbell had then said, 'You are going to be indicted. I am not fooling. There are five witnesses against you.'

"I said that I was not fooling either," the account continues. "Mr. Campbell then said, 'This is your government speaking.' "

Hiss reported all this to the grand jury the same afternoon, trying to make the point that Campbell had gone beyond his authority in determining what the grand jury was going to do, since the decision to indict belongs as a matter of law to the jurors, and not the prosecuting attorney, who is supposed to avoid any kind of coercion. But it was a lawyer's point, and the jurors did not seem to have been impressed.

The indictment was based on two questions asked in the final session for the purpose. The first was, "Mr. Hiss, you have probably been asked this question before, but I'd like to ask the question again. At any time did you, or Mrs. Hiss in your presence, turn any documents of the State Department or any other Government organization, or copies of any documents of the State Department or any other Government organization, over to Whittaker Chambers?" Hiss answered, "Never. Excepting, I assume, the title certificate to the Ford."

The second question was; "Can you say definitely that you did not see him after January 1, 1937?"

Hiss answered, "Yes, I think I can definitely say that."

The indictment alleged that both answers were false in that Hiss had delivered State Department documents to Chambers in February and March of 1938. As McLean commented when he got the news, the jury indicted Hiss for perjury because they couldn't indict him for espionage; that was barred by the statute of limitations, as Nixon had noted on December 8. But to defend himself against the perjury charge, Hiss would have to bring proofs that he hadn't committed espionage eleven years before, just as though the statue of limitations didn't exist. By the grand jury's action, Hiss had been deprived of the statute's protection, and in McLean's view, it was "a sleazy trick."

15

THE SEARCH FOR EVIDENCE

IT is generally true that in a criminal trial the burden of proof is on the prosecution, and the defendant gets the benefit of any reasonable doubt. This principle is well established in constitutional law and many rules of judicial procedure, and it usually means that a defendant will go free if he can show that the government's case isn't all it pretends to be, and a reasonable man can have serious doubts about it.

Alger Hiss thought that was going to be easy. The government's chief witness, Whittaker Chambers, had told lies under oath before the House Un-American Activities Committee (HUAC) and the grand jury that brought in the indictment, and he had admitted doing so—how could a trial jury take his word after that? Chambers had told a farcical story about stealing government documents in the 1930s that had no relation to the way government really operated in those days, as Hiss knew from his own experience—how could anybody believe that? Chambers was a self-confessed former spy, Communist, and traitor to his country—why should anyone believe what he said about anything?

Chambers had produced not a single witness to corroborate his story, except his wife and Henry Julian Wadleigh. His wife could be expected to back him up for personal reasons, and there were plenty of precedents in law for rejecting testimony of that kind. Besides, even his wife said she didn't know anything about

272

the spy story that Chambers had told. As for Wadleigh, if he said he had given documents to Chambers, that didn't prove Hiss had done so; nor did it prove that Chambers had given the documents to the Russians, whatever Chambers might have told Wadleigh. The documents in evidence clearly hadn't been given to the Russians; they had been kept by Chambers for some purpose of his own, whatever that might prove to be.

True, Chambers's story had been believed by the House Committee and a small majority of the grand jury, but under conditions that had prevented Hiss from offering a carefully prepared rebuttal. And the trial jury would have to be unanimous to convict him; a bare majority wouldn't do. True, most of the press and public believed Chambers too, but they hadn't yet heard Hiss's answer. So Hiss was confident that he would win acquittal when he had his day in court. Indeed, that was what he had been trying to achieve from the beginning; he had demanded a hearing from the House Committee, and when he found that wasn't working, he had challenged Chambers to a libel suit. To be a defendant in a criminal trial was not as good as being plaintiff in a libel suit, but at least it would give him his day in court. Hiss looked forward to it with confidence and undiminished hope.

Edward C. McLean, his lawyer, knew better. McLean had not been conditioned from childhood, like Hiss, to suppress his fears by pretending there was no danger; at forty-four Hiss was so accustomed to doing this that the habit had become part of his nature. He didn't know he was doing it, and his friends couldn't figure out why he did it. Hiss had never had any experience with juries, but McLean had; he had been Deputy Assistant District Attorney under Thomas E. Dewey in 1935–1936, when Dewey was beginning the racket-busting campaign that took him eventually to the Governor's Mansion in Albany and gave him ever-to-be-frustrated hopes of the White House. McLean knew that no jury was going to see this thing the way Hiss saw it, and that the evidence against him was going to be tough to beat.

In particular, McLean knew that this was not a case where the usual "burden of proof" and "reasonable doubt" rules would apply. They might be honored in form, but as a practical matter they weren't going to carry much weight with the jury. After the excitement over Crosley's teeth and the old Ford car at the House Committee hearings, the midnight trip to the pumpkin patch, the air-sea rescue of Representative Nixon, the strips of microfilm that Nixon had dangled before the eyes of newspaper reporters and grand jurors, and the public battle waged by Nixon against the Department of Justice over whether Chambers or Hiss was the real criminal, the indictment had been presented to the public as a kind of denouement of the drama. It put an end to the suspense; Nixon had been right all along, Hiss was the guilty one after all, and the grand jury was only doing its obvious duty by saying so. The trial jury was expected to do the same.

Under the circumstances, the burden of proof was clearly going to be on the defense; in such a case you can't convince a jury that things aren't what the government says unless you can prove they are something else instead. McLean didn't believe Hiss had given Chambers the pumpkin papers, because Hiss said he hadn't, and McLean trusted Hiss. But he didn't have any idea where Chambers had got them or how, and he had only a few months to find out. It wasn't going to be time enough, and McLean knew it.

Even before the indictment, McLean tried unsuccessfully to persuade Hiss of the trouble he was in. When he found Hiss didn't believe him, he asked Richard H. Field, who had been much closer to Hiss in their Harvard Law School days, to see what he could do. Field had lunch with Hiss at the Harvard Club, and told him he agreed with McLean that Hiss would probably be indicted, and there was grave danger that he would be convicted.

Hiss replied, as Field later recalled it, " 'I just can't believe that. I simply don't believe that twelve jurors are going to listen to Chambers and me and believe Chambers and not me. I just don't believe it.' "

And Hiss stuck to this view. After the first trial ended in a hung jury, he expected to be acquitted in the second. When the second trial ended in his conviction, he expected to win on appeal. Hiss remembers McLean saying to him that day. " 'Alger, I just don't understand you, your optimism is boundless,' " and as Hiss commented later, "He also implied it was groundless, meaning I had no right to feel that way." But he did, and the feeling influenced his actions throughout the trial and even afterwards, when he embarked on the confident quest for vindication which he has carried on ever since.

After the indictment Bill Marbury, who had handled the pretrial depositions in the libel case, dropped out, saying he had had no experience with criminal cases and could be of no further help. But the libel suit wasn't over yet, and he accompanied McLean to a few more sessions with Chambers, during which McLean tried to find out more about the pumpkin papers, without much success. Chambers's answers were vague; he stuck to the story that Hiss had given him the documents, but he couldn't remember when or where Hiss had done so in any particular case, what had been said about them at the time, or whether anyone else had been present. Priscilla might have been there sometimes, he said, but he wasn't sure. He had no recollection of what had actually happened on any occasion; he merely described what he thought "would have happened," judging by the dates on the various documents. So long as he avoided saying he had done anything at any particular time or place, it was impossible for the defense to bring evidence to show that he hadn't.

Chambers did, however, describe a general routine for his operation. Beginning about January 1937, he said, he went to Hiss's home every "seven to ten days" shortly after 5:00 P.M., and picked up documents from Hiss, which he gave to a fellow conspirator to photograph on microfilm. He described two photographers, whom he met at various unspecified places and times, and who worked sometimes in Baltimore and sometimes in Washington, but always got the documents back to Chambers the same night, in time for him to return to Hiss's home around 1:00 A.M., ring the bell, and give the documents to whomever answered, Hiss or his wife. Sometime in the middle of 1937, he said, Bykov told him to "increase the flow" of material; picking up documents once every seven to ten days wasn't enough. There was no suggestion that Chambers should visit Hiss more often, however, and Hiss couldn't keep the documents away from his office longer than overnight, Chambers said. The solution Bykov proposed, according to Chambers, was for Hiss to bring home documents every night and for Priscilla to make typewritten copies or summaries of them. Then Chambers could have the typewritten papers photographed instead of the originals. This was Chambers's explanation of the typewritten papers; it didn't fit the internal evidence of the papers and documents themselves, as will be seen,* but nobody knew that at the time.

Hiss didn't see how any juror could believe that Chambers could have come so often to his home on Thirtieth Street without being seen by the neighbors, especially if he was ringing the doorbell at 1:00 A.M.; or that Priscilla could have banged away at her old typewriter night after night in that little house with its paper-thin walls without being heard by the Robbs on one side or the Mays on the other. But twenty jurors did, eight at the first trial and twelve at the second; for as McLean well knew, the fact that neighbors hadn't witnessed it didn't prove it hadn't happened. And anyway, Chambers said it happened not only at Thirtieth Street, where the Hisses lived in 1937, but for three months more at Volta Place, where the Hisses had moved at the end of that year, and the neighbors weren't so close and might not have noticed.

Chambers said a lot of other things, too, that were all vague and uncertain and not very helpful to the defense. He didn't remember exactly where or when he had first met Hiss, or who else had been there, or what had been said; he said he had seen Hiss once a month or more from sometime in 1934 until the meeting with Bykov in January 1937, after which they saw each other more often, but nobody else had been present at any of those meetings except sometimes Priscilla; he had never met any of Hiss's personal friends, except for a woman with the memorable name of Plum Fountain, whom he said he met by chance at an unnamed restaurant on some occasion he couldn't remember; he thought he had spent the night a few times at Hiss's house on

---

* Chapters 19 and 21.

Thirtieth Street, but wasn't sure; he said the Hisses had visited him several times at his various homes in Baltimore, but the only occasion he could date was either New Year's Eve or New Year's Day 1938. He said Priscilla had visited Mrs. Chambers at a summer place in Smithtown, on the Delaware River, for about ten days in 1935, but he wasn't sure which end of the summer; and that Priscilla had spent a day at the Chambers home in Baltimore, in the fall of 1935, minding Mrs. Chambers's baby while she went to New York, but again he wasn't sure of the date.

Chambers said he had "no detailed recollection" of any of these things; he said, "I am testifying wholly on the reconstruction of events." He explained that the whole operation "was set up for the purpose of indefiniteness," so he couldn't be expected to remember anything definitely. At the trial, when Hiss and Priscilla proved that they couldn't have been in Baltimore for the 1938 New Year's party, Chambers said it must have been some other occasion, but it was certainly a party of some sort.

Chambers also described a trip he said he had taken with Hiss and Priscilla to Peterborough, New Hampshire, in 1937. When he first mentioned it in Baltimore, he said the purpose of the trip was for Chambers to deliver a message to Harry Dexter White, Assistant Secretary of the Treasury, at his summer home.* Alger and Priscilla sat in the car while Chambers walked up the driveway to talk to White, according to Chambers; he returned in fifteen or twenty minutes, he said, and they went to a tourist home in Peterborough for the night, and saw a play at a local summer theater. In Baltimore Chambers was vague about the tourist home, didn't identify the play, and couldn't remember the date.

It was Chambers's habit to add new details to his stories each time he was questioned about them, somewhat like Pooh-Bah in Gilbert and Sullivan's *Mikado*, who explained when one of his fancifully inventive tales went awry that it was "merely corrob-

---

*Chambers had not mentioned this trip while White was alive; he told HUAC, on August 7, 1948, that he had never stayed overnight on any of the trips he took with Hiss. White's fatal heart attack occurred the following week, so by March 25, 1949, when Chambers told the Peterborough story, he had no fear of contradiction.

orative detail, intended to give artistic verisimilitude to an otherwise bald and unconvincing narrative." Usually Chambers's "corroborative detail" was merely colorful, and impossible to check; he said that he remembered driving with the Hisses to Long Eddy, New York, on Easter Sunday, 1935, for example, because "at a red light in Norristown we passed a policeman carrying an Easter lily." Sometimes the new details were variations to get around the contradictions in his testimony; it may not have been a New Year's party after all, but he was quite sure they'd drunk champagne, because he remembered it made him sick. And so on.

But only in the case of the Peterborough trip did the added details give the defense something to work on. In the first trial Chambers remembered the date—August 10, 1937—and the name of the tourist home where they had stayed—it was called Bleak House. By the second trial Hiss had accumulated abundant evidence that neither he nor Priscilla could have been in Peterborough on that date, and the proprietor of Bleak House was called to produce the registration book showing that neither Chambers nor the Hisses could have stayed there that night, or any other night. Claude Cross was sure this proof would demolish the prosecution's case, since it demonstrated so clearly that Chambers was lying about an important issue. The Peterborough trip was the nearest thing to direct evidence the prosecution could bring to show that Hiss had seen Chambers after January 1, 1937, as charged in the indictment; everything else was vague or circumstantial. But the jury wasn't impressed; they had become accustomed to Chambers's habit of changing his story whenever he was caught in a contradiction, and anyhow, even if he lied about Peterborough, that didn't prove he had lied about the pumpkin papers. By that time Chambers had confessed to telling so many lies under oath for so many reasons that the jury was used to it.

So the information McLean got from the pretrial examination in the libel suit wasn't very useful; its main result was to involve the defense in an enormous amount of time, work, and expense trying to check it out and find evidence to refute it. Hiss and Priscilla denied that they had ever done the things Chambers described, or seen him on the occasions he described; but short of accounting for every minute of their time from early 1934 until April 1938, there was no way of proving that they hadn't. They were up against the very problem that the "burden of proof" rule and the statute of limitations are designed to prevent—the prosecution must prove what happened because the defense can't be expected to prove what *didn't* happen, and if an accuser produces evidence he's kept carefully hidden for ten years, the accused cannot be expected to find the evidence to the contrary that would have been available ten years before. By that time too much of it has been lost or forgotten.

But when McLean brought this point up in pretrial motions before Judge William Bondy in the U.S. District Court it got him nowhere. Later, Stryker argued it in the first trial before Judge Samuel H. Kaufman, and Cross did the same before Judge Henry W. Goddard in the second, with the same lack of success. Robert M. Benjamin argued it before the U.S. Court of Appeals and was turned down; there weren't enough precedents in the history of American jurisprudence to support him, because nothing quite like the Hiss case had ever happened before.

Then Benjamin tried the U.S. Supreme Court, but the Justices refused to hear the case by a vote of four to two, with three abstentions. As Justice William O. Douglas pointed out in *Go East, Young Man*, the trouble was that Justices Felix Frankfurter and Stanley Reed had appeared as character witnesses on Hiss's behalf in the trial, and therefore had to disqualify themselves. Justice Tom C. Clark, who had been Attorney General at the time of the trial, also disqualified himself, which left six Justices to hear the petition, a bare quorum of the Court. "Normally it takes four votes out of nine to grant a petition for certiorari," Douglas wrote. "But if there are only seven Justices qualified to sit, the votes of three are enough to grant a petition. . . . If either Reed or Frankfurter had not testified at the trial, we would doubtless have had three to grant; and in my view no Court at any time could possibly have sustained the conviction." There wasn't enough trustworthy evidence to support the verdict, the

Justice wrote; this was a point the Appeals Court had not considered, relying instead on the doctrine that the jury were entitled to trust the evidence if they wanted to.

Those arguments, of course, came much later. In the early months of 1949, the period of preparation before the first trial began, Alger and Priscilla Hiss set about gathering what evidence for their defense they could find. Hiss searched for old appointment diaries, address books, and records kept by his secretaries. Priscilla wrote endless letters to everyone she could think of, asking what they could remember about the old Ford car, when the Plymouth was first acquired, what New Year's parties they had been to, where they had been at various times in the summers of 1935, 1936, and 1937, and so on. It produced some leads that were followed up at considerable expense and led to many witnesses appearing at the trial, and much testimony and argument. But in the end it didn't add up to anything very effective.

Among other things this research established the scope of Priscilla's activities during 1937, when Chambers claimed she was busy at her typewriter copying out the documents Hiss was accused of bringing home from his office. Instead of that, she was occupied with the double responsibility of taking care of Tim during the long months after his accident, and running the Bryn Mawr Club of Washington as its president. Besides the regular monthly meetings she organized two fund-raising benefits and a three-day conference of the Bryn Mawr Alumnae Council, which took place while Tim was in the hospital, and involved, among other things, a tea at the White House with Mrs. Roosevelt, from which Priscilla had to rush away for her daily visit with Tim. Assistant Secretary Sayre came to dinner one night with his niece, and they were guests of the Hisses at a Katharine Hepburn production of *Jane Eyre*, the main fund-raising event of the season. All this was evidence enough of Priscilla's energetic and active life, but it didn't exactly prove she hadn't found time to do some typing as well.

Hiss, meanwhile, went to work with Lloyd Paul Stryker, who

had been retained as trial counsel, and gave him every detail he could remember of his life in those days, and the names of everyone he could remember who might shed any light on the problem. Stryker had been selected as the outstanding criminal defense lawyer of his day, a man with the best record in New York for handling difficult cases and doing the best that could be done for his clients. His most famous case had also been one of his rare failures, involving a former Democratic district leader named Jimmy Hines, whose conviction as a racketeer was also the most famous achieved by Thomas E. Dewey in his gang-busting District Attorney days. McLean, having worked for Dewey in those days, had reason to know Stryker and respect his abilities.

Stryker was a short, burly man with the springy step of a prizefighter and a manner that ranged from bulldog to sentimentalist. He had a round Roman head with sparse, short-cropped gray hair and a courtroom style that borrowed from both the pulpit and the operatic stage. He was a son of the Reverend Melancthon Woolsey Stryker, president of Hamilton College for twenty-five years, and his own rhetorical style was sometimes hellfire-and-damnation, sometimes poetic. He was a man who could tell the Devil from an honest man, and who knew how to make the Devil real to a jury; and if he never exactly identified Chambers as the Devil in so many words, he spared no effort to show that he was far from an honest man. Hiss was somewhat embarrassed by Stryker's histrionic ways, but as Harold Shapero, Stryker's assistant, said of him, "Stryker was a man who would become aroused if a hue and cry was on and he thought someone was getting a raw deal." And that was a fair description of the way he saw the Hiss case.

Hiss decided that the crucial evidence must be Priscilla's old typewriter; if they could find that, it would surely prove in some way that Priscilla hadn't typed the documents on it. The experts compared Chambers's papers with some of her old letters, and said it looked as though they were all done on the same machine; but that wasn't conclusive. The experts said they couldn't tell whether Priscilla had done the typing or not, but that wasn't very reassuring; some said the chances were she had. The government had Chambers's papers now, but maybe the defense could get the typewriter. It ought to prove something.

Neither Hiss nor Priscilla could remember what had happened to the old machine. Priscilla had made several different guesses in talking to the FBI and the grand jury, and so had Alger; they thought it might have been sold to a junk man, or given to the Salvation Army, but they couldn't remember when. Later, it turned out that they had given another typewriter to the Salvation Army, a portable Priscilla had bought for Timmy in September 1937, on his eleventh birthday.

Priscilla didn't like typing and didn't do it often; Alger had never done it at all. The old Woodstock had been given to Priscilla by her father, Thomas Fansler, in the early 1930s when she was collaborating with her sister-in-law Roberta Fansler on their book about fine arts for the Carnegie Foundation. It was a big, heavy office machine, which had originally belonged to the insurance company where Priscilla's father worked. Priscilla didn't like it, and wrote most of her manuscript in longhand. The only desk she had to use the typewriter on was the old-fashioned, slant-top kind with pigeon holes and a flap that opened down and rested on two little panels of wood that came out above the drawers below; much too unsteady for such a heavy machine. The portable suited Timmy better, and when she'd bought that Priscilla certainly didn't need two typewriters.

Besides, the Woodstock had developed the characteristic faults of its kind, and Priscilla didn't have enough experience of typewriters to know when repairs were needed. What happens to old manual typewriters that are used rather inexpertly is that two keys sometimes jam together in the little steel V that guides them to the ribbon; for example, if you hit the "h" in "the" before the "t" has time to fall back, the "h" will either hit the back of the "t" or get wedged alongside it, and if that happens too often the "h" key will develop a little burr on its side, and get twisted a bit, so that it tends to get stuck in the narrow end of that steel V almost every time you hit it. This can be annoying, especially if you don't notice it because your eyes are on the keyboard, and in a moment several more keys get piled up behind that stuck "h" and you have to pull them all down by hand, getting typewriter ink on your fingers in the process. It was reason enough to give the damn thing away and buy a nice, light portable in better condition.

This is apparently the sort of thing that happened to Priscilla's Woodstock, along with a tendency of the ribbon to stick, which may have been nothing more than Priscilla's unfamiliarity with the mechanism. She says she doesn't know how to change a typewriter ribbon and doesn't think she's ever done it; if it has to be done, she gets somebody else to do it for her. In any case, she got rid of the machine, but eleven years later she couldn't remember how or exactly when she'd done so.

McLean sent investigators, some hired and some volunteer, to look in all the likely places—records of the Salvation Army, junk dealers, and used-typewriter dealers in the Washington area—while Priscilla asked friends and relatives whether they remembered anything about it. The searchers didn't get very far until one day in February 1949, two months after the indictment, when Mike Catlett, a young black man, called Hiss's brother Donald. Catlett had done odd jobs for the Hisses when he was a teen-ager and his mother Claudia Catlett was their maid. His brother, Perry Murphy Catlett, known as Pat, had also worked for the Hisses as a boy. They all knew Donald Hiss quite well, and they lived not far away from his home in Washington.

Mike Catlett told Donald Hiss that the FBI had been asking about the old typewriter and that he knew where it was but hadn't told them. (Later, at the trial, Prosecutor Tom Murphy said twenty-five or thirty FBI agents had searched Washington for the typewriter, a considerably larger force than the defense could afford, but they couldn't find it, even though they "shook the city of Washington down to a fare-thee-well.") The Catlett family sided with the Hisses in the battle; they liked the Hiss family, had been well treated by them, and had no reason to help the FBI.

Catlett remembered that the typewriter was one of many things—cast-off clothing, furniture, and household equipment—

that the Hisses had given the Catletts from time to time, when they were moving. He couldn't remember whether the Hisses had given them the typewriter when they moved from P Street to Thirtieth Street or at the time they left Thirtieth Street for the house on Volta Place, where they moved at the end of 1937, but he knew it was at one or the other time.

He thought the typewriter was still in a closet at his home at 2728 P Street, two blocks from where the Hisses had lived in 1935. But when he and Donald Hiss went to look for it, it was missing. It turned out that Pat Catlett had taken it for a while, but since it hadn't worked very well, he had given it to his sister Burnetta. She had given it to a Dr. Easter, who had died, and after that it had come into the possession of a man named Marlow, who had moved Dr. Easter's belongings out of his home. Sometime later, Ira Lockey, doing another moving job for Marlow, had found the typewriter sitting out in the rain in the backyard, and asked if he could have it as partial payment for the job. Lockey gave it to his daughter Margaret, but it was in such bad condition she couldn't use it and didn't think it was worth repairing.

It took a long time for Donald Hiss and McLean to interview all the people involved in the chain, and then it took even longer to persuade Lockey to get the typewriter back from his daughter and to sell it to them. The deal was finally arranged with the help of Charles Houston, a black attorney who was able to gain Lockey's confidence, and who was willing to help because he remembered an occasion some years before when Hiss had helped him in one of the early cases involving racial discrimination in real estate covenants. So the defense finally acquired the typewriter on April 16, 1949, two months after Catlett first called Donald Hiss, and seven weeks before the trial began.

The machine wasn't actually in such bad shape as one might have expected after such a history; with a little oiling it performed well enough to type out some samples of its work for comparison with the photostats of Chambers's papers. The result was another blow; the experts who examined the two sets of typing said they

284

couldn't tell the difference. All they would say was that this looked like a machine that could have typed both Chambers's papers and Priscilla's old letters.

However, the evidence seemed clear enough that the machine had been given to the Catletts before Chambers's papers were typed, so they couldn't have been typed on it by Priscilla. Mike Catlett and his mother both remembered that the typewriter was given to them when the Hisses were moving; it couldn't have been when they moved to Thirtieth Street in 1936, because Priscilla had typed a letter on it dated May 25, 1937—the latest date of any of her work that was found. And it couldn't have been when they moved out of Volta Place in 1943, because by that time the Catletts weren't working for the Hisses anymore. So it had to be when they moved to Volta Place, at the end of December 1937, a week before the earliest date on Chambers's papers.

Hiss was well content with this explanation, and made no further efforts to find out who had actually typed the papers produced by Chambers, or why they looked so much like the work of Priscilla's old Woodstock. Whoever it was, however it was done or why, it was clearly not Priscilla's doing, and under the "burden of proof" rule the defense was under no obligation to go further. Or so Hiss thought; it didn't work out that way at his trial, however.

Meanwhile there was another development that Hiss found extremely disturbing. His stepson Timothy called McLean's office one day with quite a story to tell. Timothy was now in New York again, and for some time he had been getting calls from homosexual friends who told him the FBI had been interviewing them about him. Tim wasn't surprised when the FBI came to see him too. The agents were polite enough, but they went out of their way to mention all their visits to his friends and the information they had gathered about his way of life. It was a clear warning that if he chose to testify they would make this information public and use it to discredit him.

Tim regarded this as simple blackmail to keep him from testifying; and in the nearly thirty years since the trial he hasn't changed this view. But he told McLean he was willing to testify anyway; he wanted to tell the jury what he had told the FBI, which was that Chambers was a liar and he knew it. Tim had been living at home all through the period that Chambers claimed to have known Hiss; he remembered the period when the Chambers family stayed a few days on the top floor at P Street, because Tim had been sick in bed at the time, and Chambers's wife had painted a picture of him, which he didn't like, nor did Alger and Priscilla, so they had thrown it away. But as for the visits Chambers described, at least once a month in 1935–1936 and every "seven to ten days" in 1937 and the first three months of 1938, Tim knew they had never happened. He had been in the house at these crucial times of 5:00 P.M. and 1:00 A.M., when Chambers said he used to ring the bell. In 1937, in the tiny house on Thirtieth Street, Tim had been laid up for months with his leg in a cast, in a bedroom overlooking the front door, where he could see and hear everyone who came and went. In early 1938, when Chambers said he had picked up the papers that were in evidence at the trial, Tim was eleven, going on twelve, an age when little that goes on around the house escapes a boy's attention. That was the Volta Place house, and Tim remembered distinctly that the bell didn't work; Chambers would have had to use the big brass knocker. If Chambers had been there, Tim would have known it; Tim never saw him there, and knew he'd never come.

Tim thought this would be effective testimony, and wanted to give it at the trial. In retrospect it can be argued that if he had done so, the prosecution could have discredited him in the jury's eyes by arguing that the word of a homosexual couldn't be believed, and that he was only lying to protect his stepfather. But there was plenty of evidence that Chambers had been through homosexual experiences of his own, and the prosecution knew it. If Tim had been attacked on those grounds, Chambers could have been, too, and the defense, with the more lurid tales to tell, might have come out ahead. There were plenty of rumors on the subject during the trial, but no facts were made public; Tim was never called to the witness stand, and the lurid tales about Chambers remained untold.*

It was Hiss who made the decision; he refused to even consider allowing Tim to testify, so that his lawyers never considered whether it might be helpful or worth the risk. Hiss took the view that Tim was under such an emotional strain that the experience of testifying would be destructive to him. Once his life-style was in headlines across the front page of every newspaper in the country and broadcast over radio and television, Tim might never be able to back down from it again. Hiss wanted him to change, and believed that some day he would; it was his most earnest wish, stronger even than his own hope for acquittal. He said to McLean, "I'd rather go to jail than let that boy testify." He didn't think it would come to that, but it turned out to be a realistic appraisal; and he never regretted the decision.

Hiss's hopes for Tim's return to normal living were realized too, though it took a little time, and was not complete until after Hiss came out of jail. But Tim's success was a source of great comfort to Hiss in those difficult years after his release, and has continued to be so in the long and often discouraging years of the struggle for vindication. A close relationship has grown up between Hiss and his stepson and step-grandchildren. "We've agreed," Hiss said once in his shy way, "that while there may be no such thing as a perfect son or a perfect father or stepfather, we can be very good friends, and we are."

In 1949, however, the wisdom of Hiss's decision was by no means clear, and there was no time or reason for examining his motives. To a degree he was protecting his own sensitivities as well as Tim's by avoiding those sensational headlines, and to a perhaps more significant degree, he was trying to protect Priscilla's feelings. Alger regards Priscilla as a very apprehensive woman, and speaks of her as suffering from "free-floating anxie-

---

* At least they weren't told at the trial; some of them have been documented since then by Meyer A. Zeligs in his book, *Friendship and Fratricide.*

ties," meaning that she can always find something to worry about. Priscilla, on the other hand, doesn't consider herself apprehensive at all, and resents what she regards as Alger's overprotectiveness.

According to Priscilla, she wasn't thinking about Tim's problems in 1949, nor was she worrying about her own privacy. Her only concern, she says, was that her husband might be convicted. She knew that Alger was supremely confident that the trial would prove his innocence, but she couldn't share his confidence; she was too distressed. In any case, the lawyers working for Hiss found her impossible to deal with, and found Hiss so protective of her that they gave up trying.

Yet her testimony was going to be important, because she was the one accused of typing Chambers's so-called pumpkin papers. If she could prove she hadn't done it, her husband would almost certainly be acquitted; but if he should be convicted, the jury's verdict would condemn her, too, as a member of a Communist spy ring. Priscilla doesn't seem to have understood that; "I probably didn't take it in," she says today. And when it happened she refused to believe that the verdict implied any guilt on her part; she insists that no one could accuse her of being part of such a conspiracy, no matter what the jury found.

In preparation for an important trial it is customary for lawyers to give the witnesses a certain amount of preliminary rehearsal, so they will know what to expect when they are called upon to testify. There are many rules governing what a lawyer may do in these rehearsals; a witness may not be "coached," or told what to say, or given any information the witness doesn't already have from her (or his) own knowledge. But the attorney is entitled to find out what the witness knows, so as to be able to ask the right questions in court, and the witness can be shown how to answer questions intelligently and effectively, and in the proper legal form, without getting all confused or confusing the jury. The practice is sometimes known as "horseshedding," from the horse-and-buggy days when lawyers would take their witnesses out to the horse shed behind the court house to do the necessary interviewing out of earshot from each other and the judge. During cross-examination at the trial, the opposing attorney has an opportunity to find out if any illegal coaching of the witness has gone on in the horse shed.

According to Hiss, it was Harold Shapero's job to do the "horseshedding" of Priscilla during the first trial, but when interviewed in later years he couldn't remember doing it, and he was sure he hadn't done very much. She was reluctant, he recalled, and Hiss was protective; he concluded that Priscilla wouldn't make a very effective witness no matter what was done to help her. Harold Rosenwald had the same recollection; Claude Cross, who took Stryker's place at the second trial, said he never talked to Priscilla very much, it wasn't worth it. For her part, Priscilla feels that the lawyers didn't tell her enough and treated her distantly, with a kind of exaggerated deference; they wouldn't let her help, she says.

Apparently Hiss's lawyers never fully understood why Hiss was so protective toward Priscilla; they felt there must be some reason for it, as did the press and public watching them at the trial, and no doubt the jury too. But neither the lawyers, jury, nor public knew what the reason was, and it was all too easy to assume that maybe Priscilla had been mixed up in Chambers's spy plot after all, and that Hiss knew it. This was essentially the conclusion that Marbury had arrived at in the beginning; by the end of the trial it was common gossip around the court house and in the press.

The Hisses were quite unaware of all this; Alger remembers Priscilla worrying about the possibility that she might have to answer questions on the witness stand about her private life and the illegal abortion she had had so many years before, but Priscilla insists that those were his worries, not hers. Considering the research that the FBI had done into Tim's private life, there were grounds for anxiety. So Alger kept Priscilla's secret.

Even after the trial and the appeal were over, and a new legal team, headed by Chester Lane, was looking for new evidence on which to base the motion for a new trial, Hiss dodged the question when Lane seemed to be getting too close to it. "After all," he said to Lane, "you must let Priscilla and me have some secrets."

Lane pressed for details, and Hiss offered a compromise—he would tell the story in confidence to a psychiatrist who knew him and his wife very well, and the psychiatrist could decide how much Lane should be told. This was done, and the psychiatrist assured Lane that the matter had nothing to do with any of the issues in the trial, or with the particular bit of evidence Lane was trying to track down. That was all; and with that Lane had to be content.

Under these circumstances Hiss's lawyers were never able to learn anything very useful from Priscilla, who could not remember clearly what she had done with her typewriter or what letters she had typed on it. And at home Alger and Priscilla were constantly harassed by phone calls from strangers, some obscene, some threatening that came at all hours of the night, as though part of a deliberate campaign to weaken them by destroying their sleep. Priscilla hated to go out the door for fear of the news reporters and photographers, who were always outside once the trial began. Alger wouldn't talk to the press; he didn't want to "try the case in the newspapers," as he said, and anyhow he found most of the press was hostile to him. But he couldn't prevent them from taking pictures as he and Priscilla walked along the sidewalk, and once a press photographer followed them into a subway car and popped his flashbulb, sending Priscilla and some of the other passengers scurrying in alarm to the other end of the car, as if there had been an explosion of some kind.

The opening of the trial on May 31 found the defense with some assets and some liabilities. They had the typewriter, the government had the pumpkin papers; of the three key defense witnesses, Tim was not going to be allowed to testify, Priscilla's position was ambiguous and unclear, and it would be only Hiss's word against Chambers's, with most of the public, from whom the jury would be drawn, already conditioned to believe in Chambers rather than Hiss. In Lloyd Paul Stryker they had the best trial lawyer in the business; and they were going to need him.

16

TRIAL BY JURY AND
THE PRESS

IF Alger Hiss didn't want to try his case in the newspapers he had a right to say so, but that didn't prevent it from happening. When the trial opened in one of the great oak-paneled courtrooms of the Federal Building on Foley Square, a stone's throw from the Brooklyn Bridge and New York's City Hall, there were more newspaper reporters present than all the lawyers, judge, and jurors together. There were eight major newspapers in New York in those days, besides three national wire services, three news magazines, four radio networks, countless specialized feature services, and the young television networks, not to mention neighborhood and suburban papers and radio stations. The major papers and services sent their staff people every day, and from time to time top columnists and broadcast commentators would drop in for color stories or moments of high drama, as did correspondents of foreign newspapers and wire services. On opening day it seemed as though everyone was there.

Among the crowd was the author of this book, representing the *New York Herald Tribune*. So far I have kept myself out of the book as much as possible, since I was not present to witness most of the events I have described and have relied on accounts of those who were. (See Sources, Bibliography, and Notes on page 443.) But I was present at the trials, every day and all day for the six weeks of the first trial and nine weeks of the second. My observations and reactions at the time cannot fail to influence this account, so it's only fair to give some indication of what my feelings were.

I knew nothing about Alger Hiss when I was assigned to cover the first trial. I had been off on other assignments while he was appearing before the House Un-American Activities Committee (HUAC) and the grand jury, and too busy with my own stories to pay more than passing attention to this one. Consequently, when I got the assignment, I read through the news clippings in the *Tribune*'s morgue and the whole transcript of the Committee hearings in order to fill in the background. It was quite an eye-opener.

Neither the transcript nor the clippings told me what had been going on behind the scenes, of course, because neither Nixon's *Six Crises* nor Chambers's *Witness* had yet been written. But what I read made it clear that the Committee had been pro-Chambers and anti-Hiss from the beginning, and that a lot of questions remained to be examined at the trial. I had known people like Chambers before and didn't trust them; I had never known anybody quite like Hiss, but I knew a good many New Dealers and State Department people and had come in contact with a lot of Communists in the course of my work and, before that, in my student days. From the account Hiss had given of himself before the Committee, he didn't sound much like a Communist to me, or a spy either.

I didn't know much about espionage, though some of my friends had been in the Office of Strategic Services (OSS), the precursor of today's CIA, during the war, and I had spent several weeks with OSS missions when I was a war correspondent on the Mediterranean front in 1944–1945. They hadn't talked much about their work or let me see much of it, and anyhow it wasn't at all like the kind of espionage Chambers had described, so it didn't prove anything about Chambers one way or the other. It just made him sound amateurish.

I thought I knew something about Communists, though, because I had written my senior thesis in college on the events that led up to the Russian Revolution. I was in the class of 1936; in those days most people seemed to think the Soviet Union would never amount to anything, and history majors at Princeton were allowed to research the subject if they wanted to, though it wasn't encouraged. The experience hadn't turned me into a Communist or fellow traveler, but it had taught me a lot about the Russian Communists and how they operated, as well as what they believed in and what some of their main strengths and weaknesses were. After that I was never quite convinced that the Communists were such a threat to America—neither the Russians nor the home-grown variety—as some people seemed to think.

In the course of my research I had spent six weeks in the Soviet Union in 1935, making the grand tour of European Russia and riding the Trans-Siberian Railroad from Moscow to Manchukuo, and from there traveling mainly by Japanese trains to Peking. I came home persuaded that the Communists were doing what they wanted in the Soviet Union and were going to build that vast but crippled nation into a major world power; and that the Communist system would never work in the United States, and anybody who thought it would, or who joined the Communist Party or any of its branches and "fronts" in the United States, had to be some kind of a nut. I didn't get a very good grade on my thesis (my adviser commented that I had done as well as could be expected on an unsuitable subject), but I didn't care about that; I already had my Phi Beta Kappa key, and graduated *cum laude* anyhow.

None of this had anything to do with the Hiss–Chambers affair, of course, but it influenced the way I looked at it. I was skeptical about Chambers from the beginning; he said he had been a Communist in 1935, the year that I came back from Russia, and he reminded me of some of the people I had argued with in those days who wanted to duplicate the Russian Revolution in America; he had to be a nut like them, as far as I was concerned.

Hiss seemed to be a different type; I had never heard of him before, because I had been at the Mediterranean front while he was making his name at Dumbarton Oaks, Yalta, and San Francisco. I had covered the UN Preparatory Commission and the first General Assembly Session in 1946 as a member of the *Tribune*'s London Bureau, but I hadn't met Hiss there because Bert Andrews had come over from Washington to follow the U.S. delegation, and I had devoted myself to the UN proceedings and the other forty-nine delegations. So all I knew about Hiss was what I found in the clippings and the transcripts; and if he had been a Communist or a Communist agent, I wanted to see the evidence at the trial. I was glad to get the assignment.

Since Andrews had been so involved in the pumpkin episode, I went down to Washington at one point in my preparations to get his own account of it. I knew Andrews quite well; he had been my boss when I worked in the *Tribune*'s Washington Bureau in the early stages of the war. I had spent a good deal of time there in 1941–1942 on temporary assignments to help out when the load was extra heavy and had been transferred there permanently at the beginning of 1943. That ended when my turn came to go overseas; the *Tribune*, like other newspapers, was following the same order of priority as the draft boards—first young bachelors, then childless husbands, then fathers of children born after Pearl Harbor, and finally the pre-Pearl Harbor fathers, which included me. Andrews never made it; he was past the age limit and an executive in an essential industry.

Anyhow I had a lot of respect for him, and for his capacity to smell out a good story and follow it wherever it might lead. But when he told me about his radiograms to Nixon on the SS *Panama*, I thought he had gone too far. He had got a great scoop, but if he wanted to help Nixon get ahead in his political career—and Andrews was highly impressed by the young Congressman from California, about whom I knew nothing at the time—it seemed to me he ought to join Nixon's staff, not front for him as a *Herald Tribune* bureau chief. Andrews didn't like it when I brought that up.

His story of the midnight visit to the pumpkin patch was so vivid that for a long time I thought he had been there himself. But it also reminded me of a classic newspaperman's joke I had first heard during the war in Italy—the beauty of a scoop that isn't true is that you get two exclusives instead of one: first, when you break the story and, again, when you reveal what was wrong with it. Andrews wasn't exactly in that position; Nixon certainly had the microfilms, and nobody was ever going to prove that they hadn't been in the pumpkin. But I didn't think they would prove Hiss guilty of espionage or perjury, either. There was nothing to connect him with them, so far as I could see, except Chambers's dubious word.

The *Tribune* valued its reputation for fairness, and so long as Andrews was going straight down the line with Nixon and the House Committee, it gave the paper needed balance for me to take a different viewpoint. It wasn't necessary to be pro-Hiss in my reporting of the trial; all I had to do was follow the traditional *Herald Tribune* style, here's-what-was-said-in-court-today-and-let-the-reader-draw-his-own-conclusions, and it would be a standout contrast to what Andrews in Washington, and most of the other reporters, were writing about the trial.

In those days charges of bias and prejudice were thrown around quite freely by people who felt strongly about the Hiss–Chambers affair, and I wasn't particularly surprised when some people said my reporting was pro-Hiss. Westbrook Pegler was one; he denounced me for it in his nationally syndicated column, although he had praised me during the war for my reports of Communist influence in the French underground's resistance to the Germans. Prosecutor Tom Murphy was another; he said it in an affidavit filed with the court before the second trial, opposing a defense argument that it was impossible to get a fair trial in New York because so much of the press coverage had been unfair to Hiss.

In his affidavit Murphy wrote that the defendant "has been fairly and honestly treated and no possible prejudice could exist in this district because of such [press] coverage. If a line is to be drawn on the side of prejudice or sympathy, the Court will find some of the newspapers favored the defendant. The Court's attention is called particularly to all of the stories in the *New York Herald Tribune* by John Chabot Smith." On Murphy's analysis, 68.5 percent of the news stories published during the first trial were "completely factual; 8.3 percent pro-Hiss; 6.1 percent anti-Chambers; and 17.1 per cent pro- and anti- the trial judge."

The defense, of course, argued that these figures were all wrong, and when Murphy came to make his oral argument in court, where I was sitting there watching and listening, he edited his remarks in a way I wholly approved of. After describing how satisfied he was with the coverage of all the other New York papers, his next words, as I recall them, were: "Now the reporter from the *New York Herald Tribune*, why you'd think he was covering an entirely different trial!" There were times when that was exactly how I felt about it, too.

It seemed to me that my stories were as fair and middle-of-the-road as anybody could expect; they simply didn't look that way to people who were committed to believing everything Chambers said about Hiss and who thought Hiss's conviction was a foregone conclusion. Maybe it was, but a lot had to happen before that conclusion would be reached.

The trial got off to an uncommonly swift start for such an important case. A jury of ten men and two women was selected in two hours and fifteen minutes, and two women alternates were added after another fifteen minutes had passed. Judge Samuel H. Kaufman complimented Murphy and Stryker for acting with such dispatch, and Stryker answered with a grin, "It is quite a contrast to—er—well, it's quite a contrast." Everyone knew what he was referring to; the eleven top officials of the Communist Party of the United States were on trial in another room of the same court house, in an action to test whether the party could be outlawed altogether as a criminal conspiracy to overthrow the government by force and violence. That was a political trial in every sense, and the wrangling over who should sit on the jury had lasted nine weeks.

In the public mind the Hiss case and the trial of the Communists were inevitably linked together, and the arguments in each of the two courtrooms helped strengthen the prosecution's case in the other. For if Hiss was guilty of perjury, he must also be a Communist, spy, and traitor, which showed how terrible Communists could be, and how guilty the eleven Communist leaders must be. Similarly, if Communists were really criminal conspirators and revolutionaries, as the government was trying to prove in the other courtroom, that would make it easier to show how associating with people like Chambers had turned a respectable public servant like Hiss into a liar and a spy. Both propositions were a shock to traditional American ideas of political freedom and individual responsibility, but trying them both at once gave them each a kind of spurious credibility. They seemed to corroborate each other.

The trial of the Communist leaders was the bigger and better known of the two, because it involved so many people and had already been in session for so long. It attracted rival picket lines of Communists and anti-Communists through which Hiss and the lawyers, the witnesses, judge, and jury had to make their way into the court house. The pickets helped in a subtle way to strengthen the popular view that the crimes of which Hiss was charged were so heinous, so terrifying and unforgiveable, that they must not be allowed to go unpunished. And in their eagerness to punish the crime, many found it difficult to entertain any question about the criminal, and whether it was really Hiss or somebody else who had done the deed.

Under the circumstances, Stryker wanted his client's case to be as big a contrast to the Communists' trial as he could make it. He didn't have much hope of getting a jury that would be favorably disposed toward Hiss, or uninfluenced by the enormous publicity that had surrounded the case for the last eight months. The science of picking jurors by psychological profiles was not as advanced in those days as it is now, and in any case, the government's resources for digging into the backgrounds of prospective jurors were so vastly greater than Stryker's that he didn't attempt to do the same. All he looked for was people who seemed intelligent enough to know a reasonable doubt when they saw one.

The jury he got consisted of a junior executive, a marine accountant, the office manager of a funeral home, a gasoline delivery superintendent, a credit analyst, a real estate broker, a clerk, a dressmaker, a production manager, an unemployed hotel manager, a retail executive, and an employee of a mail-advertising agency with unspecified functions. Only the real estate broker and the dressmaker were women; all were white. Hiss felt that such people were not his "peers," and would be unfamiliar with the ways of State Department employees and his life in Georgetown; but it was a jury that Stryker thought he could work with.

After the jury was sworn in and dismissed from the courtroom, Stryker made the usual motions for dismissal of the case, relying heavily on the argument that the perjury indictment was a subterfuge to frustrate the purpose of the statute of limitations. Judge Kaufman would deny the motions some days later, but at this point he reserved decision. Then the court was adjourned until the following day, when Stryker and Prosecutor Murphy were to make their opening statements, and the jury would get their first good look at these two attorneys, the major protagonists of the long battle that was to follow.

Trial by jury is an ancient institution, owing some of its origins to the medieval "ordeal by combat," and this aspect of the proceedings was to become increasingly apparent as the weeks went by. In medieval times an accused person had a choice of several "ordeals" by which he might be tried, and one of them was to challenge his accuser to a life-and-death duel, to be fought not by the two principals themselves, but by champions each could choose to defend his cause. Both sides prayed to God for vindication, and it was believed that God would defend the right by giving victory to the just man's champion, while the other would be killed. Punishment of the unjust man, normally by death, would then follow, if he weren't able to flee the district in time. In theory the system discouraged false accusations, for what champion would lay down his life for a false accuser? But in time people concluded that the champion's skill in battle more often decided the issue than God's justice, and more sophisticated ways of arriving at the truth were developed.

In the modern trial by jury the opposing attorneys perform a function not unlike that of the medieval "champions"; their lives are not at stake, but to some degree their careers are, especially in important cases. And the fate of the accused depends in considerable measure on his champion's skill in the battle, whatever the evidence may be. Thus the skills of Murphy and Stryker were to be of crucial importance in the weeks that followed; the jurors saw much more of them and heard much more from them than they did from Hiss or Chambers.

Thomas Francis Murphy was a tall man who towered over everyone else in the court room. He looked like an overgrown bear in a double-breasted suit, with abundant dark hair and a drooping mustache long enough to chew on. His arms and legs were long, his back was tall and straight, his shoulders massive, and his mild eyes china blue. He had a folksy style and paid no particular regard to formal rhetoric or syntax, but leaned heavily on unfinished sentences and suggestive remarks left dangling in the air. He projected an air of untutored common sense, a down-to-earth friendliness that seemed to contrast as much with Stryker's polished oratory as it did with Hiss's patrician reserve. Murphy was a man of the people, or so he seemed to be saying in his deep, rumbling voice; a man you could trust, the very opposite of the arrogant defendant and his foxy lawyer.

Murphy was forty-three, a year younger than Hiss, an Assistant United States Attorney of seven years standing, and graduate of two well-known Catholic universities—receiving his A.B. degree from Georgetown and his LL.D. from Fordham. He had a wary respect for the battle-scarred veteran he was matched against, but he clearly wasn't afraid of him. This was a case that could be the making of Murphy's career if he won it, and he seemed to have every expectation of doing so.

He began in a simple, uncomplicated way, explaining to the jury what the case was about. He said the government would seek to prove that Hiss had handed over "secret and confidential documents to him—Chambers, a Communist . . . in wholesale fashion." He said he would produce the documents for the jury to look at, that is, all but one, which he said was still so secret that he would ask Judge Kaufman not to let the jury see it. He described the typewriter on which sixty-four pages of the alleged spy papers had been typed—an old Woodstock machine with pica type, ten letters to the inch. He said Mrs. Hiss had been given such a machine by her father and had used it until the end of

1938 and then sold it to a second-hand dealer in Washington, or at least that was what Hiss had told the grand jury. And he told how the FBI had searched for the machine without success, but had found letters and other documents typed on it by Mrs. Hiss, which would prove that it was the same machine on which the spy papers had been typed. So said Murphy, and he repeated in detail the story Chambers had told about the whole spy operation.

"Now," said Murphy, coming at last to the charge in the indictment, which was not espionage but perjury, "if we prove to you, as Mr. Chambers will, that he got the documents from Hiss, and we prove that they were typed on a typewriter in his possession or control, and that the documents themselves came from the State Department, and some of them right from his office, I daresay you will be convinced that Hiss lied in the grand jury."

Then Murphy conceded, as he had to concede, that the case against Hiss rested on the word of Chambers, who had made the original accusations; the typewriter, the documents, and all the other evidence to be presented by the government would be used solely to corroborate Chambers's word. The jury, therefore, must decide first of all whether to believe Chambers.

"When you have heard all of this testimony I want you then to go back and consider your oath that you took yesterday and see on which side the truth lies," he said to the jury. "I want you to examine Chambers. I want you to listen attentively; watch his conduct on the stand; watch the color of his face; watch the way his features move, because if you don't believe Chambers, then we have no case under the Federal perjury rule. . . . You need one witness plus corroboration, and if one of the props goes, out goes the case."

It was a modest opening; simple, direct, and to the point, the clearest explanation of what the case was about that the jury would receive. It had taken only half an hour. Murphy folded his long arms and legs into a chair and sat down, and the court took a brief recess before Stryker rose to reply.

Stryker, too, began in a disarmingly modest style, saying he was glad the case was at last being tried in a "dignified, calm and quiet and fair court of justice," away from the "klieg lights, the television, and all the paraphernalia, the propaganda which surrounded the beginning of the story."

Then he picked up the theme with which Murphy had ended, "If you do not believe Chambers the government has no case. . . . What you here are going to determine is whether or not you believe Chambers." And for more than an hour, he painted a word-picture for the jury of Chambers as a scoundrel on whose word no man could rely, and Hiss as a paragon of excellence whom all must admire. It was a virtuoso performance that made Hiss squirm in his chair, but on at least some of the jurors it must have made a considerable impression.

"First, let me tell you who the accused is," Stryker said, and proceeded to recite Hiss's career in terms of glowing praise. He went over his early education, the honors he had won at school and college, the crowning achievement when he was chosen, out of some five or six hundred Harvard Law School students, for a post "given only to a young man not only of signal scholarship but of character, to the outstanding boy of the class . . . the post of secretary to the great Justice Oliver Wendell Holmes."

Then he turned and pointed across the room to the defendant, sitting calmly beside his wife, just inside the well of the court. "Alger Hiss," he declared, "was good enough for Oliver Wendell Holmes, and of the many character witnesses I shall call, if the case gets that far, I shall summon with all due reverence the shade of that great member of the Supreme Court." (Hiss must have restrained him after that, because he never invoked the spirits of the dead in the trial again. However, he did summon two living Justices, Reed and Frankfurter, whose testimony as character witnesses may have impressed some of the jurors, but whose appearance cost Hiss the chance for Supreme Court review of his case.)

And there was much more about Hiss and the distinctions he had won. At Dumbarton Oaks he "was weighed in the crucible and not found wanting." At San Francisco "in his hands were countless secret documents of the most important character belonging to this country." And who was the man chosen to carry the original United Nations Charter to the President of the United States? "Why, it was Alger Hiss."

"I will take Alger Hiss by the hand," Stryker cried in his best pulpit manner, "and I will lead him before you from the date of his birth down to this hour even, though I would go through the valley of the shadow of death I will fear no evil, because there is no blot or blemish on him."

Then he was silent for a moment, walking up and down in front of the jury to give them time to absorb the impact of his rhetoric before he changed the subject. "Now," he asked, turning again, "who is the accuser?"

Chambers, he said, a man who "began changing names early," was for twelve long years, "alias Adams, alias Crosley, alias Cantwell, alias a great many other things . . . a member of this low-down, nefarious, filthy conspiracy . . . against the land that I love and you love . . . a confirmed liar before he joined the band [of Communists] that believes in lying . . . a thief . . . blasphemer . . . Communist, conspirator and thug . . . destitute of honor, destitute of credit."

Stryker said it was Chambers who had committed perjury in his story about the documents; when he found his defense against Hiss's libel suit "going on the rocks," he "screwed his courage to the sticking point to go through with this arrant perjury." In his final peroration at the end of the long morning Stryker stood facing the jury in the attitude of a father giving his children confidential advice and exhortation, and said, "I am going to let you get lunch, ladies and gentlemen, although I have not yet gone into the way in which Mr. Hiss [met] the man that at that time was falsifying and sneaking around by the name of Crosley . . . suffice it to say [that] when he met him he found before him a glib and interesting talker. Mr. Chambers is all that. You will hear him . . . Alger Hiss was interested in what he thought was another Jack London. No one was there to warn him about this man as I now am alerting you.

"In the warm southern countries, you know, where they have

leprosy, sometimes you will hear on the streets perhaps among the lepers a man crying down the street, 'Unclean, unclean!' at the approach of a leper.

"I say the same to you at the approach of this moral leper."

It was powerful stuff; vintage Stryker at his best. But among the exhortations and denunciations was one piece of information that created a sensation in the court, just before Stryker went into his peroration. That was when he announced that the defense had found the missing typewriter. He teased Murphy first about how the FBI had "turned Washington upside down" hunting for the machine; that wasn't the phrase, but Murphy accepted "shook it down," and Stryker went on, "Well, we have not the opportunities for shaking anything down that Mr. Chambers had, but we happened to have a stalwart, honest man, who was Ed McLean, who was no FBI man at all, just a lawyer . . . he found it and produced it from the then owner, a truckman who had gotten it through a long series of colored servants they had."

Stryker stuck his thumbs in his vest and announced, "We have the typewriter in our possession, and I think now that we will consent under such reasonable provisions as his Honor may prescribe to let these FBI eyes who couldn't find it come down and look at it all they want." And then in triumph he turned to the jury and said, as he had said before when he described how Hiss had insisted on turning over Chambers's papers to the government for investigation, "Is that the conduct of a guilty man?"

It made a good refrain, though it prompted a wag at the press table to note out of the jury's hearing that Hiss had hired Lloyd Paul Stryker, defender of the notorious Jimmy Hines, to be his lawyer, and "was that the conduct of an innocent man?"

These opening statements established what was going to happen in the ensuing weeks of the trial, and the battle pretty well followed the outline the protagonists had announced. Murphy put Chambers on the stand that same afternoon, following a few preliminary witnesses who disposed of some minor details and served to build suspense. Chambers began telling the story of his life, but the day's session ended before he reached the date that he met Hiss. Thus, it was the performances of the two attorneys that got that day's headlines.

The next day Chambers continued his story, or as much of it as he was allowed to, while Stryker kept up a steady barrage of objections, most of which were upheld by Judge Kaufman, to prevent him from retelling all the colorful details of spy plots and Communist activity which HUAC had made so much of. But Chambers repeated in court the main accusations on which the trial was based—that Hiss had given him State Department documents and copies of such documents in the first three months of 1938, pursuant to the instructions of the mysterious Russian, Colonel Bykov. Chambers also gave his explanation of the Oriental rug—that it was a gift from the Soviet people in gratitude for the work of American Communists—and added some other details that had not been part of his earlier testimony. The most significant was a statement that Hiss had lent him four hundred dollars to buy a used car in 1937, over Colonel Bykov's objections.

Throughout the constant interruptions of both defense counsel and the judge, Chambers remained calm and imperturbable. He was a short, fat man in a rumpled suit, with a round, pudgy, sad-looking face. Usually he stared at the ceiling, sometimes turning his pale gray eyes blandly on the prosecuting attorney. He frequently opened his mouth and closed it again with an almost soundless "ah-hum."

He was never rattled, even when Stryker began his cross-examination late that afternoon and tried to tie him up with rapid-fire questions. He answered them all in the same flat, emotionless, and often barely audible voice. Judge Kaufman rebuked him on occasion for speaking so softly, and for offering his opinions instead of answering questions directly and factually.

Several times, while Chambers was under Murphy's direct examination, the judge criticized his answers as being too vague, and examined him with further questions of his own. Chambers invariably answered the Judge in the same expressionless tones.

When Stryker's turn came, he launched at once into what was to be the main theme of his defense—that Chambers was too great a liar to be believed about anything. His first question, delivered in a high tenor after a few moments of stretching his arms and flexing his knees like a prizefighter warming up, was, "Mr. Chambers, do you know what an oath is?"

Attorney and witness exchanged a few definitions, and Stryker summed up his point. "In our courts," he said, "it is an affirmation made by a man who calls on Almighty God to witness the truth of what he says, is that right?"

Chambers agreed.

With this beginning, Stryker read the oath that had been a routine part of Chambers's application for his WPA job in 1937, in which he swore he would "support and defend the Constitution of the United States against all enemies, foreign and domestic, and that I will bear true faith and allegiance to the same; that I take this obligation freely, without any mental reservation or purpose of evasion, and that I will well and faithfully discharge the duties of the office which I am to enter, so help me God."

Stryker tossed the document onto the table in front of Murphy and said to Chambers, in tones of an irate schoolmaster, "You took and subscribed to that oath, did you not?"

"Yes," said Chambers.

"And it was false from beginning to end, was it not, Mr. Chambers?"

"Of course," said Chambers mildly.

"What?" Stryker roared.

"Of course."

"And it was perjury, wasn't it?"

"If you like."

"And you did it in order to deceive and cheat the United States Government . . . is that not true?"

"That is correct," said Chambers in his soft, expressionless voice.

"Yes or no?"

"Perfectly true."

There was more of the same that afternoon, on matters large and small about which Chambers had on various occasions told lies or perjured himself under oath, and Chambers admitted them all with ready candor. And there was a great deal more of it the following morning, when Stryker hammered at the same theme without letup for an hour and a quarter, while Chambers answered in his customary blank manner.

In that second day of cross-examination, Chambers found occasion to declare emphatically that his way of life had changed since he broke with the Communist Party, and he now considered himself an honest, God-fearing man. Styker wouldn't accept that, but it gave him opportunities for abundant sarcasm.

"During all this period from 1924, I think you told us, up until 1938," he asked [the period when Chambers said he was a Communist], "your point of view was . . . that an oath had no binding quality on you at all?"

"That is right," Chambers answered.

"So, had you been called upon as a witness in any of those years you would have with perfect readiness committed perjury?"

"That is right."

"You were, if not an actual perjurer, a potential perjurer during more than half of your life?"

"That is correct."

"Well, to be fair with you," said Stryker, "more than half of your adult life, not your whole life."

"Yes."

"Then there came a time, did there, Mr. Chambers, when you repented and reformed and became a God-fearing citizen, is that right?"

"That is right. I tried to."

"Just when did you reform and repent? What month?" The question was important, because Chambers had first told the House Committee and the grand jury that he had broken with the Communist Party in 1937, but after producing the spy papers, which were all dated in the first three months of 1938, he had changed his story and said the break didn't come until April 1938.

"I couldn't possibly set a month," Chambers answered. "That repentance continued over a period of months and took its final form in April 1938, when I broke with the Communists."

"All right," said Stryker. "April 1938, then, at any rate, in April you became a God-fearing, honest man?"

"One doesn't become that all at once," said Chambers.

"Your repentance and regeneration were slow?" Stryker persisted.

"Perhaps it was comparatively fast," Chambers replied.

"Has it been completed now, do you think?"

"Well, it never stopped. It never is in any man's life, is it?"

"Well, all right. At all events, there came a time, sometime after April 1938, when you turned from the ways of treason, disloyalty, crime and perjury—" but Murphy interrupted to object to the word "treason." Stryker gave in unwillingly, protesting that Chambers "says he was a traitor in his own words," but Murphy argued that that didn't make him one; he hadn't "given aid and comfort to the enemy."* The Judge agreed, and Stryker rephrased the question.

"There came a time then in April, you think 1938, when you became an honest man who no longer believed in lying, cheating, and stealing, is that right?"

"That is right," said Chambers.

"From that point on you had the same decent attitude toward an oath an honest man would have, is that right?"

"That is true."

"Whatever you did in the matter of giving testimony after that you would say was not due to the shield and cloak of being a Communist?"

"No, it would have been through my being a Christian." [Chambers had already testified that he had been baptized an Episcopalian in 1940 and joined the Quakers in 1942.]

"You became a God-fearing Christian?" Stryker asked.

"That is right."

"With the same ethical sense, is that right?"

"I believe so."

"And you did away with lying and stealing and all that?"

* This discussion took place in a whispered conference at the bench, which the jury and spectators couldn't hear; but it was all taken down by the court stenographer, and included in the stenographer's minutes of the trial.

"Yes, I thought so."

"Now I should like to ask you this: You will agree, will you not, that lying takes many forms?"

"Yes, it is around us all the time."

"You say, 'It is around us all the time,' " said Stryker.

"Yes, I think so."

After much more testimony of this sort, Stryker gradually built up to his point. It was that, on numerous occasions after Chambers's break with the Communist Party, beginning with his interview with Adolf Berle in 1939 and including his testimony before the grand jury in October 1948, he had concealed his knowledge of the alleged espionage he was now talking about, even though he was under oath to "tell the truth, the whole truth and nothing but the truth" before HUAC and the grand jury, as well as in his pretrial examination in the libel suit. Chambers admitted these charges reluctantly, one by one.

Stryker left the grand jury incident to the last. As defense counsel he did not have access to the transcript of the grand jury proceedings, but there had been references to them in the libel suit proceedings, so he knew he was on solid ground. A few minutes before 1:00 P.M., when the court was scheduled to adjourn for the weekend, he introduced the subject that was to be his clincher of the day.

"Did you in October 1948, testify before the grand jury in this building?" he began, "and were you asked before the grand jury as to whether or not there had been any espionage?"

"Yes, in effect," said Chambers.

"Were you under oath?"

"I was."

"And did you answer there was not?"

"I answered I had no knowledge of it."

"Let's see about that." Stryker then read from his transcript of the libel suit proceedings and continued, "The fact is, is it not, that you were asked directly by the grand jury under oath whether there was any espionage, and you said you had no recollection?"

"That is right," said Chambers.

"Was that answer true or false?"

"The answer was false."

"Then you admit that you testified falsely and committed perjury before the grand jury in this building, is that right?"

"That is right."

And that was that, for the time being, at least. The subject was to come up many times in the following weeks, but now Stryker had given the jury a good curtain line to think about over the weekend. He glanced at the clock and said, "Your Honor, it is a few minutes to one, and if I turn to another topic I won't finish by the usual adjournment time, and I would like to stop right there."

Murphy made no objection, and the Judge agreed, admonishing the jury as usual not to discuss the case with anyone. Occasionally in these end-of-the-day admonitions, the Judge also reminded the jury not to pay attention to anything they read about the case in the papers or heard on the radio, but he didn't do that often.

17

"A MIDDLE-CLASS FAMILY"

WHITTAKER CHAMBERS was on the witness stand in the first trial for four full days and parts of two more, after which his wife testified for the better part of two days, supporting his story in some of its details and adding more of her own. By the time they had finished, the jury knew a great deal more about Chambers than his habit of telling lies, although this was the aspect which Stryker emphasized most heavily and consistently. A fairly complete story of his life was put into the record, but in such a disjointed and fragmentary way, interrupted by so many objections and arguments between counsel, that it must have been difficult for the jurors to form any coherent picture of what kind of man he really was. It's a fair guess that they concluded he was unusual, to say the least, and a complicated personality whose behavior would be difficult to understand under any circumstances.

All the time Chambers was on the stand, except for his brief appearance the first afternoon, a tall, heavy-set man with thinning hair and rimless glasses sat inside the rail of the court, directly opposite the witness chair, watching Chambers intently and taking notes, and from time to time handing slips of paper to members of defense counsel. Prosecutor Murphy called the court's attention to his presence soon after he first appeared, and Stryker identified him only as a man he had already told Murphy and Judge Kaufman about in conference before the session began.

Rumors quickly circulated through the courtroom that the stranger was a psychiatrist observing Chambers's behavior, and that the defense planned to call him as an expert witness. That day the stranger refused to talk to the press, saying the court had ordered him not to reveal his identity or what he was doing. The rumors spread and grew more detailed, and after the next day's session the stranger announced that he had the court's permission to identify himself. He was Dr. Carl Binger, a practicing psychiatrist and associate professor of clinical psychiatry at the Cornell University Medical School. Later, when he took the witness stand at the first trial, Judge Kaufman wouldn't let him testify, but he was to do so at great length in the second trial.

Binger's presence was in support of Hiss's contention that there must be something mentally wrong with a man who could say the things Chambers had said about him, a view that he had expressed before the grand jury and relied on as one of his main lines of defense. It was also one of the reasons for the exhausting, if not exactly exhaustive, detail in which Chambers's past life was examined at the trials.

The question of whether or not Chambers really was "of unsound mind," as Hiss put it, and if so how much that had to do with the case, was not finally resolved by the trials. But it was examined in great detail afterward by Dr. Meyer A. Zeligs, a San Francisco psychiatrist who devoted six years to his research and concluded that Chambers was indeed plagued by profound emotional disturbances—mental illness, to use the common term —and that his charges against Hiss were the product of psychotic fantasies. Zeligs's book, *Friendship and Fratricide*, was roundly denounced by supporters of Chambers when it was published, as well as by many fellow psychiatrists who felt Zeligs had embarrassed his profession and brought discredit on himself by tangling with a political issue. There were others, psychiatrists and lay people both, who accepted his conclusions, and no answering study of comparable scope has been published to challenge Zeligs's findings. But the matter remains in dispute, and the psychiatric evidence, such as it was, didn't save Hiss at either trial.

The story of Chambers's life, however, was a fascinating one, and Judge Kaufman allowed as much of it to be told as he found relevant to the issue of Chambers's credibility. The questioning and arguments were tediously long-drawn-out and repetitious, but in the end the Judge excluded many interesting parts of the story on the grounds that they were irrelevant or immaterial, and the jury heard only an abridged version. Chambers added many more details after the trial, when he wrote his own uninterrupted version in *Witness*—particularly in the chapters entitled "The Story of a Middle-Class Family" and "Flight." Some of the gaps that still remained were filled in by the research of Zeligs and others. For the following account, I have drawn on both the trial transcript and this additional material, which contains much that the jury never heard.

Chambers was born April 1, 1901, in Philadelphia, and was thus three and a half years older than Hiss. He was the son of Jay Chambers and Laha Whittaker Chambers; "Laha," he explained, was a Malay word for "princess," and the name caused his mother "acute discomfort all her life. But she promptly contrived an even more distressing name for me. She named me Jay (for my father) Vivian (for the surname of the English branch of the family of one of her childhood schoolmates and lifelong friends) . . . As soon as I knew anything I knew that I loathed that name. I determined that as soon as I was able, I would take any other name in preference to it."

When he was two or three, his parents moved to a big tumbledown house in Lynbrook, Long Island, eighteen miles from New York City, where as Jay Vivian he spent his childhood and to which he later returned as Whittaker Chambers on many occasions. His father was a staff artist for the New York *World* at first; later he became a book and magazine illustrator, and still later an advertising artist and manager of the art department of Frank Seaman and Company, a New York advertising agency. His mother had been an actress, and he described her as "possessed of a soulful beauty uncommon anywhere." In later years, after many quarrels between his parents in which Chambers's sympathies were with his mother, his father moved out, apparently for a lengthy period, and sent the family only eight dollars a week. To supplement this income his mother baked cakes for sale, and raised vegetables and chickens, while young Chambers would "go out and hustle for orders." He also "developed a regular route for eggs," but killing the chickens for broilers was too much for him. He found the poverty "humiliating" because it was "unnecessary"; his father was simply not sharing his salary with the family.

At school he was acutely embarrassed by the name "Vivian," and made no real friends. He spent a lot of time reading, and at the age of eight or nine discovered Victor Hugo's *Les Miserables*, that monumental romance about crime and poverty in early nineteenth-century France. The book made a great impression on him; he thought of it as "a full-length picture of the modern world—a vast, complex, scarcely human structure, built over a social abyss of which the sewer of Paris was the symbol, and resting with crushing weight upon the wretched of the earth." He described Hugo's novel as "the Bible of my childhood," saying that it gave him his first impression of Christianity and also contained the "play of forces" that drove him first into the Communist Party and then out of it.

While his father was away, his mother kept an axe under her bed at night because she was afraid of marauders, and Chambers began sleeping with a knife under his pillow, though he hid it from his mother. These were comparatively happy years, according to *Witness*; when his father came home again there was more hostility, and Chambers wrote that the "chill of his presence spread through the house." He stayed in his room behind closed doors, even taking his meals there on a tray; one Sunday he quietly emerged and cut down the clematis vine that grew up the pergola. Of this incident Chambers wrote, "he had to perpetrate some violence on us or the tensions of his hostile home would have driven him mad."

In high school Chambers felt he was an outcast and tried "desperately" not to learn anything, except English and Latin, which interested him. He began studying languages by himself at home; first Gaelic, Arabic, Persian, Hindustani, and ancient Assyrian, then the more practical German and French, which he mastered, and Spanish, Italian, and a little Russian. His high school career ended in some disgrace; he was chosen to write the class prophecy, and his first draft contained material which offended the principal, so that he was instructed to rewrite it. He did so, but at the graduation ceremonies read the original offensive version instead.

His mother wanted him to go on to college, but his father didn't, nor did Chambers want to go. He solved the dispute for himself by leaving home and heading for Mexico, but he stopped in Washington when he got a job as a laborer tearing up street railway tracks and laying new ones. This was the job that made such an impression on Hiss when Chambers described it to him in 1935; at the time it was a grueling ordeal for a boy of eighteen with no experience of such heavy manual labor. It lasted for some months, and impressed him as being his first experience with the "proletariat," with whom he was to identify in later years when he became a Communist.

From Washington he went to New Orleans, and lived in a "wretched kind of dive" where his landlady, the wife of a peanut vendor, was virtually drinking herself to death, and one of the other occupants was a prostitute named One-Eyed Annie; at the trial Stryker made much of this episode, and Chambers insisted he hadn't been "living with" the prostitute; in *Witness*, he called her "as ugly a woman as I have ever seen." Throughout this experience he called himself Charles Adams, choosing the name because of his regard for John Quincy Adams.

Chambers couldn't get a job in New Orleans, so that when his money ran out he wrote home, and his father wired him "the price of a ticket to New York and a few dollars more." It was too late to go to college that year, but Chambers promised to do so the following year. Meanwhile his father got him a job at Frank Seaman but because he didn't want it known there that this was his son, Chambers combined his mother's maiden name with his new choice of first name, which was also the first name of his mother's father, and called himself Charles Whittaker.

In the fall of 1920 Chambers enrolled at Williams College and used for the first time the name he came to like best, combining the family names of his mother and father to become Whittaker Chambers. A day or two after his arrival he decided that Williams was not for him, and his family couldn't afford it, so he transferred to Columbia, which was near enough to Lynbrook for him to live at home. There he became editor of a student publication called *Morningside,* and published in it, under the pseudonym of John Kelly, what he called "an atheist playlet" entitled *Play for Puppets,* in which he satirized the life of Christ. It brought him a storm of criticism. Thereupon he resigned from Columbia, "entirely by my own choice," as he says in *Witness,* and tried to get a job with the American Friends Service Committee as a relief worker in the famine areas of Russia. This was late in the fall of 1922, five years after the Communist Revolution; Chambers didn't get the job because, as he explained in *Witness,* the Friends heard about his atheist play and told him in effect, "You are an outcast." But he did go to Germany the following summer with two friends from Columbia, and came home via Belgium and France in September.

On his return Chambers got a night job at the New York Public Library, and started devoting his days to a major work of poetry. The job lasted on and off for more than three years, then ended rather abruptly when he was accused of stealing books from the Library. His locker was searched and found to contain Communist pamphlets but none of the missing books; Chambers maintained at the trial that it was the Communist materials the investigators were looking for, and the charge of stealing books was merely an excuse. In any case, the detectives searched his home and found twenty or thirty books belonging to the Columbia Library but none from the New York Public Library. Stryker argued that this constituted theft, but Chambers said he simply hadn't got around to returning the Columbia books.

Meanwhile Chambers decided, in the fall of 1924, to apply for readmission to Columbia, and was accepted, but he didn't last the year. Early in 1925, sitting on a cold concrete bench in the winter sunlight on the Columbia campus, he decided that the world he lived in was dying and that Communism was the only solution. He decided to join the Communist Party, and asked one of his Columbia friends how to go about it; a few days later a stranger came up to his desk at the Public Library, where he was still working part time, and after a few questions said he would take Chambers to a "meeting." This was the beginning of Chambers's career as a Communist, and he soon gave up Columbia and went to work for the *Daily Worker*, though continuing his part-time job at the Public Library as long as it lasted.

At some time during this period there took place a series of events which were touched on only briefly in the trial, but described in great detail in *Witness*, and which must have had profound effects on Chambers's life. One "misty midnight," he doesn't say just when, Chambers found his Grandmother Whittaker on the street in Lynbrook, waiting for the trolley to Brooklyn, though she lived at the time at a YWCA in Jersey City. He spoke to her briefly, and her answers were so weird that he concluded she must be insane. She wouldn't come home with him, so he helped her board the trolley car. When he asked his mother about it, she told him a story of an unhappy love affair which she thought had "unsettled" Grandmother's mind in her old age.

Sometime after that, Chambers's mother took him with her to Jersey City to "pick up" Grandmother Whittaker from the insane ward of the city hospital. The old lady had been found wandering in the street in her nightgown at two o'clock in the morning, talking about someone pumping gas into her room.

"We took her home and gave her a room," the account in *Witness* continues. " 'You will have to stay up tonight,' my mother said to me. 'She may try to kill us all.' " Chambers obeyed, and periodically through the night found his grandmother wandering around opening windows and complaining, " 'They're pumping gas in here. The house is full of gas.' " Each time he got her back into bed and went back to his reading. "This kept up all night," he wrote. "For years, in addition to our old tensions, this dark, demoniac presence sat at the heart of our home." Years later, when Chambers was at *Time* magazine, she was finally committed to a mental institution, where she died.

Meanwhile—the exact sequence of events is not clear in *Witness*—Chambers's younger brother Richard dropped out of Colgate University, apparently in his freshman year, and came home.

316

Richard was two and a half years younger than Whittaker, his only brother; they had no sisters. His brief experience of college had apparently been highly disturbing to him; when he returned, Chambers wrote, he was very quiet; "He slept most of the day and was gone most of the night."

The account continues, "One day I came in and found him lying on the old couch, where we had suffered the toothaches of our childhood. His eyes were open and he was staring at something ahead of him. His face was pinched and white. After a while, he raised his arm and pointed to the old print that still hung at the end of the couch: *Il Conforto—Death, the Comforter.*

"Then he asked slowly without looking at me: 'If I kill myself, will you kill yourself with me?'

"I said: 'No.'

" 'Why not?' he asked.

" 'You are not going to kill yourself,' I said.

"He laughed meanly. 'You're a coward, Bro,' he said." ["Bro," short for "Brother," was Richard's nickname for Whittaker.]

Richard was engaged at the time in remodeling the old house, and when he had finished, he built himself a workshop behind it, "a little house in itself with a gabled roof and a fireplace of its own. He piped in gas from the main house so that he could use his workshop after dark. He moved in a couch and sometimes slept there, surrounded by his tools, his pipe wrenches, vises and dies."

Richard took to drinking, according to *Witness*, and bringing girls to his "workshop." His mother told Whittaker to watch over him, saying, " 'I do not know what he is going to do next. But I am afraid that he is going to try to kill himself.' " So Whittaker went with his brother on drinking bouts at speakeasies all over Long Island and at the Manhattan end of the Queensboro Bridge, enjoying them at first but losing his pleasure when they developed into bloody fights. "I could not see what good my supervision did," he wrote. "I began to go my own ways again."

Then one evening Whittaker came home to find Richard in the kitchen with his head in the oven and all the gas jets on. He pulled him out, turned off the gas, and revived him. His brother's reaction, as described in *Witness*, was, " 'You're a bastard, Bro. You stopped me this time, but I'll do it again.' "

Another evening Whittaker came upon his father and his brother fighting in the same kitchen, his brother drunk and his father "blind with rage." They were pummeling each other, and Whittaker couldn't pull them apart; he struck at his father, wrestled with him, and finally "flung him against a cabinet."

Then "the ferocious strength drained out of him. His face was ashen and twitching. He was an old man, fighting for breath and panting: 'He—has been taking girls—into that little house—at night. Your mother—I won't stand for it.' "

Once more, in the winter, Whittaker rescued Richard from a suicide attempt, this time going to his "little house" at midnight to find Richard lying on the couch with the gas turned on. After that the gas was disconnected from the little house, and Whittaker's mother told him to "sit up and watch through the nights." By this time the grandmother was in the house, and Whittaker would sometimes have to deal with her during the night. "I used to wish that the house would burn down with all its horrors," he wrote.

Finally Richard married, against Whittaker's urging, and took an apartment with his wife in a neighboring village. For a time, Whittaker didn't see his brother. During the summer Richard's wife went back to her parents, and Richard remained alone in his apartment. On the night of September 9, 1926, two weeks before his twenty-third birthday, he put his head into the oven again with the gas on, and this time there was no one to stop him. Whittaker, as he wrote in *Witness*, was in New York that evening, "chatting with a Communist friend." Richard had gone to the station to meet him, but he was not on his usual train. "I failed my brother for the last time," he wrote.

Whittaker Chambers wrote a great deal about the impression this experience made on him, in poetry at the time and in *Witness* later. For a long time he went to the cemetery every morning and every night to visit his brother's grave. He wrote that he "had to fight an all-pervading listlessness of the will. I would lie for hours and watch the leaves, heaving gently in the wind. To do anything else seemed, in the face of death, gross and revolting, seemed a betrayal of my brother because any activity implied that life had meaning." He testified at the trial that for a couple of months he found it physically difficult to move. He wrestled with the question of whether he should kill himself as his brother had done; finally, one night after a visit to the grave-yard, he looked inside the little house his brother had made, and decided he had to go on living. But, he wrote, "I added to myself: 'I shall be sorry that I didn't go with my brother.' "

On New Year's Eve, almost four months after Richard's death, Whittaker visited his grave for the last time and wrote a long poem which he later destroyed, but remembered well enough to quote snatches from it in *Witness* some twenty-five years later. It was a poem about "the meaning of my brother's death, the rightness of the act for him, his courage in retiring from the hub-bub of the world to that silence which the world abhorred because it betrayed the world's inconsequence." It ended with the lines:

> *Let me see only in the light of another year*
> *The roofs and the minds that killed him,*
> *And the earth that holds him,*
> *Forever dead.*

In *Witness*, the quotation is followed by this solemn com-ment which ends the chapter, "I was already a member of the Communist Party. I now first became a Communist. I became irreconcilable."

After that Chambers overcame the "listlessness of the will" from which he had suffered, and threw himself more actively into the work of the Communist Party. He wrote for the *Daily Worker*, for a nominal salary of ten dollars a week, which often went unpaid, but was later increased to twenty-five or perhaps thirty-five dollars a week. By 1929 he had contracted what he called a "party marriage" with a "Communist girl," and lived with her in a cottage near Lynbrook. Then his father died, of apparently natural causes though the exact nature of them remained in dispute, and was buried beside Richard. Chambers's reaction was that "Our line seemed to be at an end. Our famiiy was like a burnt-over woods, which nothing can revive and only new growth can replace. The promise of new growth lay wholly within me—in my having children. No need was so strong in me as the need to have children.

"But," he added in the next sentence, "by then I agreed with my brother that to repeat the misery of such lives as ours would be a crime against life."

It was apparently about a year after his father's death, according to Zeligs's research, that Chambers's Communist "wife" became pregnant, and at some time during this period he moved with her into his mother's house. In his testimony at the trial he said this arrangement was permitted by his mother because she "had lost one son and did not want to lose another." In *Witness*, he doesn't mention the arrangement at all; Zeligs was told by one of the girl's relatives that it lasted for most of their two-year "marriage," and that the girl lived in constant "apprehension" of Grandmother Whittaker, who was kept locked in the attic. The pregnancy ended in a miscarriage, and soon afterward the relationship ended as well.

In April 1931, about a month after he had broken up with his Communist "wife," according to his testimony, Chambers married Esther Shemitz. He described her in *Witness* as "not a Communist, but a pacifist" when he first met her, "on the staff of *The World Tomorrow*, a pacifist magazine."* The occasion was a demonstration of strikers at a Passaic, New Jersey, textile mill, involving battles with the police, which Chambers was covering for the *Daily Worker*. "With her black bobbed hair, she looked like a Russian," Chambers wrote. "She was very forthright and militant."

That was some time in 1930. Later, in the spring of 1931, Chambers wrote, he met her again through mutual friends on the *Daily Worker* staff, and recognized her as "the girl with the black

---

* At the trial, Mrs. Chambers testified that she was a Communist but didn't specify how or when she became one.

bobbed hair I had seen walk toward the police clubs in the Passaic strike." Chambers was then going through his period of differences with the Communist Party; he had left the *Worker* and not yet entered the underground.

"Few courtships can have been much stormier than ours," he wrote. "For the Communist Party, too, soon actively intervened." Esther told him the Party had told her never to see him again, but Chambers, climbing in through her window one night, argued at her bedside "that she must make a choice, and that that choice was not between the Communist Party and renegacy, or between any political viewpoint and any other, but between life and death."

He didn't think that declaration impressed her but concluded, "she had begun to realize that if a man was intent enough on marrying her to climb through her window at five o'clock in the morning, even putting a bolt on it was probably not much use." So they were married, and in Chambers's words, "We never quarreled again." They remained together for the rest of his life, and had two children. It was she who testified on his behalf in the trials.

Chambers's career as a Communist has been summarized in earlier chapters—how he disagreed with the *Daily Worker*, turned to free-lance writing, joined the *New Masses* and then the underground, and how he learned some of the techniques of espionage and became a spy; how he met Hiss in Washington, according to his testimony, in 1934 or 1935, and continued his espionage until he broke with the party, which was either in 1937 or 1938.

But which year was it? The matter wasn't settled by the brief cross-examination described in Chapter 16; Stryker and Murphy returned to it again and again. The explanation that the "break" had simply taken a long time wasn't enough, because the change in dates was too obviously tied in with that other more damaging change of testimony: until November 1948, Chambers had maintained that his Washington "apparatus" was not involved in espionage; then, under pressure of the libel suit, he had suddenly said it was, produced his papers and microfilms to prove it, and changed his story of the "break" to fit the dates on the documents. His explanation, repeated at the trial, was that he had lied for years about the espionage to protect Hiss and the others involved, but was this accusation of espionage itself a lie? That was the whole issue.

It was a case where the jury had to decide which of Chambers's different stories to believe; had he been lying then and was he telling the truth now, or was he lying now after telling the truth before, or was he perhaps lying both then and now? Should the jury decide that Chambers was lying now, then the government's case against Hiss would be lost; because as Nixon had pointed out, you can't convict a man of perjury if your only accusing witness is proved to be a perjurer himself.

There was nothing for the jury to go on but Chambers's word. No other witness could be found to corroborate this part of his story, except his wife, who was too uncertain about it to be much help. Chambers's own testimony on the subject was all-important.

What the jury heard from him was as fragmentary and disjointed as the rest of his testimony and as often interrupted by arguments between counsel. There is no knowing what the jury made of it, or whether Chambers would have told them the story in as much detail as he told it later in *Witness* if he had been allowed to. In any case, the following summary is based on the account in *Witness*, as Chambers's fullest, final, and considered version, though it wasn't all tested in cross-examination.

According to *Witness*, Chambers began to "break away from Communism" in 1937, though he doesn't explain what prompted him to do so or why he did it at that time. He dated his first such impulse as far back as the summer of 1935, after he had moved out of Hiss's apartment on Twenty-eighth Street, when it occurred to him, watching his baby daughter smear porridge on her face as she ate breakfast in her high chair, that people were created by some Design of God, rather than "any chance coming together of atoms in nature," which he defined as "the Communist view." His reasons for leaving the Communist Party, like his reasons for joining it, he described in metaphysical terms; he became a Communist when he thought Man could exist without God, and abandoned Communism when he concluded that Faith in God was the answer to life. By 1937 he had apparently reached this conclusion or was at least approaching it.

"There is a difference," he wrote, "between the act of breaking with Communism, which is personal, intellectual, religious, and the act of breaking with the Communist Party, which is organizational. I began to break with Communism in 1937. I deserted from the Communist Party about the middle of April, 1938."

He used the word "deserted" deliberately, he wrote, because he regarded the Communist Party as a "semimilitary discipline" and his own position in it as under the command of a Russian officer in the Red Army. He expected that the Party would kill him, if it could, as punishment for his desertion and to guarantee his silence, to prevent him from telling what he knew. He reflected on the number of such "deserters" who had been murdered by the Russian secret police, two of whom he apparently knew. And he remembered a saying in the "Soviet apparatus," which was, "Any fool can commit a murder, but it takes an artist to commit a good natural death." He determined to avoid this fate, and to "fight the Communist Party as a Communist would fight, to prepare my break carefully, using against the conspiracy all the conspiratorial methods it had taught me."

He decided there were five main points essential to success: a weapon, a hiding place, an automobile "for swift movement"; an "identity, an official record of the fact that a man named Chambers had worked in Washington in the years 1937 and 1938"; and "a life preserver, in the form of copies of official documents stolen by the apparatus, which, should the party move against my life, I might have an outside chance of using as a dissuader."

For his weapon he bought a long sheath knife; for his hiding place he rented two back rooms in a big house on Old Court Road near Pikesville, Maryland, just outside Baltimore, reasoning that since the Communists would expect him to flee his former haunts, it would be a good idea to stay near them.

For his automobile, he said, he traded in an "old and ailing" car the Communist Party had bought for him some years before, and bought a new Ford sedan, borrowing four hundred dollars from Hiss for the purpose. (Hiss denied this at the trial, and in spite of much argument and production of witnesses and documents by both sides, it was impossible to prove one way or the other.) To establish his "identity," he got the WPA job, which was the occasion for the oath of office Stryker read at the trial, by which Chambers admitted he had perjured himself. In *Witness*, he wrote of this job that it was "important to have some proof that I had worked as a Communist in Washington. There could be no more official proof, it seemed to me, than to let the Communist Party get me a job under my own name in the United States Government." Through his Communist connections, he said, he was employed by the WPA National Research Project, where all his bosses for three levels above were Communists. (The fact that he got the job was readily proved at the trial; whether his bosses were Communists and whether the Communists had anything to do with getting him the job remained in dispute.)

Last came his "life preserver," which he described in *Witness* as follows, "Shortly before my break, I began to organize my life preserver. I secreted copies of Government documents copied in the Hiss household, memos in the handwriting of Alger Hiss and Harry Dexter White, microfilms of documents transmitted by Alger Hiss and the source in the Bureau of Standards." (This "source" was never identified; the microfilms ascribed to him were undeveloped when Chambers produced them from the pumpkin, and proved so badly light-struck that they were impossible to read when they were developed, according to HUAC. These films were not submitted as evidence at the trials.)*

* In 1975, however, the Justice Department released copies of them, in response to suits brought by Hiss and others under the Freedom of Information Act. One of the films turned out to be totally blank, and the other two contained "faintly legible copies of Navy Department documents relating to such subjects as life rafts, parachutes and fire extinguishers." (*The New York Times*, July 31, 1975.)

"This selection was not aimed at any individual," *Witness* continues. "There was much of the Hiss material because he was the most productive source. There may actually have been more of the material from the Bureau of Standards, but . . . much of it could not be read. There was no material from Julian Wadleigh because, in the spring of 1938, he was out of the country on a diplomatic mission to Turkey, though I believe he had returned by the time I broke.

"I was now ready to desert."

One day in April 1938, according to *Witness*, Chambers moved his family to their hiding place on Old Court Road, which was so small that "our goods were stacked against the walls and we had somewhat the feeling of sitting in a sandbagged dugout. The blinds were drawn. . . . All night I would sit up watching while my family slept. I would sleep for a few hours in the daytime. Fortunately I had found work—translation—that I could best do in the still nights."

The work he referred to was the translation of Martin Gumpert's *Dunant—The Story of the Red Cross*, and he soon found it difficult to concentrate in such crowded quarters. So he moved his family to Florida, driving in the new Ford, and renting a bungalow on the beach. A neighbor lent him a revolver to ward off prowlers, and thereafter, he wrote, "I worked with the heavy gun lying on the table beside my typewriter." When he finished the book he returned the revolver to the neighbor and took his family back to Pikesville, buying a shotgun on the way to replace it.

From then on Chambers devoted himself to his fight against the Communist Party. It was not his only interest, he wrote in *Witness*, but it was "a necessity of the 20th century, and I, by an accident of individuality and history, and hence by my special experience, happened to be the one man who could make it. . . .

"I carried on the fight against the Communist Party on more than one level. I carried it on for ten years before the world at large ever noted the name of Alger Hiss. I carried it on, in Marx's phrase, by 'now open, now hidden means.' For most of those ten years, the files of *Time* magazine reflect my fight week by week. The secret files of more than one security agent would reflect it more explicitly."

He got his job with *Time* later in 1938, through his old friend Robert Cantwell, and it was the following year that he told his story to Adolf Berle, setting into motion the events that ultimately led to the trial. By that time his position as an anti-Communist was well established, and his fears of being murdered by the Communists had diminished, but not disappeared.

When Chambers took the stand to testify in the trial, he had, as Prosecutor Murphy pointed out, been questioned many times before on the issues at stake—by the FBI, the House Committee investigators, the Committee members in their hearings, Hiss's lawyers in the Baltimore libel suit proceedings, the grand jury, and Murphy and his staff in preparation for the trial. He had his answers ready and stuck pretty well to the questions he was asked; while he often added new details or altered his story to meet the needs of the question, he hardly scratched the surface of the material that occupies so much of *Witness*. The jury had to be content with a more limited version of his life story, and the additional light his wife shed upon it, when she followed him to the stand.

Esther Chambers was a small, soft-voiced woman of forty-nine, with dark hair almost hidden under a large-brimmed, black hat. When she took the stand on the morning of June 10, the ninth day of the trial, her face looked thin in comparison with her husband's pudginess. She had her husband's habit of looking at the ceiling between questions and fluttering her eyelids as she started to speak. She recounted a two- or three-year period of friendly relations with Alger and Priscilla Hiss, extending a full year beyond the date when Hiss had sworn that such relations had ended. Thus, her testimony tended to strengthen the government's case on the second count of the indictment,* but she said

---

* The first count alleged that Hiss had given the documents to Chambers; the second alleged that he had seen Chambers after January 1, 1937. Both counts alleged that he had lied when he denied the allegations. See Chapter 14, page 271.

she knew nothing about her husband's underground activities, so that she wasn't able to corroborate the espionage story.

She testified in a voice so soft it was often barely audible, and while Murphy was questioning her, Judge Kaufman got down from the bench and sat in the clerk's chair to hear better. Murphy repeatedly asked her to keep her voice up, and she sometimes did but for a few minutes only. Then Stryker began cross-examining her, and she not only talked louder but retorted with considerable heat to some of his questions. She particularly objected to his efforts to establish the date of Chambers's break with the Communist underground.

"I don't have a very good head for figures or dates," she said. "I don't know why you are trying to stump me on dates."

"Now, Mrs. Chambers," Judge Kaufman said to her kindly, "no one is attempting to stump you at all."

"Well, it is very easy," she answered.

"The Court resents any such implication, and I am certain the jury does," the Judge went on more severely. "The Court will not permit anybody to be stumped. We are here attempting to get the facts in a case that is important for the government and very important for the defendant. And it comes with a very bad grace for you to indicate that anyone is trying to stump you."

Esther Chambers tried to interrupt with a meek "I think so too," and when the Judge finished admonishing her she said, "I am sorry, sir." Stryker resumed his cross-examination:

"Is it the fact, then, that on October 4, 1937, your husband was no longer a Communist?"

"I don't know," she said. "I don't remember. I don't remember the date on which he broke with the party."

"Wouldn't you as the man's wife know when he got out of this underground criminal conspiracy known as the American Communist Party?" Stryker persisted. "As his wife wouldn't you know when he started to reform from that criminal activity?"

She was silent, and Judge Kaufman said to her, "Can't you answer that question, Mrs. Chambers?"

"Oh, I didn't know there was any question," she said. The

clerk read the question again, and Murphy objected that it was two questions, but the judge allowed it. Stryker pressed her for an answer, and she stammered, "It wasn't all—it didn't all occur on a special date, at a certain time. It was—"

Stryker interrupted impatiently, Murphy objected and Stryker argued; the clerk read the question again, and Esther Chambers went on, as if there had been no interruption, "—or it was not a special hour. It was a long time in coming and thought out very thoroughly and suffered through, and he finally broke. That particular moment of breaking has been unimportant in my life and I have long since forgotten it."

Stryker, still not satisfied, pressed her further, but all he got was, "I can't remember—1938 or '37—I have forgotten."

Esther Chambers had difficulty in remembering almost everything. In her purse she had a list of the dates and places where she and her husband had lived, and the names they had used, but she wasn't allowed to look at it. She said she and her husband had prepared it together six months before, when she was questioned in the libel suit proceedings in Baltimore. She tried to answer most questions about dates and places by connecting them with the addresses where she had lived at the time, but without her list she was continually confused. She even got the date of her own wedding day wrong.

Nevertheless, she mentioned more than twenty occasions on which she had seen Priscilla Hiss, and on many of them she said the two husbands were also present. She said Priscilla had stayed ten days with the Chambers family one summer at Smithtown, Pennsylvania, taking care of the Chamberses' baby while Esther painted landscapes. She remembered visiting the Hisses in Washington on one occasion when her youngest baby wet the floor and Priscilla gave her a "very lovely old linen towel" to use as a diaper. She described the various houses in which the Hisses had lived in Washington, and there was much discussion of the colors of the wallpaper and the furnishings. Her recollections on these points were different in many respects from those of her husband and of Alger and Priscilla Hiss, and the result was endless repetitious and contradictory testimony by all four of them, which left this reporter at the press table thoroughly confused. I concluded that apart from shakiness of memory and the likelihood that somebody was lying, it sounded as though somebody must be color blind; Esther had painted a picture of Timothy in 1935, which Priscilla said she didn't like because the face was green. But the cumulative effect of all this was that the Chambers family must have seen a good deal of the Hisses at one time or another, and that was the point the government wanted to make.

On the second day of Esther's testimony, she wrestled with her memory for five grueling hours, altering many of the details in her previous testimony, but sticking to the main lines of her story. She stood proudly by her husband, saying she shared his Communist viewpoint when they married, and they had never suffered from lack of money, despite the fact that when they met the Hisses they had no furniture of their own and accepted gifts from the Hisses of a patched rug, a dining room table, and other things for the child. She said she was worried about giving her child false names when her husband changed his name to Cantwell to Breen to Dwyer, but it didn't trouble her conscience.

She said the reason why she couldn't remember when her husband broke from the Communist Party was that it had been his own struggle, and she had been more concerned with "the details of housekeeping and raising two babies." She knew he was "struggling," she said, but she had not helped him to make up his mind. "He himself made it up."

Stryker tried to get her to admit that this decision involved "repentance" from the "criminal conspiracy" and "lying and deceiving" her husband had been engaged in, and she protested that "repentance" was not the right word. "We had begun to break away from the work in which we were engaged and from the party," she said primly.

Stryker persisted, reminding her that in applying for a kindergarten scholarship for her daughter at a private school in October 1937, she had concealed her husband's connection with the Communist Party. Esther said she didn't think that was very pertinent. "It was simply not telling the whole facts," she said. "If I were asked point blank I probably would have told the truth."

"In other words," Stryker retorted, "you didn't think it was very much of a misrepresentation to present your husband to this school as a decent citizen whereas he was—"

"I resent that!" Esther Chambers fairly shouted. Her voice, so often almost inaudible, suddenly carried to the farthest wall of the courtroom. "My husband is a decent citizen, a great man."

"Was he a great, decent citizen in October, 1937?" Stryker asked sarcastically.

"When he was in the underground?" she asked, with a moment's seeming uncertainty.

"I just asked a simple question. Was he a great and decent citizen in October 1937?" Stryker repeated in his bull-like voice. "Yes or no?"

"Yes, and always," she said. Her voice was strong and clear.

"And so that the jury will understand your conception: is it your idea that a man who was plotting and conspiring by any and all means to overthrow the Government of his country, who had been sneaking around for twelve years under false names, that is your conception of the great, decent citizen, is that right?"

"No," said Esther Chambers, "but if he believed that is the right thing to do at the moment, I believe that is a great man, who lives up to his beliefs. His beliefs may change, as they did."

"In other words, if he believed it was all right for him to sneak around the country under aliases using the means he described, you think if a man believes that kind of criminal activity is all right, you think that makes it right, is that it?"

"No," she began, "he was not—" but the Judge intervened, telling Stryker he was being argumentative. He had made his point; Esther Chambers had stated her husband's philosophy very neatly. He believed he was his own judge of what was right or wrong, and that what he did was always right, no matter what others might think, and no matter what results might follow. It was a good summary of what Chambers had said before, and would say again in the second trial, when all these questions had to be asked and answered again. Meanwhile, the testimony in the first trial moved on to other things.

18

THE DOCUMENTS

AFTER the confusion and theatrical excitements of the testimony by Whittaker and Esther Chambers, it was something of a relief, on the morning of June 14, to see a new face on the witness stand and some new scenery in the courtroom. It was time to introduce the celebrated "pumpkin papers" into evidence and to show the jury the documents upon which the case was based. A seven-foot-high easel was brought in and placed next to the witness stand and on it were hung enlargements of the incriminating documents so huge that the most myopic juror in the back row would have no difficulty reading them. The type was forty-nine times its original size.

The jury and public were already familiar with the documents in a general sort of way, because so much had been said and written about them since the pumpkin was opened. There were the four scraps of paper with notes scribbled on them in Hiss's handwriting; sixty-five typewritten pages, all but one of them apparently typed on the old Woodstock machine once owned by his wife; and fifty-eight pages of official State Department documents photographed on microfilm. Only the microfilms had ever been in the pumpkin, but the whole set of documents was popularly referred to as the "pumpkin papers" because of the midnight drama through which they had first been brought to public attention.

The contents of most of the papers had already been made

331

public by the House Un-American Activities Committee (HUAC); they had been read into the *Congressional Record* by Rep. John E. Rankin; they had been the subject of speeches by Representative Nixon and of newspaper articles by Scripps–Howard's Nelson Frank, Hearst's Howard Rushmore, and dozens of others. The idea was firmly fixed in the public mind that all were highly secret government papers of the greatest importance, which had been turned over to the Russians and thereby caused immense harm to the American national interest, endangering the lives of American servicemen in World War II. Rankin had even talked about "the American boys who were killed, who lost their lives as a result of this treason," and had suggested that if action had been taken in time "we might not have had a Pearl Harbor." It was a wildly irrelevant surmise, but not greatly different from what many people were thinking.

Actually, Chambers never said he had turned these particular papers over to the Soviet spy ring that he claimed to have served; he only said he had turned over others like them. But in the public mind this was just as bad, perhaps worse; who could tell what dreadful things Chambers had given our enemies if these were a sample? Chambers said these were papers that he had held back when he decided to quit the spy ring; they were in the pipeline, so to speak, turned over to him by his sources but not turned over by him for delivery to Moscow.

These were the "life preservers" Chambers had testified about and was to describe later in greater detail in *Witness*; a device for blackmailing the Communists into leaving him alone, by threatening exposure of their spy ring if he were to die or disappear. It was for this purpose that he had left them with his wife's nephew, who had put them in the old dumbwaiter shaft for safekeeping for so long. A weird idea, which could only have worked if the Russians or their Communist agents in America had known about the papers, though Chambers never gave any indication that they had. But in the fevered state of public opinion in 1949 the story was readily believed, and, in some respects, what was happening at the trial corresponded very well with the plan Chambers described. For he hadn't been murdered by the Russians, and his "life preservers" had saved him from a libel suit and transformed him into a prosecution witness, protected by the United States Government and immune from any punishment he might otherwise have received for the illegal activities of his Communist days.

In these circumstances the production of the documents in court was a momentous event. The jury was to be made privy to government secrets, displayed before them on a scale as huge as a highway billboard. These documents were the heart of the case; either they had been given by Alger Hiss to Whittaker Chambers for delivery to the Soviet Union in 1938, or they had not. And if they had not, how had Chambers got hold of them? How could the very existence of the typewritten copies be explained? What were they?

Walter H. Anderson, Chief of the Records Branch of the State Department's Division of Communications and Records, was the new face on the witness stand. His was the laborious task of identifying the State Department originals from which the pumpkin papers had been made, and explaining the procedures by which they were handled in the State Department and the various offices to which copies had been distributed. Anderson was the perfect picture of the experienced bureaucrat, bespectacled and gray-haired, with a soft, patient voice. He kept everything in order.

Murphy read some of the documents to the jury in full, while the jury read the corresponding text on their billboard to satisfy themselves that the documents there matched the pumpkin papers. This was a tedious business, and after a while Murphy contented himself with reading only a few identifying lines from each document. At the end of the day, only thirty-six of the State Department documents had been introduced, and the last half-dozen were accepted without being read at all. This was Judge Kaufman's suggestion, to save time. After the midmorning recess Stryker apparently lost interest and left Edward McLean to follow the proceedings, while he attended to other business outside the courtroom.

It took most of the next day to complete the introduction of the documentary evidence, and although Stryker was on hand early for arguments in the Judge's chambers, he didn't stay long after the testimony began. He made no objections to anything, and left McLean to do the cross-examining, which was not particularly exciting. It was as though Stryker wanted nothing to do with those incriminating documents, except to get them hauled down off their billboard and hidden from the jury's eyes as soon as possible. Nor did Stryker go into much detail about the documents in his summation at the end of the trial; his theme was, that regardless of what they showed, there was nothing but Chambers's unsupported word that Hiss had given them to him, and Chambers was a practiced liar whose word could not be believed.

But there the documents were, tangible evidence that something extraordinary had happened in 1938, if only the evidence could be correctly read and fully understood. Stryker's approach worked well enough to get him a hung jury, but it left eight of the twelve jurors unconvinced. His successor as counsel in the second trial, Bostonian Claude Cross, worked much harder on the documents, but left his jury bewildered and confused, and all twelve of them regretted his arguments. In the twenty-five years since then, the documents have been open to the inspection of scholars and investigators of all points of view, and a great deal more is now known about the evidence they have to offer.

They are a part of history, photographically reproduced in three 8½-by-11-inch paperback volumes that stand together three-inches thick—a far cry from the "four-foot stack" of microfilmed documents that HUAC pretended to have when the pumpkin was opened—but still a ponderous collection of volumes. Through the years they have been pored over by experts of every kind—documents examiners, lawyers, judges, State Department officers and clerks, historians, journalists, typewriter makers and typewriter users, amateur sleuths and professional investigators. Every date stamp, pencil mark, initial, every typographical error, every typed or handwritten correction, every discrepancy of text or typing or type face among the various versions of each document has been analyzed, questioned, examined, and debated. Every word has been read, not once but dozens of times and by dozens of people. And a great deal more has been found in them than was ever shown to either jury.

When Walter Anderson took the stand for the second time at the second trial, he confronted the same seven-foot billboard and the same heroic enlargements, and was questioned about them from 11:15 A.M. Thursday, December 1, until late afternoon the following Monday, interrupted only by the weekend recess and the brief appearance of two minor witnesses after lunch on Friday. It was an utterly bewildering experience for this reporter and, no doubt, for the jury as well; it was tedious, frustrating, at times ludicrous, and often exasperating. There were at least three versions of most of the documents—the pumpkin paper itself, the "action copy" of the State Department original on which it was based, and the "code room copy," which carried a list of the offices within the State Department to which "information copies" had been distributed.

All three versions of each document had to be introduced, discussed, examined, assigned its exhibit number, and in some cases argued about. Cross and Murphy referred to the documents by exhibit numbers; Anderson referred to them by the names and dates on the originals, which the jury couldn't see. The pumpkin paper versions hung on the easel for them to study, but in some cases these were abbreviated summaries that didn't show the names and dates Anderson referred to. Defense Attorney Cross, a benign, gray-haired man with a scholarly air and a gentle manner, sometimes tried to clarify the discussion by referring to the documents by name, date, and exhibit number at the same time, but that only confused the listeners more.

To complicate matters further, some of the original documents were telegrams from abroad, some were interoffice memos that had never left Washington, and some were dispatches sent by mail from as far away as the Netherlands and Japan.* The exhibit

* The telegrams were uniformly referred to as "cables" in the testimony, but identified as "telegrams" on the documents themselves, so that the latter style is used here. I have spelled "dispatches" as it appears in the Trial Record, although the State Department preferred "despatches." Anderson

numbers assigned to them corresponded roughly to the chrono-
logical order of the dates when they were written, which was quite
different from the order in which they were obtained by Chambers, who had no access to them until some time after each was
received in Washington. But this point was never explained in the
trials.

In my report of Anderson's cross-examination in the *New
York Herald Tribune*, I commented that most of the first day
"was devoted to attempts of the two lawyers and the witness to
understand what each other was talking about." When the bare
text of the printed transcript is studied today, away from the
tensions and high drama that gripped all of us in the courtroom,
parts of it read almost like a Marx Brothers comedy script—confusion compounded by absurdity. Yet it is also clear from the transcript, as it was not in the courtroom, that Claude Cross was
going after a very important point.

Chambers had testified that the typewritten papers were
copied from State Department originals which Hiss brought home
from his office each evening; Priscilla copied them on her typewriter, he said, and then Hiss took them back to the office before
they could be missed. To corroborate this story the government
was trying to show that all the documents had come from Hiss's
office; Cross was trying to show that the government was manu-
facturing false evidence to support this point.

Cross's argument dealt with a set of five documents on
related subjects, four of which had been copied in full in the
pumpkin papers, though only two of them bore the necessary
rubber-stamped dates to show that they had been in the office of
Assistant Secretary of State Francis B. Sayre, where Hiss worked,
and that Hiss had thus had access to them. Two others bore the
date stamps of other offices, and one didn't show any date stamp at
all. When they were produced in court by the prosecution, they
were stapled together in two groups, each with a document on top
bearing the date stamp of Sayre's office. Cross sought to demon-

---

used the term for anything sent by mail, without distinguishing between a
covering letter and a report enclosed with it; this was a further source of
confusion for Claude Cross.

strate that they had not been stapled together that way when they traveled through the State Department in 1938; the prosecution had grouped them in the wrong order to make it appear that they had all gone to Sayre's office although, Cross believed, some of them had not.

This would have been a telling point if the jury had understood and accepted it, because it put the government in the position of relying on false evidence, whether the falsification was done deliberately or not, and whether Prosecutor Murphy knew it was false or not. But the point was subtle and difficult to establish, especially when the witness and attorneys couldn't agree on what documents they were talking about, and the jury couldn't see what was in their hands.

The reporters at the press table couldn't see any more than the jury, but now that the documents have been published in the Trial Record they can be examined. They concern a Japanese plan to raise money from American investors for the economic development of Manchukuo, the former Chinese province of Manchuria, which the Japanese had conquered in 1931–1932. There was a twenty-two-page report on the subject with a covering letter from Richard F. Boyce, U.S. Consul in Yokohama, Japan; an eight-page analysis of the Boyce report by Joseph N. Jones, of the Far Eastern Division of the State Department; a one-page note by Stanley K. Hornbeck, Political Adviser on Far Eastern Affairs; a two-page follow-up dispatch from Boyce, and a one-page note from Jones summarizing it.

It was clear that some of these documents had been attached to others in various ways as they moved from one office to another, but they did not necessarily all travel together, nor all go to the same places; they were apparently shuffled into a different order at each stop. Jones's one-page note, which bore no date stamps, must have been attached at all times to the two-page Boyce dispatch which it summarized, and which bore the date stamps of other offices but not Sayre's. It was questionable whether the Hornbeck note, which bore the date stamp of Sayre's office, was also attached to the Jones one-page note in 1938, as it was when the prosecution produced it in court.

Cross demonstrated, in his marathon cross-examination of Anderson, that the Hornbeck note had nothing to do with Jones's one-page note; it must have been attached instead to Jones's eight-page analysis, which is what it referred to. And in that case there was nothing to show that Jones's one-page note had ever gone to Sayre's office, or that Hiss had ever seen it. But there it was in the pumpkin papers, copied in full. How had it got there?

Anderson could not afford to concede a point that would have damaged the government's case so severely, but he was able to dodge the issue in a way that made it ludicrously incomprehensible to the jury. For example, when at one point Cross was about to pin him down he changed the subject by lifting up one of the documents and saying, "It is my belief that this memorandum of Mr. Hornbeck's actually refers to this memorandum here."

"Yes," said Cross, and tried to help the jury by adding, "and when you say 'this memorandum here' that is the memorandum of February 7, 1938, a memorandum of Mr. Jones?"

"That is correct, sir," Anderson answered.

"Now," said Cross, "what was this Jones memorandum of February 7, 1938, attached to when you brought the papers here?"

"It was attached to this file."

"By 'this file' you mean the January 6, 1938, one that did go to Sayre's office?"

"Yes."

"And the other two papers here, the January 18, 1938, Boyce report, and the February 9 went, as we have already seen, to different offices?"

"Yes."

Cross turned to Murphy and said, "Now, may I have either the photostat or the original of this Dr. Hornbeck* memorandum of February 11, 1938?"

"Do you know the number, Mr. Cross?" asked Murphy.

"Well, it should be State Exhibit—between 15 and 12."

At this point Judge Kaufman interrupted to say, "Did you

---

* Cross was apparently applying to Political Adviser Hornbeck the title of "Doctor" used by Economic Adviser Feis.

want a recess now?'', and the usual mid-morning recess was taken. It enabled the judge and jury to go to the bathroom and the spectators to do the same or to stretch their legs in the marble-floored hallway outside the courtroom and maybe have a smoke. For Cross, it was pure frustration since his point was only half made, and after the recess he had to begin over again. But the Judge had to keep his eye on the clock, and the necessity of hunting through documents for the one Cross wanted next was already an interruption, perhaps as good a time as any for a break.

In any case, Anderson was too experienced a bureaucrat to concede that there was anything unusual about stapling two State Department documents together that had nothing to do with each other. In a bureaucracy there are always things being done that don't seem to make sense, and so long as they don't violate any regulations a good bureaucrat doesn't inquire into them. A week later, when it was the defense's turn to call witnesses, the Dr. Hornbeck referred to in this exchange testified positively from his recollection that Cross was right; Hornbeck's own note had not been stapled to Jones's note the way the government claimed. But by then it was too late. The whole business only gave jury and spectators a headache, and the point of it was lost.

It would have been no use for Cross or Stryker at either trial to have argued that the pumpkin papers did not look like the sort of thing a competent spy would be expected to turn over to a foreign government—much less that ruthlessly professional and highly disciplined intelligence organization known variously in history and fiction as OGPU, NKVD, and SMERSH. The idea that these were genuine spy papers was too firmly fixed in the public mind. Yet, further examination since the trials has raised the question whether they may not have been that at all; at the very least, it has become clear that they were highly unsuitable for the purpose.

Most of the information the pumpkin papers contained could have been more easily collected in other ways if any foreign government cared to know about it. Of the forty-four telegrams involved, only twenty were confidential enough to be sent in a secret code, while twenty-nine were of sufficient public interest to be distributed to the Current Information Division of the State Department, where the press had access to them.

The "Boyce report" about Manchukuo that gave Cross so much trouble was based on the published reports of a Japanese business enterprise and a series of articles in a newspaper called the *Japan Advertiser*. The subject may have interested the Russians because Manchukuo was on the eastern border of Siberia; but the Russian consul in Yokohama could have read the business reports and newspaper articles as easily as Boyce had. They might have wanted their spies in Washington to tell them what the State Department was going to do about the matter, but there was nothing in the pumpkin papers to tell them that. The series ended before any decision was reached.

In the first trial there was one document that the government did want to keep secret, for reasons that only became apparent when the secrecy was lifted in the second trial. This was the one that Murphy referred to in his opening statement as being too secret for the jury to see. When it came time to introduce it into evidence along with the others in the first trial, Murphy simply stated that "Mr. Stryker and Mr. McLean have agreed we won't introduce the cable from Mr. Bullitt," and gave no further explanation to the jury; to reporters after adjournment that day he said it had been withheld at the request of the State Department, and he understood that the Department's request was based on "security reasons."*

---

* There was no explanation of what these "security reasons" might be, and around the courthouse the gap was naturally filled by rumors. One of the most popular was that the State Department was mainly interested in protecting the secrecy of the code Bullitt had used, but that wasn't very convincing because the codes used in 1938 would hardly be still in use in 1948, and in any case there were plenty of other documents in evidence that involved the same code. The State Department codes in the 1930s were not particularly sensitive; they were a convention of diplomacy and a means of saving the taxpayers' money, since the telegrams were sent by commercial cable at the lower rates charged for code material. The Department's "Gray" code was no different from ordinary commercial codes used by businessmen; the "secret" codes, ranging from A to D, were largely a matter of official prestige and gaining attention. Code D was transmitted ahead of Codes

Two paragraphs from the lengthy telegram had to be shown to the jury on the billboard, because they were quoted verbatim in the pumpkin papers. They didn't seem particularly dangerous; they described a conversation, which took place on January 25, 1938, between Ambassador William C. Bullitt in Paris and the then French Foreign Minister Yvon Delbos, about French hopes for a reconciliation with Hitler's Germany. It was hard to imagine that the Russians would have relied on American spies to find out Delbos's views on the subject, when their own Ambassador could talk to Delbos himself; and if there was something else more important and more secret in the rest of the telegram, why had the spy left that part out? The mystery was left unexplained; the defense made no attempt to probe it, and didn't point it out to the jury.

In the second trial the government changed its tactics without explanation and apparently caught the defense by surprise. The whole telegram was read to the jury, and the "secret" thus disclosed could have hurt the government's case if the defense had been quick enough to see it. But it wasn't until after the jury's verdict that the defense put its argument together and used it before the Court of Appeals; and by then it was too late.

What had happened was that Bullitt's telegram had been transmitted in two sections, both of which had gone to Hiss's office, but only one of which was copied in the pumpkin papers. The other section contained the disclosure that the Soviet Ambassador did indeed know all about Delbos's hopes for a reconciliation between France and Germany; Delbos had discussed them with him, even before mentioning them to Bullitt, and had already received the Soviet government's answer before Bullitt reported the matter to Washington.

Thus, it was clear from section two of the telegram that there was nothing in section one that the Soviet government hadn't already known, and therefore no need for the information

---

C, B, A, and Gray, and was read first on arrival. Bullitt, a bit of a snob about such things, habitually used C and D; Ambassador Joseph Grew in Japan sometimes used A; most of the others represented in these papers were generally content to use Gray.

in section one to be sent back to Moscow by a spy. If the pumpkin papers were indeed the work of a spy, it had to be someone who didn't see section two of the telegram. But there was the record of the code room copies to show both sections of the telegram had gone to Hiss's office, and on the same day.

Here was a case where the evidence showed that Hiss had nothing to do with it. But it was evidence that had been withheld in the first trial and passed unmentioned in the second; the Appeals Court found it insufficient to upset the verdict, and it is idle to speculate what effect it might have had on the trial jury if they had known about it.

The more sensational disclosure in section two, which earned the story of the day a two-column headline on the front page of the *Herald Tribune*, was what the Soviet Ambassador had said to Delbos. It gave a startling insight into the history of a crucial period in world affairs, a bit of information which may not have been news to scholars of the period but certainly was to the general public. For the Soviet Ambassador had warned Delbos that "if France should begin serious negotiations with Germany, the Soviet Union would come to terms with Germany at once." This occurred in January 1938, when the official policy of the Soviet Union was one of implacable hostility toward Hitler's Germany, and Hitler's main claim to support in democratic countries like France and the United States was his own implacable hostility toward the Soviet Union, Communism, and all their works. Such a reversal of policy on the part of the two main protagonists in the great Nazi–Communist ideological warfare of the 1930s seemed impossible to Delbos, and in different diplomatic ways he said so to the Soviet Ambassador and to Bullitt. Delbos frankly didn't believe it.

As history later proved, the Soviet Ambassador knew what he was talking about, and Delbos didn't. Nineteen months after their conversation, Stalin and Hitler signed the nonaggression pact that made World War II inevitable and led to Hitler's invasion of Poland. That pact also threw confusion and dismay into the ranks of Communists and liberal anti-Nazis the world over, and played its part in Whittaker Chambers's decision to tell his story of Communist infiltration to Adolf Berle and to start the long process that culminated with the production of these pumpkin papers in court. It had been the ultimate disillusionment for Chambers, confirming his decision to switch from anti-Nazi (the ideology that had bound him to the Communists) to anti-Communist—the ideology that bound him for the next ten years to *Time* Magazine, the FBI, HUAC, and the pumpkin papers.

One cannot help wondering what might have happened had Chambers seen section two of the Bullitt telegram in January 1938—or if he perhaps did see it, and was so shocked he didn't want anyone to know he had. This was during the time when, according to the testimony of Chambers and his wife, he was going through the tortuous and terrifying process of breaking away from the Communist Party, with all the hesitation, self-doubt, fear of the unknown, and changes of mind and mood, opinion and decision, recounted in *Witness*. His "break" with the party only anticipated what thousands of other Communists and their supporters did in less melodramatic ways when the news of the Hitler–Stalin pact was published in 1939. Was it knowledge of this telegram that finally turned Chambers against the Communism he had believed in for so long? He never explained what it was, and the truth may never be known. The evidence suggests that Chambers never saw the significant portion of the telegram; if he did, he never admitted it.

There are other passages in the pumpkin papers, too, that seem inconsistent with the idea that they were prepared by a spy for transmission to the Soviet Union or any other foreign power. Exhibit no. 1, a scribbled note in Hiss's handwriting that looks like something picked out of a wastebasket, quotes a telegram that had gone from Washington to Moscow in plain English and back to the State Department in the nonconfidential Gray code, so that the Russians had ready access to it if they were interested; it was a cryptic affair which, after some research, was found to have to do with a traveler using a false passport, but had no relation to international affairs of any consequence. It looked significant because it was so cryptic; but it had no significance.

Exhibit no. 2 was a similar handwritten note, mentioning the purchase of some French fighter planes by the Chinese; it was based on a cable which also discussed the available evidence of Japanese intentions to attack Russia, a subject which would have been more interesting to the Russians, but was ignored in the note. As in the case of the Bullitt cable, if this were written by a spy, he either hadn't seen the whole message or didn't understand his job.

In any case, handwritten notes were an unlikely device for a spy to use. The handwriting would incriminate him if it fell into the wrong hands, and was difficult enough for an American to read, much less a Russian; and the notes were too cryptic to be of much value, even if they had dealt with important subjects. These points were brought out clearly in both trials, but the juries were apparently unimpressed. They must have thought that even if Chambers lied about these documents, he might have told the truth about the others.

Unfortunately for the spy theory, the others present problems too. In Pumpkin Paper no. 11, for example, nine telegrams from the Far East are briefly summarized on two pages, with their dates and, in some cases, verbatim excerpts. Among them is the information under the date of January 27 that the Japanese had decided to take over some of the buildings of Tsinhua University for use as military barracks; distressing news to Americans who helped support the University, but of no apparent importance to the Russians. On the next page are two further telegrams on the same subject: on January 29 the Japanese yielded to American protests and decided not to take over the buildings, and on February 2 they changed their minds and decided to take over the buildings after all. What Chambers's papers didn't report is that the following day Ambassador Grew made a further protest at the Japanese Foreign Office, and for all that the documents in evidence at the trial showed, the Tsinhua students remained undisturbed in their buildings.

And so on. A similar absurd sequence of telegrams was summarized on one page in no. 46: on March 30 the State Department cabled the U.S. legations at Costa Rica and Panama to investigate a rumor of Japanese efforts to purchase a manganese mine on Cocos Island; on March 31 Panama replied that it couldn't be confirmed; on April 1 Costa Rica replied that there was no manganese on Cocos Island. There was some at Cocos Bay, but whether that was what the Japanese were interested in or whether there was any truth to the rumor, Chambers's papers were unclear.

As spy papers, these clearly weren't much; not worth risking anyone's neck for, as Chambers feared he was doing, and not worth the subsequent forty-four months that Hiss spent in jail. An odd collection: the four wastebasket scraps, the bundle of papers about the Manchukuo business enterprise, innumerable vague reports about Japanese troop movements in China, lacking enough detail to give a clear picture of how the Japanese invasion was going; numerous reports from Europe in the second week of February 1938 about what the ambassadors were saying to each other about the prospects of Hitler taking over Austria and uniting it with Germany; many more conversations of the same kind at the end of March, after Hitler had done exactly that in the famous Anschluss; but oddly enough nothing to show how Hitler accomplished it or what the ambassadors were saying to each other while it was being done. If the Russians were trying to find out from all this what American and European reactions would be to their plans for "coming to terms with Germany," they wouldn't have learned much this way; their own ambassadors could have told them more, as could the newspapers.

But if the typewritten papers in Chambers's collection weren't spy papers, what were they? The defense didn't know; it wasn't until long after the trials that enough evidence was found to answer the question, as we shall see in Chapter 21. Certainly, if the spy papers weren't genuine they were a sufficiently good imitation to convince eight members of the first jury and all twelve of the second. For all the defense knew, they could have been just that and nothing more—forgeries, deliberately created to frame Alger Hiss, and never intended to be sent to Russia at all. But the theory wasn't much use to them until they could find the evidence to support it, and by the time they did that it was too late to save Hiss.

The microfilms were a different matter. There was no doubt that they were photographs of genuine State Department documents, and nobody disputed Chambers's statement that they were typical of the material he said he had given the Russians. Everybody knew that spies used this technique to smuggle secrets out of the country, hiding two-inch squares of celluloid in the backs of pocket mirrors, or squeezing six-foot rolls of it into pill bottles. It was and had been a popular theme of spy fiction and thriller movies since the miniature camera was invented in the 1920's.

The question was whether Hiss had given the original documents to Chambers or not; Chambers said he had, Hiss said he hadn't. Three of them were mimeographed "information copies" of incoming telegrams, showing the date stamp of Sayre's office and the initials of Alger Hiss. To Prosecutor Murphy this was evidence that Hiss had given them to Chambers; to the defense attorneys, Stryker at the first trial and Cross at the second, it was proof that he had not—they must have been stolen from Sayre's office after Hiss initialed them and without his knowledge. Who ever heard of a spy carefully putting his initials on a stolen document before it was microfilmed, so that it could easily be traced to him if it fell into the wrong hands?

The rest of the microfilmed material consisted of five documents relating to negotiations with Germany over a proposed trade agreement, totaling forty-eight pages. Chambers said the whole lot had been photographed in a single operation, and nobody disputed him; it looked that way from the two strips of film that had been used.

The significant thing about the trade agreements documents is that the set was incomplete; it showed all the work done on the subject in the Trade Agreements Section of the State Department, where Julian Wadleigh worked (see Chapter 14), but it didn't match the set of documents on the same subject in the office of

Assistant Secretary of State Francis Sayre, where Hiss worked. Four of the microfilmed documents were carbon copies that had never gone to Sayre's office; they did not show the various rubber stamps, penciled initials, and other distinguishing marks on the hard copies that had gone to Sayre and Hiss. The fifth was an aide-memoire that had been forwarded by Sayre to Wadleigh's boss in the Trade Agreements Section. Missing from the set were two other documents that made up part of Sayre's file on the subject but were not seen by the Trade Agreements Section.

Wadleigh testified about these matters in both trials, admitting that he had often taken papers from the Trade Agreements Section, given them to Chambers to be microfilmed, and then returned them to their proper places without anyone else knowing about it. He said he couldn't remember whether he had handled the German trade agreement papers, but in the second trial he did identify them as being among those he "might possibly have seen and given to Chambers." It took long hours of cross-examination to draw this admission from him, and he never made it without qualifying it in various ways, so that it seemed a rather weak statement that fell short of taking responsibility for the crime Hiss was accused of. But it was an important admission nonetheless.

Wadleigh was a lanky, bony man, with a thin face, large glasses, and hair that stood up straight, and he looked younger than his forty-five years. He spoke in a soft, cultured voice, with a faintly English accent. Stryker, at the first trial, labeled it an "Oxford accent" and teased him about it; Cross, at the second trial, was equally sarcastic about his "Oxfordian" diction, by which he meant the practiced ease with which Wadleigh blunted Cross's attack by quibbling over words.

Wadleigh was indeed an Oxford graduate, and had lived in Europe from the age of three until he was twenty-five, studying at Kiel University in Germany and the London School of Economics as well as at Oxford. He had been a Fabian socialist in London; the term sounded ominous to many American ears in 1949, but it represented the views of the party of George Bernard Shaw, Clement Attlee, and Harold Wilson, which has by turns over the years formed the government of Great Britain and His (or Her) Majesty's loyal opposition. Wadleigh said he was not and never had been a Communist, but he had volunteered to help the Communists in the late 1930s because, like Chambers at the time, he saw in the Soviet Union the world's main defense against Hitler and Nazi Germany.

In the course of two years as a purveyor of government documents, Wadleigh testified, he turned over about four hundred of them to Communist agents, including Whittaker Chambers. Having handled so many, he said, he couldn't be expected to remember any of them in particular or which ones he had given to Chambers. The best he could do, looking over the documents in court, was to indicate which ones he might have seen in the course of his work, and which of these looked interesting enough to the Communists to be worth turning over to them. In this category, he identified the set of papers on the German trade agreement; he didn't remember working on them, but he might have seen them, and if so, he would certainly have given them to the Communists, he said.

As for the three telegrams that filled the rest of the strip of microfilm, Wadleigh said they would have been a "rich find" for him, exactly what the Communists wanted. The first two were estimates of the Japanese military situation in China, a subject the Communists had specifically asked him to look out for; the third was a long telegram from Bullitt in Paris, in three sections this time, describing what the Chinese Ambassador to Moscow had to say when he stopped in Paris on his way back to China.

Wadleigh apparently had a special interest in telegrams from Bullitt; the only document he could remember selecting for the spy ring was a 1937 telegram from Bullitt in Moscow, parts of which Wadleigh quoted in verbatim style. It had nothing to do with Wadleigh's work on trade agreements, and he didn't know how it had come into his hands, but he remembered deciding that the Communists must have it because he found it so interesting. Its contents, as he described them on the witness stand, were as follows:

"Bullitt said to the German Ambassador, who, according to

Bullitt, was drunk, 'Your government is pursuing a very strongly anti-Soviet policy, isn't it?'

"The Ambassador agreed.

"He said, 'On the other hand I have information that your government is allowing submarine parts to be shipped from Germany to Russia. Isn't that rather inconsistent?'

"And the German Ambassador answered, in effect, that he did not know what his government's policy was."

This light note was welcome enough relief in the complexity of Wadleigh's two long days of testimony, but why it had seemed so important and stuck in Wadleigh's mind so long he didn't explain. Its real significance seems to be what it tells about Wadleigh's access to telegrams which were none of his business. It's a fair enough inference that if he could pick up one fascinating Bullitt telegram, he could get another; which is the simplest explanation of how those three telegrams that were such a "rich find" got on the same microfilm with the German trade agreement papers.

The dates fitted neatly; the three telegrams, according to their date stamps, arrived at Sayre's office on January 14, 1938, only a few days after the last of the trade agreement papers had been completed in Wadleigh's section, so that all the carbon copies were ready for delivery to Chambers. It was a Friday afternoon; Sayre had left for the weekend, and Hiss was in his office. Wadleigh had in those days what he called a "roving assignment" and wasn't very busy. It was not unusual for him to drop into Hiss's office when he had nothing else to do and sit down for a chat, whether Hiss was busy or not. After all, they had known each other on the Eastern Shore, and Wadleigh made the most of the acquaintance; he also frequently had business with Hiss, or waited in Hiss's office to see Sayre.

There were three desks in Hiss's office, two of them piled high with papers, as lawyers' working desks normally are, and the third reserved for occasional use by others assigned to special tasks. Telegrams, dispatches, reports, memoranda, documents of all kinds came to Hiss in a constant flow, a fresh batch delivered by messenger every hour. On his own desk were his overflowing "in" and "out" baskets and the papers that required immediate attention; others which might need to be looked at later tended to pile up on the extra desk, where they would wait sometimes for weeks before any attention was paid to them. Visitors often sat at the extra desk while they waited to be called into Sayre's office. And whoever sat there had an opportunity to notice whatever documents happened to be lying on the desk, forgotten by Hiss while he worked on something else.

A month after the three Bullitt telegrams reached Hiss's desk, another batch of documents arrived in which Wadleigh had considerable interest. These were the Manchukuo papers that were to give Claude Cross such problems at the second trial. Cross thought that some of them had never reached Hiss, but further examination after the trial showed that the whole bundle came to him together—though not arranged in quite the way the government contended—on Wednesday, February 16, 1938. By that time action on the matter had been completed, there was nothing Sayre was required to do about them, and they were exactly the kind of papers Hiss would shove on to his extra desk to wait until he had time to look at them.

The file contained altogether thirty-seven pages, which the typist of the pumpkin papers reduced to twenty-one pages by typing single-space instead of double-space, though every word and figure was copied, including the handwritten parts. Indeed, since some of the original file was handwritten, it was clear that the pumpkin version was copied from this particular set, and not from someone else's carbon copies. When Wadleigh was asked to look through the original papers at the second trial, he picked out this set as documents he might have seen in the course of his work and would have given to Chambers if he had.

The question left unanswered at the trial was how this set of documents came to be gathered together in one place, and set down under Wadleigh's nose on that extra desk in Hiss's office. With so many other more pressing issues at the trial, it didn't seem particularly important; but over the years since then there has been time to study the documents more closely and work out the only answer that is consistent with all the evidence. It is also consistent with State Department procedures and practices in 1938, and it's an intriguing example of the arcane intricacies of bureaucratic paper shuffling, as well as the nature of the material Chambers and Wadleigh said they were turning over to the Russians. If it had been understood at the trials, it might have made quite a difference.

The sequence begins with the arrival at the State Department of Boyce's report, which was entitled "New Economic Organization of 'Manchoukuo.' "* It was dated January 6, 1938, and was received and stamped in by the State Department Division of Communications and Records (DCR) at 11:15 A.M. on Monday, January 24. Attached to it were carbon copies which did not need to be stamped.

The DCR routinely stamped a file number on the side of page 1 (in this case, 893.50 Manchuria/39) and indicated in green pencil on the upper right-hand corner the offices to which the document should be routed: FE, A-M/C, EA.† The document duly arrived in the Far Eastern Division (FE) the following day and was date-stamped by the receptionist there. A handwritten notation was made over the date stamp to show that a carbon copy was detached and held in the FE.

Maxwell M. Hamilton, chief of the FE, assigned one of his staff, Joseph N. Jones, to study the report and prepare a summary and comments. This Jones did, taking not quite two weeks for the job, and passed his work to Hamilton for approval on Monday, February 7. Hamilton signed his initials on it, and marked it for routing to the PA/H, A-M/C, and EA.‡

The Jones memorandum, as it came to be called, was essen-

* Presumably the quotation marks around "Manchoukuo" reflected the fact that the State Department didn't recognize the country's new name, or the right of the Japanese to rename it; the spelling used by Boyce was the one preferred by the Japanese, but the State Department and Americans generally spelled it without the "o" in the middle, so it was closer to the traditional name of "Manchuria," by which it is again known today.
† Far Eastern Division, Assistant Secretary Messersmith's Commercial Office, and International Economic Adviser (Herbert Feis).
‡ PA/H refers to Political Adviser Hornbeck, who was not on the distribution list for the Boyce report.

tially an eight-page summary of the twenty-two-page Boyce report, reaching the same conclusion: the new development corporation that the Japanese were setting up in Manchukuo (as Jones spelled it) looked like a highly risky proposition for American investors. A Mr. Yoshisuke Aikawa was due in the United States shortly to seek American capital for the venture, and Jones agreed with Boyce that American investors should be warned of the risks.

The Jones memorandum and the Boyce report were both stamped in at PA/H, the office of Political Adviser Stanley Hornbeck, on Wednesday, February 9. It was Hornbeck's responsibility to decide what action, if any, should be recommended to Secretary of State Cordell Hull in the matter; in making up his mind, he would consult the International Economic Adviser (EA) and the Commercial Office of Assistant Secretary Messersmith (A-M/C). Assistant Secretary Sayre, Hiss's boss, would be kept informed, because he was responsible for foreign economic policy.

While the papers were on Hornbeck's desk, Jones in the FE received another letter from Boyce saying that Aikawa was leaving for the United States by ship on February 24, which meant he would be here in early March, and that he hoped to raise $300 million of American capital. This was before the days of jet planes crossing the Pacific; but a month was little enough time for the State Department to make up its collective mind about what to do when Aikawa arrived. So Jones and his boss Hamilton decided to bring Aikawa's travel plans to Hornbeck's attention.

The standard procedure for calling a document to somebody's attention was to summarize it briefly on a small slip of notepaper, and to attach the summary to the document. Jones dictated such a summary of Boyce's letter, mentioning Aikawa's travel plans and fund-raising goal; but while his secretary was typing it he noticed a comment at the end of the letter to the effect that Aikawa's chances of success would depend on the "attitude of the American government toward his venture." So Jones copied that statement by hand at the bottom of his typed memo, underlining the key phrase, and he underlined it on the original letter as well. It was, after all, the main point. Then the memo and the letter were clipped together, and Hamilton apparently walked into Hornbeck's office with them, without giving Hornbeck's secretary a chance to date-stamp them.

Thus alerted, Hornbeck studied the papers and dictated a brief memo of his own two days later, February 11, formally calling the work of Jones and Boyce to the attention of Secretary Hull, Undersecretary Sumner Welles, Assistant Secretary Sayre, Economic Adviser Herbert Feis, and Messersmith's commercial officer, James J. Murphy. On the same day, Friday, the longer Jones memo was stamped in at Dr. Feis's office, and on Saturday the short Jones memo, along with the letter about Aikawa's travel plans, was in James Murphy's office. On Monday Feis collated all the papers, ticked off his name on the distribution list at the head of Hornbeck's covering note, and wrote across it the comment: "A very interesting report."

The set of papers was now ready for Secretary Hull to see— the two little memos by Hornbeck and Jones showed that the lengthy documents had been carefully studied by the people responsible; the longer memo by Jones, if Hull cared to read it, would save him the trouble of reading the even longer report from Boyce; the comment from Feis indicated that the report was "interesting," but didn't suggest that anything be done about it. So it's not surprising that the papers moved in quick succession through the offices of Hull and Welles, date-stamped by both on Tuesday, February 15. The following day they were stamped into Mr. Sayre's office, where they soon landed on Hiss's extra desktop. The Secretary of State had made no comment, there was nothing Sayre need do about it; the matter was for Hornbeck to handle however he liked, and he obviously had copies of his own of the whole file, since the covering note had come from his office. Everybody had seen it who needed to; all the names were ticked off on Hornbeck's distribution list.

There remained, however, the matter of making sure all the routing indications on all the documents in the file were properly checked off, and matched with appropriate office stamps. This was a routine that Eunice A. Lincoln, one of the two secretaries in Sayre's office, was very particular about, and when Hiss finally put the papers in his "out" box she sorted and inspected them before returning them to the DCR for permanent filing.

According to the date-stamps, this happened on March 11, twenty-five days after the file reached Sayre's office, so there had been plenty of time for the documents to be taken out and brought back again without attracting Hiss's attention. On March 11 the original letter from Boyce was stamped into James Murphy's office; he had certainly seen it when Hornbeck sent it to him a month earlier, but it hadn't passed under his receptionist's rubber stamp at the time. And it wasn't until March 17 that he got around to initialing it and putting it in his "out" box so that it could go down to the DCR and be filed.

Much the same happened to the letter about Aikawa's travel plans; it wasn't stamped by Dr. Feis's secretary when he saw it in February, so that it was sent back to be stamped on March 16, and filed in the DCR March 21. Thus did the two sets of documents get separated from each other, and cause so much confusion twenty years later, with so much damage to Hiss's defense. Not knowing what had really happened to these documents, Cross missed the opportunity to prove that it was Wadleigh, not Hiss, who stole them; at the time he could only speculate about it. And if Cross had known the facts presented here, he would not have had such difficulty proving that the documents were grouped in the wrong order when the government produced them in court. This would have been proof that the government was relying on false evidence—the Hornbeck note had been stapled to the wrong Jones note—and once that was proved, the question would have arisen whether the government knew the evidence was false or was itself responsible for the falsehood.

19

THE OLD WOODSTOCK
TYPEWRITER

WHEN the testimony and the arguments about the documents were over, there remained the question of the typewriter. Had sixty-four of the sixty-five pages of typewritten copies, excerpts, and summaries of the State Department documents been done on the old Woodstock machine that Priscilla had got from her father? There it sat on a table in front of the jury, a clumsy old-fashioned machine, big and awkward to use, bearing the serial number N230099. It had been produced with a flourish by Stryker at the beginning of the first trial, as though it would be the clincher to prove Hiss's innocence; by the time the second trial was over it was to become one of Murphy's "immutable witnesses" that persuaded the jurors he was guilty. Rarely in the history of American trials had a piece of evidence boomeranged so badly.

Murphy approached the typewriter rather gingerly in the first trial. He didn't accept Stryker's invitation to examine it; he just let it sit there, never so much as touching it or looking at it. He didn't introduce any evidence to show it was the one used for the pumpkin papers; he relied instead on the opinion of the FBI documents expert, Ramos C. Feehan, that the pumpkin papers had been typed on the same machine as some other papers in evidence that Priscilla Hiss said she had typed. For, at the very beginning of the case, before the typewriter was found, Hiss had turned over to the Justice Department all the typed material he and Priscilla could find, for comparison with the pumpkin papers, and the FBI had hunted for more, inquiring of everyone they could reach who might have had any correspondence from the Hisses.

Four samples of the old Woodstock's work were found in this way, and referred to in the trial as "Hiss standards," because they served as standards for comparison with Chambers's papers. The latest date on any of them was May 25, 1937, more than seven months before the earliest date on any of the pumpkin papers. This was a point on which Stryker laid great stress, since it supported his contention that the machine was out of the Hisses' possession when the "pumpkin papers" were typed. The sample was a letter from Priscilla to the director of admissions at the University of Maryland applying for entrance into the summer course in chemistry she took that year. The other "Hiss standards" were Priscilla's report to the Bryn Mawr Club as its president in the year 1936–1937; her "Description of Personal Characteristics of Timothy Hobson," which accompanied an application for his admission to the Landon School, dated September 9, 1936; and her sister Daisy Fansler's letter to the Philadelphia Free Library of December 6, 1931.*

Feehan testified that in his opinion all these papers were typed on the same machine as the pumpkin papers, and he used huge enlargements of portions of each paper to show how he had arrived at that conclusion. His enlargements were displayed on the same seven-foot easel as the documents had been, but now the typewritten letters were of even more enormous size, for only a few words appeared in each photograph. Stryker asked a few questions as Feehan went through his presentation but didn't cross-examine him; he accepted Feehan's view that Priscilla's machine had been used to type the pumpkin papers. It was entirely consistent with the defense view that the machine wasn't in her possession at the time; somebody else must have done the typing.

---

* A fifth sample, a letter from Alger Hiss to the Equitable Life Assurance Society, was ignored by Feehan without explanation.

In later years, after the trials were over, new evidence was found to show that Feehan's analysis was all wrong, and that old N230099 may have been a fake. But Stryker didn't know this at the time nor did Cross in the second trial. They had no way of breaking down Feehan's testimony, so they didn't try.

As a matter of trial tactics, they had no choice. They couldn't tangle with Feehan because they hadn't been able to find a rival documents expert who would dispute Feehan's testimony. Many cases involving expert testimony have to do with such questions as whether it was an automobile accident that caused the plaintiff's backache, or muscular weakness resulting from a previous pregnancy; whether the signature on some embezzled bonds was forged, or did the defendant sign it himself; and so on. In such cases each side produces its own expert and they express contrary opinions. Then the lawyers argue about it, and the jurors make up their minds on a common-sensical basis, deciding who they are going to believe. A lawyer who doesn't have an expert to back him up in such an argument can be in a difficult position indeed.

In 1949 the defense couldn't find such an expert, although three years later, when the excitement had died down, they found several. For this was no ordinary accident or embezzlement case; the allegations of treason and conspiracy against the United States were producing a storm of public excitement. Anyone who said a good word for the defendant, no matter how accurate or well founded, was promptly excoriated by press and politicians, and his career put in jeopardy. Even Judge Kaufman became a victim of this tactic when the first trial ended in a hung jury. Representatives Nixon and Case, of South Dakota, a new member of the House Un-American Activities Committee (HUAC), demanded an investigation of Judge Kaufman's "fitness to serve on the bench"; Nixon accused him of "prejudice against the prosecution," and said that "when the full facts of the conduct of this trial are laid before the nation, the people will be shocked." While Judge Kaufman escaped the impeachment that Nixon and Case were threatening, he rose no further in the judicial hierarchy. Secretary of State Dean Acheson, who told a press conference he "wouldn't turn his back" on Hiss, paid for it in a reputation for being "soft on Communism" which bedeviled him the rest of his political life; while John Foster Dulles, who chose to give his highly ambiguous testimony as a witness for the government rather than the defense, boasted of this distinction in the election campaign of 1952, and won Acheson's old office in the Eisenhower Administration.

So there was every reason for documents experts to be cautious when they were approached by the defense lawyers, and to limit themselves to the sufficiently obvious comment that all the typewritten papers in evidence looked a good deal alike. None of them wanted to tangle with Ramos C. Feehan of the FBI; after all, the government was their best client, and win or lose, Alger Hiss could never bring them much business, or protect them against defamation or attack. Besides, nobody thought he'd win.

In any event, Feehan's task was a simple one; he was a Justice Department employee, asked by his employers to point out any similarities he could find between the pumpkin papers and the acknowledged work of Priscilla Hiss's old Woodstock. This wasn't difficult; typewriters are essentially machine-made machines, and any two taken off the same production line at approximately the same time will produce work as nearly alike as two mechanical adding machines or cash registers of the same make and model. The differences, if there are any, will come from the way the machines are used—and who used them.

Murphy ignored all this; he argued that it was impossible to tell the work of one typist from another, but that individual typewriters were as different from each other as people's fingerprints. This was an argument that Nixon was to use in *Six Crises*; the fallacy in it passed unchallenged, because the defense lawyers, so unfamiliar with typewriters themselves, didn't recognize it. A fingerprint is a mark of individuality which a human being receives at birth, and however much he grows and changes the fingerprint doesn't change, because the living cells are renewed in exactly the same pattern year after year. Typewriters at birth— that is, when they come off the production line—are identical, except for any microscopic or chemical irregularities in the metal they are made of or any handwork that has been done on them. They may develop differences over the years as a result of wear, but these are not as useful to the detective as Murphy and the jury seemed to think.

What happens to old manual typewriters, as all old newspapermen know, is that the keys get a little loose, and tend to flop about. A letter may hit the page slightly above or below the line, or lean slightly to the right or left. Or it may be properly vertical and in line, but slightly angled as it strikes the page, so that one side hits harder and makes a heavier impression than the other. It may do some of these things more often than others, but it won't do any of them consistently; it will do sometimes one and sometimes another, or sometimes a combination of two or more, depending on how loose the keys are, and how hard the typist strikes them. It gets worse the longer the typewriter is used, if it isn't properly repaired. But it isn't a distinguishing mark of any particular typewriter's "fingerprint."

It was easy enough for Feehan to find a number of instances where a letter on the two sets of documents—the pumpkin papers and the "Hiss standards"—showed the same flaw. There was an "i" slightly below the line in various places, an "o" printed more heavily on the right side than the left, an "a" heavier at the bottom than the top; and an "r" leaning to the right, an "l" and an "A" printing heavier on the right than the left.

What Feehan didn't say was that there were plenty of other places in the two sets of documents where these letters didn't show exactly these flaws, and where the documents didn't match at all. There were instances where these and other letters could have been used to show the differences between the documents, if the defense had had an expert of their own to point them out. Feehan covered himself in the first trial by conceding that there were "variations" in the similarities he had pointed out, but in the second trial he didn't even bother to do that. He simply stated flatly that the documents all came from the same typewriter; he had no doubt about it.

Feehan also found places where the "d" and "u" showed similar defects on both sets of documents: the serif, that little decorative line at the bottom right-hand corner of each of these letters, seemed too short on the "d" and slightly crooked on the "u." The bottom half of the "e" sometimes looked irregular, and so did the bottom loop of the "g." These defects, which might have resulted from wear (or from dirt or imperfections on the ribbon or paper) were not dependable either; sometimes they showed up and sometimes they didn't. But Feehan contended they showed up often enough to prove his point, and nobody argued with him.

It wasn't until two years after Hiss's conviction, when his lawyers unsuccessfully moved for a new trial on the basis of newly discovered evidence, that two independent document examiners disputed Feehan's analysis. By this time the defense had gone to the expense of having another old Woodstock altered to duplicate the work of the one Priscilla had used, simply to demonstrate that this could be done and therefore might have been what Chambers had done to type the pumpkin papers. The defense challenged the government to examine the work of the two machines and see if they could tell the difference; this the government refused to do, arguing that it wasn't new evidence, it was just a new theory of the case, and if the defense wanted it taken seriously they should have brought it up at the trial. The judge denied the motion, and that closed the case, so far as the courts were concerned, except for the appeal to the Supreme Court, which that court refused to hear. But the evidence supplied by the document examiners sheds new light on other aspects of the case, which didn't happen to be involved in the new trial motion.

Miss Elizabeth McCarthy, documents examiner for the City of Boston and the Massachusetts State Police, examined the work of the new machine and compared it with that of the one produced at the trial; she found that she could tell them apart, but not by the techniques Feehan had used. Feehan's affidavit didn't argue the point; the government simply refused to put the matter to the test. Then Miss McCarthy went on to make her own comparison of the pumpkin papers and Priscilla's work, using her own more sophisticated techniques. And she found that they might have been typed on the same machine, but then again they might not. It was altogether uncertain, inconclusive, and unsatisfying.

Miss McCarthy scorned Feehan's methods as revealing nothing more than the kind of flaws that might be found in any old typewriter of the same age and make, and explained in a detailed footnote how she arrived at that conclusion. Then she pointed out that she had found plenty of discrepancies between the two sets of documents to offset the similarities Feehan had found. The only reason she couldn't say definitely the documents were typed on two different machines was that she couldn't find a sufficiently consistent pattern of discrepancies to prove it. In other words, it's easy to show that two similar typewriters do similar work; to distinguish between them with certainty is more difficult.

It was Mrs. Evelyn Ehrlich, a typography expert for Harvard's Fogg Museum of Art, who was first to recognize the importance of the flimsy paper and fresh typewriter ribbons that had been used for the pumpkin papers. These details hadn't been apparent to the other documents examiners hired by the defense before and during the trials, because they had had to work from photostats and photographic copies instead of the actual pumpkin papers themselves. The originals were occasionally shown to witnesses on the stand, but the defense motion to examine them before the trial had been turned down by Judge William Bondy, and the only concession the defense won during the trial was permission to cut off a three-inch square from the bottom of one of the pages, where nothing was typed, and submit it to chemical analysis to see if the age of the paper could be determined. It couldn't.

Late in the proceedings on the motion for a new trial, on March 21, 1952, the government withdrew its objections to letting the defense examine the original papers, and they were made available to the defense experts to work on under continuous FBI supervision for a little over two weeks. Mrs. Ehrlich discovered on examining them that the typewritten letters were smudged and had such blurred outlines that it was impossible to measure them with the precision necessary to determine whether or not they were the product of the same machine Priscilla had used. She explained that they were "all on poor types of paper with inadequate sizing and a high degree of absorbency. In many instances the ribbons were apparently moist." Miss McCarthy had discovered that at least four typewriter ribbons were used, perhaps more, and she couldn't understand why the ribbons had been changed so often in the course of sixty-four pages.

Priscilla's letters, done with normally dry ribbons on proper typewriter paper, could be compared with the work of the machine produced in court, and Mrs. Ehrlich found they had not been typed on it after all. This would mean that the machine that had been recovered from Ira Lockey after so much trouble, and had been accepted at both trials as the original Hiss machine, wasn't that at all. It was some other old Woodstock, whether or not it had been deliberately altered to do work that looked like Priscilla's. And which of the two machines had typed the pumpkin papers, or whether the typing had been done on a third old Woodstock which nobody knew anything about, Mrs. Ehrlich couldn't tell. The use of the absorbent paper and the moist typewriter ribbons had made that impossible.

None of this was known when first Stryker and then Cross confronted Feehan at the trials; and when it came to arguments on the motion for a new trial in 1952, it was too late to pursue the implications of Mrs. Ehrlich's discovery. Hiss's new attorney, Chester Lane, was following a different approach. He was trying to prove that the typewriter produced at the trial was a deliberate fake, planted on the defense by Chambers or by the prosecution; he didn't know how the trick had been done, but it would obviously mean Hiss's immediate vindication if it could be shown that the prosecution had known about it or the FBI had helped do it.

When Lane looked for the evidence that would show whether his theory was right or wrong, he found that everywhere he went the FBI had been there before him. The serial number of the machine, N230099, didn't seem to match the numbers for the date when Priscilla's father had purchased the one he gave her; it suggested a typewriter manufactured at a later date. But the records of the Woodstock Typewriter Company which had made it, the Philadelphia dealer who had sold it, and the Northwestern Mutual Life Insurance Company which had bought it for Priscilla's father, were all in some confusion. The FBI had been through them, taken some records away, and talked to the people Chester Lane and his investigators wanted to talk to. Lane found that every time a line of investigation seemed promising the story would suddenly be changed, or the records become unavailable, or the individual concerned would decide not to sign the affidavit.

Thus, when it came to arguing the motion for a new trial, Chester Lane couldn't prove anything; all he could say was that the government evidently knew more about the matter than he did, and he couldn't get the evidence he needed unless the court would let him issue subpoenas and bring witnesses in for questioning under oath. This the court refused to do; after all, it was the same judge, Henry W. Goddard, who had heard all the evidence and arguments at the second trial, and he was unimpressed by the new theory.

There was nothing more Chester Lane could do, or Hiss either, and the matter might have rested there if Nixon had not made his startling statement, in the first chapter of *Six Crises*, that the FBI had found the Hiss machine on December 13, 1948, four months before the defense found old N230099.* Hiss and his attorneys had some other bits of evidence on this point in their files that suddenly seemed to gain new significance; there was the passage in the report of HUAC, dated December 31, 1951, in which the Committee formally commended the FBI for its work on the case, and particularly for "the location of the typewriter." And there was a letter from Rep. John R. McDowell, one of Nixon's colleagues on the Committee in 1948, giving "a generous amount of credit . . . to the FBI for finding the typewriter that typed the letters found in the pumpkin."

What did this mean? Had the FBI actually found old N230099, and discovered from examining it that the serial number

* See page 269.

was wrong, and that the type bars showed signs of having been tampered with, as Daniel P. Norman, a specialist in the chemical analysis of metals and papers, discovered when he examined the machine for the defense lawyers in 1952? And had the FBI, concluding the machine was a fraud, taken it back to Ira Lockey and told him to let the defense have it without saying anything more about it? Or had the FBI perhaps found the real Hiss machine, and discovered that it proved what Hiss originally expected it to prove, that it hadn't been used on the pumpkin papers after all? And had the FBI then altered it themselves, or altered some other old Woodstock that looked like it, and planted the fake machine on Ira Lockey? The questions were tempting, but the answers were as elusive as ever.

Nixon repudiated the whole idea when he was challenged in 1962, and altered succeeding editions of his book to conform to the trial record on this point. But he never quite got rid of the idea that he and the Committee had got the typewriter first, even if he eventually ceased to give the FBI credit for helping. When the first White House-edited version of the famous Watergate tapes was published by Nixon in April 1974, they contained a half-dozen references to the Hiss case, including Nixon's injunction to his aide, John W. Dean, III, to "go back and read Chapter 1 of *Six Crises*." And in that same conversation, on February 28, 1973, Nixon was quoted as saying, "We got the evidence, we got the typewriter, we got the pumpkin papers. We got all of that ourselves. The FBI did not cooperate. The Justice Department would not cooperate."

So perhaps it was Nixon and his HUAC investigators, not the FBI, who first found the typewriter. Could they have altered it too? No one knows, except Nixon and whoever he included in that "we," and Nixon isn't telling. There may be some evidence on this point in the files of the FBI or the old records of HUAC, which are now in the custody of the House Judiciary Committee, but if so neither the FBI nor the Judiciary Committee has agreed to release it.*

* As of this writing, September 1975. Efforts to gain full access to these files and records are continuing.

Whatever the truth about the typewriter, there was still only Chambers's word that Priscilla had done the typing of the pumpkin papers, and neither side produced any expert testimony about that. Murphy said no expert would be able to tell, and when the defense lawyers consulted one, he said it looked to him as though Priscilla might have done it. So that was no help.

The normal thing that a defense lawyer might be expected to do in such a case would be to take the documents to Priscilla, and let her sit down and see what she could make of them. After all, any one who uses a typewriter quickly learns to recognize her own work (or his, as the case may be) and to distinguish it from that of other typists. Maybe a document expert can't do that, or couldn't in 1948, but a habitual typewriter user can, especially if the work in question is done by someone who isn't a professional typist.

A newspaper reporter, for example, can fish his own work out of a pile of miscellaneous copy in an instant, simply by noting its appearance without reading a word of it, even if the rest of the pile is typed on machines of similar make and age, which is not unusual in newspaper offices. We all have our characteristic frequency of errors, and frequency of leaving errors uncorrected. Touch typists work at a fairly even rhythm, striking each letter with about the same pressure and making relatively few errors; hunt-and-peck artists may work either faster or slower, and strike the keys harder or more lightly; if they work too fast, the capital letters tend to be above the line, because the carriage doesn't shift up and down fast enough. Some hard-punching typists really make the machine bounce, especially if the table it's on is a little creaky in the joints, so that almost every letter is out of line, and there's often an extra space between letters or words. All this makes a distinctive pattern on the page; no experienced typist of this kind could fail to recognize his own work or have much difficulty pointing out the differences in style of somebody else's. It's as easy as recognizing the handwriting on an envelope.

Unfortunately, neither Hiss nor McLean nor any of the other defense lawyers knew this, because they had never used a typewriter or looked at a typewritten page in this way. They were accustomed to the montonously perfect work of their secretaries and stenographers, which if they were good enough was almost as indistinguishable in the days of manual typewriters as it is today on electrics. So the lawyers took the experts' word for it, without inquiring further.

There were other reasons, too, why it may not have occurred to them to take the question to Priscilla. An outside lawyer doesn't abandon such questions easily; he has a professional skepticism, and much as he puts his faith in his client, he never quite trusts him. But it's hard to confront your own friend's wife with the statement, "This document expert says you typed these papers; see if you can prove to me that you didn't." It's particularly hard when the wife in question is in the confused and frightened state Priscilla seems to have been in. And if the lawyers had asked her, she says today, she probably would have told them she couldn't prove anything about the papers one way or another. She had never used a typewriter often enough to notice anything distinctive about her own work, she says; she wasn't a "habitual" typewriter user, she only used it occasionally.

Priscilla says she felt terrible when she took the witness stand, and to this reporter at the time she seemed to be holding herself together by an effort of will, frightened half to death and not quite able to understand what was going on around her. She was a slight figure in a gray dress with white hat, white gloves, and white collar and cuffs; a dainty, delicate woman. She looked and sounded like a discreet and silent Quaker, a Puritan maiden in simple dresses with her neat blond hair drawn demurely back from her face, lips tight together, and great liquid, hazel eyes turned on her husband.

All through the trial, except when she was testifying, Priscilla sat next to her husband, the defendant, just inside the rail of the court, facing the witness stand. It was a special privilege for one who was to be a witness; all the other witnesses except the defendant and Dr. Binger, the defense psychiatrist, were barred from the courtroom when they were not on the stand, so that they could not hear what the other witnesses said. Dr. Binger was allowed to hear Chambers, but no one else. Priscilla, like her husband, was allowed to hear everything; and this was not for any reasons of compassion or sentimentality on the part of the judge at either trial. It was because Priscilla was an unindicted co-conspirator, although the grand jury had made no formal statement to that effect. For Hiss to be guilty as charged, it had to be Priscilla who had typed the documents, an accessory to the alleged crime who should have been indicted if the government thought they had a strong enough case. So along with the defendant she was entitled to listen to the evidence against her, as though she were co-defendant as well as alleged co-conspirator. It was a circumstance that might have given her cause for anxiety if she had been aware of it, but she says she was not.

On the witness stand she spoke in as soft and inaudible a voice as Esther Chambers had done, and the lawyers repeatedly had to ask her to speak up. Stryker and Murphy treated her for the most part with unaccustomed gentleness; Cross, who was by nature gentle, avoided questions that might give her pain, though sometimes he seemed to find her answers rather frustrating. She was on the stand barely six hours in the first trial; at the second, she began her testimony late on the Friday afternoon before New Year's Eve, then was on the stand the whole of Tuesday, January 3, and for intervals on Wednesday and Thursday as well. Everything was more thorough at the second trial; it lasted nine weeks where the first lasted six.

It was not until that first Tuesday of 1950, when the second trial was nearing its end, that Priscilla ever looked at the typed pumpkin papers or held them in her hand; she didn't even remember having seen the photostatic copies of them until shortly before the second trial began. She remembered typing something on the old Woodstock in McLean's office before the trial, but she didn't remember what she had typed or why she had been asked to do it, or what the machine was doing in that office. "I am sure I wasn't told anything about it," she said.

Priscilla told the jury she didn't have any idea how long it would take her to type a page like the ones shown her, or whether she typed fast or slowly. She said she wasn't a "touch typist" because she had to look at the keyboard; she wasn't exactly hunt-

and-peck either, because she used more than two fingers, though not all ten. She couldn't remember how many she used.

That must have sounded like a silly answer to the jury, but it's a little like the story of the man with a long beard who was asked whether he slept with it inside the covers or outside. He stayed awake all that night trying to find out. Examining my own habits as I type this manuscript, I can report that I hardly ever use the little fingers of either hand, because when I do they usually make mistakes; but I do sometimes use them to press a shift key, or an "a" or "p" if I'm in good form and full of confidence. So counting one thumb, let's say I use seven or eight fingers as a rule, rarely nine.

Priscilla had never made this kind of analysis, and didn't attempt it in her white gloves on the witness stand. The point she wanted to make was that she really didn't type very much, and never had. That's what she said, in so many words, and she formally denied that she had typed the pumpkin papers. But she didn't dramatize it with illustrative detail. Instead, when Murphy opened his cross-examination by saying to her in his don't-be-afraid-of-me-I-may-look-like-a-bear-but-I'm-not-going-to-eat-you voice, "You could type them, couldn't you?", Priscilla simply blinked her eyes in embarrassment and answered shyly, "I beg your pardon?"

"Could you have typed them," Murphy repeated; "were you physically able to type them?"

"Yes, I can type," said Priscilla.

"And were you sufficiently familiar with a typewriter to have typed them?"

"Yes, I think so," Priscilla conceded, and with that admission her whole defense tumbled to the ground.

Looking back on the experience, Priscilla contends that she was misunderstood; all she meant was that she was perfectly capable of typing out A, B, C, on a typewriter if anybody asked her to. She certainly didn't mean that she could have typed all those sixty-four pages Murphy was talking about, for that would have taken her "years and years." But she didn't realize at the time that the typing job involved was so complicated; nobody had shown the papers to her or gone over them with her.

That twenty-two page report on the "New Economic Organization of 'Manchuoukuo,'" for example, which attracted so much of Claude Cross's attention earlier in the trial, was a monumental typing job that must have taken hours to do, and was filled with interesting clues that made it seem a most unlikely product of Priscilla's fingers. It was reduced in the pumpkin papers to sixteen pages of single-spaced type, plus a title page and table of contents that were done with considerably less skill than the professional stenographer's work on the State Department original, but nevertheless showed a certain amount of experience and know-how, not to mention a typewriter equipped with workable tabulator keys and a typist who knew how to use them. Priscilla hadn't done anything like that on the manuscript she and her sister-in-law wrote in the early 1930s for the Carnegie Foundation; she had written a lot of it in longhand, typed some, and hired a professional stenographer for the final draft.

There were pages in the Manchukuo report that required as many as four separate indentations for numbered subparagraphs and lettered sub-subparagraphs, all involving use of those tricky tabulator keys; there were long columns of figures carefully lined up, each in its correct position on the page, and only one typographical error to be corrected in the lot. When Priscilla said she thought she could have done all this, she genuinely didn't know what she was talking about. When she tried to type one of the easier pages in McLean's office it took her almost three-quarters of an hour, and the resulting page looked quite different.

For one thing, the typist of the pumpkin papers had moved along at a good fast pace, and a lot of his capitals were above the line, as happens in such cases. But that hardly ever appeared in Priscilla's work, since she typed more slowly. Nor did Priscilla ever transpose letters in her work, as the pumpkin typist did, writing "prupose" for "purpose," "veiw" for "view," and "teh" for "the." Such differences might not have convinced Ramos C. Feehan, the government's documents expert, but they would have made a big impression on the jury if Priscilla's letters, too, had been enlarged to seven feet high and hung on an easel in front of the jury while Priscilla pointed them out.

But Priscilla didn't know this, and neither Hiss nor McLean nor Cross nor Stryker knew enough about the typist's art to realize it could be done. Nor had Hiss yet noticed some other peculiarities of the pumpkin papers that later leaped to his eye when he looked at them years afterward.

There was the spelling of that word "Manchoukuo," for instance. Richard F. Boyce, U.S. Counsul in Yokohama, spelled it with the extra "o" in the middle, or his typist did, but the accepted spelling in the United States in those days was "Manchukuo," and that's the way the pumpkin papers typist spelled it in the transcription of Boyce's covering letter, title page, table of contents, and the first page of the text. Then suddenly near the bottom of the page the pumpkin papers started adopting Boyce's spelling, except for a few lapses on page 2, and stuck to it the rest of the way, following copy as Boyce had done in quotations from the *Japan Advertiser*.

When Joseph N. Jones in the Far Eastern Division wrote his summary and analysis of the Boyce report, he spelled the word "Manchukuo," like everybody else in the State Department; and if the pumpkin papers had been prepared for Hiss's use or under his supervision, perfectionist Hiss would have done the same. Or perhaps, if his purpose was to reproduce the Boyce document exactly, he would have followed the Boyce spelling; but he never would have tolerated a mixture of the two. Nor would he have allowed such careless errors as "Mitsuibishi" for "Mitsubishi," or "Yoskisuke" for Yoshisuke Aikawa's first name; Hiss has a sharp eye for such things and does not allow them to pass uncorrected.

Most interesting of all, in the light of what was later to be discovered by Mrs. Ehrlich and Miss McCarthy, was the thinness of the paper. Murphy drew attention to it, asking Priscilla to take off her gloves and feel how thin it was. Priscilla declined; "I can see that it is thin," she said. She remarked somewhat remotely that it looked like cheap tissue paper, "the kind that is in dress

THE OLD WOODSTOCK TYPEWRITER

boxes," and she didn't think that she had ever seen any "writing paper" like that.

"You never saw it before in connection with typewriting or receiving carbon copies or typing paper?" Murphy asked incredulously.

"Possibly," said Priscilla, "but I don't think so."

"Mrs. Hiss," Murphy pursued with an air of patience becoming strained, "don't you know that it is the common garden variety of seconds that is used all over the country?"

"No, I don't know it, Mr. Murphy," said Priscilla. "I simply have no experience with it."

To the jury this must have seemed a deliberate and probably untruthful evasion; how could anyone go through life without ever seeing a carbon copy of something? But Priscilla's description of it as "tissue paper" wasn't bad, for it was close enough to tissue paper to be the grade known in newspaper offices as "flimsy." Why the pumpkin papers should have been typed on flimsy was a question never raised in either trial, but it is important enough to examine here.

Flimsy makes excellent paper for carbon copies, because it is cheap and light; you can put up to ten sheets of it in a typewriter with leaves of carbon paper between, and come out with readable copy on the tenth sheet. In the days before Xerox machines this was a valuable trait. But to put a single sheet of it in a typewriter and type directly on it is inviting trouble. It is too thin for the machine to hold properly, so it slips around and the lines are uneven (as they were on the pumpkin papers). It tends to crease when you put it in the typewriter, especially if you have typed halfway down it, pulled it out of the machine so you can type something else on another page, and then put it back in. (This kind of crease shows up in an interesting way on two of the pumpkin papers.)

Most important, flimsy is soft and spongy, just right for taking the impression of carbon paper; but when typewriter ribbon hits it the ink tends to smudge and spread, almost like a fountain pen (not a ball-point pen!) on newsprint, so that the outline of the letter is blurred. This makes a poor impression, and strains the reader's eyes; it also, as Mrs. Ehrlich pointed out, makes it impossible to tell for certain which one of a number of similar typewriters was used for the job.

The blurred effect is, of course, much greater if the typewriter ribbon is new and wet; an old ribbon will do almost as well on flimsy as on proper typewriter paper. Priscilla didn't mind using old, dry ribbons on her letters, including some of those introduced as evidence; but the pumpkin papers typist, as Miss McCarthy noticed, used no less than four different ribbons on sixty-four pages, changing them often enough so that the ribbon was always fresh and wet, the impression on the page always blurred and smudgy.

Thus, the evidence of the pumpkin papers themselves, if the defense had been able to discover it in time and use it in the trial, showed that they could not have been typed by Priscilla at all. They must have been done by someone who typed a lot faster than she did, with somewhat less regard for accurate spelling, and who went out of the way to use an unsuitable kind of paper and change the ribbons before they showed any wear. All of which supports the view that the typist wanted it to look as though the work was done on Priscilla's typewriter, when it really wasn't. But this was a view that the defense was never able to offer to the jury; Judge Bondy's ruling had prevented that, when he refused to let the defense examine the papers before the trial.

20

THE CASE FOR THE DEFENSE

THE main line of defense offered by Hiss and his attorneys was that the typewriter had been given away before the pumpkin papers were typed, so whoever had done the deed, it had nothing to do with Hiss or his wife. This should have been conclusive if the jury had believed it; there was nothing very convincing to connect Hiss with the microfilmed documents, which pointed more clearly to Wadleigh; and the handwritten notes had so obviously been pinched from Hiss's desk or wastebasket that the prosecution paid little attention to them.

The trouble was that the evidence of when the typewriter was given away depended on the testimony of the Catlett family, and they didn't remember the details very clearly. Moreover, they were black, and the jurors were all white, a circumstance which produced reactions in 1949 quite different from what they might be today. There was Claudia Catlett, known as Cleidie (or Clydie; there were many ways of spelling the name, and nobody bothered to standardize it), who had been the Hisses' cook and maid at P Street, Thirtieth Street, and Volta Place; and her two sons, Perry Murphy Catlett, known as Pat, and Raymond Sylvester Catlett, known as Mike. They all remembered the incident, but they didn't agree about the details, and their recollections were too vague to stand up under Murphy's cross-examination. When they took the stand and told their story,

Murphy shot it down easily, and there was no way for the defense to repair the damage.

Part of the trouble was Mike Catlett's truculent attitude toward Prosecutor Murphy and the FBI, which couldn't have gone down well with the jury. Mike Catlett was a "Washington nigger," in the language of the 1940s, very different from a "New York nigger" or such radio stereotypes as The Two Black Crows, Amos 'n' Andy, and the Mills Brothers, which the jury had grown up with. He wasn't at all like the black elevator operators, Pullman porters, redcaps and shoe-shine boys that middle class New York whites met in their daily lives. For while Washington was a Southern city in its high ratio of black to white residents, it affected many liberal attitudes of racial equality for political reasons. So "Washington niggers" tended to be more "uppity" than most, and you had to know Washington to understand it. Which the jury didn't.

Thus when, at the beginning of his cross-examination in the first trial, Murphy asked the witness if he could call him Mike, as McLean had done on direct examination, the witness replied coldly:

"My name is Raymond Sylvester Catlett."

The bold gesture did him no good; the power of White Authority was too strong. As Murphy tried to pin Catlett down on dates and details of the typewriter story, he became more and more confused and resentful. He complained that Murphy was getting him "all balled up," deliberately trying to confuse him.

"Now that is what I don't want to do," Murphy said.

"That is what you are trying to do," Catlett retorted. "You ask me the same questions over and over again."

"I don't want to confuse you. Do you believe me when I say that?" Murphy persisted.

Catlett shook his head, and a moment later tried to explain. "You know," he began, "I was told, I mean—"

Murphy cut in sharply: "You were told what?"

"That there is a whole lot of things you believe and a whole lot of things you don't believe," Catlett continued, but Murphy cut in again, advancing toward the witness chair with fire in his eye.

"What were you told?"

"I mean this, I mean, you know what I mean."

"No."

"When I was brought up young."

"What was that? What were you told when you were brought up young?"

"To believe a whole lot of things like God, and about fellows like you, I mean—"

At that point Judge Kaufman intervened, curtly informing the witness, "We will not get into a discussion of that." Catlett, suddenly all meekness, said "Excuse me," and for the next few minutes the Judge took over the questioning, trying to establish whether Catlett remembered the date when he had taken the typewriter away from the Hisses' home some dozen years before. Catlett said "Yes, sir" and "No, sir" in a chastened voice, but when it came to actually remembering anything all he could say was "Judge, it is kind of hard. I mean that is a big problem for me."

When the cross-examination resumed the next morning, Murphy drew from Catlett the statement that Donald Hiss had posted a $50 reward for the finding of the typewriter, and although Catlett hadn't found the machine himself he was paid $40 for "a month's good work" helping to track it down. Then McLean, who took Stryker's place when the three Catletts were on the stand because McLean had been involved in the search for the typewriter and knew all the details, began redirect examination. He asked Mike Catlett how much the FBI had offered him, and suddenly there was another explosion.

Catlett testified that one of the FBI agents had said he would give "two hundred dollars or more" for the typewriter, and McLean promptly sat down. Murphy, his towering frame trembling with anger, sprang from his chair shouting, "What agent told you that?"

"What agent?" Catlett repeated.

"Yes, sir," Murphy snapped. "What was his name? What did he look like?"

"Jones!" Catlett shouted back.

"Jones told you that?" Murphy roared, in tones of incredulity mixed with rage.

"That's right."

"Jones is a big tall fellow, isn't he?"

"Yes, sir."

"And he said he would pay you two hundred dollars?"

"Yes, sir!"

"And that is your oath here?"

"That's what I said."

The exchange continued hot and heavy, until McLean quietly objected to "this screaming at the witness." Judge Kaufman responded with a noncommittal rebuke; Mike Catlett stuck to his story.

Later, of course, Murphy put FBI agent Courtland J. Jones on the stand, to deny that he had ever said anything to Mike Catlett about the two hundred dollars. Defense Attorney Stryker cross-examined him for more than an hour, accusing him of taking unfair advantage of "those poor little colored boys," meaning Mike and his brother Pat. He asked if Jones had questioned them for long hours without letting them have anything to eat, and without telling them of their constitutional rights or giving them a transcript of the interrogation. Jones refused to admit he had done anything wrong; the net effect of the whole incident was to impair Mike Catlett's credibility without earning him much sympathy from the jury. By now the proof that Priscilla hadn't typed the pumpkin papers was lost in the excitement.

Mike Catlett was twenty-seven years old in 1949, and he had been fifteen when he got the typewriter. He testified that he had done odd jobs for the Hisses in those days, washing their car, washing windows and floors, cleaning the yard and so on. He and his brother had been given the typewriter when the Hisses moved from one address to another, he said, but he couldn't remember which move it was. The typewriter had remained in a little room called "the den" in the Catlett home at 2728 P Street for three or four years, but nobody used it very much, he said.

Cleidie Catlett's recollection was just as vague, and it became still more confused under cross-examination. She said that when the FBI first asked her she had forgotten all about it and told them she didn't know anything about any typewriter. Later, when it was found, and her son showed it to her, she remembered that the Hisses had given it to the Catlett family when they were moving, but like her son she didn't remember which move it was.

Perry Murphy Catlett, known as Pat, was the last of the three to testify, and it turned out he was hard of hearing. His story was much the same, until on cross-examination he was confronted with a statement he had made to the FBI saying it "could have" been several months after the Hisses moved into Volta Place before they gave away the typewriter. That would have meant it was still in the Hiss home when the pumpkin papers were typed, so that the admission was highly damaging to the defense.

Prosecutor Murphy said to him, "Is that correct?"

"They could have," said Pat Catlett.

"Yes?"

"And they couldn't."

"In other words?"

"I still don't say whether they were living there or on Thirtieth Street. All I know it was in between there," Catlett finished lamely.

This wasn't much help, and he made matters worse by saying he had taken the typewriter to a repair shop on K Street, which, according to Murphy, didn't open for business until September 1938. Pat Catlett wasn't at all sure that he and Murphy were talking about the same repair shop, but Murphy used the incident to suggest that the whole transaction of giving the typewriter to the Catletts might have taken place much later than the defense claimed, late enough for the pumpkin papers to have been typed in Hiss's home after all. It was all very confusing and fatiguing, and by the time it was over there wasn't much left of Hiss's main line of defense.

This was a low point in Stryker's presentation, and after the luncheon recess that day he called two witnesses to the stand to provide a much-needed upbeat, though they contributed little to the main arguments in the case. First came Charles Fahy, former Solicitor General of the United States and legal adviser to the State Department, who had known Hiss for ten or twelve years and said his reputation for integrity, veracity, and loyalty was "excellent"; then Malcolm Cowley, author and literary critic, gave his recollections of an interview with Whittaker Chambers in 1940, in which Chambers had mentioned, not Hiss, but his boss, Assistant Secretary of State Francis Sayre, as "the head of a Communist apparatus in the State Department." Stryker interrupted as soon as Sayre's name was mentioned to repudiate the idea that there might be any truth in the statement, and said "We strongly understand and believe that Mr. Sayre was a completely loyal member of the Government at all times." Judge Kaufman commented that "this conversation is only offered for the purpose of showing inconsistent statements made by Chambers," and Cowley continued with his recollections.

"Chambers said to me that he had joined the Episcopal Church," Cowley went on. "I said to him that that was a strange church for a former Communist because the church had taken no active stand in political matters. Chambers said to me, 'I joined the Episcopalians because it was—it is there that you will find the most powerful enemies of the Communist movement.' "

"Yes," Stryker prompted, and Cowley continued, "I said to Chambers that I was very, very glad that I had never joined the Communist Party because I said to him that it seemed to me that all former Communists had been warped by their experience, that they felt the loss of something, and could be likened to a bunch of de-frocked priests. Chambers said to me, 'I am glad that I joined the Communist Party because I learned their methods, and I'm going to use their methods against them.' "

That was the point Stryker wanted to bring out—that Chambers was using the methods of the Communist conspiracy in attacking Hiss—the methods of lying and deception Stryker had spoken of so often and would speak of again in his summation.

And there was a second point, to which he returned a moment later—that the documents Chambers had could have been used against Sayre as well as Hiss, and that, in 1940, it was Sayre rather than Hiss that Chambers had in mind as his victim. Did Chambers in the 1940 conversation ever mention the name of Alger Hiss, Stryker asked. No, said Cowley.

It wasn't much, but it was a way of leading up to the main event in the defense presentation—the moment when the defendant himself took the stand to testify. He did so at 3:20 P.M., following Cowley after a five-minute recess. It was the moment for which everyone had been waiting; for four long summer weeks, Hiss had sat in the well of the court beside his wife listening attentively to what went on, occasionally whispering something to his wife or his lawyers, saying nothing aloud in court, avoiding the press as much as he could in the corridors and the streets outside. Now he was to say his piece, make his own defense, tell his own story. What would it be?

There was only a little more than an hour left of that day's session, and Stryker used it to draw some ringing declarations of innocence from his client, followed by a review of his career, from his education and early law practice through his work for the Agriculture Department, the Nye Committee, the Justice Department, and finally the State Department, and the Dumbarton Oaks, Yalta, and San Francisco conferences. This was laying the groundwork; building a picture in the jury's mind of what kind of a man the defendant was, in preparation for the next day's discussion of how Hiss became involved with the man he had known as George Crosley.

Hiss on the witness stand appeared as calm as he had been for the four weeks of listening to others. He was a handsome man, lean and trim, with level, deep-set eyes and neatly brushed hair, his manners formal and slightly patrician, his head tipped to one side as though to hear the questions better. He seemed completely composed, if a little pale, and perhaps a little boyish for a man of forty-four. Eagle Scout, choir boy, that was part of his reputation, held against him by some and to his credit by others;

and he looked the part. He spoke deliberately, choosing his words with care, at first in a soft voice, then louder as he warmed to his subject. In the first few minutes he glanced several times at the jury, as if trying to guess what was in their minds. Then he concentrated on his testimony.

Stryker began with an almost formal catechism. "Mr. Hiss," he said, in loud tones to warn the jury of the solemnity of the question, "are you now or have you ever been a member of the Communist Party?"

"I am not and I never have been," Hiss answered firmly.

"Or a fellow traveler or a sympathizer?"

"No, Mr. Stryker, I never have."

Stryker called his attention to the four handwritten notes and asked Hiss if they were in his handwriting.

"Yes, Mr. Stryker," he answered, "they all are."

"Mr. Hiss, did you in the months of February and March 1938, or any other time in your life, ever furnish, transmit or deliver those exhibits to Whittaker Chambers?"

"I did not."

Then the typewritten papers. "Did you ever furnish, transmit or deliver those documents, or any of them, to Mr. Chambers, ever in your life?"

"I did not, Mr. Stryker."

"Did you in your lifetime ever furnish, transmit or deliver to Whittaker Chambers or any other authorized person any restricted, secret or confidential documents of the State Department of any kind, character, or description whatever?"

"I think you meant 'unauthorized'?" Hiss inquired.

"I did," said Stryker.

"As amended the answer is I did not," Hiss replied. It was the first of many such small corrections and precise answers he was to make in the four days he was on the stand in the first trial, and five days in the second. His testimony was always most precise. When it came time for cross-examination, his recollection of what he had said on direct examination was precise. So was his recollection of the transcript of his statements to the FBI and his testimony before the House Committee, which he had studied carefully before taking the stand. Sometimes his recollection was more precise than Murphy's.

Hiss's use of the English language was also most precise, even to the point of correcting Murphy on occasion. Once he made a very fine distinction—he knew Chambers had come to the door of his house, because he had entered the house, but Hiss had not seen him come to the door.

"I thought you said he came to the door," Murphy said, seeming to sense an opportunity to tangle the witness in a contradiction of testimony.

"That is the way he entered the house," Hiss replied calmly. There was loud laughter from the spectators' benches, and Murphy angrily asked the Judge to "ask some of the clowns to stop laughing." Judge Kaufman replied, "There is no justification for that remark, Mr. Murphy."

"I think it is getting ridiculous, your Honor," said Murphy, but the Judge answered coldly, "I think we have preserved order here very well. There have been a few spontaneous outbursts, but I don't think there is any justification for that remark of yours at all." And at that point the Judge called a five-minute recess.

It was a small triumph that seemed to demonstrate nothing except that Hiss's appearance on the stand had brought a lot of his supporters to the courtroom. But his habit of answering questions so precisely and remembering what had been said so exactly worked against him in the long run. For the whole story of his relationship with Chambers in 1935–1936 involved details which he didn't remember with anything like the same precision; indeed, the account of it he had first given the House Committee had proved on examination to be full of mistakes. Why had Hiss remembered all that so imperfectly when his recollection of other details was now so perfect? The inference that he was now telling carefully rehearsed lies was all too easy to draw; and the more precise Hiss's answers on the witness stand were, the stronger the inference became.

Hiss wasn't aware of this problem; he thought it perfectly natural that he had forgotten about his dealings with Crosley, which had seemed unimportant to him at the time. Now that he was on the witness stand everything was important, and he was extra careful, but in spite of his occasional glances at the jury he didn't sense the impression he was making on them.

On his second day of direct examination by Stryker, Hiss went point by point over the testimony against him given by Chambers earlier in the trial, and denied it in every detail. Over and over again, as Stryker asked him if he had done one thing after another Chambers said he had done, Hiss answered: "Certainly not!" or "Of course not!" or sometimes, very bitterly and deliberately, "I . . . did . . . not."

Sometimes his denials were tossed off scornfully as if they referred to allegations beyond belief, too incredible to merit a reply. Sometimes his denials were firm, defiant, and challenging. Always they were immediate, unhesitating, and determined.

Only in one respect were any of his denials qualified. Stryker reminded him of Chambers's testimony about going with him to "some remote part of Brooklyn to a moving picture theater" to meet the mysterious Colonel Bykov, and asked, "Is there a word of truth in that?" Hiss replied with his meticulous care, "Insofar as it refers to me, Mr. Stryker, there is not a word of truth in it."

The denials occupied about half of Hiss's two and a quarter hours on the stand that day. The rest of it concerned accounts of his own actions and explanations of some of the points raised in Chambers's testimony. He described his working procedures in the State Department, his "in" and "out" boxes, and the extra desk in his office. He told of the lack of security controls in the Department in the 1930s, and how easy it was for other people to come into his office when he wasn't there. He mentioned coming into his office one day and finding an old friend from Harvard there alone, waiting for him. The friend was Charles E. Wyzanski, Jr., who in 1949 was a judge of the United States District Court in Massachusetts, and Hiss's testimony was interrupted a little later for Judge Wyzanski to take the witness stand, corroborate the story, and testify to Hiss's reputation for "integrity, loyalty and veracity," as Charles Fahy, Francis Sayre, Justices Reed and Frankfurter, and many other distinguished public men did before the trial was over.

Hiss told his own story of the apartment, the car, the rug, his small loans to Crosley and his meetings with him to give him information about the Nye Committee under the impression that Crosley was a free-lance writer. The uncertainty about details that had marked his appearance before the House Committee the previous summer was gone now, he explained, because he had had a chance to consult his records and straighten out his recollections. But it sounded like a warmed-over version, different both from what he had said before and from what Chambers had said about it earlier in the trial. These differences had been written about so often in the newspapers and talked about so much on the radio before the trial began that it all seemed rather old stuff now; there was nothing really new for Hiss to make an impression with. On Monday morning, June 27, Hiss's third day on the stand, Stryker sat down and Murphy began his cross-examination.

Murphy worked calmly and methodically, with none of the flamboyance Stryker had shown in cross-examining Chambers. Hiss remained as calm and poised under Murphy's questioning as he had been before. There were times when he even seemed to be enjoying it. Occasionally he smiled; sometimes his expression was earnest, but it remained untroubled. For long periods his face showed no expression except perhaps patience. In the corridor during a recess he repeated what he had said before; "I have waited a long time for this."

Murphy wasn't able to draw any statement from Hiss that was inconsistent with what he had told Stryker on direct examination, but there were dozens of details on which his testimony now was inconsistent with what he had earlier told the FBI and the House Committee, and Murphy spent a good deal of his two-day cross-examination going over them. Each time Hiss gave essentially the same answer; now he had checked his recollection and it was accurate; the earlier testimony was simply poor memory.

The old Woodstock typewriter and the crucial question of when it had been given to the Catletts took up a lot of time, too. Hiss remembered the machine only vaguely; he hadn't realized it was a Woodstock when it was in his house because "it normally sat under a cover, a dust cover, which did not have any name on it at all." He had no "independent recollection" of how or when the machine had been disposed of; when he had talked to the FBI and appeared before the grand jury in December 1948, it had been his impression that "we still had the typewriter at sometime on Volta Place."

"Isn't that your impression today?" Murphy asked.

"It certainly is not, Mr. Murphy," Hiss replied.

"Your impression today is what?"

"My knowledge today," said Hiss, making another distinction without exactly drawing attention to it, "is that we gave the typewriter to the Catletts at the time when we moved from Thirtieth Street to Volta Place in December of 1937."

Murphy restated Hiss's answer as though Hiss had been the one who gave the typewriter away, and Hiss corrected him again. "My wife gave it to the Catletts," he said.

"Your wife gave it?" asked Murphy, as though he'd never heard that detail before.

"Yes, sir," said Hiss.

"Is it your testimony she gave it to them before or after the move was completed?"

"Before the move was completed. One does not carry an old typewriter to a new house only to give it away." Murphy objected to the comment, and the Judge said, "Strike it out." Murphy went on, and soon was engaged in a semantic tangle with Hiss over how he knew when the typewriter was given away.

"In any event," Murphy said, "you say now, as a matter of your own knowledge, that that typewriter was given by your wife prior to moving to Volta Place?"

"I did not say of my own direct independent recollection," said Hiss. "I say I know from what the Catletts have told us."

"But did you use the phrase 'knowledge' a few minutes ago?" Murphy persisted. Hiss wasn't sure whether he had said "knowledge" or "I know."

"Well, no matter whether you used the verb or the noun, it is knowledge of some type?"

"Yes."

"And it is knowledge that has been recalled or refreshed because of the testimony of the Catlett boys?"

"That is not a matter of refreshing a recollection. It is knowledge of an independent fact."

Murphy persisted, and Hiss added: "It was not recalled. It was established." Murphy changed the subject after that; if the Catletts' testimony had established anything as a fact that was for the jury to decide, not Hiss; and Murphy didn't want the jury to accept Hiss's view of the matter. In the end, of course, only four of the jurors did at the first trial, and none at the second.

Murphy questioned Hiss at length about what he had said to John Foster Dulles on various occasions, when he was first appointed President of the Carnegie Endowment in 1946 and again when Chambers's charges against him were made public in 1948. Hiss refused to concede that he had in any way misled Dulles about the rumors of Communist activity that were first circulated against him, and he indignantly denied that Dulles had asked him to resign in August 1948. He also denied that he had told Dulles at that time that he wanted to put off any question of his resignation while the hearings of the House Committee were going on. He conceded that in fact that had happened—he ultimately resigned in May 1949, shortly before the trial began—but he denied that he had asked for the delay.

Two days later, after the defense rested its case, Murphy called Dulles to the stand on rebuttal to give his version of these conversations. His recollection wasn't exactly the same as Hiss's, but the differences were subtle: Dulles said there had been some discussion about whether or when Hiss should resign, and "either he intimated or I intimated, I would not now be prepared to say where the initiative came from, but we agreed it would not be wise for him to resign while the hearings were still going on."

It was all a very fine point, and Stryker insisted that there was no real conflict between the two versions. But it served to demonstrate a quite different and more obvious point to the public and the jury: Dulles, who had been Hiss's boss in this crucial period, had chosen to appear as a prosecution witness against

Hiss, instead of joining the long list of dignitaries who had appeared as character witnesses on Hiss's behalf. The implication was clear, even if the details of the testimony were fuzzy—Hiss must have lied to his boss, because obviously Dulles believed the charges against him. As one of the last few witnesses to appear at the very end of the trial, just before the final summations of the opposing attorneys, Dulles's appearance must have had considerable impact on the jury.

The last defense witness to take the stand earlier that day was Dr. Carl Binger, the psychiatrist who had sat in the well of the court listening to Chambers's testimony five weeks before. He was prepared to give an expert opinion on Chambers's mental condition, based on all he had seen of Chambers's behavior on the stand, all he had heard Chambers say, and his study of all that could be found of Chambers's writing, including his poetry, the "atheistic playlet" that had got him into such trouble at Columbia, and his translations, as well as his work for *Time* magazine. It wasn't the face-to-face personal examination of a cooperative patient that would be necessary for the treatment of mental illness, but Binger considered it sufficient for a diagnosis of the general category of illness Chambers was suffering from.

Normally, an expert witness charges a fee for his professional services, but psychiatrists come high, and this job required an enormous amount of work. Binger was a friend of the Hisses, and he found Chambers a challenging subject for a psychiatrist to study, so that he charged no fee. It was another case of the defense relying on friends for lack of money to hire outsiders, though psychiatrists can be just as susceptible to the kind of emotional pressures they talk about as anybody else. As it turned out, this made no difference in the first trial, but it became important in the second.

Murphy objected to allowing Binger to take the stand, as he had objected earlier to his presence in the courtroom, but Judge Kaufman ruled that Stryker should at least be allowed to ask him the hypothetical question, If all that has been put in evidence about Whittaker Chambers is true, what is the doctor's professional opinion about the state of Chambers's mental health? The question had to be put in that form because it was up to the jury, not the lawyer or the witness, to decide which parts of the evidence were true and which were untrue. And Judge Kaufman allowed Stryker to ask the question so as to establish a record on which an appeal might be based if necessary.

When Stryker finished, Murphy renewed his objection, and the Judge replied, "Mr. Murphy, this matter as to the admissibility of Dr. Binger's testimony was discussed by us some time ago. My first indication, predicated on the briefs submitted, was that I was going to admit the testimony because the tendency of the law is that this type of testimony be admitted. However, there is one other thing about which the government and the defendant agree, and that is that the question of the credibility of Mr. Chambers is one of the crucial elements in this case. I have determined, notwithstanding the trend of the decisions, to exclude Dr. Binger's testimony because I think the record is sufficiently clear for the jury, using its experience in life, to appraise the testimony of all of the witnesses who have appeared in this courtroom." In plain language, Judge Kaufman was telling the jury they shouldn't need a psychiatrist to tell them whether Chambers was crazy; they could answer Stryker's hypothetical question for themselves. At Murphy's prompting, he added to the jury, "You may disregard the question. It is not proof of any of the facts except insofar as you remember the testimony."

Nevertheless, as Murphy pointed out in his argument, the hypothetical question had given Stryker an opportunity to spend forty-five minutes reminding the jury of every unsavory detail of Chambers's character and behavior that had appeared so far—his habit of telling lies, many of which he had admitted on the stand; his habit of using false names, so many that he couldn't remember them all; the obscurely pornographic nature of some of Chambers's poems that had been read to the jury; the "class prophecy" that had got him into trouble at high school, and the atheism at Columbia; the "wretched kind of a dive" where he had lived in New Orleans, and One-Eyed Annie; his brother's suicide and how it had affected him; the "Communist woman" he had lived with in his mother's home; his panicky behavior when he broke with the Communist Party; even his habit of looking at the ceiling while he answered questions on the stand. And much more.

Murphy argued that all this gave the defense an unfair advantage, because it was "not a complete summary of the witness's testimony here by a long shot," and the government had no opportunity to respond to it. "He left out his marriage to his wife, his only wife," Murphy complained. "He left out the fact that the man is now a member of the Quaker religion and has been for many years. He left out the fact that he is the father of a boy and a girl; he left out other writings, particularly the child's book *Bambi*,* and innumerable things, so I think the question is not a fair summary upon which the doctor could base his opinion."

The damage, said Murphy, was done, and he pressed the point no further; but as it turned out the prosecution gained more than it lost from this exchange. For Murphy had now heard the hypothetical question, and knew what aspects of Chambers's career Binger had intended to talk about to support his diagnosis, whatever it might be. Murphy could take that question and the testimony on which it was based, all of it recorded in the trial transcript, and find an expert psychiatrist of his own to give him a different opinion. For there was no lack of dispute among psychiatrists about diagnostic questions in 1949.

Here was another case of an opinion by an expert, who might be countered by other experts with contrary opinions. But Murphy did better than that; instead of calling his experts to testify, he got them to coach him for his cross-examination in the second trial. So that by the time Binger took the stand in January 1950, Murphy was loaded for bear.

Again, there were long arguments in the Judge's chambers about the admissibility of the testimony, and briefs citing legal precedents were submitted by both sides. Judge Henry W. Goddard, presiding at the second trial, ruled that the psychiatric testimony should be heard, and wrote a memorandum on the subject

---

* Murphy was a little hasty here—*Bambi* was not one of Chambers's "writings" but a book by Felix Salten, which he had translated from the German.

for inclusion in the trial record. When Binger was called to the stand Murphy rose and renewed his objections.

"I do ask your Honor to reconsider your ruling and not permit the psychiatrist to testify," he said, "because, as I read the cases and the textbooks, this is the first time in the history of Anglo-Saxon jurisprudence that the testimony of a psychiatrist is being admitted to impeach the credibility of a mere witness, when there has not been one scintilla of proof indicating that the witness, Mr. Whittaker Chambers, has had any institutional confinement or treatment by a doctor other than for his teeth and heart, and because it is a direct encroachment on the province of the jury. I submit that it is for the jury and the jury alone to determine where the truth lies, and that duty, under our system of law, cannot be usurped by a medical expert."

This was essentially the position Judge Kaufman had accepted in the first trial, but Judge Goddard had a different view. "Mr. Murphy," he said, "as you know in our conference in chambers I advised you that in my opinion it should be admitted. You know that I have given it very thorough consideration. I think that perhaps you are mistaken when you say it has never been introduced in any court in this country. It has not been introduced in the federal courts, but it has in a number of state courts.

"Now, I shall endeavor to tell the jury how much weight they may give this opinion testimony, impressing upon the jury always that it is their opinion, not the opinion of anyone else, that controls their decision."

Murphy thanked the Judge, and while Binger was testifying he sat quietly in his chair, taking notes and making only occasional further objections on minor points. Defense Attorney Claude Cross asked a hypothetical question even longer than Stryker's, covering the same ground and adding new details because there had been so much more testimony in the second trial. The question took Cross sixty-five minutes to read; halfway through it he interrupted himself to ask for the usual mid-morning recess. At the end of it he asked Binger for his opinion "as to the mental condition of Mr. Chambers."

"I think Mr. Chambers is suffering from a condition known as psychopathic personality," Binger replied, "which is a disorder of character, of which the outstanding features are behavior of what we call an amoral or an asocial and delinquent nature."

Binger defined these terms in answer to Cross's questions, and then was asked to describe "some of the symptoms of a psychopathic personality."

"Well," he said, "they are quite variegated. They include acts of deception and misrepresentation; they include alcoholism and drug addiction*; abnormal sexuality; vagabondage; panhandling; inability to form stable attachments, and a tendency to make false accusations.

"May I say," he added, "that in addition to what is commonly recognized by the layman as lying, there is a peculiar kind of lying known as pathological lying, and a peculiar kind of tendency to make false accusations known as pathological accusations, which are frequently found in the psychopathic personality."

Cross asked for more details, and Binger went on: "First of all, a psychopath is quite aware of what he is doing but he does not always know why he does it; and to characterize the acts in a qualitative way, they are frequently impulsive and very often bizarre, so that they do not make much sense to the casual observer who does not understand what the particular fantasy or imagination there is behind these acts; because the acts represent something private to the patient, but from a point of view of common sense and understanding apparently making no sense. . . .

"These unfortunate people have a conviction of the truth and validity of their own imaginations, of their own fantasies without respect to outer reality; so that they play a part in life, play a role. They may be a hero at one moment and a gangster at the next. They act as if a situation were true which, in fact, is true only in their imaginations; and on the basis of such imaginations they will claim friendships where none exist, just as they

* Here Binger was quoting the textbook; there was nothing in the evidence to suggest that Chambers was an alcoholic or had used drugs.

will make accusations which have no basis in fact, because they have a constant need to make their imaginations come true by behaving as if the outer world were actually in accord with their own imagination."

Cross interrupted to ask, "By that, Dr. Binger, do you mean that a psychopath is insensible to the feelings of others?"

"Well, he is amazingly isolated and egocentric," Binger replied. "He does not really establish a rapport with other people, and he never knows how other people feel because he is always playing a part as if what he thought to be true was true of others."

This was the diagnosis, essentially completed just before adjournment time that afternoon. The following morning Cross spent an hour or so going over it in more detail, and then it was Murphy's turn.

For the next three days, Murphy engaged in a battle of wits with the psychiatrist that developed into a studied campaign of ridicule and sarcasm on Murphy's part, and prompted one spectator to say, "this will set psychiatry back twenty-five years." But the jury seemed to love it. Murphy cut the poor psychiatrist into ribbons, scorning his every word, teasing him about the number of times he, too, looked at the ceiling, and going over the points in the hypothetical question one by one to show that no one of them by itself was so unusual that a normal person might not sometimes do it.

Binger tried to insist that that wasn't the point; it was the whole picture that mattered. Murphy took the picture apart, and showed the jury how absurd each part of it looked in isolation. Psychiatry was a much newer and less well understood art in 1950 than it is now; intellectuals like Alger and Priscilla Hiss might know about it, but plain people like the jury were afraid of it. In Murphy's hands the psychiatrist's testimony became an insult to the jury; an insult not to their intelligence, but to their ignorance of psychiatry, their fear of it, and their sensibilities.

The defense had anticipated an attack of this sort, and had even considered putting a different psychiatrist on the stand instead of Binger, so that Murphy would not be so well armed against him. But Binger wanted to testify; he had been frustrated in the first trial, he had done a great deal of preparation, and he thought he could handle it. He had already exposed himself to the abuse of scoffers at the first trial, and he had done it out of friendship and belief in the rightness of the cause. He was entitled to his day in court now, too, and it couldn't be denied him. But at least the defense could strengthen their case by calling another expert witness to buttress Binger's testimony. He was Dr. Henry A. Murray, lecturer in psychology and former director of the Harvard Psychological Clinic.

Murray supported Binger's view in general but differed from it in some details, approaching the subject from the viewpoint of a psychologist rather than a psychiatrist, although he was professionally qualified in both fields. The distinction was a technical one, difficult for the public and the jury to grasp, but Murphy made it all sound simple and absurd.

"Let me ask you this, Doctor," he said before Murray was allowed to give his testimony. "Do you propose merely to give an opinion merely as to Mr. Chambers's personality? Is that what you are going to tell us? Don't tell us what it is, but do you propose to tell us something about his personality?"

"I propose to make a diagnosis," said Murray, "and that diagnosis has to do with personality."

"Well now, your Honor," said Murphy to Judge Goddard, "I submit that if this doctor is going to tell us merely about his personality that that is far and beyond anything that the Court or the jury either should have or desires."

Defense Attorney Claude Cross interrupted to repeat the question he had asked Murray, which was, "Now, Dr. Murray, assuming the facts stated in the question which I read to Dr. Binger, and which you heard and have a copy of, to be true, and taking into account Mr. Chambers's writings and translations which you have just enumerated, have you as a psychologist an opinion, within the bounds of reasonable certainty, as to the mental condition of Whittaker Chambers?"

Murphy brushed that aside. "Yes, I have no doubt that is the question," he said. "What I had in mind, if your Honor pleases, and which the witness has confirmed, is that he is prepared to testify to a personality. Now I submit if we get into the question of personalities any further we will be trying a lawsuit which will go down in history, your Honor, as just a burlesque on something we have never seen before."

Judge Goddard didn't think so. "Mr. Murphy," he said, "I think the witness should be permitted to testify. What weight, if any, is to be given his testimony is solely for the jury."

Murray concurred in Binger's diagnosis; Chambers, he said, was a psychopathic personality. He described the affliction much as Binger had done, and added that psychopaths hardly ever go to mental institutions or seek a doctor's treatment for their affliction, because they "are satisfied with themselves"; they don't see anything wrong with their own behavior. Murray said he had learned a lot about such people during the war when he was a lieutenant colonel in OSS (Office of Strategic Services), the American espionage agency. Psychopaths, he said, were attracted to espionage work because of "the sensation of it, the intrigue of it, the idea of being a mysterious man with secret knowledge and working as an intelligence officer." It had been part of Murray's job to weed out such people from among the applicants for OSS jobs, and to see that they weren't accepted.

Murray was a difficult witness for Murphy to attack, because he stuck to his opinion with confident assurance, and his experience in the OSS made him all too knowledgeable about espionage as well as psychopathic personalities. Murphy let him off with a mere four hours of cross-examination, compared to the better part of three days he had spent working on Binger. But it was Binger's performance he hammered away at in his summation two days later, and he made it all seem too much for the jury. The impression Murphy left was that Hiss had to be crazy himself to think this kind of attack on Chambers would help. Like the typewriter the defense had found with so much effort, the psychiatric evidence turned out to be a boomerang.

21

ADDING IT UP

THE Fourth of July fell on a Monday in 1949, which was convenient for Stryker and Murphy because it gave them a three-day weekend to prepare their summations for the following week, the sixth and final week of the first trial. The jury must have been glad of the rest, too; they had heard twenty-three days of testimony and argument, and there were still more witnesses to testify, though their testimony was to be relatively brief and unimportant, a cleaning up of last-minute details. Altogether the jury heard seventy-three witnesses and three depositions in the first trial; they were shown 257 exhibits, and the typewritten transcript ran to 2,851 pages, or about 570,000 words. The second trial was even longer; the jury heard almost 1,200,000 words of testimony and argument in thirty-nine court days spread over nine weeks; there were 110 witnesses and 423 exhibits. Under the court rules the jurors could not take notes as they listened, and they could not take any of the exhibits into the jury room without the express permission of the judge and counsel for both sides.

It was the task of the opposing attorneys to take this enormous mass of disputed information and add it all up, each in his own way and from his own viewpoint, as the basis for his final arguments. The defense attorney spoke first, then the prosecutor; the judge had the last word, but his function was to explain the law to the jury, not to comment on the evidence. So the defense attorney had no opportunity to reply to the prosecutor's final arguments; he had to anticipate them, and try to make such a strong impression on the jury that the prosecutor would be unable to undermine it. Stryker was an old hand at that game.

On the Saturday of that Fourth of July weekend Harold Shapero, then a young lawyer working for Stryker as researcher, leg-man, and general assistant, spent the morning in his office on the thirty-sixth floor of 40 Wall Street digging through the transcript for useful bits of testimony that Stryker might want to refer to in his summation, and making notes and a kind of outline for him to be sure he would be well equipped and not overlook anything. It was a comfortable office, furnished expensively but in simple taste; the carpets were blue and very thick. There was no air-conditioning yet at 40 Wall, but the windows overlooking the Upper Bay at the foot of Manhattan were open, and the outer doors were ajar to keep the fresh air moving. It was a hot day. Shapero was to take his notes to Stryker's home in Locust Valley, on Long Island, early that afternoon, joining a party Stryker was giving for a few friends.

Alger and Priscilla Hiss spent most of the morning with Shapero, going over the transcript with him and offering their own ideas about the important points Stryker should make in his summation. Along toward 1:00 P.M. Hiss reminded Shapero of his appointment in Locust Valley, saying it was pretty near time for him to leave. Shapero bundled his papers into his briefcase and said good-bye to Alger and Priscilla, who left through the open door to go down the hall to the elevator. A few minutes later Shapero came out too and saw his clients standing by the elevator, their backs to him, talking to each other. It was a moment Shapero never forgot, because he overheard what they were saying, and knew that it was a moment of privacy which, even as their lawyer, he wasn't meant to hear.

"Alger," Priscilla was saying, "what if they convict you?"

"Well," said Alger, "I am innocent. Someday they will find that out, and it will be on their consciences the rest of their lives."

Then the elevator arrived, and the Hisses disappeared into it. Shapero said nothing; he was so struck by what he had heard that he didn't want to make his presence known. For Shapero was not one of the old friends of the Hisses who had been recruited to help; he was simply a junior member of Lloyd Paul Stryker's staff, who had sweated through the six weeks and half a million words of testimony without any preconceived notions of what the trial was about or where the truth might lie. Suddenly he felt that the defendant must be an honest man, whatever the evidence showed and whatever the jury might decide; no one in the privacy of an empty thirty-sixth floor lobby on a quiet Saturday afternoon would say something like that to his wife unless he was not only an honest man and an innocent one, but an extraordinary man, who could look at his predicament in terms of its effect on other people, not just its effect on himself.

It was a most unusual quality, and after working with Hiss through the six long weeks of the trial and the four long months of preparation before it, Shapero recognized that the attitude Hiss had just expressed was genuine and characteristic of him—not some kind of pretentious hypocrisy intended to fool his wife. And it disposed forever, in Shapero's mind, of the theory that Priscilla might be the guilty one and Hiss might be deliberately shielding her. His protective attitude toward her appeared in a new light; he was trying to reassure her in his own peculiar way, but concerned now with the jurors' consciences, not with Priscilla's or his own. Shapero hurried to Long Island with his notes for Stryker in a new mood of enthusiasm and encouragement.

Stryker's summation the following week—it began just before noon on Wednesday and continued after the luncheon recess and for the first hour on Thursday—was built around the same theme as he used for his opening remarks six weeks before: Chambers was a liar whose word could not be trusted, and without Chambers's word the government had no case. Stryker called Chambers a "psychopathic . . . sadist," a "liar by habit, by training . . . and by preference." He said the charges against Hiss were "preposterous," that Chambers's story was "fantastic," that it was "absurd" to imagine that a real spy engaged in a real conspiracy would have publicly associated with his fellow conspirators the way Chambers and his wife claimed the Hisses had done. He made much of the initials "A. H." that appeared on some of the microfilms, arguing that since they had been put on the documents by Hiss when he was finished with them, they showed that "some other thief or rogue conspired with Mr. Chambers and got [them] after they left Mr. Hiss's possession."

It wasn't enough for Hiss to "tear all around Washington" with Chambers, Stryker pointed out sarcastically in his wind-up on Wednesday afternoon; it wasn't enough to give him the handwritten notes, he had to establish his guilt "beyond a peradventure of a doubt" by giving Chambers documents with his initials on them. "I tell you that story is preposterous!" Stryker shouted.

It was an appeal to the jury's common sense, and for four of the twelve jurors it worked. But for six weeks the jury had been living in the weird world of Chambers's fantasies, where people changed their names whenever it suited them, and thought nothing of driving all the way from Washington to Peterborough, New Hampshire, just to sit in the car for twenty minutes while Chambers walked up a driveway to say something to an Assistant Secretary of the Treasury. They had become accustomed to Chambers changing his story as often as his name, and to the stamp of approval placed on his strange conduct by the U.S. government in the persons of Prosecutor Thomas F. Murphy, the members of HUAC, and the FBI. Common sense was pitted against authority, and it was authority that won.

Murphy had his answers to Stryker, too. He dared the jury to acquit the defendant if they thought the FBI had done anything wrong. "If any juror thinks—not all twelve of you or even six—but if any one juror thinks that the FBI at any time in this case with respect to the Catlett boys or anybody else—if any juror thinks that the FBI was unfair in any wise—acquit this man!" he said. Murphy's voice could be louder than Stryker's when he cared to use it, and he fairly shouted, "That's how confident I am that you won't be taken in by this sideswipe at the FBI."

And Murphy had his appeal to common sense, too, in his "three solid witnesses"—the typewriter, the documents he said were typed on it, and the State Department originals from which they were copied. These were "undisputed, uncontradicted facts," he said—the pumpkin papers were copies of State Department originals, they were in Chambers's possession before the trial, and they were all dated in the first three months of 1938. He also said it was an "uncontradicted fact" that sixty-four pages of the pumpkin papers were typed on "the Hiss typewriter." As far as the testimony in the trial went, he was right; it was certainly uncontradicted, and because the defense didn't yet have the evidence with which to contradict it, it was accepted at the time as a fact. All Murphy had to do was discredit the Catlett testimony, and when it became necessary to choose between the Catletts and the FBI, it was easy for the eight jurors who believed in Chambers to make their choice.

Stryker's trial ended in a hung jury, and Alger and Priscilla Hiss went to Peacham, Vermont, for the summer to think about what to do next. Within hours after the jury was discharged, Attorney General Tom C. Clark announced that the case would be tried again as soon as possible, and U.S. Attorney John F. X. McGohey announced that Murphy would again handle the prosecution.

Hiss wasn't sure he wanted Stryker to handle the defense again, however. There were a lot of things that worried him; as a matter of personal taste he didn't like Stryker's flamboyant style, and he worried sometimes that the sixty-five-year-old lawyer might be stricken with apoplexy or a heart attack. He didn't think Stryker had paid enough attention to the documents, or made a sufficient showing to the jury that the pumpkin papers couldn't really be spy papers at all, and certainly hadn't been given to any spies with Hiss's knowledge or consent, much less participation.

Hiss also worried about the enormous publicity the first trial had received, and the jurors he had seen reading the New York *Journal–American*, *World–Telegram*, and *Mirror*, all of which were solidly against him, supplementing their coverage of the trial with feature stories supporting Chambers's side of the argument.*

* Unlike the juries in some of the Watergate trials in 1974–1975, the juries in the Hiss trials were not locked up to keep them from this kind of publicity until the testimony was complete and they started to consider their verdict. The rest of the time the jurors went home at night and came to work every morning like anyone else, and Hiss often saw some of them on the subway he rode to the courthouse.

Hiss didn't think he could get a really fair trial in New York under these circumstances, and wanted his second trial moved to Vermont, where he was also a resident by virtue of his summer home at Peacham, and which was in the same Federal Judicial Circuit for appeals purposes as New York.

Early that summer Hiss asked his friend Richard Field, who had a lot of contacts in Vermont, to look into a change of venue for him. Field consulted a former Vermont Attorney General, who told him that a Vermont jury was "more likely to acquit Alger, and more likely to convict him, but less likely to be deadlocked. Vermont juries have a way of thrashing things out and reaching a decision," Field was told. He reported this to Hiss, who said that was the way he wanted it; he'd rather take his chances on going to jail than have another long trial end in a hung jury. Besides, he never believed he'd be convicted.

This decision meant parting company with Stryker, for two reasons. One was that Stryker didn't mind a hung jury if a case was impossible to win; after Hiss was convicted Stryker said to Field, "I'm not saying I could have got Alger acquitted, but I am saying that I could have kept trying that case until hell froze over and they could never have got twelve jurors to convict him. You've got to make up your mind whether you're really going for unanimity or trying to be divisive and get some of the jurors on your side—and you do it quite differently."

Stryker's approach would have meant that Hiss might not have gone to jail, but would have lived under the cloud of a charge that had never been proved against him and never disproved either. Hiss didn't want that; he wanted a lawyer who would go the all-or-nothing route and try for acquittal even at the risk of conviction.

Once the decision was made to apply for a change of venue to move the trial to Vermont, Hiss had to find another lawyer. Stryker was an expert at handling New York juries, but he didn't think he knew enough about Vermont juries. There was no assurance that the change of venue would be granted, but Hiss was confident as usual, and there was no time to lose. Nor was there money to keep two lawyers at work on the case at the same time:

Stryker to handle it if the change of venue were denied, and another lawyer to handle it in Vermont should the court approve. So Hiss broke the news to Stryker, and was deeply moved when the fatherly lawyer said to him, "All right, if that's what you want. But don't forget, if you change your mind or don't find anybody else, you can always come home to me."

At that point Hiss didn't have another lawyer, and there was no certainty that he could find one with sufficient skill and experience who would take the case for the modest fee that he could afford. Field introduced him to Claude Cross, then one of the leaders of the Boston bar, a graduate of Harvard Law School and native of Mississippi, who had tried cases all over the country. Cross was a gentle, gray-haired man of fifty-six, with a cherubic face and a short, stocky figure, who felt quite at home with New England juries, and had no anxieties about trying the case in Vermont.

So the decision was made; and then the change of venue was denied by Judge Alfred C. Coxe on October 14, barely a month before the second trial began. Cross had no experience of New York juries, and had wondered at first whether New Yorkers might be prejudiced against his Boston background. He had made some inquiries and been reassured about that; but when the trial began he found Murphy saying and doing things in front of the jury that he would never have dared, and didn't know how to answer. He thought them most improper, and concluded Judge Goddard must have been asleep to allow them.

Cross was a demon for detail, with a solid background in corporate cases involving complex documents, and to Hiss it seemed that his handling of the documentary evidence was masterful. Indeed, although the results of the second trial were exactly the opposite of what Hiss expected and hoped for, he still admired the way Cross had handled it, and thought he'd done it exactly right. Though he lost the case he had fought fairly and honestly and brought out all the evidence the defense could find; in Hiss's view he had been defeated only because they hadn't been able to find out in time how Chambers had worked his frame-up. Cross's conclusion, which he held to until he died in

1974, was that "the temper of the times" had made acquittal impossible—"You can't win them all," he said. He hadn't been able to prove how Chambers had got the documents, but he felt he had proved beyond any doubt that Chambers had lied about the Peterborough trip, and in any ordinary perjury case that would have been enough. This just wasn't an ordinary case.

The second trial seemed interminable, especially to the reporters at the press table. We were hearing it all for the second time, all those dreary arguments and contradictions and repetitions and disputes about the color of the wallpaper and whether it was a New Year's Eve party or a wedding anniversary when the champagne (or was it port wine?) made Chambers sick. In the first trial Murphy and Stryker had been on their feet a good deal of the time shouting objections at each other, but in the second Murphy and Cross apparently both decided to let the other side have its say ad nauseam. And Judge Goddard allowed virtually every scrap of evidence and testimony to be used that Judge Kaufman had excluded. William Rosen, the man whose name appeared on the title certificate of Hiss's old Ford roadster, was allowed to take the stand and refuse to answer questions for fear of being incriminated. Hede Massing, former wife of a German Communist named Gerhard Eisler, who had recently fled the country, was allowed to testify that she had once met Hiss and knew him to be a Communist; after that the defense called Henrikas Rabinavicius, a former Lithuanian diplomat, to testify that Mrs. Massing had given him an entirely different account of her meeting with Hiss at the time.

These were all side issues, bearing little or no relationship to the question of whether Hiss had given Chambers the incriminating documents. But after the first jury failed to reach a verdict, it was evidently decided that the second jury should be given more information so that they would be better equipped to make a decision. Every conflict of testimony had to be explored, no matter how remote or unimportant it might seem, until the wealth of detail about these extraneous issues became overpowering.

Hours went by without objections from either side or interruptions from the judge, while the attorneys persisted with their questions and the witnesses patiently answered, going over the same ground time after time to catch the little discrepancies and subtle differences of emphasis that might produce something new to argue about. Repeatedly the homes in which the Hisses had lived in Washington were described, but nobody seemed to remember very clearly what they had looked like a dozen years earlier, and the descriptions given by Hiss and Chambers and their wives differed enough to make it difficult to tell which house was under discussion at any particular moment. It became clear that the tree which had been in front of the Volta Place house in 1938 was no longer there in 1948; Priscilla Hiss remembered it as a silver maple, and Esther Chambers couldn't remember it at all. Esther said the wall in front of the house was white; Priscilla said it was red brick, while the contractor who had remodeled the house testified that Priscilla was right.

The same contractor produced wall scrapings from another house, bearing out Priscilla's contention that a wall which Esther said was pink was really green, though at the press table we wondered if Esther might have confused it with another wall which she had said was either a faded plum color or had a plum pattern on it. (When she heard this testimony, Priscilla was convinced the FBI had bugged their apartment, because only the night before, she and Alger had been talking about that wallpaper, and Esther had never mentioned it before.)

The arguments over the houses had to do with the question of whether Chambers had ever been inside the Thirtieth Street and Volta Place houses while the Hisses were living there in 1937–1938, or had only seen the inside of the Twenty-eighth Street apartment and the P Street house, where the Hisses lived in 1935–1936. Whittaker and Esther Chambers were sometimes wrong in their descriptions and sometimes right, but the jury must have found it as hard as the press did to know what the right answers were, or which house was which. The impression was left that, right or wrong, the Chamberses seemed to know a lot about all four houses, and therefore might have been in them all. The defense tried to suggest that the FBI had told them what to say, or that they had looked through the windows or revisited the houses in 1948 and perhaps got into the wrong one by mistake. All that could be proved was that the FBI had taken them to see the outsides of the houses, and shown them floor plans of the insides; but that didn't account for their descriptions of the wallpaper. The more the defense tried to bring out the errors in the Chamberses' testimony the more confused everybody got. And all the time the main issue of the trial was buried more deeply under these extraneous details.

When it came time for Cross's summation at the end of the second trial, he had little more to go on than Stryker had before. There was the psychiatric testimony, which Judge Goddard had allowed; but it had been so mercilessly chewed up in Murphy's cross-examination that Cross avoided making too much of it. Indeed, he gave it less than five minutes in a five-hour summation, just enough to remind the jury that Chambers had been called a psychopathic liar by two experts on the subject.

Cross's main theme was that Chambers couldn't have obtained the documents from Hiss, and must have got them from other people—his "confederates"—in the spy ring. He said some of them came from Julian Wadleigh, and he had evidence to support that; of the others, he said some must have come from an unnamed person in the State Department's Far Eastern Division, but he didn't know who it was, and the evidence on this point was mainly supposition. He could show that Hiss hadn't had access to all the documents involved, but he couldn't get away from the fact that Hiss had access to some of them, and that was what hurt. He argued, as Stryker had, that the typewriter was not in Hiss's house when the spy papers were copied on it, but he had to concede, as Stryker had, that it was Hiss's typewriter, and he could only guess how Chambers had got hold of it after Priscilla had given it to the Catletts. It wasn't a very good guess, and Murphy the next day ridiculed it as effectively and unmercifully as he had ridiculed the psychiatric testimony. But with no real evidence to go on, it was all Cross had to offer in argument.

"How did Chambers know about that [typewriter]?" Cross asked rhetorically. "How did he get it? . . . He did not do it himself, you can bet your life on that. He gets [things] through

confederates, anybody who can get [things] through confederates and steal top secret documents from the State Department
would not have much trouble locating a big office typewriter.

"Now I can suggest there might be several ways. I can suggest a way that he could easily have found out. Suppose someone
had called up, or come over, when he knew the Hisses weren't
there, and asked Clidi [Claudia Catlett], saying that they were a
typewriter repair man and had come to repair the Woodstock
typewriter. What would she have said? 'Why, they have given it
to my boys.' He wouldn't have much difficulty locating Clidi's
place, and with that open house, with the cellar there, I mean
the closet; with all the people coming and going, all the people
living there, and their friends, and the dances and all. How easy.
Am I talking through my hat? Have I got any basis for that?"

It was an appeal that the jury didn't respond to, especially
after Murphy got through with it the next day. Murphy handled
the Catlett testimony essentially the same as he had in the first
trial, by making it an issue between the Catletts and the FBI,
and suggesting that a jury that acquitted Hiss would be attacking
the FBI. "It is the thing to do today—call the FBI conspirators,"
he said. "It sounds good. A lot of the press like it—some of the
press. Smart. The intelligentsia like it, love it."

The comment had more meaning than appears on the surface, because alleged misconduct by the FBI was one of the
sensational issues in another trial in the same courthouse that
was going on at the same time. That was the trial of Judith
Coplon, a former Justice Department employee accused of stealing documents and giving them to Russian spies; she was convicted two months after Hiss, but her conviction was reversed on
appeal and the charges against her were eventually dropped.
When Murphy delivered his summation, the case was still underway and making headlines; and Murphy's implication to the jury
was clear. This was a case where the jury's loyalty would be at
stake when they considered their verdict.

With this reminder by way of introduction, Murphy
launched into his lacerating ridicule of Cross's suggestion. "Now,"
he said, "let's get back to the theory No. 103 as to who did it.

This is No. 103. And how was it proved? Well, you start off with the fact that the Catletts had the typewriter, and here is a picture of their hall." (He wasn't really showing them a picture, he was able to draw it in words and gestures.) "You see how these things follow. The Catletts had it. Here is the hall where they used to keep it. Here is the picture of the back entrance. You see all that space back there, people come in and out there all the time. Then there is the den, then there are the dancers.

"Now, what probably happened, Mr. Cross testified, is that somebody, not Chambers—he is too smart, but one of his conspirators, one of his confederates—those are good names, 'conspirators,' 'confederates'—he went up to the Volta Place house and asked innocent Clidi Catlett, 'I am the repair man. Where is the machine?'

"I can just see it now. It's terrific. You can have this guy coming with a Woodstock hat on, 'Woodstock Repair,' with a jumper 'Woodstock,' ringing the bell—no, it isn't a bell, you have to pull that one I think—and saying to Mrs. Catlett, 'I am the repair man to fix the typewriter.'

"Then Clidi says, 'Well, which one do you want? The Remington, the Royal, the L.C. Smith? Which one?'

" 'No, we want the Woodstock.'

" 'Oh, that's over in my boy's house, over at P Street.'

"And then the next scene, it is the middle of one of these dances. And you see Chambers sneaking in at night, mingling with the dancers, and then typing, typing the stuff, holding the State Department document in one hand—Oh, Mr. Cross, you got better than that!"

"Poppycock," Murphy called it, and in the end the jury agreed with him. They were guessing, of course, just as much as Cross was guessing, because neither Murphy nor the jury nor Cross nor Hiss knew what the whole truth really was. It may never be known in all its details, for much of what Chambers did in 1938 may have been known to no one else but himself, and he died without telling it all. Yet enough is known today, twenty-six years after the jury's verdict, to put together an explanation that is more likely to be true than the guesses made by either Murphy or Cross, because it is based on more solid evidence. It is the only explanation that fits all the undisputed facts, and is consistent with most of Chambers's testimony, though not all. Nothing could be consistent with all of Chambers's testimony, because he contradicted himself so much.

The first clue to be considered is the WPA job Chambers got on October 25, 1937, the job that was the occasion for his perjured oath of office. It wasn't much; it paid not quite forty dollars a week, but it gave him the title of report editor in the National Research Project. In his testimony and in *Witness*, Chambers described it as part of his system of "life preservers" when he broke with the Communist Party. The job gave him an identity, which he hadn't had before as a faceless member of the Communist underground. "I wanted to establish an identity for myself because I was afraid that I would be killed," he told Murphy at the second trial. "I knew it was more difficult to kill a man who has an identity, or, at least, the consequences may be greater for the killer."

The car he bought in November 1937, was another part of his life preserver system, he said, providing the means to escape from his Washington–Baltimore haunts and hide out for a month in Florida. On April 1, 1938, the date of the last of the pumpkin papers, his wife had the new car serviced in Randallstown, Maryland, in preparation for the Florida trip.

Another item which may have been part of the life preserver, though Chambers didn't identify it as such, was a typewriter which he subsequently abandoned on a "streetcar or elevated" in New York City—he didn't know which—in 1940. He made a special trip to New York for the purpose, according to his testimony; the typewriter had been given to him by the head of the "Soviet apparatus" he had first worked for in the underground, and he wanted to get rid of it because it reminded him of those experiences. He conceded that by disposing of it in this way he made sure it would never be traced back to him, though he said that wasn't what was in his mind at the time. And he said it was a Remington portable, not a Woodstock.

Given Chambers's habit of contradicting himself on the witness stand and inventing details which he later confessed were lies, it would be incautious to accept this story at face value and equally incautious to disregard it altogether. Chambers's testimony generally touched the truth somewhere and had some basis in reality; and as Doctors Binger and Murray pointed out, it also generally contained elements of fantasy which suited Chambers's purpose at the moment, and could be repudiated later should they be proved untrue.

Certainly Chambers had a typewriter of some kind in 1938; he couldn't have done his translation of Gumpert's book about Dunant and the Red Cross if he hadn't. But other than Chambers's story about the Remington portable there is no evidence to show what kind of typewriter he had, or if he had more than one. Stryker and Cross were unable to prove anything about it one way or the other so that it remains a matter of speculation. But it is speculation that must be undertaken, because it leads to consideration of those three cardinal principles by which mysteries of this kind are solved—means, motive, and opportunity.

The first point to notice is that when Whittaker Chambers spent a few nights with the Hiss family at 2905 P Street in the spring of 1935 and then moved in for a three-month stay in their empty apartment at 2831 Twenty-eighth Street, he must have noticed Priscilla's old Woodstock. He never said he did, to be sure; but how could a professional writer, a former editor of the *Daily Worker* and *New Masses*, a man who made his living by pounding a typewriter, fail to notice this big, awkward office machine that looked so out of place in Priscilla's home? He didn't notice Priscilla's piano, but then he wasn't a pianist; he could hardly have failed to notice such a prominent tool of his own trade. Moreover, the Woodstock seems to have been at the Twenty-eighth Street apartment at the time, at least Priscilla thought it probably was. She had no immediate use for it at P Street, and most of the Hisses' belongings weren't moved out of Twenty-eighth Street until after Chambers left, because the rented P Street house was still full of its owner's furniture. And if that was the case, Chambers had three months to use the old machine himself, and perhaps type papers on it which he carried away with him when he left.

Chambers apparently carried quite a lot of things away with him from that Twenty-eighth Street apartment, and over the years accumulated other objects of one kind or another that had belonged to Hiss. Among them were an old, broken loveseat, a table which he later had refinished, a rug, a wing chair, a small child's rocker which he said Alger and Priscilla had given his daughter, and a chest that once belonged to Timmy. When Edward McLean visited his home in Westminster, Maryland, before the trial, Chambers showed him a small, tattered piece of cloth, saying it was part of the fabric that had once covered Hiss's wing chair. Chambers had removed it, had it dry cleaned, and kept it for thirteen years "as a memento of a former friendship," according to Dr. Zeligs, who described the incident in *Friendship and Fratricide.*

Zeligs found a good deal of meaning in Chambers's attachment to objects associated with Hiss. He referred to them as "fetishes," and said for Chambers to have taken over Hiss's Woodstock typewriter was "psychologically equivalent" to his purchase, in 1937, of a small farm in Westminster which Hiss had once tried to buy as a summer place.

It would not be inconsistent with this analysis if in January of 1938, while Chambers was working on his WPA job as report editor, he had in his possession either the old Woodstock typewriter he had seen in Hiss's home, or another very like it. There are many ways this could have happened; Claude Cross's suggestion that Chambers might have found out that the Catletts had the machine is not impossible, stripped of the ridiculous details added by Murphy; and it is quite possible the Catletts wouldn't have missed it if he had taken it from their "den" one night and returned it three months later. Chester Lane's theory that Chambers's allies in the Communist underground could have faked another old Woodstock for him to match the Hiss machine is not impossible either; and it would have been easy to do if Chambers had brought samples of the Hiss machine's work with him from his stay at the Twenty-eighth Street apartment. Zeligs and the late

Professor Herbert Packer of Stanford University have suggested that Chambers might have switched such a fake machine with the real Hiss machine in late 1937 without the Hisses knowing it, and Priscilla would have given the fake to the Catletts, which would explain how it turned up at the trial; Beatrice Gwynn, an English archaeologist whose specialty is deciphering ancient manuscripts, has developed the same idea in detail. Others have suggested that the fake machine might have been made for either Chambers or the FBI at various times before November 1948, in order to produce the pumpkin papers when they were needed to support Chambers's story.

It's a sound rule of real life as well as detective fiction that the simplest explanation is most likely the right one. And the simple explanation is that, during 1935–1938, Chambers had an easy way of buying himself an old Woodstock just like the Hiss machine, from a dealer in used typewriters who advertised regularly in *New Masses*, the magazine Chambers had recently worked for, and which was still "must reading" for Communists. The dealer, Martin K. Tytell, did all the repairs and servicing for the *New Masses*' own typewriters, and the weekly advertisements were his pay for this work. They brought him a lot of business, according to his recollection in later years. Woodstocks were part of his stock in trade; and, in 1939, he took a full page in *New Masses* to advertise a special sale of rebuilt Woodstocks for $29.75—they cost $115.50 new in those days.

Whether Chambers bought an old Woodstock out of what Zeligs called his "fetishism" when he left the Twenty-eighth Street apartment or bought it later out of sentimentality or for the express purpose of typing the pumpkin papers, he could have had it when he needed it in 1938. He had only to type his documents on flimsy paper and use fresh typewriter ribbons, as Mrs. Ehrlich has pointed out, and nobody would ever know the difference. They would look like the work of Hiss's own machine.

This possibility is particularly appealing because it gets around the objection of Myles J. Lane, the U.S. Attorney who opposed the defense's Chester Lane on the motion for a new trial. Myles J. Lane argued that old N230099 might not be a fake at all, even though it looked like one. The point was never settled because the court refused a hearing on the evidence, so there's no way of telling whether Myles J. or Chester Lane was right. But if the pumpkin papers typist didn't use old N230099, it doesn't matter whether those tool marks and metallurgical discrepancies found by Daniel Norman* were the result of deliberate faking of the machine, as Chester Lane thought, or simply the result of repairs or carelessness at the factory, as Myles J. Lane contended.

So much for the means; by any of the means suggested Chambers could have typed the pumpkin papers himself. Each of them is consistent with some of the conflicting evidence; the theory advanced here is consistent with all the undisputed evidence. Unfortunately for the defense, they didn't discover the advertisements in *New Masses* until Elinor Ferry, a free-lance writer doing volunteer research in connection with the new trial motion, ran across them in the New York Public Library, when she was working on a different aspect of the case. The trial was long since over, and it was too late to question Chambers again.

The problem of motive is more complex. The question was first raised by Representative Mundt in the House Committee hearings—what motive would a man like Chambers, a $25,000-a-year editor of *Time* magazine,† have to tell lies about Alger Hiss? Hiss didn't know, and that counted heavily against him at the time; if he were telling the truth, he was expected to know why Chambers was lying. The obvious explanation—that Chambers was protecting his job by sticking to a story he had been telling the FBI for years—escaped both Hiss and Mundt at the time because neither of them knew about it.

When Chambers produced the pumpkin papers, the question of motive was suddenly changed; now Chambers was asked what motive he had had for concealing this evidence for so many years. He had a ready answer; as Miss Gwynn has noted, Chambers "could produce new stories when needed like juice from a

* See page 364. Norman's affidavit was part of the proceedings on the motion for a new trial.
† Chambers said it was $30,000, including bonus.

squeezed orange." He had not lied about Hiss being a Communist, he said, so there was no question of motive for that; he had lied when he said Hiss was not a spy, because he was a man of compassion and didn't want to hurt him. So here was Chambers apparently confessing to a previous lie and supplying a motive for it; nobody then asked what motive he might have for inventing a false confession, telling a lie now when he had said the truth before. It was brilliant; as Zeligs says in more professional language, Chambers may have been mad but he was a genius.

Yet, if Chambers lied about the pumpkin papers when he produced them, his motive for doing so was again obvious—he was on the losing side of a libel suit and if he couldn't convince the court that Hiss was a Communist, he stood to lose not just the $75,000 damages Hiss was seeking, but his whole career and means of livelihood. Quite apart from his feelings as the man of destiny, described so eloquently in *Witness*, his position at *Time* depended on his reputation as an expert on American Communism and Communists. The pumpkin papers saved him, putting an end to the libel suit and sending Hiss to jail, but they wouldn't have done so if Chambers hadn't sworn that they were given to him by Hiss and typed on Priscilla's typewriter. True or not, it was a statement he had to make people believe.

Behind this question of the motive for lying come the more interesting questions of the motive for typing those papers in the first place, and Chambers's motive for attributing them to Hiss. Could it be that they were really typed between August and December of 1948, for no other reason than to give Chambers the documentary evidence he needed then? Some investigators have argued this possibility; Ronald Seth, a British writer of fiction and non-fiction spy stories, developed it in a highly imaginative way in *The Sleeping Truth*. But there is a simpler explanation supported by more of the evidence.

Chambers wrote in *Witness* that he accumulated the spy papers in 1938 as his main life preserver, a means of blackmailing the Communist Party by threatening to expose the espionage conspiracy, and thus to protect himself from the assassination he feared.* Assuming this statement to be true, as some of Chambers's testimony seems to have been, the papers had to point to somebody in particular, or they would not have been much use as blackmail. And if Chambers already had a typewriter that matched the Hiss machine, what better target for his blackmail than Hiss?

Chambers apparently believed at the time that Hiss was a Communist, and he acted on this belief as though it were true; it seems to have been one of the fantasies described by Dr. Binger, the psychiatrist, at the second trial. Whether Dr. Binger's analysis is correct, what better target for Chambers's blackmail than this promising young State Department official who had already made a name for himself as one of the radical New Dealers, the "Frankfurter hot dogs" who frequented the "little red house on R Street"; a man who had identified himself with the "Communist line" by standing up for sharecroppers' rights in the great 1935 "purge" of the Agricultural Adjustment Administration, and by attacking such notables as Irénée Du Pont and Bernard Baruch before the Nye Committee; a man against whom, moreover, Whittaker Chambers had special reasons for nursing a sense of personal resentment and desire for revenge?

The special feelings Chambers had toward Hiss have been exhaustively documented in *Friendship and Fratricide*, the psychiatric study in which Dr. Zeligs develops in detail the system of fantasies that Dr. Binger and Dr. Murray referred to in general terms at the trial.† Some of Chamber's feelings had rather obvious

*Chambers was not asked about this at the trials, apparently because the prosecution had everything to lose and nothing to gain by bringing out this part of the story, and the defense didn't know enough about it to ask the right questions.

† Zeligs came to the conclusion that Chambers's whole life was "one prolonged span of psychic conflict," in which he was forever seeking to destroy himself, as he occasionally said in so many words; and for reasons of which Chambers himself was quite unaware, he felt compelled to drag Hiss to destruction with him. Or try to; in the end it was not Hiss who was destroyed, for he survived his three years and eight months of jail, learned many things from the experience, and emerged to make a new life for himself, find new friends, and labor for vindication. It was Chambers who

sources; he had offered Hiss his friendship in 1935, for example, and it had been refused. Chambers had sponged briefly off Hiss as he had off Robert Cantwell, his friend at *Time*, Maxim Lieber, his literary agent, and others. He had used Hiss's apartment without paying rent, used his car and sold it under mysterious circumstances that caused endless argument but were never fully explained, and hit him for small loans, which were never to be repaid. This was the kind of support Chambers was accustomed to getting from his Communist friends, and if he therefore assumed, in 1935, that Hiss was a Communist, the mistake was perhaps a natural one. But Hiss was neither a Communist nor did he become Chambers's friend; there came a time when he turned down Chambers's request for a loan and refused to see him, and years later he was to repudiate that friendship altogether.

Hiss was everything Chambers was not; a golden boy making a name for himself in public life, a man of family, a modest inheritance, education, good looks, a Phi Beta Kappa key, and a law degree. Chambers in 1935 was a nobody from nowhere, with no family (feuding parents and an insane grandmother), no money, always broke, a twice-interrupted college experience with no degree, lots of talent but no recognition, and decayed front teeth that needed fixing. Chambers was a man without a name; he didn't like the one he was born with and never could settle on another he wanted to stick with until *Time* put "Whittaker Chambers" on its masthead and he was stuck with it. He couldn't even sell the products of his own best talent, his imagination; he wrote what the Communists wanted him to for the *Daily Worker* and *New Masses*, and what Henry Luce wanted him to for *Time*,

---

lived as a frightened recluse for eleven and a half years after Hiss's conviction and in self-imposed confinement after Hiss was freed from jail. Chambers died in carefully contrived secrecy on July 9, 1961, the twelfth anniversary of the first Hiss jury's decision that they could not agree; his body was secretly cremated without examination to determine the cause of death and without notification to the State Health Department. Zeligs concluded that Chambers had finally succeeded in the suicide he had attempted so often before, and in the style he had foreshadowed in *Witness*: "Any fool can commit murder, but it takes an artist to commit a natural death."

and between those jobs he translated the works of more successful writers.*

So Chambers had abundant reasons to resent Hiss, quite apart from the unconscious drives suggested by the psychiatric evidence. Moreover, of all the people in the government whom Chambers identified at one time or another as members of his "conspiracy," Hiss was the only one he seems to have known much about—the only one in whose home he had stayed, or who had lent him a car, taken him to lunch, or introduced him to his wife. He really had no choice; if his "life preserver" was to blackmail anyone, it had to be Hiss.

So much for Chambers's motive; now let us consider the intriguing question of opportunity—the opportunity to lay his hands on those State Department documents that were the raw material for his pumpkin papers. This is where Chambers's job as a report editor for the National Research Project becomes important.

The beauty of that job, from Chambers's point of view, was that it gave him the necessary credentials for wandering around government buildings and looking at documents. The work actually assigned to him wasn't very demanding; he told the House Committee that "I sat in the office and made up some kind of index"; and since it was a WPA job, he was encouraged to take his time over it in order to make the job last. WPA jobs were essentially make-work affairs—"public service employment," as it is called today—designed to give otherwise unemployed people a chance to do something at least marginally useful and to earn a small wage at public expense.

* The only thing of his own that Chambers ever published, apart from the pornographic poems and atheistic playlet of his youth, was *Witness*, a work which he described as autobiography but which has been criticized as largely fiction. According to Joan Worth, an English researcher who has made an exhaustive study of the subject, *Witness* was heavily plagiarized from the novels of Dostoevsky, the gloomy Russian novelist who was one of Chambers's favorite authors and indisputably a major influence on his style. After *Witness*, published in 1952, there were a few articles in the *National Review*, and some letters to friends and fragments of rambling, introspective essays, published posthumously by his admirers for limited distribution. That was all.

Indeed, Chambers's job didn't last very long. On February 23, 1938, he was notified that "due to the reduction in volume of work" he had been "furloughed without prejudice," as of February 1, and his "last working day was January 31, 1938." That meant he wasn't going to get any February paycheck; it didn't mean that anyone had picked up his credentials on January 31, or called him in to surrender them when the furlough letter was written on February 23. Nor did it mean that a notice was circulated to all government offices saying "Jay V. David Chambers doesn't work for us anymore; don't let him in your office, don't answer his questions or let him see any documents." He hadn't been fired because of any suspicion of espionage; he was simply laid off for lack of work.

By this time Chambers had had plenty of opportunity to make his face known wherever he wanted to in the offices and hallways of the Old State, War and Navy Building, that monstrous gray Victorian wedding cake across Seventeenth Street from the White House that is now the Executive Office Building. And there was nothing to prevent Chambers from letting people think, as he was so fond of doing, that the work he was engaged in was much more important and high level than it really was; that he wasn't merely indexing a ponderous tome about the Railroad Retirement Board but working on some highly confidential history of State Department operations and foreign policy for the National Research Project. After all, his job title called him an editor and referred to "reports"; it didn't say anything about making indexes.

With these advantages, it couldn't have taken Chambers long to find out, if he didn't already know, some of the State Department procedures that Walter Anderson testified about in the trials. For example, it was useful for a spy to know that incoming telegrams were reproduced on a mimeograph machine and that copies were distributed to every office that might have any conceivable interest in them; that extra copies were kept in DCR (Division of Communications and Records) for anyone else who might ask for them; that a record of which offices received copies of each cable was marked on three of the DCR copies,

415

and while one of these marked copies was kept as a permanent record, the others were thrown away once a week; that a messenger circulated through the building every Monday to pick up the copies discarded by DCR and every other office during the week; that the messenger piled these discarded copies in wire baskets on a handcart which he pushed through the halls and down to the basement, where the papers were burned; that copies of telegrams that weren't of great interest to the offices to which they were sent were normally discarded quickly to get them out of the way; and that mailed dispatches and interoffice memos were circulated with carbon copies attached, but when they were finally filed by DCR, any carbon copies that hadn't already been removed would be discarded in the usual way.

A spy who knew all this and was free to circulate through the building as the editor of a National Research Project wouldn't need to take the risks Julian Wadleigh took, removing documents from someone's desk and sneaking them back after they'd served his purpose. He could pick up all the information copies or discarded carbon copies he needed, by pinching them out of one of those wire baskets on a Monday morning when the messenger left his handcart briefly unguarded. For that matter, if Wadleigh had turned Communist spy out of confused political idealism, what lowly messenger might not have cooperated with Chambers in his own way, without fully realizing what he was doing but perhaps thinking it did no harm—the papers were going to be burned anyway—and collecting a small tip? Security was not strong in the State Department or anywhere else in the government in those days; there was no screening for loyalty, no investigation of people in unimportant jobs. If there had been, Chambers would not have had his job.

It wouldn't matter if Chambers got more documents than he needed each Monday; they were piled by the hundreds in those wire baskets, and a handful or so wouldn't be missed. He wouldn't have to return them; he could copy the ones he wanted and burn the rest himself. If the pickup was made at the right point on the messenger's route it would include DCR copies showing the distribution of each telegram, and from the symbol "A-S" he could identify the ones that had gone to the office of Assistant Secretary of State Francis B. Sayre and into the hands of Alger Hiss. Chambers wouldn't need to do it this way, because everybody knew Sayre's assignment was foreign economic policy, and every telegram that had anything remotely to do with that subject was routed to Sayre's office. But there are interesting clues to suggest that perhaps he did.

One is in Exhibit number 38, a telegram which was somewhat garbled in transmission. As originally decoded, the message said Germany was secretly buying cereals and linseed in Argentina, "presumably for excessive fees." But this made no sense, so that the last two words were corrected on the action copy of the telegram to read "military service." The DCR distribution list copy remained uncorrected until routine confirmation arrived by mail nearly two months later, and the correct wording was found to be "war purposes." Meanwhile, the typist of the pumpkin papers had copied the original meaningless phrase, and never caught up with the correction; clearly the action copy hadn't been seen. The typist must have worked from a carbon of the DCR distribution list copy or from an uncorrected information copy based upon it.

The evidence of Exhibit number 47 points even more strongly to the DCR as the place where Chambers got his copies of the documents. The pumpkin papers version of number 47 is a single typewritten page quoting from three telegrams dated March 29, March 30, and April 1, and a mailed dispatch from The Hague dated February 26. In 1938 April 1 was a Friday so that discarded information copies of the three telegrams would have been in the messenger's wire baskets on Monday, April 4; each had been distributed to at least fourteen different offices. But there was no such distribution of the February 26 dispatch from The Hague; it was circulated with four carbon copies attached, three of which were accounted for by Military Information, Naval Information, and Messersmith's commercial officer, James Murphy. That left one carbon to be discarded by the DCR when the original was returned for filing, which happened, significantly enough, on Wednesday, March 30. So the last carbon copy would have been in the messenger's wire basket after he made his pickup from the DCR on April 4 and not before.

At whatever point on the messenger's route the pickups were made, the weekly pattern is clear from the dates on the documents, though it wasn't clear from the exhibit numbers assigned to them at the trial. The reason is that the exhibit numbers followed the same sequence assigned to Chambers's papers by his lawyer Richard Cleveland, when they were first produced in Baltimore during the libel suit proceedings. Cleveland sorted them into the approximate order of the dates they showed, which were the dates the original documents had been written, not necessarily the dates on which they were received at the State Department or found their way into Chambers's hands.

First, Cleveland assigned the numbers 1–4 to the four handwritten notes; numbers 5–8 were the Boyce dispatch of January 6, 1938, about Manchukuo and its enclosures; number 9 referred to three telegrams from Bullitt dated January 5 and 12; on number 10, the date January 7 was handwritten at the top; number 11 was based on sixteen telegrams from various places with dates running from January 22 to February 2, covering four single-spaced typewritten pages; numbers 12 and 13 were Jones's summaries of the two Boyce dispatches, dated February 7 and 9; number 14 summarized two telegrams dated February 11; number 15 was Hornbeck's note of February 11 about the Manchukuo papers; numbers 16–35 were complete texts or summaries of telegrams dated from February 12 through February 18; number 36 was a memorandum of a conversation between Assistant Secretary Sayre and the Czechoslovakian Minister to Washington, Vladimir Hurban, on February 18; and numbers 37–47 were copies, summaries or excerpts from seventeen telegrams dated March 18–April 1, and a mailed dispatch dated February 26.

From this list, we can identify Exhibit numbers 5–8, 12, 13, and 15 as the set of Manchukuo papers picked up by Julian Wadleigh, who also picked up the microfilmed documents, as described in Chapter 18. The four handwritten notes were evidently picked out of a wastebasket, which could have been done by anyone who wanted to, and there is no way of telling whose wastebasket it was or when they were taken. All we know is that it wasn't Wadleigh who picked up number 4, because it refers to a telegram dated March 11, the day he sailed for Turkey.

Apart from Wadleigh's contributions, all but two of the exhibits in this series fall into four weekly groups, so that they required no more than four pickups in the whole three months. Exhibit number 11 covered the weeks from Friday, January 21, through Thursday, January 27, and from Friday, January 28, through Wednesday, February 2; and there are creases on the first and third pages to show when the flimsy paper was taken out of the typewriter and put back in again between those two pickups. The telegrams in this collection are organized by place of origin as well as date, in a rather awkward way; two pages are headed "Far East" and two are under "Europe," oddly subtitled "England," "Spain," "Great Britain," and "France," in that order.

Exhibit numbers 14 and 16–36 were all dated between Friday, February 11, and the following Friday, February 18; the pickup date would have been Monday, February 21, for the lot. Then came a gap of five weeks: Exhibits 37–47 carried the dates from Saturday, March 26, to Friday, April 1, plus the mailed dispatch of February 26 from The Hague already discussed. All of them were therefore ready for pickup on Monday, April 4.

This was the last of the pickups; by that time Chambers had started on his translation of Gumpert's book, and by the end of the week he was in Florida, perhaps taking the last set of documents with him to type in greater safety.

There remain two other exhibits to consider, numbers 9 and 10. Exhibit number 10 was ignored at the trial because it obviously wasn't typed on the Woodstock machine, and it wasn't done on flimsy paper with a wet ribbon either. How it got mixed up with the others Chambers never explained; on examination it proved to be a few paragraphs excerpted from a military intelligence report on the Japanese invasion of China, sent routinely by the War Department to the Far Eastern Division of the State Department. Evidently someone in that division had selected four paragraphs, or parts of them, from that nine-page report, and read them off to his secretary as being worthy of someone's attention; the secretary had typed them out on standard government typewriter paper misspelling three Chinese place-names, as one might do when working from dictation instead of a typed copy, and making only one typographical error; an "l" typed over an accidental comma. Routine office work; the date of the original memo, 1/7/38, was noted by hand at the top of the page, but there was nothing to indicate who had dictated it or why. It wasn't a matter of record, and needed no office stamps or file number; somebody, perhaps Wadleigh since he had friends in the Far Eastern Division as well as occasional business there, had picked it up and given it to Chambers, who slipped it in with his other pumpkin papers without giving it a thought. Evidence that proves nothing that we don't already know.

Exhibit number 9 was apparently the first of the whole series to be typed, and thus perhaps an experiment in technique. It referred to three long telegrams from Bullitt, one dated January 5 and the others January 12. The pumpkin papers version referred only to parts of the information in the telegrams, and not the most interesting parts by any means; one of them was badly garbled, with misstatements that didn't appear in the original; another contained a numerical error, and the third was obviously based only on sections one and two of a four-section telegram. It looks as though the pumpkin papers typist had only a brief look at these three telegrams and wasn't able to take them away for careful copying. However he did it, that obviously wasn't what he wanted; he never tried that again. By the end of January he had a much more efficient system.

Means, motive and opportunity—Whittaker Chambers, or Jay V. David Chambers as he called himself in his National Research Project job, had them all. That doesn't prove he did it, of course, but it shows he was in a much better position to do it than either Alger or Priscilla Hiss. Certainly, these typewritten papers are not typical examples of a well-established routine, as

Chambers pretended; they are a mixed bag of different materials put together in different ways, as though somebody was catching what he could and trying various techniques in a hastily improvised scheme. They fit Chambers's description of a "life preserver" manufactured for blackmail purposes, but they don't look like the work of an espionage ring with more than a year of experience working together, such as he described. There is nothing to connect them with Hiss except the fact that they were typed on a machine much like one his wife had owned; but his wife couldn't have done the typing if she'd wanted to, and nor could Hiss. Chambers could have done it, and only Chambers had compelling reasons for wanting to.

This wasn't the way the story was presented to the jury, because the defense didn't have the evidence until after the trial was over. They could have had some of it if they had examined the papers more thoroughly when Chambers first produced them in the Baltimore libel suit proceedings; and if Mrs. Ehrlich and Miss McCarthy had made their discoveries at that time, things would have been different. But at that early stage neither Hiss nor his lawyers had any suspicion of what Chambers was really up to; and when they asked permission to examine the papers in their pretrial motion three months later, Judge Bondy turned them down. He accepted the government's argument that they had had their opportunity at Baltimore and weren't entitled to a second chance. Though the defense finally got access to the papers in 1952, when they moved for a new trial, Judge Goddard then took essentially the same position as Judge Bondy; they'd had their chance in two trials, and the new evidence wasn't enough to entitle them to a third.

Even in 1952, the defense hadn't found all the evidence presented here; some of it depended on a study of typewriting techniques that they never undertook, and more of it came from a thorough study of the original State Department documents, which the defense had access to during the trials, but didn't have time to examine carefully enough.

So the best the defense could do at the trials was cast doubt on Chambers's story, and in this case "reasonable doubt" wasn't enough. They couldn't disprove what Chambers said, because they didn't know what had really happened. And as Claude Cross said, the "temper of the times" was against them. The burden of proof was on the defense rather than the prosecution, in spite of all the constitutional and procedural law on the subject, and the burden was too heavy for the defense to bear.

22

EPILOGUE

At the end of the first trial the jury wrangled, argued, worried, and slept over the questions left unanswered by the testimony for a total of twenty-eight hours and forty minutes, of which fourteen hours and ten minutes were formally devoted to "deliberations," according to the clerk's statement to reporters. At the end of that time, having twice been told by Judge Kaufman to try again when they said they could not agree, they finally convinced him that further efforts would be futile, and were discharged. The vote in the jury room, as Edward McLean quickly learned from one of the departing jurors, was eight to four; in the first half-hour of deliberations four waverers had joined with those who wanted to convict, and for the rest of the time nobody's opinion changed in the slightest, the juror said. The New York *Journal–American* the next day quoted one of the jurors as saying, "Eight of us pounded hell out of the four since Thursday night, but we couldn't get anywhere."

The second jury, consisting of eight "housewives" and four business executives, one of them retired, wrangled for almost as long before they reached a verdict. They had the case twenty-three hours and forty minutes, of which nine hours thirteen minutes were recorded as "deliberation" time. The verdict came on the fortieth day of the trial, at 2:50 P.M. on Saturday, January 21, 1950. Hiss heard it with the same stoic calm he had shown throughout the two trials, sitting in his usual seat just inside the rail of the court, with Priscilla beside him.

When the jury entered the courtroom, Joseph Toner, clerk of the court, formally called the roll of their names for the record. Priscilla looked straight ahead as though seeing nothing. Hiss sat with head high, chin up, his expressionless face turned toward the jury, seeming to turn his eyes from one juror to the next as their names were called and each answered, "present." His right leg was crossed over his left, his arms akimbo; it was a posture that looked oddly and artificially unconcerned. Priscilla was at his left, her hands clutching the black leather handbag in her lap.

Then Toner asked the forelady of the jury Mrs. Ada Condell whether she and the jury had reached a verdict. "Yes, we have," she answered.

"How say you?" asked the clerk.

"We find the defendant guilty on the first count and guilty on the second."

Hiss showed no sign of emotion; Priscilla looked straight ahead as before. There was a sudden rush of newsmen for the door, and voices were heard from spectators, but their words were lost in the hubbub. The clerk said, "Quiet, please."

Cross asked for the jury to be polled, and the clerk asked each juror if his verdict was the same as that of the forelady. Some said "Yes," some said "I do," and some said "It is."

Again Hiss's eyes rested on each juror in turn. Then, his arms now crossed, he touched his wife's folded hands with his own right hand. For an instant he smiled, and she smiled back.

Judge Goddard thanked the jury for their services, and told them he thought they had rendered a "just verdict." Then he dismissed them, first cautioning them not to talk to the press. They took his advice, emerging from the jury room a few minutes later in a solid phalanx with mouths sealed, answering all queries with no or no comment. Outside, on the steps of the courthouse, they lined up two by two to be photographed, and again refused to speak.

The courtroom emptied slowly, spectators crowding around

Hiss and his wife as they walked silently out. In the corridor they were met by Harold Shapero, Stryker's assistant at the first trial, who had come to be with them for the verdict. Shapero walked between Alger and Priscilla, one arm around each, and they went into the defense counsel's room. The door closed behind them and word was sent out that Hiss would make no comment. Within half an hour they appeared on the courthouse steps and walked across the sidewalk to enter a maroon sedan, pushing their way through a crowd of photographers and newsreel men. A microphone was thrust inside the car, and Hiss said, "I have no comment." Then the car rolled away, followed by another containing friends and relatives.

Murphy, whose voice had seemed choked with emotion when he first spoke after the verdict was announced, received congratulations and reporters' questions with an air of combined fatigue and jubilation. "It was the toughest case I ever had," he said.

Four days later, on Wednesday, January 25, Hiss was back in the courtroom for sentencing. Cross made the usual motions for arrest of judgment and a new trial, and Goddard routinely denied them, having already heard them argued in chambers. Then Cross pleaded for mitigation of sentence, speaking for only a few minutes in a voice that trembled slightly.

"There are certain matters that I feel it my duty, and also privilege, to call to your Honor's attention before imposing sentence in this unusual and very important case," he said. "It is a case that has even greater interest than national interest. It has international interest. People have followed the case perhaps more closely than any other case that has been tried for many, many decades. The final outcome of the case has been awaited by many who have believed, and still believe, in the innocence of Alger Hiss.

"As to the matter of punishment, if your Honor please, I think from any corrective standpoint no further punishment would ever have any effect on Alger Hiss. For a year and a half since this matter first broke in August of 1948 he has suffered, his family have suffered. As to what he has done, certainly since the

Stalin–Hitler Pact in 1939, we have had documentary evidence; his contribution to the interests of the United States, and in fact our international relations are matters beyond dispute.

"As to his financial condition, what little savings he has had were gone long before the conclusion of the first trial. . . . His financial ruin is long since an accomplished fact; a brilliant career ruined. And so I say to your Honor, with all sincerity, that any punishment further than what he has undergone is unnecessary for any effect upon the individual.

"As to any exemplary effect of any sentence, the matter of the commitment to jail where a man has undergone the worst punishment, that of mind and heart, that he can undergo, is unnecessary. So I respectfully urge upon your Honor, and I say this against the wishes of my client, because he did not want to suggest anything pointed toward a mitigation of punishment, but I feel it my duty to tell your Honor . . . what I said to the jury, I have believed, and I still believe, in the innocence of Alger Hiss. But I accept the verdict of the jury; that is our judicial system.

"There are only two or three people who know the real facts. The jury believed him guilty or they would not have returned a verdict. They don't know, and I don't know, and until the true and complete facts come out there will always be the lingering doubt, which was manifested by a hung jury at the first trial . . . and by the manifestation of doubt when [this] jury came in after twenty hours and asked your Honor to re-read parts of your charge having to do with reasonable doubt. . . .

"I have attempted to present all the facts within my command. I have done it, and I did not convince the jury, and I feel that I should tell your Honor frankly that I still believe in Alger Hiss."

The gray-haired lawyer sat down, and Judge Goddard answered quietly, "Mr. Cross, I am inclined to think the fact that the jury considered this case for nearly twenty-four hours or more is not any indication of any snap judgment but does indicate a very full consideration and conscientious effort on the part of the jury to arrive at the right verdict."

Then it was Murphy's turn, and he bristled at the idea that

426

the full facts had not been brought out. "Under our system of jurisprudence the defendant has now had two opportunities to bring out the full facts," he said, "and I know of no other way than trial by jury to disclose the full facts. To add now some air of mystery I think is not quite fair." Then Murphy recommended that sentence be imposed of five years on each count—the maximum —to run concurrently. "I think the public should be told that in this country perjury cannot be committed with impunity," he said.

Judge Goddard agreed, and turning to Cross he repeated Murphy's statement, even in some of the same words. "It is not in my opinion a case where sentence should be suspended," he said. "There should be a warning to all that a crime of this character may not be committed with impunity."

Cross asked if Hiss could make a brief statement, and Judge Goddard said, "Yes, certainly. You may come up closer if you wish."

"No, there is no need to, unless your Honor would like me to," Hiss said, but he approached the bench anyhow. Then he said in a loud, firm voice, "I would like to thank your Honor for this opportunity again to deny the charges that have been made against me. I want only to add that I am confident that in the future the full facts of how Whittaker Chambers was able to carry out forgery by typewriter will be disclosed. Thank you, sir."

Judge Goddard made no comment. Hiss turned to go back to his seat, but two marshals detained him. They stood on either side of him as Judge Goddard said, "The defendant is sentenced to five years on each count, sentences to run concurrently." There was a brief discussion of Hiss's bail, which had been $5,000 during the trial; Judge Goddard now increased it to $10,000 pending the appeal.

It was 10:50 A.M.; the proceedings had taken twenty minutes. Hiss and his wife waited in the defense counsel's room until the additional bail was posted by Manice deForest Lockwood III, one of their friends. It took nearly an hour to arrange through the National Surety Company.

Outside the courthouse a crowd of about five hundred people waited for the Hisses to appear. A lane down the long stone stairway from the door to the street was secured by wooden barriers, behind which press photographers stood. The bulk of the crowd was on a traffic island facing the steps in the middle of Foley Square. At 12:21 P.M. Hiss and his wife appeared in the doorway; voices cried, "Here they come!" and the crowd left the traffic island and surged forward into the street.

Alger and Priscilla walked down the steps, heads high, looking straight ahead, both smiling. Reporters closed in behind them, mingling with a group of friends, relatives, and attorneys who were following. At the bottom of the steps they were surrounded by the crowd. Alger and Priscilla pushed their way forward, walking rapidly. The crowd parted to let them through, and photographers rushed ahead to get more pictures.

Somewhere in the crowd someone muttered in a low voice, "Hang the traitor." There were no shouts. For several minutes it seemed as if nothing could be heard but the clicking of heels on the pavement, and photographers trying to get out of each other's way. Priscilla linked her right arm in her husband's and her left arm in that of Mrs. Phelps Soule, a close friend from Peacham, Vermont, who had appeared at the trial as a character witness. Mrs. Soule linked arms with Mrs. John Alford, the former Roberta Fansler. Mrs. Alford wore a sad and worried expression; Mrs. Soule looked angry; Priscilla had her chin up and her lips set in a tight, forced smile; Alger looked depressed and unbelieving, his expression for once preoccupied as though the meaning of the experience had finally become clear to him.

Behind them, struggling through the crowd as best they could, walked Miss Ann Winslow, of the Carnegie Endowment staff; Robert M. Benjamin, a friend and attorney who was to help with the appeal; Manice Lockwood and his wife Agnese, who had first met Hiss through the Carnegie Endowment; Mrs. Margaret Fansler, Priscilla's sister-in-law; Miss Berthol E. Sayre, a friend; Mrs. Julie D'Estournelles, director of the Woodrow Wilson Foundation; Mrs. Helen L. Buttenwieser, a friend and attorney, who was to be Hiss's counsel through the long struggle for vindication that was about to begin; Mrs. Harold Rosenwald and Mrs. Robert von Mehren, whose husbands had been part of the defense legal team since the case began in August 1948, and who were now separated from them by the crowd; Cross, McLean, and Daniel West, of McLean's staff.

They walked two and a half blocks, the whole crowd of spectators following at their heels. In front of the State Office Building at 80 Centre Street, Alger and Priscilla got into a taxi, while a man walking by them said "Boo" once, loud and long.

There remained the appeal, and Hiss threw himself into the work of helping Robert Benjamin write the brief, while Chester Lane took charge of the search for new evidence. McLean's firm, having served Hiss for eighteen months at considerably greater cost than the fees they were paid, was unable to do more. Hiss thought he had unbeatable grounds for his appeal—prejudicial conduct by both the judge and the prosecutor, errors in admitting testimony that should have been barred, and a record that showed insufficient evidence to support the verdict.* But Judge Harrie B. Chase, who wrote the opinion denying the appeal eleven months later, thought otherwise. The Supreme Court refused to review the case, and on March 22, 1951, Hiss went to prison.

Five years' imprisonment: with time off for good behavior, that meant three years and eight months inside the walls, one year and four months outside on "conditional release." Theoretically he would be eligible to apply for parole after twenty months in prison, but when that time came Hiss wasn't particularly surprised to find that his successive applications were turned down without explanation. It was, after all, a case with political implications; there would have been an angry hue and cry if Hiss had served a day less than the maximum allowed by law.

Hiss prepared himself for the experience as if he were going to a strange country to live, by consulting an expert on the language and customs of the country—Austin H. McCormick, head of the Osborne Association for prison reform. McCormick told him some of the conventions of prison life—don't speak to strangers, mind your own business, don't get too friendly with the

* For a fuller description of the appeal, see Hiss's own account in *In the Court of Public Opinion.*

guards, don't talk about your own case, don't take a job in the prison hospital or you'll be in danger of getting into trouble over drugs—and so on. McCormick reminded him he'd be "the new boy in school," with a lot to learn from "experienced upper class-men." Hiss learned quickly and made a lot of friends in prison, some of whom he has often seen since, and some who correspond with him fairly regularly.

At the detention center on West Street in New York, where he spent the first few days before being transferred to the federal penitentiary at Lewisburg, Pennsylvania, he met Morton Sobell, who had been convicted with the Rosenbergs of conspiracy to steal atomic secrets for the Russians—another trial which had been going on in the same courthouse and added to the general public excitement. Sobell assured Hiss that he and the Rosenbergs had been framed, and Hiss admired the courage with which Sobell faced the thirty-year sentence that awaited him, much of it to be served at Alcatraz, a much tougher institution than Lewisburg. Julius Rosenberg was at West Street, too, awaiting execution; he wasn't allowed to mingle with the other prisoners, but Hiss occasionally saw him getting his exercise in the walkway between the cages.*

At Lewisburg Hiss met two of the Communist leaders who had been convicted in 1949, and found them pleasant, cheerful men who took a little ragging from the other inmates but didn't make any trouble. It never occurred to Hiss to ask them what, if anything, they knew about Chambers and his story of espionage; Hiss was so sure in his own mind that Chambers was a fake that he never thought to bring the subject up. In any case he had few contacts with the Communists at Lewisburg because he had nothing in common with them. Years later, when Hiss returned to Johns Hopkins University for a public lecture, one of the people who came up to congratulate him afterwards was a prosperous business man who had been a fellow inmate at Lewisburg. He told Hiss he was still wrestling with doubts about the case, since

---

* Rosenberg and his wife Ethel were executed June 19, 1953; Sobell was released from prison January 14, 1969.

he had been so impressed by Chambers's testimony about the documents, the old Ford car, and the famous prothonotary warbler; but the one thing he found most in Hiss's favor was that while at Lewisburg he had "never talked to those Communists except to exchange the time of day."

The trial was all part of another world to Hiss while he was in prison; he would lie awake at night thinking about it and imagining other ways it might have been handled, things that might have been done differently to make it more successful. His favorite dream was that a prosecution witness who claimed to have seen Priscilla at the Chamberses' house could have been proved a liar by a simple trick—someone else instead of Priscilla could have been sitting beside Hiss when the witness was asked to point her out. It wasn't until years after he was released from jail that Hiss realized the trick couldn't have worked; if Priscilla hadn't been sitting beside him, Murphy wouldn't have asked the witness to point to her.

Another fellow inmate at Lewisburg was William Remington, who had been accused of espionage by Elizabeth Bentley, and like Hiss was convicted of perjury when he denied it. Remington was asleep on his cot one day when another prisoner, a violent mountaineer from Kentucky who was generally regarded as crazy, started going through his bathrobe pockets looking for cigarettes. Stealing is not popular in prison, it's one of the things you don't do, even if you make your living that way outside. But that's what the man was doing, and Remington had the bad luck to wake up and catch him at it. He started to jump out of his cot, but he never made it; the other prisoner had a rock in a sock, and he pounded Remington on the head with it until the blood spurted over the walls. Remington lingered for a couple of days, and several men volunteered to give blood transfusions, but he never regained consciousness.

This happened only about two weeks before Hiss was due for release, and when it became known, it created such a storm of protest that the Justice Department in Washington decided that Hiss should be given protective custody for the remaining weeks to make sure something similar didn't happen to him.

Hiss was summoned to the warden's office and told he was to be moved into the isolation wing. By that time he had enough prison savvy to know what to do.

"That's absolute nonsense," he said to the warden. "It's not going to happen to me; my relations with my fellow inmates are totally different. This is a helluva way to treat me the last two weeks, how do I know some of them won't think I asked for it? Anyway, I'm not going to do it."

The warden persisted, because he had orders from Washington. The captain was called in and assured the warden that Hiss was perfectly safe where he was. Finally, a compromise was reached; Hiss wasn't isolated, but a guard was assigned to follow him around. He was an old guard, about to retire, and generally liked by the prisoners because he was "absolutely harmless, a flat-footed cop," in Hiss's description. Hiss accepted the arrangement, provided that the guard didn't come within twenty paces of him. "I'm not going to have him joining in all my conversations," he told the warden.

Those forty-four months in jail were an experience Hiss doesn't like to remember, though he sometimes jokes about it as a kind of "postgraduate college education." He avoids the words "jail" and "prison" when he is talking about his own experience, and never refers to "Lewisburg" if he can help it; he speaks of when he was "away" and when he "came back." While in jail he wrote endless letters to his family and friends, but said very little in them about life in jail. He wrote to his brother Donald about current affairs; to Priscilla, Tony, and Tim he offered moral support, affection, encouragement, intellectual ideas, and personal messages. But he was hating it all the time, and the depth of his feelings about it sometimes come out. Donald remembers an occasion in 1974, when he and Alger and a group of friends were discussing the Watergate scandals and the resignation of Vice President Agnew, and somebody said that both Nixon and Agnew ought to go to jail. Alger broke in and said, "Never! Don't ever send anybody to jail, it's a terrible place!"

"Not even Agnew and Nixon?" Donald asked.

"No!" said Alger. "Jail doesn't do anybody any good."

"What about those people you helped," Donald persisted, "the one you taught to read—" (One of the ways Alger had occupied himself at Lewisburg was to help an illiterate prisoner learn enough to write his first letter to his wife.)

"Some of them went straight, some of them didn't," Alger answered shortly, "but jail is a terrible place." And that's all he would say about it.

Those forty-four months must have been a terrible experience for Priscilla, too, though she denies it now; she remembers only that she did a great job and felt she was "carrying the flag for the family." She was alone with a ten-year-old son and no money; there was no question of going back to her career as a teacher at Dalton School, although Tony remained there as a pupil. Through a friend she got a job in a book store, but it paid far less than she could have earned in other circumstances.

Priscilla traveled to Lewisburg once a month—which was all the regulations allowed—to visit Alger, and took Tony with her except when he was away at camp. Alger, Priscilla, and Tony all have different recollections of these visits. Priscilla was allowed to write to her husband three times a week and remembers that she wrote about "everything lovely and beautiful I could think of." Alger kept the letters, and brought them home with him when he came out of jail. Priscilla treasures them now, along with the letters Alger wrote to her, but will not allow anyone to see them.

When Hiss came out of jail, the day after Thanksgiving in 1954, there was a brief period of exaltation. But he had changed and so had Priscilla, and the exaltation didn't last.

For the first sixteen months Hiss was on conditional release, which meant reporting once a month to his parole officer and remaining inside the jurisdiction of the court that had sentenced him—the Southern District of New York. He could live in Manhattan; he could go to Peekskill but he couldn't go to Brooklyn or New Jersey without his parole officer's permission; when he visited friends in Nyack, New York, he couldn't cross the Hudson on the George Washington Bridge but had to travel over the Bear Mountain Bridge.

He spent these sixteen months writing his book, *In the Court of Public Opinion*, which was essentially a lawyer's argument about the evidence that had already been found insufficient to prove his innocence. It was abundantly documented, cogently reasoned, but as coldly restrained as Hiss had been in his own testimony on the stand. It added nothing new to the story, and though it had a modestly successful sale, it made no observable impression on public opinion.

By the time the book was published, in early 1957, Hiss had a job as assistant to the President of Feathercombs, Inc., a small company that produced a patented ornament for women's hair, a kind of expensive novelty or elaborate piece of costume jewelry. The company was in trouble, and Hiss's job was to help reorganize it; but the troubles of the company kept getting worse, along with Hiss's troubles at home. By 1959 both came to a climax; Alger left Priscilla and soon afterward quarreled with his boss at Feathercombs, which was soon in bankruptcy; then he was out of a job for six months. It was the low point of his life, and it came when he was four and a half years out of jail, nearly eleven years after the ordeal had begun.

Then began the long climb back—the finding of a new job, a new home, new evidence to prove his innocence—a whole new way of life. His old friends stayed with him, and he made many new ones. He became a salesman of office supplies and printing, a business he had learned something about when he worked in the supply room at Lewisburg. He suddenly found that his fame as an ex-convict, a man believed to have been a perjurer, spy, and traitor, could be helpful to him as a salesman. Curiosity opened many new customers' doors; he needed no introduction because his name was well known. Among the buyers of office supplies in New York he found a lot of old New Dealers, old Lincoln Brigade fighters, even ex-Communists of a very different stripe from Whittaker Chambers, as well as plain people who were glad to make his acquaintance and buy from him. And he has made a reputation as a reliable salesman for a reliable firm, so that customers with very different backgrounds and viewpoints have no hesitation in dealing with him.

For the last dozen years, Hiss has also been in considerable demand as a lecturer on New Deal Washington, the founding of the United Nations, the McCarthy era, and other aspects of history of which he can speak from personal experience. He has addressed student and public audiences at Harvard, Johns Hopkins, Princeton, Columbia, New York University, Brandeis, Wesleyan, the University of Virginia, Cortland and Oneonta Colleges of the State University of New York, Kenyon, Trinity College (Hartford), Olivet, Franconia, Peter Cooper Institute, the New School for Social Research, and the New England College of Law; and in England he has lectured at the Universities of London, Nottingham, Hull, East Anglia, Reading, Lancaster, and Keele. He has been interviewed on television in England, Belgium, and Canada, as well as on many occasions in the United States.

English audiences have been interested in Hiss ever since the late William Allen Jowitt, then Lord Chancellor of England and that country's highest legal authority, wrote *The Strange Case of Alger Hiss* in 1953. Jowitt was somewhat scathing about the way the trials had been handled, and suggested with evident satisfaction that such things would never happen in England. Writing soon after the publication of Chambers's *Witness,* he pointed out that that book provided a lot of new evidence that had not been heard at the trial, and raised new questions about Chambers's mental condition and the importance of the psychiatric testimony. "I should be profoundly interested," he wrote, "to hear the opinion of distinguished American psychiatrists on all the new circumstances revealed in *Witness.* I wonder what conclusions they would reach. . . . Surely it should be put to the test."

It was this comment that aroused the interest of Dr. Meyer A. Zeligs, the San Francisco psychiatrist who wrote *Friendship and Fratricide,* and led him to undertake the six years of research on which the book was based. Zeligs tracked down and interviewed everybody he could find who had ever known Whittaker Chambers or Alger Hiss or had anything to do with the case; he studied old letters and records of births, deaths, and baptisms which the defense lawyers had never seen; he read everything

435

Chambers had ever written and everything written about him up to the time he finished his book, in 1966. Chambers refused to see him, despite repeated letters, phone calls, and approaches through his friends; his death occurred two years after Zeligs began his research. Zeligs concluded, as Binger and Murray had done, that while it would have been impossible to give Chambers any psychiatric treatment without his cooperation, that wasn't necessary to arrive at an adequate diagnosis.

Nixon also refused to see Zeligs, as did a few others who had known Chambers. Esther Chambers saw Zeligs only after her husband's death. He found her "worshipping and sustaining" her late husband's image as a "martyr, savior and hero." She didn't tell Zeligs much, but he was very sorry for her. He had a great deal of sympathy for Chambers, too, who had first attracted his interest as a study in psychopathology. But as his research proceeded he became convinced that Hiss was innocent, and stepped out of his role as psychiatrist to argue the case.

Another writer who came to the same conclusion is Fred J. Cook, who declared in *The Unfinished Story of Alger Hiss*, in 1958, that "Either Alger Hiss was a traitor to his country and remains one of the most colossal liars and hypocrites in history, or he is an American Dreyfus, framed on the highest level of justice for political advantage." In later articles for *The Nation*, Cook dropped the "either-or" approach and argued that Hiss had clearly been framed, and that the FBI appeared to have been involved in the frame-up.

Cook's first article on the subject in *The Nation*, a preview of his book, caught the attention of Raymond A. Werchen, a New York attorney who had had no previous connection with the case or knowledge of it. Werchen became interested and undertook some research of his own, visiting the Brooklyn home where Nathan Levine had hidden Chambers's papers in the old dumbwaiter shaft, checking the records of the Ford Chambers bought in 1937, and going over the testimony and affidavit of Ramos C. Feehan, the FBI documents expert who had testified that the papers were typed on the Hiss machine. The result was another *Nation* article on May 28, 1973, signed jointly by Cook and Werchen, concluding that "The Hiss case cries aloud for fresh and thorough examination, for here is where it all began; here was the genesis of the unscrupulous power that has brought the nation to the disgrace of Watergate."

These were heartening developments for Hiss, although they weren't enough to bring him the vindication he seeks. It is too late now for another trial, however much new evidence is gathered; Hiss has never applied for a Presidential pardon, for that would imply an admission of guilt, and he has stated that he will only accept a pardon that overturns his conviction as a miscarriage of justice. He has, however, won reinstatement to the bar in Massachusetts, where he first practiced law in 1930–31, but was automatically disbarred when he was convicted. In a unanimous decision on August 5, 1975, the seven judges of the Massachusetts Supreme Judicial Court found that regardless of Hiss's perjury conviction twenty-five years before, he had demonstrated the "moral and intellectual fitness" required of an attorney-at-law, and should therefore be readmitted to the bar.

Judge G. Joseph Tauro, who wrote the opinion, carefully avoided passing judgment on the question of whether Hiss had in fact been guilty of perjury; the Judge said he was bound by the United States District Court's "adjudication of guilt" even though "nothing in the record* in any way corroborates the fact of guilt." He accepted Hiss's argument that "miscarriages of justice are possible," and that "innocent men can conceivably be convicted," though he avoided saying whether he believed that had happened in Hiss's case.

* Judge Tauro was referring here to the record of the proceedings in his own court, in which no one had argued that Hiss was in fact guilty of the perjury for which he had been convicted. Indeed, as Judge Tauro pointed out in another footnote, no witnesses opposed Hiss's reinstatement at all. "When duly notified," he wrote, "the Attorney General of the United States indicated that he did not 'wish to be heard or to be represented at the hearing' . . . The prosecutor of the Hiss perjury case, the Honorable Thomas F. Murphy, did not respond to the communication of the board's counsel." The Bar Associations of Massachusetts and New York City had responded the same way as the Attorney General, as had the clerk of the United States Supreme Court. Former Supreme Court Justice Stanley Reed, however, had sent a letter recommending Hiss's reinstatement.

One of the questions Hiss had been asked in the preliminary hearing before the Massachusetts Board of Bar Overseers was whether he looked upon reinstatement to the bar as a form of vindication. His answer was no; it is not for the Overseers or the Supreme Judicial Court of Massachusetts to set aside the judgment of a United States District Court. There is no court that can do that now, simply on a showing that documentary evidence was manufactured by Chambers and his testimony perjured; it would be necessary to show that the government *knew* about the fraud and perjury, or at least some of it, and was not simply deceived by Chambers like the jury and most of the public. That isn't likely to happen, as long as fuller access is not allowed to the old FBI and HUAC files.*

Yet, if a Committee of Congress today should use its investigative powers to undertake a new study of the case, it seems more than likely that the remaining mysteries would be cleared up and these issues laid to rest. Was the typewriter produced in court a fake, for example, and if it was, did the FBI have anything to do with it? Were the microfilms really made before 1938, or perhaps a decade later? Did those papers really lie together in that envelope in the dumbwaiter shaft for ten years, as Chambers claimed? Was Chambers really a Communist spy, or was it all his fantasy? How much did Nixon know about the fraudulence of Chambers's story?

However, the main issue is now clear enough; whatever Chambers did and whatever Nixon and the FBI knew about it at the time, Hiss had nothing to do with it; he wasn't a Communist and he didn't give Chambers any of the incriminating documents.

Certainly Hiss believed in 1938 that any American had the

---

* As of September 1975, a series of suits under the Freedom of Information Act had resulted in the release by the Justice Department of selected materials from the FBI files which added nothing significant to the evidence in the case, but led to further inquiries. In general, the Department's policy has been to deny access to any information which the Department decides to withhold for "national security" or other "compelling reason." A lengthy appeals procedure is provided, and litigation was continuing. Meanwhile the HUAC files had been turned over to the House Judiciary Committee, which had not established any procedure by which researchers could gain access to them.

right to be a Communist if he wanted to, and in those days many Americans shared the same view. It was difficult to believe in 1938 that the tiny handful of domestic Communist "agitators" could ever overthrow the government of the United States by force and violence, or that the Soviet Union would ever be a threat to American security. The Communists in America were just another political party; wrong-headed in other people's eyes, and occasionally troublesome in labor disputes, but only a right-wing minority seemed to be actually afraid of them. Most people believed that America's institutions of political freedom were protection enough against a bunch of crackpots who didn't have votes enough to effect a change.

Certainly Hiss believed in maintaining friendly relations with the Soviet Union during and after World War II; so did President Roosevelt as long as he lived. It was part of the foundation on which Roosevelt built his strategy for peace in the post-war world. The great powers were to work together in the United Nations to settle their disputes and keep order.

But by 1948, three years after Roosevelt's death, many things were different. There was a large body of opinion in America that rejected Roosevelt's philosophy, and preferred to rely on the military power of the United States, now so much greater than ever before, instead of the peace-keeping authority of the United Nations, which was new and relatively untried. Many people feared the military strength that the Soviet Union had demonstrated during the war, and felt that the domestic Communists might be instruments of a Soviet attack on American institutions.

Not everybody in America agreed with this frightened view of the world in 1948, by which the defeat of world Communism was given a higher priority than the pursuit of world peace, and hostility toward the Soviet Union and all Communists everywhere was considered the necessary cornerstone of American policy. But it was soon to become the majority view and to furnish support for the policies of the Cold War and the shooting wars in Korea, Vietnam, and Cambodia.

Within the perspective of this historic shift of American attitudes, the Hiss case has a special significance. Hiss fought against

439

the role in which he was cast, and his defeat became a dramatic turning point in America's repudiation of Roosevelt and acceptance of the Cold War. It was precisely because Roosevelt and his policies could be attacked through Hiss that Richard Nixon made such a spectacle of Hiss before the HUAC and hounded him into jail. Nixon and his supporters made Hiss a symbol of what the public feared, because the symbol suited their purposes, although it didn't fit the man.

Hiss's role in these events, which he blundered into without understanding, was to dramatize to the world something he didn't believe himself—the idea that Communism was an almost supernaturally corrupting influence, endangering the nation in unimaginable ways, extending into the highest councils of government, bent on destroying everything good in America; and the proof of all this (as presented by the HUAC and the prosecution at the trials) was that even Alger Hiss, golden boy and Eagle Scout, pillar of the State Department and supposed darling of President Roosevelt, had been corrupted by Communism and turned into a traitor and a spy. The idea was wildly untrue to Hiss's real nature, which is one reason he didn't recognize it for what it was; but that only made it more difficult for him to defend himself, and the public accepted these accusations without question.

The effect of the Committee hearings and the trials was not so much to convert the waverers and opponents of the anti-Communist policy as to create a climate of opinion in which they were frightened into submission. For the hearings and trials created an illusion of treason and conspiracy in high places that confirmed the public's worst fears. And there were other trials in the same period that added to those fears, helping to create the atmosphere of hysteria which pressed upon the jury that convicted Hiss and the Court of Appeals that upheld the verdict—Klaus Fuchs, Alan Nunn May, Judith Coplon, the Rosenbergs, William Remington—some clear-cut cases, some still disputed.

The policy of opposition to the Soviet Union was perhaps historically inescapable, given the natural tendency of great empires to oppose each other. The destruction of the British, French, and Japanese empires and the Nazi–Fascist Axis in World

War II had left the United States and the Soviet Union alone in the field. But that policy was accepted by the nation more as a matter of fear than of reason, and much of the violence and bloodshed that has happened since can be understood as to some degree a product of this circumstance.

The use of fear as a political tool was not new to America in 1948; many politicians were already using it before Hiss was accused. After his conviction, it became for a time the dominant influence. Sen. Joseph McCarthy of Wisconsin built a briefly meteoric career on the popular fear of Communism, borrowing some of Nixon's ideas and platform props ("I hold in my hand . . ."). He succeeded in clouding the issue by giving the public something else to be fearful of—his own ruthless and irresponsible use of power—and was ultimately brought down and censured by the Senate. Nixon, more astute, built a more durable career on the anti-Communist slogan, going in 1950 to the Senate, 1952 to the Vice Presidency for two terms, and, after an eight-year interruption, to the Presidency, always trading on his anti-Communist credentials as the man who exposed "the traitor Hiss."

The Hiss case dramatized, too, the idea that the United Nations was a danger to the United States, because membership in it was shared with the Soviet Union and other Communist nations, and "the traitor Hiss" had been (or seemed to have been) one of the architects responsible for giving the Communists so much power in it. Even today, a pressure group calling itself "American Opinion" periodically mails out postcards showing a picture of the UN buildings, captioned "The House That Hiss Built," and "Get US Out!"

It was easy to be afraid of the Communists in 1948; the world was full of fears, and full of things to be afraid of. The war, then only recently ended, had revealed a capacity in human beings for murderous behavior on a massive scale never before dreamed of; more than ever before since the Dark Ages it had been a war not just between armies but against civilians, first with explosives dropped from the sky, then with fire bombs, then napalm, then the atom bomb, which seemed the ultimate. But already the superultimate hydrogen bomb was being built in

American research laboratories and factories, and Americans wondered what would happen if the Russians got those dreadful weapons too. For a time, people nourished the dream that the secret could be kept from the enemy, and that's what the Coplon and Rosenberg trials were about, and what Fuchs and May tried to prevent. But the laws of nature cannot be kept secret from those who go after them, so that the Russians soon had the bomb too; then the "balance of nuclear terror" became the ultimate foundation of American policy.

Then, as now, the dangers the world faced were real, and could be dealt with successfully only by courage and intelligence; but the very frightening nature of the dangers tended to undermine courage and to cloud intelligence. The Hiss case made a major contribution to this rule of fear; and it contributed also to the popularity of fraud and deceit as instruments of politics and sometimes policy, because it was through the use of these instruments that the prosecution was successful.

The panic fears that were so strong in 1948 are less obvious today, though they are still with us, and the dangers are still abundant. The uses of fraud and deceit are perhaps better recognized now, if not more widespread; but so long as the conviction of Alger Hiss stands unreversed it is a reminder that the consequences of fraud and deceit are still with us, working their harm on America.

Justice remains to be done, and it can be done by an act of Congress. It needs to be done, not only to vindicate Alger Hiss but to vindicate America's institutions of freedom. For they are human institutions, subject to human error, and can survive only if errors, once discovered, are corrected.

SOURCES, BIBLIOGRAPHY, AND NOTES

Three main sources of material have been relied upon for this book:

1. The official records of the two trials of Alger Hiss, his appeal and motion for a new trial, and the hearings before the House Un-American Activities Committee in which he was involved.

2. Interviews with Hiss, his family and friends (most of them recorded on tape), and a study of the correspondence, notes, and memoranda in his personal files and his attorneys'. files.

3. My own observations of the trials as a reporter for the *New York Herald Tribune*, as recorded in my notebooks at the time, and my scrapbook of clippings for the period May 19, 1949–January 26, 1950. (These issues are available on microfilm at the New York Public Library and many other major libraries.)

For background material about the history of the United States and the United Nations, I have relied mainly on standard sources and occasionally on my own observations as a student in 1932–1938 and a newspaper reporter in 1939–1951.

The Bibliography below does not pretend to be exhaustive, but I have listed all the works referred to in the Notes and some others which I found particularly helpful. Nor is it a critical bibliography; some discretion is recommended in reading the more argumentative and self-serving works listed.

OFFICIAL RECORDS

The official records and the code letters by which they are referred to in the notes are as follows:

HUAC. Hearings Regarding Communist Espionage in the United States Government—Part Two: Hearings before the Committee on Un-American Activities, House of Representatives, 80 cong., 2 sess., July 31–December 14, 1948; and 81 cong., 2 sess., August 28–31 and September 1 and 5, 1950. (These are available in major public and university libraries.)

BALT. The so-called Baltimore Depositions of Whittaker and Esther Chambers, November 4–5 and 16–17, 1948; and February 17–18 and March 25, 1949, in the case of *Alger Hiss* v. *Whittaker Chambers*, U.S. District Court for the First District of Maryland, Civil No. 4176.

The stenographic transcript was obtained through the courtesy of Attorney Helen Buttenwieser of New York.

FIRST.   Stenographer's minutes of the first trial, *U.S.A.* v. *Alger Hiss*, before Hon. Samuel H. Kaufman, D.J., C. 128–402; available through the courtesy of Attorney Helen Buttenwieser of New York.

SECOND.   Transcript of Record, On Appeal from the District Court of the United States for the Southern District of New York, in the U.S. Court of Appeals for the Second Circuit, *U.S.A.* v. *Alger Hiss*. In ten volumes, available at major public and university libraries, and from Attorney Helen Buttenwieser of New York. It contains full text of proceedings at second trial and pretrial motions before both trials and reproductions of documentary evidence.

APPEAL.   Brief for Appellant, *U.S.A.* v. *Alger Hiss*, U.S. Circuit Court of Appeals for the Second Circuit; available through the courtesy of Attorney Helen Buttenwieser of New York.

NEW.   Appendix to appellant's brief on appeal from order denying motion for new trial on ground of newly discovered evidence; U.S. Court of Appeals for the Second Circuit, No. 22478, *U.S.A.* v. *Alger Hiss*. Available through the courtesy of Attorney Helen Buttenwieser of New York. The appellant's brief in the same docket contains additional details and arguments, which are summarized in the Appendix. This, and the complete file of all legal papers in the case, including the unsuccessful petitions to the U.S. Supreme Court, are also available through the courtesy of Attorney Buttenwieser.

INTERVIEWS

In addition to Alger Hiss, who was interviewed repeatedly from April 1974 to July 1975, for periods ranging from a couple of hours to a full day at a time, the principal sources interviewed were his brother Donald, his son Anthony, his wife Priscilla Hiss (from whom he is living apart), his stepson Timothy Hobson, his cousins, Elizabeth Hiss Hartman and the late Mary C. Hiss, Hobson's aunts, Miss Katherine Thayer Hobson and Mrs. Eleanor (George M.) Mackenzie; his friends, Donnell Tilghman, Richard Field, John Lowenthal, Oliver Lundquist, Charles F. and Laurie Reese, George and Simone Boas, John Sutro, and Edward G. Chandler; his lawyers, William Marbury, Harold Rosenwald, Helen Buttenwieser, Harold Shapero, Robert von Mehren, and the late Claude Cross; and others interested in the case, including Benjamin V. Cohen, George A. Eddy, Elinor Ferry, Matthew Josephson, Barbara Kerr, Dr. Morton Levitt, William Reuben, Stephen

Salant, Professor Allen Weinstein, Raymond Werchen, Alden Whitman, and Dr. Meyer A. Zeligs. Additional information was obtained in correspondence from Dr. Viola Bernard, Beatrice Gwynn, Peter Irons, Manice Lockwood III, Hannah Quinn, Meyer Shapiro, Edmund F. Soule, Harlan H. Vinnedge, and Joan Worth, and from the study of Hiss's personal correspondence with these and many others. Dean Rusk, who succeeded Hiss as director of the Office of Special Political Affairs (then renamed Office of United Nations Affairs), wrote to me that he made it a policy not to comment on the case; Prosecutor (now Judge) Thomas F. Murphy did not reply to my requests for an interview; and efforts to obtain an interview with Richard M. Nixon were also unsuccessful. The Reverend John F. Cronin replied in general terms to my first letter, but not to the more detailed questions in my second.

BIBLIOGRAPHY

Andrews, Bert, and Andrews, Peter. *A Tragedy of History*. Washington: R. B. Luce, 1962.

Bernstein, Irving. *The Lean Years: A History of the American Worker, 1920–33*. Boston: Houghton Mifflin, 1960.

―――. *The Turbulent Years: A History of the American Worker, 1933–41*. Boston: Houghton Mifflin, 1970.

Challener, Richard D. "New Light on a Turning Point in U.S. History." *University: A Princeton Quarterly*, Spring 1973.

Chambers, Whittaker. *Cold Friday*. Edited by Duncan Norton–Taylor. New York: Random House, 1964.

―――. *Odyssey of a Friend, Letters to William F. Buckley, Jr., 1954–61*. Edited with notes by William F. Buckley. New York: National Review, Inc., 1969.

―――. *Witness*. New York: Random House, 1952; Chicago: Regnery, 1969.

Clubb, O. Edmund. *The Witness and I*. New York: Columbia University Press, 1975.

Compton, James V., "Anti-Communism in American Life Since the Second World War," in *Forums in History*, Saint Charles, Mo.: Forum Press, 1973.

Conrad, David Eugene. *The Forgotten Farmers: The Story of the Sharecroppers in the New Deal*. Urbana, Ill.: University of Illinois Press, 1965.

Cook, Fred J. *The Unfinished Story of Alger Hiss*. New York: William Morrow, 1958.

————. "Nixon Kicks a Hole in the Hiss Case." *The Nation*, April 7, 1962.

————. "Haunting the Hiss Case: The Ghost of a Typewriter." *The Nation*, May 12, 1962.

———— (with Raymond A. Werchen). "New Light on the Hiss Case." *The Nation*, May 28, 1973.

Cooke, Alistair. *A Generation on Trial*. New York: Knopf, 1950; Baltimore: Penguin Books, 1969.

De Toledano, Ralph, and Lasky, Victor. *Seeds of Treason*. New York: Funk & Wagnalls, 1950.

Dilling, Elizabeth. *The Red Network*. Chicago: privately printed, 1934.

Douglas, William O. *Go East, Young Man*. New York: Random House, 1974.

Fiedler, Leslie. *An End to Innocence: Essays on Culture and Politics*. Boston: Beacon Press, 1955.

Goodman, Walter. *The Committee: The Extraordinary Career of the House Committee on Un-American Activities*. New York: Farrar, Straus and Giroux, 1968.

Gwynn, Beatrice V. *The Discrepancy in the Evidence*. London: privately printed, 1972–1973.

Halsey, Margaret. *The Pseudo-Ethic*. New York: Simon and Schuster, 1963.

Harbaugh, William H. *Lawyer's Lawyer: The Life of John W. Davis*. New York: Oxford University Press, 1973.

Hiss, Alger. "Yalta, Modern American Myth." *The Pocket Book Magazine*, November 1955.

————. *In the Court of Public Opinion*. New York: Knopf, 1957; Harper & Row, 1972.

————. "An Apartment Dweller's Guide to Fine Wines." *The Real World*, Early Winter 1973.

Hiss, Anthony. "I Call on Alger." *Rolling Stone*, September 13, 1973.

Holmes, Oliver Wendell, and Laski, Harold. *Holmes-Laski Letters*. Edited by Mark DeWolfe Howe; abridged by Alger Hiss. New York: Atheneum, 1963.

Hull, Cordell. *The Memoirs of Cordell Hull*. New York: Macmillan, 1948.

Irons, Peter Hanlon. *"America's Cold War Crusade: Domestic Politics and Foreign Policy, 1942–48."* Ph.D. dissertation, Boston University Graduate School, 1973.

Josephson, Matthew. *Infidel in the Temple*. New York: Knopf, 1967.

Jowitt, William Allen. *The Strange Case of Alger Hiss*. Garden City, N.Y.: Doubleday, 1953.

446

Keeley, Joseph. *The China Lobby Man*. New Rochelle, N.Y.: Arlington House, 1969.

Kempton, Murray. *Part of Our Time: Some Monuments and Ruins of the Thirties*. New York: Simon and Schuster, 1955.

Kornitzer, Bela. *The Real Nixon*. Chicago: Rand McNally, 1960.

Krivitsky, Walter. *In Stalin's Secret Service*. New York: Harper & Bros., 1939.

Lewis, Flora. *Red Pawn*. Garden City, N.Y.: Doubleday, 1965.

Liebling, A. J. *The Press* (rev. ed.). New York: Ballantine Books, 1964.

Lurie, Leonard. *The Running of Richard Nixon*. New York: Coward, McCann and Geoghegan, 1972.

Miller, Merle. *Plain Speaking: An Oral Biography of Harry S. Truman*. New York: G. P. Putnam's Sons, 1973.

Nixon, Richard M., *Six Crises*. New York: Doubleday, 1962.

Packer, Herbert. *Ex-Communist Witnesses*. Stanford, Calif.: Stanford University Press, 1962.

Pearson, Drew. *Diaries, 1949–59*. Edited by Tyler Abell. New York: Holt, Rinehart and Winston, 1974.

Philip, Cynthia Owen, ed. *Imprisoned in America: Prison Communications, 1776 to Attica*. New York: Harper and Row, 1973.

Popkin, Richard H. "Ellsberg: Hiss Story Repeats Itself." *University Review*, April 1974.

Reuben, William A. *The Honorable Mr. Nixon*. New York: Action Books, 1956.

Schlesinger, Arthur M., Jr. *The Age of Roosevelt*: vol. I, *The Crisis of the New Order*; vol. II, *The Coming of the New Deal*; vol. III, *The Politics of Upheaval*. Boston: Houghton Mifflin, 1957, 1958, 1960.

Seth, Ronald. *The Sleeping Truth: The Hiss–Chambers Affair Reappraised*. New York: Hart Publishing, 1968.

Sherwood, Robert E. *Roosevelt and Hopkins*. New York: Harper & Bros., 1948.

Stein, Rose M. *M-Day: The First Day of War*. New York: Harcourt, Brace, 1936.

Stripling, Robert. *The Red Plot Against America*. Drexel Hill, Pa.: Bell, 1949.

Terkel, Studs. *Hard Times: An Oral History of the Depression*. New York: Pantheon, 1970.

Tetlow, Edwin. *The United Nations: The First 25 Years*. London: Peter Owen, 1970.

Trilling, Lionel. *The Middle of the Journey*. New York: Viking, 1947.

———. "Whittaker Chambers and 'The Middle of the Journey,' " *The New York Review of Books*, April 17, 1975, pp. 18–24.

447

Truman, Harry S. *Memoirs*. Garden City, N.Y.: Doubleday, 1958.
Tugwell, Rexford G., *The Democratic Roosevelt*. Garden City, N.Y.: Doubleday, 1957.
———. *The Brain Trust*. New York: Viking, 1968.
Tytell, Martin (as told to Harry Kursh). "The $7,500 Typewriter I Built for Alger Hiss." *True*, August 1962.
Voorhis, Jerry. *The Strange Case of Richard Milhous Nixon*. New York: P. S. Eriksson, 1972.
Wadleigh, Julian. "Why I Spied for the Communists." *New York Post*, July 12–24, 1949.
Weinstein, Allen. "Reappraisals: The Alger Hiss Case Revisited." *The American Scholar*, Winter 1971.
———. "Opening the FBI Files: An Interim Report," in Smith College *Alumnae Quarterly*, February 1975, pp. 11–14.
Werchen, Raymond A., and Cook, Fred J. "New Light on the Hiss Case." *The Nation*, May 28, 1973.
Weyl, Nathaniel. "I Was in a Communist Unit with Hiss." *U.S. News & World Report*, January 9, 1953.
White, Nathan I. *Harry Dexter White: Loyal American*. Waban, Mass.: Bessie (White) Bloom, 1956.
Wills, Garry. *Nixon Agonistes*. Boston: Houghton Mifflin, 1970.
Zeligs, Meyer A. *Friendship and Fratricide: An Analysis of Whittaker Chambers and Alger Hiss*. New York: Viking, 1967.

NOTES

Abbreviations used in the Notes (for more details, see page 445):

HUAC.   House Un-American Activities Committee hearings
BALT.   Baltimore Depositions
FIRST.   Minutes of the first trial
SECOND.   Transcript of the second trial
APPEAL.   Brief for Appellant, U.S. Court of Appeals
NEW.   New trial motion, appendix to Appellant's Brief
W.   *Witness*, by Whittaker Chambers
SIX.   *Six Crises*, by Richard M. Nixon
NYHT.   *New York Herald Tribune*
NYT.   *The New York Times*

CHAPTER 1

PAGE

1–4 It was on a Saturday . . . : Interviews with Hiss, and Priscilla Hiss.

5–7 . . . They have been described . . . : Josephson, 174–178; Josephson, interview.

7 . . . Fourth Section . . . : W., 288.

7 Chambers had joined . . . : W., 164, 201–263.

7 This success earned . . . : W., 271.

7 Bedacht denied . . . : Ferry, interview.

7–9 Chambers described . . . : W., 275–321.

CHAPTER 2

10–15 When Hiss got . . . : Hiss, interviews; memoranda in Hiss's attorneys' files.

14 . . . Pressman was the one . . . : De Toledano and Lasky, 41; Schlesinger, vol. II, 53, quoting a letter from Jerome Frank to Charles Brand.

15–16 . . . Pressman made no bones . . . : HUAC, 2845ff.

17 These were the days . . . : Schlesinger, vol. I, 267.

17 Then there was the tricky problem . . . : Schlesinger, vol. II, 42–44.

17 The solution was . . . : Hiss, interviews.

18 Roosevelt and his brain trust . . . : Schlesinger, vol. II, 2–23 gives a concise summary of the Hundred Days.

19–21 This was the kind of problem facing AAA . . . : Schlesinger, vol. II, 27–67; and Conrad, 19–36 are good sources.

21–23 These were essentially questions of policy . . . : Hiss, interviews; Conrad, 37–63.

23–24 Hiss still remembers . . . : Hiss interviews.

24–30 What Hiss hadn't recognized . . . : Hiss, interviews; Conrad, 65–153; Schlesinger, vol. II, 68–84.

26 . . . "reign of terror" . . . : Conrad, 154–176.

30 . . . Raymond Clapper . . . : *Washington Post*, Feb 7, 1935.

30 The fracas . . . : *Washington Post, NYT*, Feb. 6 and 7, 1935.

CHAPTER 3

PAGE

31–46 Alger was born . . . : Interviews with Hiss, his brother Donald Hiss, and his cousins Elizabeth Hiss Hartman and the late Mary C. Hiss; memoranda in Hiss's personal and attorneys' files. Genealogical data compiled by the late Anna and Mary C. Hiss. For some additional details, see Zeligs, 135–155.

CHAPTER 4

47–49 Camp Wildwood . . . : Hiss, interviews; *Frondes Silvestres* for 1919, courtesy of George A. Eddy.

49–54 There was never any question . . . : Interviews with Hiss, Charles F. Reese, George and Simone Boas; and Johns Hopkins 1929 yearbook, courtesy of Charles F. Reese.

54–56 On this trip . . . : Interviews with Hiss and Priscilla Hiss.

56–58 Law school . . . : Interviews with Hiss, Marbury, Sutro, Chandler, Field, and Rosenwald.

58–61 Beyond all these . . . : Hiss, interviews; *Holmes–Laski Letters* (abridged) vol. II, 336, 333, 313, 325, 329–330.

CHAPTER 5

62–63 Alger Hiss had been . . . : Interviews with Hiss and Priscilla Hiss. Priscilla's marriage . . . : interviews with Hiss, Katherine Hobson, and Eleanor Mackenzie.

63–69 Hiss's emotional life . . . : Interviews with Hiss and Priscilla Hiss. For some additional details, see Zeligs, 167–183.

69 Priscilla made . . . : Interviews with Mrs. Elizabeth Hiss Hartman, Mrs. Laurie Reese, Hiss, Priscilla Hiss, and others.

70–71 Alger took his new responsibilities . . . : Interviews with Hiss, Timothy Hobson, Anthony Hiss, and Priscilla Hiss.

PAGE

71–72 None of these considerations . . . : Interviews with Hiss, Priscilla Hiss, and Rosenwald.

72–74 This was the winter of 1931–1932 . . . : Interviews with Hiss and Priscilla Hiss; letter to Hiss from Robert Cruise McManus, Oct. 18, 1948, quoting an unnamed friend.

74–76 When spring came . . . : Hiss, Priscilla Hiss, and Donald Hiss, interviews.

76 From time to time . . . : "Description of personal characteristics of Timothy Hobson," Government's Exhibit 46–B (SECOND, 3373); Timothy Hobson, interview.

77 After her year of . . . : Interviews with Hiss and Priscilla Hiss.

CHAPTER 6

78–86 In the spring of 1934 . . . : Hiss, interviews.

81 There was United Aircraft . . . : NYT, Sept. 18–19, 1934.

83 He spent weeks . . . : NYT, Dec. 14–15, 1934.

83 Hiss had a lot of tough questions for Baruch . . . : NYT, March 30, 1935.

84–85 Carpenter was taking . . . : NYT, Dec. 21, 1934.

85 . . . a list of 181 men . . . : NYT, Dec. 14, 1934.

87–91 It was in this period . . . : Hiss interviews; records in Hiss's attorneys' files; see also chaps. 10–12 and 15–17.

87 . . . three psychiatrists, who later . . . : Doctors Carl Binger, Henry A. Murray, and Meyer Zeligs.

91 When Chambers appeared . . . : HUAC, 563–584, 661–672.

91 Chambers said he had never . . . : HUAC, 975–1001; SECOND, 242–243.

92 At the trials . . . : SECOND, 248, 961–962, 1004–1005.

93 . . . When the lease . . . : SECOND, 243–245.

93 Chambers remembered driving . . . : HUAC, 666–667.

93 As for the rug . . . : SECOND, 254–255, 724–726; and Government's Exhibits, nos. 41 and 42.

94 When Chambers enlarged his story . . . : SECOND, 239, 250.

94 . . . The Soviet agent . . . : W., 375.

94 ... But the idea was revived ... : SECOND, 257–260.

94–95 As a matter of fact ... : Hull, vol. I, 400–404.

95 Hiss had left the Nye Committee ... : Hiss, interview. See also chaps. 10–13.

CHAPTER 7

97–98 While Hiss was having ... : Hiss, interviews; Schlesinger, vol. III, 470–474, 488–492.

98–99 This was not the first ... : Schlesinger, vol. III, 447–496.

99 ... A new system ... : Schlesinger, vol. III, 504–505.

99–104 After the Butler case was over ... : Hiss, interviews.

104–108 There was, for example, the problem ... : Interviews with Hiss and Priscilla Hiss; memoranda in Hiss's attorneys' files.

108 It was through the Stanley–Browns ... : interview with Tilghman.

108–113 Meanwhile Hiss was getting ... : Hiss, interviews; memoranda in Hiss's attorneys' files.

CHAPTER 8

114–116 The war brought ... : Hiss, interviews.

116–117 If Hiss's domestic ... : Hiss, interviews; memoranda in Hiss's attorneys' files.

117–118 Over the mantelpiece ... : Sherwood, 227, 360, 697, 756–757, 855, 876.

118–122 Alger Hiss was one ... : Hiss, interviews.

119 ... "Declaration of the United Nations" ... : Sherwood, 446–453.

119–120 So far the United Nations ... : Tetlow, 24–26.

121 ... "Tentative Proposals" ... : Sherwood, 854.

121 ... They had the Covenant ... : Tetlow, 27–29.

121 ... *trusteeship* ... : For the state of this issue at Yalta, see Sherwood, 865–866. It remained unsettled at San Francisco

PAGE

and was ultimately compromised at London; see NYHT, Dec. 6, 1945; Jan. 23–24, 30, and Feb. 5, 1946.

122–123 The Dumbarton Oaks Conference . . . : Tetlow, 27–29; Sherwood, 854–855.

123–127 Hiss was attached . . . : Hiss, interviews; Sherwood, 855–870; and Tugwell, 667–673.

125 . . . the United States wanted Russia . . : Sherwood, 867.

127 The basic plan . . . : Tugwell, 671–673.

127–128 The U.S. delegation had to be briefed . . . : Sherwood, 876–877.

129–130 After Yalta . . . : Hiss, interviews; Tetlow, 34–39.

130–131 The Polish issue . . . : Sherwood, 883–912.

131–132 Since the signing . . . : Interviews with Oliver Lundquist and Hiss.

132–134 A trivial incident occurred . . . : Hiss, interviews.

CHAPTER 9

135–140 After the San Francisco Conference . . . : Hiss, interviews.

140–141 According to Challener . . . : Challener, 1–3, 28–33.

141–142 But a hitch . . . : Hiss, interviews; HUAC, 648; SECOND, 1907–1908.

142–143 But it had not been dropped . . . : HUAC, 1291–1300.

143 There was a good deal . . . : HUAC, 1007; Keeley *passim*, especially 196–200.

143–144 . . . Mandel was an old . . . : SECOND, 388 (the name is misspelled Mandell in the official transcript).

143n. In 1948 William Marbury . . . : Hiss, interviews.

143n. . . . from Nathaniel Weyl . . . : NYT, Feb. 20, 1952; memoranda in Hiss's attorneys' files.

144 Another important member . . . : Irons, 177–184.

144–145 Nixon in those days . . . : Lurie, 43–52.

145 He asked Rep. Charles Kersten . . . : Irons, 183; Wills, 27; and Kornitzer, 172.

146 Hiss knew nothing . . . : Hiss, interviews.

PAGE

146 Meanwhile, Alfred Kohlberg . . . : Challener, 29; SECOND, 3082; Kohlberg's testimony before the House Committee on Tax-Exempt Foundations, 1953, p. 658; and Hiss, interviews.

146 . . . And in June 1947 . . . : The text of Hiss's statement to the FBI of June 2, 1947, has been published as Appendix C in Zeligs, 445–446.

147–148 . . . Barbara Kerr . . . : Telephone interview with Mrs. Kerr.

148 This was the second . . . : Hiss, interviews.

148–150 This was in January 1948. In March . . . : Challener, 29–30; and Hiss, interviews.

150 Hiss was not particularly aware . . . : Hiss, interviews.

150–151 There were other . . . : Interviews with Hiss, Priscilla Hiss, Timothy Hobson, and Donnell Tilghman.

CHAPTER 10

152–154 When Hiss started . . . : Hiss, interviews.

154–157 The political institution . . . : Goodman, 3–225.

156 "This Committee will not . . ." : Quoted by Goodman, 27.

158–161 The Berlin blockade . . . : Hiss, interview; and memoranda in Hiss's attorneys' files.

161–164 "Almost exactly . . ." : HUAC, 564–566.

162 This oracular sentence . . . : SIX, 3; W., 25. See also Chambers, *Odyssey*.

164–168 Robert Stripling . . . : HUAC, 566–584.

164 . . . (Nixon was . . .) : SIX, 4.

164–165 . . . whether White was . . . : HUAC, 574.

165 "I should perhaps . . ." : HUAC, 577.

165–167 "It is pretty hard . . ." : HUAC, 573–574.

167 "I went to . . ." : HUAC, 572.

167–168 A little later Mundt . . . : HUAC, 579.

168–169 All this looked . . . : Hiss, interviews.

169–170 But Hiss had to wait . . . : HUAC, 623–642.

170–171 With this introduction . . . : HUAC, 642–643.

PAGE

171–173 That concluded . . . : HUAC, 643–644.

173 Stripling then resumed . . . : HUAC, 645; and SIX, 6.

173–176 Indeed, the suppressed anger . . . : HUAC, 646–647; SIX, 7–8.

175 When Nixon wrote . . . : SIX, 7.

CHAPTER 11

177 The hearing of August 5 ended . . . : HUAC, 659.

177–180 At this point Hiss . . . : Hiss, interviews; and records in Hiss's attorneys' files.

180–183 Meanwhile in Washington . . . : SIX, 9–16.

183–188 The transcript of this session . . . : HUAC, 66–72.

188–189 That was it . . . : Hiss, interviews; records in Hiss's attorneys' files; and testimony at both trials.

189–192 Nixon didn't know . . . : SIX, 18–23; see also, Andrews, 72–73; Challener, and Stripling. Nixon's visits to Chambers's farm are not mentioned in *Witness*.

192–193 Meanwhile, the Committee . . . : HUAC, 935.

193 Hiss was beginning . . . : Hiss, interviews.

193–203 That, however, was not . . . : HUAC, 935–955.

197 "That is quite incorrect . . ." : HUAC, 945. The exchange is quoted without comment in W., 584.

197 . . . But to Hiss . . . : Hiss interviews.

199 On the train from New York . . . : Hiss, interviews.

201–203 Then Representative Hébert . . . : HUAC, 950–952.

203 More argument followed . . . : HUAC, 952–955.

CHAPTER 12

204 . . . refused to release . . . : Application has been made to the House Judiciary Committee, which inherited the records from the House Internal Security Committee in early 1975.

204 . . . calling Mrs. Hiss . . . : HUAC, 955.

PAGE

204 Hiss had used the intervening time ... : Hiss, interviews.

204–212 "The name of the man ..." : HUAC, 955–974.

206 At this point ... : HUAC, 956.

209 ... a prothonotary warbler ... : HUAC, 961–962. McDowell and Hiss had seen the bird in Arlington, several miles down the river from Glen Echo, where Chambers had placed it.

209 ... He brought a rug over ... : HUAC, 964.

210 There the matter rested ... : Hiss, interview. In later years Nixon commented that he didn't know anything about polygraph lie detectors (the type under discussion in 1948) or how accurate they were, "but I know they'll scare the hell out of people." (White House tapes, July 24, 1971, quoted in the *Los Angeles Times,* July 19, 1974.)

210–212 There was only ... : HUAC, 967–974.

212–213 Hiss flew back ... : Hiss, interviews. Some additional details in Hiss, *In the Court of Public Opinion,* 79–82.

212 ... White had been questioned ... : HUAC, 877–906 (full text in White, 20–68).

213 ... Thomas L. Stokes ... : *Boston Traveler,* Aug. 18, 1949; the article is reprinted in White, 73.

213–214 According to Nixon ... : SIX, 29–31.

214–215 Chambers meanwhile ... : W., 600–601.

215–226 ... He introduced Dollard ... : HUAC, 975–1001.

217 (As Hiss described ...) : Hiss, 85.

217n. "to do so ..." : Trilling, 20.

217–218 "I am senior editor ..." : HUAC, 978.

218 Hiss was baffled ... : Hiss, interviews; SIX, 33; SECOND, 329, 472–477, and 375–377.

218–219 Nixon interrupted ... : HUAC, 978; Hiss, 86–87.

219–221 Stripling told Chambers ... : HUAC, 978–986.

221 There it was ... : Hiss, interviews; and Hiss, 90.

221–222 Nixon intervened ... : HUAC, 986–987; Hiss, interviews; records in Hiss's attorneys' files.

222–224 Hiss was thoroughly ... : HUAC, 987–988.

224–225 There were many ... : interviews with Hiss and Rosenwald.

225–226 His anger was so ... : HUAC, 988–1001; SIX, 36.

CHAPTER 13

PAGE

227   Hiss was a gone . . . : Hiss, interviews.

227   "A great hurdle . . ." : SIX, 36.

227–228   What Hiss sensed . . . : Hiss, interviews; and memoranda in Hiss's attorneys' files.

228   . . . Before Priscilla arrived . . . : HUAC, 1003–1009.

228–229   Between these two . . . : HUAC, 1011–1013.

229–230   From that point . . . : SIX, 39–40; HUAC, 1115; Hiss, 104; SECOND, 1849; SIX, 40; SECOND, 922–923.

230n.   Chambers thought . . . : SECOND, 245, 277–278.

230–231   Hiss, meanwhile, hired . . . : Hiss, interviews; memoranda in Hiss's attorneys' files.

231–232   "This charge . . . : HUAC, 1162–1165.

232–233   The Committee were unimpressed . . . : HUAC, 1165–1206; SIX, 41.

233   . . . 131 closely printed pages . . . : HUAC, 1075–1206.

233–234   Hiss's reputation . . . : Challener, 30–32; Hiss, interviews.

234   Chambers, meanwhile, had accepted . . . : W., 705–711.

234–235   Hiss consulted with . . . : Hiss, interviews; Hiss, 157–158; W., 722.

235   The immediate political effect . . . : SIX, 45–46.

235–236   The effect on Chambers . . . : W., 723, 727, 759.

236   But it was not the money . . . : W., 725–727, 737–739, 744–747.

236   . . . But that attempt . . . : See chap. 14.

236   It was a dangerous . . . : W., 723–727.

236–237   "My No to the grand jury . . . : W., 726.

237   In any case, his denial . . . : HUAC, 565.

237–238   This was the dilemma . . . : BALT, 208–209, 211–212.

238   After the close . . . : W., 735; BALT, 271–274.

238–240   Marbury spent much . . . : BALT, 296–318.

239   . . . introduced the idea of espionage . . . : BALT, 307–308.

239–240   Again Marbury pressed . . . : BALT, 313–318.

240   The curious thing . . . : See chaps. 18 and 21.

241   Nevertheless Chambers . . . : BALT, 316–317.

PAGE

241 "A sense of the enormous . . ." : W., 20–21.

241–242 At this point . . . : W., 734–735.

242 Cleveland, his lawyer . . . : W., 735; SECOND, 291.

242 The story of what happened . . . : HUAC, 1451–1465.

242–243 In *Witness* . . . : W., 737; NEW, 166a–168a (Exhibit 2S–III, supporting affidavit of Daniel P. Norman).

243–244 But Marbury had no way . . . : Marbury, interview; BALT, 716–745.

244–245 After the numbering . . . : BALT, 738–742.

246 Marbury responded . . . : BALT, 742–744.

246 . . . meanwhile he had prepared . . . : BALT, 745–829.

246–248 There was one point . . . : Interviews with Marbury and Priscilla Hiss.

CHAPTER 14

249–252 When the session ended . . . : Interviews with Hiss, Marbury, Rosenwald, Cross, von Mehren, and Field; and financial records retained by Field.

252 On November 18 . . . : SECOND, 6–21, 40–42, 86.

253 Two quite different . . . : W., 751; SIX, 46–47.

253–254 Chambers described . . . : W., 751–752.

254 What Chambers was hinting . . . : 739–743.

254n. Stripling, in his . . . : Stripling, 142–144. See also, Andrews, 175.

254–255 Here Chambers and Nixon . . . : SIX, 47–48.

255–256 While Nixon was . . . : W., 752–754.

256–257 All this happened . . . : SIX, 48–49.

257 . . . The plane met the ship . . . : I am indebted to Harlan H. Vinnedge for sharing some of the results of his research with me.

258 Nixon worked . . . : SIX, 51–54.

258–259 "The news jolted . . ." : SIX, 54–55.

259–260 Chambers, whose account . . . : W., 768–770.

260 . . . Nixon had called a press conference . . . : SIX, 55–56.

CHAPTER 15

PAGE

275–277 After the indictment . . . : Marbury, interview; and BALT, 831–1382.

277 Chambers said he had . . . : BALT, 1113, 1067, and 1187.

277–278 Chambers also described . . . : BALT, 1321–1328.

278 But only in the case . . . : FIRST, 356–358.

278 . . . the proprietor of Bleak House . . . : SECOND, 1670–1679.

278–279 So the information . . . : Interviews with Hiss, Rosenwald, Shapero, Cross, and von Mehren.

279–280 Then Benjamin tried . . . : Douglas, 378–379.

280–281 Those arguments, of course . . . : Hiss, interviews; and memoranda and letters in Hiss's attorneys' files.

281 Stryker was a . . . : Author's observation; and interviews with Hiss and Shapero.

281–285 Hiss decided . . . : Hiss, interviews; and memoranda in Hiss's attorneys' files. For some additional details on the search for the typewriter, see Cook, "Haunting the Hiss Case: The Ghost of a Typewriter," *The Nation*, May 12, 1962, pp. 416–421.

285–290 Meanwhile there was another . . . : Interviews with Hobson, Hiss, Shapero, Rosenwald, Cross, von Mehren, Marbury, and Priscilla Hiss.

287 . . . some of them have been documented . . . : Zeligs, 212–217.

CHAPTER 16

295 In his affidavit . . . : SECOND, 128.

296–309 The trial got off . . . : NYHT, May 19–July 9, 1949.

297 Under the circumstances, Stryker wanted . . . : Interviews with Shapero, Rosenwald, and von Mehren.

299–300 He began in a . . . : FIRST, 16–25.

300–303 Stryker, too, began . . . : FIRST, 25–54.

303 . . . defense had found the missing typewriter . . . : FIRST, 52–53.

303 . . . Murphy put Chambers on the stand . . . : FIRST, 96–126.

304 The next day . . . : FIRST, 127–227.

PAGE

304–306 When Stryker's turn came . . . : FIRST, 228–251.
306–308 In that second day . . . : FIRST, 277–280.
308–309 After much more . . . : FIRST, 292–301.

CHAPTER 17

310–312 Whittaker Chambers was on the witness . . . : NYHT, June 2–5, 7–9, 11, 14.
312 Chambers was born . . . : W., 91–92.
312 When he was two . . . : W., 96.
312–313 . . . In later years . . . : W., 123–124.
313 At school . . . : W., 110–114.
313 . . . Victor Hugo's *Les Miserables* . . . : W., 133–138.
313 While his father . . . : W., 122–124, 138–141.
313 In high school . . . : W., 144–145.
314 . . . ended in some disgrace . . . : FIRST, 2451; and SECOND, 374.
314 His mother wanted . . . : W., 150–163; and SECOND, 375–376.
314–315 In the fall of 1920 . . . : W., 164–167; and SECOND, 377–380.
315 On his return . . . : W., 165; FIRST, 2455–2456; and SECOND, 223–224, 380, 3657–3658 (Defense Exhibit F).
315–316 Meanwhile Chambers decided . . . : W., 195–201; and SECOND, 382–390.
316 At some time . . . : W., 168–169; and Zeligs, 318.
316–319 Meanwhile—the exact sequence . . . : W., 174–187; SECOND, 422–426.
319–320 After that Chambers . . . : SECOND, 224–226, 426; W., 183–184; and SECOND, 397; Zeligs, 118.
320–321 In April 1931 . . . : W., 231–232, 265–268; and SECOND, 397.
322–323 According to *Witness* . . . : W., 25, 6–17.
323 "There is a difference . . ." : W., 26.
323–324 He used the word "deserted" . . . : W., 35–40.
324–325 . . . "Shortly before my break . . ." : W., 40–44.
325 The work he . . . : W., 56.

325 From then on . . . : W., 64–65.

326 He got his job . . . : W., 85–86.

326 When Chambers took . . . : FIRST, 23–24.

326–327 Esther Chambers was . . . : NYHT, June 11, 1949; and FIRST, 841–897.

327–328 "I don't have a very good . . . : FIRST, 903–906.

328–329 Esther Chambers had difficulty . . . : FIRST, 897–908, 914–1040.

329 . . . the face was green . . . : SECOND, 2406.

329 . . . "the details of housekeeping . . ." : FIRST, 926.

329–330 Stryker tried to get . . . : FIRST, 932–935.

CHAPTER 18

331–332 After the confusion . . . : NYHT, June 15, 1949.

332 . . . Rankin had even talked . . . : HUAC, 1421.

333 Walter H. Anderson . . . : FIRST, 1057–1141, 1154–1207.

333–335 . . . McLean to follow the proceedings . . . : FIRST, 1207–1237.

335–336 When Walter Anderson took . . . : SECOND, 749–772, 788–921.

336 In my report . . . : NYHT, Dec. 3, 1949.

336 Cross's argument dealt with . . . : Government State Exhibits nos. 5–8, 12, 13, 13–A, and 15, reproduced in vol. VIII of SECOND, at pages 3543, 3557, 3559, 3561, and 3565. (State no. 13–A is so numbered because it has no exact counterpart in the Baltimore series; it is a combination of State nos. 13 and 15 and a document that does not appear in the Baltimore series at all.)

336–337 . . . Cross sought to demonstrate . . . : State no. 15 was stapled to no. 13–A, as shown in SECOND, at page 3561.

337 . . . Jones's one-page note, which . . . : State no. 13, reproduced in SECOND, following page 3559, and again as the second of three documents stapled together in State no. 13–A, in SECOND, following page 3561. The other two documents in

13–A are the two-page Boyce dispatch (which does not appear in the Baltimore series) and the Hornbeck note, which is also reproduced as State no. 15, in SECOND, following page 3565.

338–339 Cross demonstrated, in his marathon . . . : SECOND, 839–853 and 915–920. Jones's eight-page analysis is State no. 12, reproduced in SECOND, following page 3557.

339 . . . A week later . . . : SECOND, 1353–1358, 1361–1363, 1378–1379.

339 Most of the information . . . : The full text of all the State Department documents involved is presented in vols. VIII and IX of SECOND, entitled *Government's State Exhibits*; the full text of the "pumpkin papers" is in vol. VII, entitled *Government's Baltimore Exhibits* (because they were first produced in the Baltimore libel suit proceedings). The same series of exhibit numbers (1–48 and 50–55) is used in both sets, so that the exhibit number of any State Department document corresponds to the number of the pumpkin paper based upon it, and the two series are distinguished by referring to them as "State no." and "Baltimore no."; thus "Baltimore no. 15," is the pumpkin paper copy of "State no. 15," and so on. In some cases a single "Baltimore" exhibit summarizes a number of State Department documents, but they all bear the same "State" exhibit number. Baltimore no. 11, for example, consists of four pages summarizing sixteen State Department documents, which are reproduced in SECOND, vol. VIII, as State no. 11, Groups I, II, III, and IV, the four groups corresponding to the four pages of Baltimore no. 11.

339–340 . . . Of the forty-four telegrams . . . : The code used in each case is shown at the head of each State exhibit; the distribution of each telegram is shown on the code room copy, which is reproduced in SECOND, following the action copy of the same telegram, and distinguished by the suffix "A" after the exhibit number; thus State no. 1 is an action copy, bearing office date stamps and initials to show who saw it on what dates, and State no. 1–A is the code room copy of the same telegram, showing the list of offices to which information copies were distributed. This procedure was not necessary for dispatches and interoffice memoranda, since they did not pass through the code room; it does not apply to State no. 13–A (see note to pages 372–373).

340 The "Boyce report" . . . : Boyce identifies his sources throughout the document; see especially State no. 8, pp. 1, 3, 5, and 10.

340 In the first trial there was one . . . : FIRST, 17, 1126; NYHT, June 15, 1949; FIRST, 1142–1153.

341 Two paragraphs from . . . : Baltimore no. 11, p. 4 (in SECOND, following p. 3447).

341–342 In the second trial . . . : SECOND, 795; State no. 11, Group IV (in SECOND, following p. 3555).

342–343 The more sensational . . . : NYHT, Dec. 2, 1949.

343 . . . breaking away from the Communist Party . . . : W., 25–88.

343–344 There are other passages . . . : SECOND, 1494–1495, 1504–1511, 1917–1924.

344–345 Unfortunately for the spy theory . . . : Compare Baltimore, no. 11 and State no. 11; and Baltimore no. 46 and State no. 46.

345 As spy papers these . . . : See also chap. 21, pp. 28–31.

346 The microfilms were . . . : Baltimore nos. 48 and 50–55. (The number 49 was used at Baltimore for a different purpose.)

346 . . . Three of them were mimeographed . . . : Baltimore nos. 54 (from Hankow) and 55 (from Tsingtao and Paris).

346–347 The significant thing . . . : Compare Baltimore nos. 48 and 50–52 with State nos. 48, and 50–52.

347 Wadleigh testified about . . . : FIRST, 1332–1364; SECOND, 1107–1153, 1164–1256.

347 . . . he did identify them . . . : SECOND, 1217–1218.

347–348 Wadleigh was a lanky . . . : NYHT, June 17, 1949.

348 In the course of two years . . . : SECOND, 1145, 1117, and 1218 (State nos. 48, 50–53).

348 As for the three telegrams . . . : SECOND, 1221 (State nos. 54–55).

PAGE

348–349 Wadleigh apparently had . . . : SECOND, 1145–1146.

349 The dates fitted . . . : State nos. 54–55; SECOND, 1518, 1113; Hiss, interviews.

349 There were three desks . . . : SECOND, 1965, 945; Hiss, interviews.

350 A month after the three . . . : State nos. 5–8, 12, 13, 13–A, and 15.

350 The file contained . . . : Compare Baltimore nos. 5–8, 12, 13, and 15 (see also note to pp. 372–373 above); SECOND, 1213–1214.

351 . . . consistent with State Department procedures . . . : as described in general terms by Anderson and Eunice A. Lincoln, Sayre's secretary, SECOND, 750–759, 949–952; and specifically by Hiss, interviews.

351 The sequence begins . . . : State nos. 5–8.

351–352 Maxwell M. Hamilton . . . : State no. 12.

352 While the papers . . . : Dispatch from Boyce, in State no. 13–A.

352–353 The standard procedure . . . : State no. 13 (also in no. 13–A).

353 Thus alerted, Hornbeck . . . : State no. 15 (also in no. 13–A).

353–354 The set of papers . . . : The date stamps appear on State no. 15, which served as covering note for the set.

354 According to the date stamps . . . : State no. 5 and Boyce dispatch in no. 13–A.

CHAPTER 19

356 Four samples . . . : Government's Exhibits nos. 34, 37, 39, and 46–B.

356 Feehan testified . . . : FIRST, 1290–1332; SECOND, 1071–1106; NYHT, June 17, 1949.

356n. A fifth sample . . . : Government's Exhibit no. 36.

357 In later years . . . : See pp. 360–362.

357–358 As a matter of . . . : interviews with Hiss, Rosenwald, Shapero, and von Mehren.

357 . . . Representatives Nixon and Case . . . : NYHT, July 10, 1949.

PAGE

357–358 . . . Secretary of State Dean Acheson . . . : NYHT, Jan. 26, 1950.

358 . . . John Foster Dulles . . . : FIRST, 2551–2567; SECOND, 3071–3083.

358–359 . . . This was an argument . . . : SIX, 60.

359 It was easy enough . . . : SECOND, 1075–1081.

359–360 What Feehan didn't say . . . : NEW, 149a fn.; FIRST, 1306; SECOND, 1074.

360–363 It wasn't until two years . . . : NEW, 16a–37a; 54a–90a; 106a–169a.

360 . . . The defense challenged . . . : NEW, 170a–208a.

360 . . . The judge denied . . . : NEW, 286a–303a.

360 . . . appeal to the Supreme Court . . . : see pp. 279–280.

360–361 Miss Elizabeth McCarthy . . . : 56a–59a; 147a–154a.

361 It was Mrs. Evelyn Ehrlich . . . : NEW, 155a–161a.

361–362 Late in the proceedings . . . : NEW, 138a.

362 . . . Miss McCarthy had . . . : NEW, 154a.

362 Priscilla's letters . . . : NEW, 157a–161a.

362–363 When Lane looked . . . : NEW, 27a–37a; 107a–119a; 134a–146a.

363 . . . Hiss and his attorneys . . . : memoranda in Hiss's attorneys' files.

364 . . . Daniel P. Norman . . . : NEW, 123a–133a.

364 . . . famous Watergate tapes . . . : Feb. 28 (twice in conversation with John Dean, once to Senator Baker); March 21, March 27, and April 16, 1973. For a convenient summary, see the *Los Angeles Times*, May 2, 1974.

365 . . . defense lawyers consulted one . . . : memoranda in Hiss's attorneys' files.

365–366 Unfortunately, neither Hiss . . . : interviews with Hiss, Rosenwald, Shapero, von Mehren, and Priscilla Hiss.

366–372 Priscilla says she felt . . . : NYHT, June 29–30, 1949; Dec. 30, 1949; Jan. 4–6, 1950; Priscilla Hiss, interviews.

367 . . . She was on the stand . . . : FIRST, 2251–2396, 2412–2445; SECOND, 2336–2414; 2483–2514.

PAGE

367–368 It was not until that first Tuesday . . . : SECOND, 2355–2356, 2361, 2490, 2495.

368–369 . . . Instead, when Murphy opened . . . : SECOND, 2362; Priscilla Hiss, interview.

369 The twenty-two page . . . : Baltimore nos. 5–8.

There were pages in . . . : Baltimore no. 8, especially pp. 2, 4, 6, 8–10.

369–370 There was the spelling . . . : Baltimore nos. 5–8.

370 When Joseph N. Jones . . . : State no. 12.

370 . . . such careless errors . . . : Baltimore no. 8, pp. 1 and 5.

370–371 Most interesting of all . . . : SECOND, 2427.

371 . . .(This kind of crease . . .) : Baltimore nos. 11 (pp. 1 and 3) and 31.

CHAPTER 20

373–374 The trouble was . . . : NYHT, June 23–24, 1949; FIRST, 1600–1791; SECOND, 1560–1638, 1655–1670, 1708–1732.

374–375 "My name is Raymond . . ." : FIRST, 1708–1712.

375 When the cross-examination resumed . . . : FIRST, 1747–1749; 1751–1754.

375–376 Catlett testified that one . . . : FIRST, 1754–1757.

376 Later, of course, Murphy put . . . : FIRST, 2497–2550.

376 Mike Catlett was twenty-seven . . . : FIRST, 1679–1757; SECOND, 1580–1638.

377 Cleidie Catlett's recollection . . . : FIRST, 1600–1678; SECOND, 1560–1580.

377 Perry Murphy Catlett . . . : FIRST, 1757–1791; SECOND, 1708–1732.

377 . . . it "could have" been . . . : FIRST, 1778.

377 This wasn't much help . . . : FIRST, 1779–1780; SECOND, 1719–1732.

378 . . . First came Charles Fahy . . . : FIRST, 1806–1810.

378–379 then Malcolm Cowley . . . : FIRST, 1811–1838.

467

PAGE

379–381 It wasn't much, but . . . : NYHT, June 24, 1949; FIRST, 1839–1874.

381 Hiss's use of the English . . . : FIRST, 1994.

381–382 Hiss wasn't aware . . . : Hiss, interviews.

382 On his second day . . . : FIRST, 1875–1944, 1960–1972; NYHT, June 25, 1949.

382 Only in one respect . . . : FIRST, 1903–1904.

382–383 . . . Hiss's testimony was interrupted . . . : 1945–1954.

383 Murphy worked calmly . . . : NYHT, June 28–29, 1949; FIRST, 1973–2116, 2126–2250.

383–385 The old Woodstock typewriter . . . : FIRST, 2062–2065.

385 . . . what he had said to John Foster Dulles: FIRST, 2151–2157, 2220–2226.

385–386 Two days later . . . : FIRST, 2551–2567.

386–388 The last defense witness . . . : FIRST, 2446–2476.

387 . . . Murphy renewed his objection . . . : FIRST, 2473–2475.

388 . . . the prosecution gained more . . . : interviews with Rosenwald, von Mehren, and Hiss; SECOND, 3218–3219.

388 Again, there were long . . . : SECOND, 2516–2519.

389–391 Murphy thanked the judge . . . : SECOND, 2519–2553, 2558–2579.

390 "I think Mr. Chambers . . . : SECOND, 2550.

391 For the next three days, . . . : SECOND, 2579–2633, 2663–2790.

391–392 The defense had anticipated . . . : interviews with Rosenwald, von Mehren, and Hiss.

392–393 Murray supported Binger's . . . : SECOND, 2792–2833, 2846–2950.

392–393 "Let me ask you . . ." : SECOND, 2811–2812.

393 Murray concurred . . . : SECOND, 2812–2817.

393 . . . Murphy let him off . . . : SECOND, 2849–2945, 2949–2950.

CHAPTER 21

394 . . . Altogether the jury heard . . . : NYHT, July 9, 1949; Jan. 1, 1950.

PAGE

395–396 On the Saturday . . . : Shapero, interview.

397–398 Stryker's summation . . . : FIRST, 2724–2844.

398–399 Murphy had his answers . . . : FIRST, 2848–2910, 2894, 2847.

398 Stryker's trial . . . : NYHT, July 9, 1949.

398–399 Hiss wasn't sure . . . : Hiss, interviews.

399–400 Early that summer . . . : interviews with Field and Hiss.

400–401 At that point Hiss . . . : interviews with Hiss, Field, Cross; SECOND, 141.

401–403 The second trial . . . : NYHT, Nov. 17, 1949, Jan. 26, 1950.

403 Cross's main theme . . . : NYHT, Jan. 20, 1950; SECOND, 3091–3175.

403–404 "How did Chambers know . . ." : SECOND, 3164.

404 It was an appeal . . . : SECOND, 3213–3262.

404 . . . "It is the thing . . ." : SECOND, 3255.

404–405 With this reminder . . . : SECOND, 3255–3256.

406 The first clue . . . : SECOND, 261–262, 528–529; W., 40; Zeligs, 294–296.

406 The car he bought . . . : SECOND, 263; W., 38–39.

406–408 Another item . . . : SECOND, 455–457.

408 Chambers apparently carried . . . : BALT, 1174–1178; Zeligs, 233–234.

408 Zeligs found . . . : Zeligs, 233–234, 376 fn., 203–205.

408–409 . . . Zeligs and the late Professor . . . : Zeligs, 372–373 (quoting Packer); Gwynn, 1–5.

409 . . . The dealer, Martin K. Tytell . . . : Tytell, interview. This is the same Martin K. Tytell, who in 1951 was hired by the defense to alter an old Woodstock to duplicate the work of the Hiss machine, as described on page 398, before the defense knew anything about his advertisements in *New Masses* in the 1930s.

409–410 This possibility . . . : NEW, 111a–119a, 170a–208a.

410 . . . advertisements in *New Masses* . . . : Ferry, interview.

410–411 . . . Chambers "could produce . . ." : Gwynn, letter to author.

410n. Chambers said . . . : SECOND, 271.

411 . . . Ronald Seth, . . . : Seth, 214–274.

411–412 Chambers wrote in *Witness* . . . : W., 38, 40–41.

PAGE

412–414 The special feelings . . . : Zeligs, 201–235, 264–307, 364–387, 415–433.

    412n. . . . apparently because . . . : interviews with Hiss, Rosenwald. When Chambers came close to the subject in the first trial, Stryker objected that it was "immaterial," and Judge Kaufman agreed. FIRST, 192, 194.

    412n. Zeligs came . . . : Zeligs, 428–432.

    414 . . . he told the House Committee . . . : HUAC, 1288.

    414n. According to Joan Worth . . . : letter to the author from Miss Worth. Her manuscript is currently unpublished. . . . letters to friends and fragments . . . : "Odyssey of a Friend" and "Cold Friday."

    415 Indeed, Chambers's job . . . : Zeligs, 296.

415–417 With these advantages . . . : SECOND, 749–759.

    417 One is in Exhibit no. 38 . . . : Compare State nos. 38 and 38–A with Baltimore no. 38.

417–418 The evidence of Exhibit no. 47 . . . : Compare Baltimore no. 47 and State nos. 47 and 47–A.

418–420 First Cleveland assigned . . . : BALT, 722–738. Compare with Baltimore nos. 1–47.

    420 Exhibit no. 9 was apparently . . . : Compare Baltimore no. 9 and State nos. 9 and 9–A, 9–B, and 9–C.

    421 This wasn't the way . . . : SECOND, 12–68, 79–86; NEW, 286a–303a.

421–422 . . . And as Claude Cross said . . . : Cross, interview.

CHAPTER 22

    423 At the end of . . . : NYHT, July 9, 1949.

423–425 The second jury . . . : NYHT, Jan. 22, 1950; SECOND, 3294–3295.

425–429 Four days later . . . : NYHT, Jan. 26, 1950; SECOND, 3297–3305.

    429 There remained . . . : Hiss, 324–362; APPEAL, 12–15.

    429 . . . Judge Harrie B. Chase . . . : Federal Reporter, second series, vol. 185, p. 822.

PAGE

429–435 Five years' imprisonment . . . : interviews with Alger, Donald, and Anthony Hiss and Timothy Hobson; correspondence and notes in Hiss's personal files.

435 For the last dozen years . . . : Hiss affidavit in support of petition for readmission to the Massachusetts bar.

435 ". . . I should be profoundly . . ." : Jowitt, 223–224, quoted by Zeligs, ix.

435–436 It was this comment . . . : Zeligs, ix–xiv, 434–435, 447–464; Zeligs interviews.

436–437 Cook's first article . . . : *The Nation*, Sept. 21, 1957; May 28, 1973.

438 One of the questions . . . : interviews with Hiss and Attorney von Mehren.

438n. . . . "compelling reason." Letter from Attorney General Edward H. Levi to Hiss's attorney K. Randlett Walster, June 25, 1975.

INDEX

AAA, *see* Agricultural Adjustment Administration
Abraham Lincoln Brigade (Spanish Civil War), 104
Abt, John, 13, 163, 164, 169, 171
Acheson, Dean, 75, 139, 357, 358
Adams, Charles, *see* Chambers, Whittaker: aliases
Adams, John Quincy, 314
Agnew, Spiro, 432
Agricultural Adjustment Administration (AAA), 11, 17, 19, 57, 82, 144, 150, 153, 171, 247–248
constitutionality, 97–100
objectives and program, 19–30
Agriculture Department, 10, 12, 82, 83, 142
purge of, 26–29, 419
Aikawa, Yoshīsuke, 352, 353, 370
Alford, Mrs. John (formerly Mrs. Roberta Fansler), 428
Alger, Russell Alexander, 32
American Friends Service Committee, 75, 179, 315
American Magazine, 88, 91
"American Opinion," 441
American Telephone and Telegraph Co., 2
Anderson, Maxwell
What Price Glory, 52
Anderson, Walter H.
Hiss trials, 333, 335, 336, 338, 415
Andrews, Bert, 128, 129, 190, 191, 192, 193, 216, 256, 257n, 294–295
Anti-Comintern Pact, 111
Anti-Semitism, 154
Appeals Court (U.S.), 279, 341, 342, 440
Appell, Donald, 183, 193, 213, 214, 215, 228, 256
Appleby, Paul, 13
Arnault, Christine (Mrs. V. Hesse), 32
Astor, Mrs. Vincent (Mary Cushing), 179
Atlantic Charter (Aug. 1941), 119
Attlee, Clement, 138, 139, 347

Balfour, Arthur, 95
Baltimore, Lord, 32

Baltimore, Md., 38, 49, 52, 55, 144
Hiss family and, 31–34
"Baltimore depositions," 237n
Barrie, James M., 101
Barrows, Gen. David P., 146
Baruch, Bernard, 412
on Hiss, 84
Nye Committee hearings, 82–84
Bayerische Motor Werke (Germany), 81
Bedacht, Max, 7
Beer, Walter E., 251
Benjamin, Robert M., 251, 279, 428, 429
Bennett, Margaret, 26
Bentley, Elizabeth, 158, 163, 164, 431
Berle, Adolf
Chambers and, 142, 143, 181, 183, 202, 228, 266n, 308, 326
Bessie, Alvah, 156n
Beverly Farms, Mass., 71
Biberman, Herbert, 156n
Binger, Dr. Carl, 210, 366
on Chambers's mental health, 311, 386–393, 407, 412, 436
Bird watching, 48–49, 192
prothonotary warbler, incident, 185, 209
Birrell, Augustine
Obiter Dicta, 60
Bleak House, 278
Bliss, Mr. & Mrs. Robert Woods, 116, 121
Bloom, Rep. Sol, 127
Boas, George, 54
"Bob," *see* Chambers, Whittaker: aliases
Bondy, Judge William, 279, 361, 372, 421
Bone, Sen. Homer T., 82
Bosley, Mary Ann, *see* Hiss, Mary Ann Bosley
Boston Herald, 179
Boyce, Richard F., 337, 340, 351, 352, 353, 354, 370
Brand, Charles, 173
Brandeis, Louis, 60, 98
Brookwood Labor College, 73
Bryn Mawr, Penn., 48

United Nations, 4, 82, 190, 439, 441
  Charter conference (San Francisco),
    127, 129–134
  Dumbarton Oaks conference, 120–
    123
  Preparatory Commission, 135–140
  Security Council veto question,
    130–131
  Yalta conference, 123–129

Vail, Richard B.
  HUAC, 231
Vandenberg, Sen. Arthur H., 82, 127,
  128, 231
Vansittart, Sir Robert, 94
Vassar College, 7
Vazzano, Nicholas, 254n
Veatch, Roy, 101
Velloso, Pedro Leão, 133
Versailles Treaty, 79, 118
Virgil
  Aeneid, 47
Volta Institute for the Deaf,
  Washington, D.C., 107
Voorhis, Jerry, 144, 145

Wadleigh, Henry Julian, 265–268,
  272–273, 325, 346–351, 354,
  373, 403, 416, 418–420
Wallace, Henry, 153–154, 169, 170
  Agriculture Secretary, 13, 17, 23,
    29, 30, 97
War Industries Board (World War
  I), 83
Ware, Harold, 163
Washingon Daily News, 192
Washington Post, 179–180, 253, 254
Watergate tapes, trials, 364, 398n,
  432, 437
Webb, Sidney, 73
Weinstein, Allen, 145n
Werchen, Raymond A., 436, 437
West, David, 429
Westminster, Md., Chambers farm,
  191, 192, 241
  pumpkin papers, 253–257
Weyl, Nathaniel, 143n
Whearty, Raymond, 267

Wheeler, William A., 193, 256
White, Harry Dexter, 164–165, 212–
  213, 214, 215, 243, 277, 324
White, William Allen, 112, 149
Whittaker, Charles, *see* Chambers,
  Whittaker: aliases
Whittaker, Grandmother, 316, 320
Whittaker, Tony, 142
Whittier, Calif., 145
Wickersham Commission, 71, 77
Wilder, Thornton, 187, 189
Wiley, John C., 240
Willard, Charlie, 68, 71
Williams College, 314–315
Wilson, Edwin R., 121, 129
Wilson, Harold, 347
Wilson, Woodrow, 82, 95, 117, 118,
  126, 127
Winslow, Ann, 428
Witt, Nathan, 13, 16, 163, 171
Women's International League for
  Peace and Freedom, 86
Wood, John S.
  HUAC, 203
Woodstock Typewriter Company,
  363
Woodstock typewriter question, 250,
  269, 281–285, 299–300, 303,
  331, 336, 355–377, 383–384,
  403–410
The World Tomorrow, 320
World War II
  America's entry into, 113
  beginnings, 110–111
Worth, Joan, 414n
WPA National Research Project, 324,
  406, 408, 414, 415, 416, 420
Wrightson, Bill, 44
Wrightson, Uncle Josh, 44–45
Wrightson, Aunt Tege, 43, 44, 59, 68
Wyzanski, Charles E., 382

Yale University, 2, 55, 67, 135
Yalta conference, 4, 123–129, 157, 190
Yost, Charles, 101

Zeligs, Meyer A., 312, 320, 409, 411
  Friendship and Fratricide, 287n,
  311, 408, 412, 435–436